Handwritten annotations:
REG.No. V98 EES

V.I.N. WVWZZZ6NZ XY389085

Date of 1st Registration 01 09 1999

Haynes
THE BOOK ®

VW Polo

Service and Repair Manual

Handwritten annotations:
Engine Number: APQ483901

oil filter No (MANN) W712/52

NGK PLUGS BUR6ET

RM Jex

(4150 - 5AM2 - 256)

Models covered

Polo Hatchback, including special/limited editions
1.0 litre (999 cc) & 1.4 litre (1390 cc) petrol

Does NOT cover GTi or Saloon (Classic), Estate or Caddy models
Does NOT cover Diesel models, or 'new' Polo range introduced Jan 2002

© Haynes Publishing 2008

A book in the **Haynes Service and Repair Manual Series**

ABCDE
FGHIJ
KLMNO
PQR

ISBN **978 1 84425 150 6**

British Library Cataloguing in Publication Data
A catalogue record for this book is available from the British Library.

Printed in the USA

Haynes Publishing
Sparkford, Yeovil, Somerset BA22 7JJ, England

Haynes North America, Inc
861 Lawrence Drive, Newbury Park, California 91320, USA

Haynes Publishing Nordiska AB
Box 1504, 751 45 UPPSALA, Sverige

Contents

LIVING WITH YOUR VW POLO

Roadside repairs

Weekly checks

Lubricants and fluids

Tyre pressures

MAINTENANCE

Routine maintenance and servicing

Contents

REPAIRS & OVERHAUL

Engine and associated systems

Transmission

Brakes and suspension

Body equipment

Wiring diagrams

REFERENCE

Index

Many people see the words 'advanced driving' and believe that it won't interest them or that it is a style of driving beyond their own abilities. Nothing could be further from the truth. Advanced driving is straightforward safe, sensible driving - the sort of driving we should all do every time we get behind the wheel.

An average of 10 people are killed every day on UK roads and 870 more are injured, some seriously. Lives are ruined daily, usually because somebody did something stupid. Something like 95% of all accidents are due to human error, mostly driver failure. Sometimes we make genuine mistakes - everyone does. Sometimes we have lapses of concentration. Sometimes we deliberately take risks.

For many people, the process of 'learning to drive' doesn't go much further than learning how to pass the driving test because of a common belief that good drivers are made by 'experience'.

Learning to drive by 'experience' teaches three driving skills:

☐ Quick reactions. (Whoops, that was close!)
☐ Good handling skills. (Horn, swerve, brake, horn).
☐ Reliance on vehicle technology. (Great stuff this ABS, stop in no distance even in the wet...)

Drivers whose skills are 'experience based' generally have a lot of near misses and the odd accident. The results can be seen every day in our courts and our hospital casualty departments.

Advanced drivers have learnt to control the risks by controlling the position and speed of their vehicle. They avoid accidents and near misses, even if the drivers around them make mistakes.

The key skills of advanced driving are **concentration,** effective all-round **observation, anticipation** and **planning.** When **good vehicle handling** is added to these skills, all driving situations can be approached and negotiated in a safe, methodical way, leaving nothing to chance.

Concentration means applying your mind to safe driving, completely excluding anything that's not relevant. Driving is usually the most dangerous activity that most of us undertake in our daily routines. It deserves our full attention.

Observation means not just looking, but seeing and seeking out the information found in the driving environment.

Anticipation means asking yourself what is happening, what you can reasonably expect to happen and what could happen unexpectedly. (One of the commonest words used in compiling accident reports is 'suddenly'.)

Planning is the link between seeing something and taking the appropriate action. For many drivers, planning is the missing link.

If you want to become a safer and more skilful driver and you want to enjoy your driving more, contact the Institute of Advanced Motorists at www.iam.org.uk, phone 0208 996 9600, or write to IAM House, 510 Chiswick High Road, London W4 5RG for an information pack.

Working on your car can be dangerous. This page shows just some of the potential risks and hazards, with the aim of creating a safety-conscious attitude.

General hazards

Scalding

• Don't remove the radiator or expansion tank cap while the engine is hot.
• Engine oil, automatic transmission fluid or power steering fluid may also be dangerously hot if the engine has recently been running.

Burning

• Beware of burns from the exhaust system and from any part of the engine. Brake discs and drums can also be extremely hot immediately after use.

Crushing

• When working under or near a raised vehicle, always supplement the jack with axle stands, or use drive-on ramps. *Never venture under a car which is only supported by a jack.*
• Take care if loosening or tightening high-torque nuts when the vehicle is on stands. Initial loosening and final tightening should be done with the wheels on the ground.

Fire

• Fuel is highly flammable; fuel vapour is explosive.
• Don't let fuel spill onto a hot engine.
• Do not smoke or allow naked lights (including pilot lights) anywhere near a vehicle being worked on. Also beware of creating sparks (electrically or by use of tools).
• Fuel vapour is heavier than air, so don't work on the fuel system with the vehicle over an inspection pit.
• Another cause of fire is an electrical overload or short-circuit. Take care when repairing or modifying the vehicle wiring.
• Keep a fire extinguisher handy, of a type suitable for use on fuel and electrical fires.

Electric shock

• Ignition HT voltage can be dangerous, especially to people with heart problems or a pacemaker. Don't work on or near the ignition system with the engine running or the ignition switched on.

• Mains voltage is also dangerous. Make sure that any mains-operated equipment is correctly earthed. Mains power points should be protected by a residual current device (RCD) circuit breaker.

Fume or gas intoxication

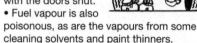

• Exhaust fumes are poisonous; they often contain carbon monoxide, which is rapidly fatal if inhaled. Never run the engine in a confined space such as a garage with the doors shut.
• Fuel vapour is also poisonous, as are the vapours from some cleaning solvents and paint thinners.

Poisonous or irritant substances

• Avoid skin contact with battery acid and with any fuel, fluid or lubricant, especially antifreeze, brake hydraulic fluid and Diesel fuel. Don't syphon them by mouth. If such a substance is swallowed or gets into the eyes, seek medical advice.
• Prolonged contact with used engine oil can cause skin cancer. Wear gloves or use a barrier cream if necessary. Change out of oil-soaked clothes and do not keep oily rags in your pocket.
• Air conditioning refrigerant forms a poisonous gas if exposed to a naked flame (including a cigarette). It can also cause skin burns on contact.

Asbestos

• Asbestos dust can cause cancer if inhaled or swallowed. Asbestos may be found in gaskets and in brake and clutch linings. When dealing with such components it is safest to assume that they contain asbestos.

Special hazards

Hydrofluoric acid

• This extremely corrosive acid is formed when certain types of synthetic rubber, found in some O-rings, oil seals, fuel hoses etc, are exposed to temperatures above 400°C. The rubber changes into a charred or sticky substance containing the acid. *Once formed, the acid remains dangerous for years. If it gets onto the skin, it may be necessary to amputate the limb concerned.*
• When dealing with a vehicle which has suffered a fire, or with components salvaged from such a vehicle, wear protective gloves and discard them after use.

The battery

• Batteries contain sulphuric acid, which attacks clothing, eyes and skin. Take care when topping-up or carrying the battery.
• The hydrogen gas given off by the battery is highly explosive. Never cause a spark or allow a naked light nearby. Be careful when connecting and disconnecting battery chargers or jump leads.

Air bags

• Air bags can cause injury if they go off accidentally. Take care when removing the steering wheel and/or facia. Special storage instructions may apply.

Diesel injection equipment

• Diesel injection pumps supply fuel at very high pressure. Take care when working on the fuel injectors and fuel pipes.

⚠️ *Warning: Never expose the hands, face or any other part of the body to injector spray; the fuel can penetrate the skin with potentially fatal results.*

Remember...

DO

• Do use eye protection when using power tools, and when working under the vehicle.

• Do wear gloves or use barrier cream to protect your hands when necessary.

• Do get someone to check periodically that all is well when working alone on the vehicle.

• Do keep loose clothing and long hair well out of the way of moving mechanical parts.

• Do remove rings, wristwatch etc, before working on the vehicle – especially the electrical system.

• Do ensure that any lifting or jacking equipment has a safe working load rating adequate for the job.

DON'T

• Don't attempt to lift a heavy component which may be beyond your capability – get assistance.

• Don't rush to finish a job, or take unverified short cuts.

• Don't use ill-fitting tools which may slip and cause injury.

• Don't leave tools or parts lying around where someone can trip over them. Mop up oil and fuel spills at once.

• Don't allow children or pets to play in or near a vehicle being worked on.

VW Polo 1.4 SE

The VW Polo range covered by this manual was introduced to the UK market in January 2000. Apparently very much a facelift of the previous highly-successful Polo range, it was still proclaimed by VW as being 75% new, with the most obvious differences being seen in the new-look interior, derived from the smaller Lupo. Other changes included a stiffer, fully-galvanised bodyshell, with new bumpers and lights.

All engines are derived from the well-proven engines which have appeared in many VW vehicles. The engine is of four-cylinder overhead camshaft design, mounted transversely, with the transmission mounted on the left-hand side. All models have a five-speed manual transmission or four-speed automatic transmission.

All models have fully-independent front suspension. The rear suspension is semi-independent, with suspension struts, trailing arms and a torsion beam axle.

A wide range of standard and optional equipment is available within the Polo range to suit most tastes. All models have electric mirrors, tinted glass, twin airbags, power steering and ABS as standard, with central locking, electric windows, and air conditioning available further up the range.

Provided that regular servicing is carried out in accordance with the manufacturer's recommendations, the VW Polo should prove a reliable and economical small car. The engine compartment is well-designed, and most of the items needing frequent attention are easily accessible.

Your VW Polo manual

The aim of this manual is to help you get the best value from your car. It can do so in several ways. It can help you decide what work must be done (even should you choose to get it done by a garage). It will also provide information on routine maintenance and servicing, and give a logical course of action and diagnosis when random faults occur. However, it is hoped that you will use the manual by tackling the work yourself. On simpler jobs it may even be quicker than booking the car into a garage and going there twice, to leave and collect it. Perhaps most important, a lot of money can be saved by avoiding the costs a garage must charge to cover its labour and overheads.

The manual has drawings and descriptions to show the function of the various components so that their layout can be understood. Tasks are described and

photographed in a clear step-by-step sequence. The illustrations are numbered by the Section number and paragraph number to which they relate – if there is more than one illustration per paragraph, the sequence is denoted alphabetically.

References to the 'left' or 'right' of the car are in the sense of a person in the driver's seat, facing forwards.

Acknowledgements

Thanks are due to Draper tools Limited, who provided some of the workshop tools, and to all those people at Sparkford who helped in the production of this manual.

This manual is not a direct reproduction of the vehicle manufacturer's data, and its publication should not be taken as implying any technical approval by the vehicle manufacturers or importers.

We take great pride in the accuracy of information given in this manual, but car manufacturers make alterations and design changes during the production run of a particular car of which they do not inform us. No liability can be accepted by the authors or publishers for loss, damage or injury caused by any errors in, or omissions from, the information given.

The following pages are intended to help in dealing with common roadside emergencies and breakdowns. You will find more detailed fault finding information at the back of the manual, and repair information in the main chapters.

If your car won't start and the starter motor doesn't turn

- [ ] If it's a model with automatic transmission, make sure the selector lever is in the P or N position.
- [ ] Open the bonnet and make sure that the battery terminals are clean and tight.
- [ ] Switch on the headlights and try to start the engine. If the headlights go very dim when you're trying to start, the battery is probably flat. Get out of trouble by jump starting (see next page) another car.

If your car won't start even though the starter motor turns as normal

- [ ] Is there fuel in the tank?
- [ ] Has the engine immobiliser been deactivated? This should happen automatically, on inserting the ignition key. However, if a new key has been obtained (other than from a VW dealer), it may not contain the transponder chip necessary to deactivate the system.
- [ ] Is there moisture on electrical components under the bonnet? Switch off the ignition, then wipe off any obvious dampness with a dry cloth. Spray a water-repellent aerosol product (WD-40 or equivalent) on electrical connectors like those shown in the photos. Pay special attention to the DIS ignition module's wiring connector.

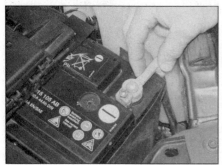

A Check the condition and security of the battery connections.

B With the ignition off, check that the spark plug HT leads are securely connected by pushing them onto the DIS module.

C With the ignition off, check that the spark plug HT leads are securely connected to their spark plugs.

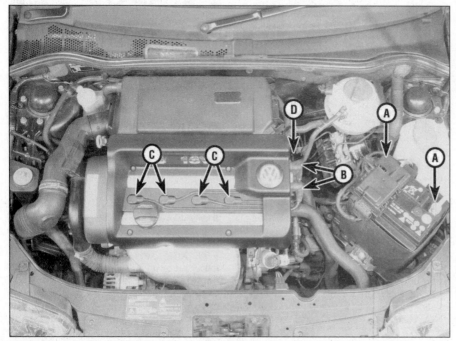

Check that electrical connections are secure (with the ignition switched off) and spray them with a water-dispersant spray like WD-40 if you suspect a problem due to damp

D With the ignition off, check that the wiring connectors are securely connected to the DIS module.

Jump starting

When jump-starting a car using a booster battery, observe the following precautions:

✔ Before connecting the booster battery, make sure that the ignition is switched off.

✔ Ensure that all electrical equipment (lights, heater, wipers, etc) is switched off.

✔ Take note of any special precautions printed on the battery case.

✔ Make sure that the booster battery is the same voltage as the discharged one in the vehicle.

✔ If the battery is being jump-started from the battery in another vehicle, the two vehicles MUST NOT TOUCH each other.

✔ Make sure that the transmission is in neutral.

 Jump starting will get you out of trouble, but you must correct whatever made the battery go flat in the first place. There are three possibilities:

1 *The battery has been drained by repeated attempts to start, or by leaving the lights on.*

2 *The charging system is not working properly (alternator drivebelt slack or broken, alternator wiring fault or alternator itself faulty).*

3 *The battery itself is at fault (electrolyte low, or battery worn out).*

1 Connect one end of the red jump lead to the positive (+) terminal of the flat battery

2 Connect the other end of the red lead to the positive (+) terminal of the booster battery.

3 Connect one end of the black jump lead to the negative (-) terminal of the booster battery

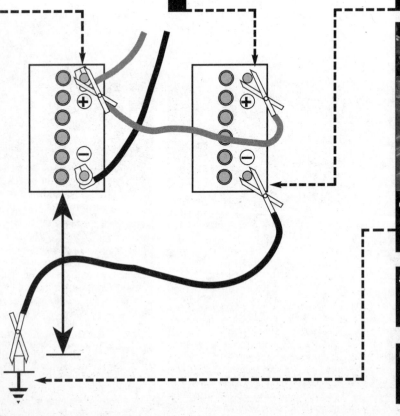

4 Connect the other end of the black jump lead to a suitable metal part of the engine on the vehicle to be started.

5 Make sure that the jump leads will not come into contact with the fan, drivebelts or other moving parts of the engine.

6 Start the engine using the booster battery and run it at idle speed. Switch on the lights, rear window demister and heater blower motor, then disconnect the jump leads in the reverse order of connection. Turn off the lights etc.

Wheel changing

Some of the details shown here will vary according to model

 Warning: Do not change a wheel in a situation where you risk being hit by another vehicle. On busy roads, try to stop in a lay-by or a gateway. Be wary of passing traffic while changing the wheel - it is easy to become distracted by the job in hand.

Preparation

☐ When a puncture occurs, stop as soon as it is safe to do so.

☐ Park on firm level ground, if possible, and well out of the way of other traffic.

☐ If you have one, use a warning triangle to alert other drivers of your presence.

☐ Apply the handbrake and engage first or reverse gear, or P on automatic transmission models.

☐ Use hazard warning lights if necessary.

☐ If the ground is soft, use a flat piece of wood or paving to spread the load under the foot of the jack.

Changing the wheel

1 The spare wheel and tools are stored in the luggage compartment, under the floor covering. A warning triangle may be provided on the right-hand side of the luggage compartment, behind a trim panel. Release the retaining strap, and lift out the jack and wheel changing tools out from the centre of the wheel. Unscrew the retaining nut and lift the wheel out of the car.

2 Remove the wheel trim/hub cap (on some models, a wire hook is provided, which is inserted through one of the holes in the wheel trim, and used with the wheelbrace handle to pull off the trim). On lower-specification models, plastic caps may be fitted over the wheel bolts, which can be hooked off with the tool provided.

3 Slacken each wheel bolt by a half turn, using the wheelbrace. If the bolts are too tight, DON'T stand on the wheelbrace to undo them – call for assistance from one of the motoring organisations.

4 Only attempt to jack up the car on firm, level ground. Locate the jack below the reinforced point on the sill, indicated by the triangular indentations (don't jack the car at any other point of the sill).

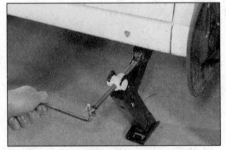

5 Turn the jack handle clockwise until the wheel is raised clear of the ground. Unscrew the wheel bolts and remove the wheel.

6 Fit the spare wheel, and screw in the bolts. Lightly tighten the bolts with the wheelbrace then lower the car to the ground. Securely tighten the wheel bolts, then refit the wheel trim/hub cap or the bolt covers. Stow the punctured wheel and tools back in the luggage compartment and secure them in position. Note that the wheel bolts should be slackened and retightened to the specified torque at the earliest possible opportunity.

Finally...

☐ Remove the wheel chocks.
☐ Check the tyre pressure on the wheel just fitted. If it is low, or if you don't have a pressure gauge with you, drive slowly to the next garage and inflate the tyre to the correct pressure.
☐ Have the damaged tyre or wheel repaired as soon as possible.

Note: *If a temporary 'space-saver' spare wheel has been fitted, special conditions apply to its use. This type of spare wheel is only intended for use in an emergency, and should not remain fitted any longer than it takes to get the punctured wheel repaired. While the temporary wheel is in use, do not exceed 50 mph (80 km/h), and avoid harsh acceleration, braking or cornering. Note that, besides being narrower than a normal roadwheel, the temporary spare wheel is of smaller diameter; therefore, since ground clearance will be slightly reduced with the temporary spare in use, take care if travelling over rough ground.*

Identifying leaks

Puddles on the garage floor or drive, or obvious wetness under the bonnet or underneath the car, suggest a leak that needs investigating. It can sometimes be difficult to decide where the leak is coming from, especially if the engine bay is very dirty already. Leaking oil or fluid can also be blown rearwards by the passage of air under the car, giving a false impression of where the problem lies.

 Warning: Most automotive oils and fluids are poisonous. Wash them off skin, and change out of contaminated clothing, without delay.

 The smell of a fluid leaking from the car may provide a clue to what's leaking. Some fluids are distinctively coloured. It may help to clean the car carefully and to park it over some clean paper overnight as an aid to locating the source of the leak.
Remember that some leaks may only occur while the engine is running.

Sump oil

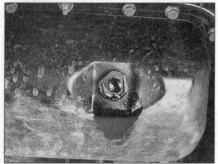

Engine oil may leak from the drain plug...

Oil from filter

...or from the base of the oil filter.

Gearbox oil

Gearbox oil can leak from the seals at the inboard ends of the driveshafts.

Antifreeze

Leaking antifreeze often leaves a crystalline deposit like this.

Brake fluid

A leak occurring at a wheel is almost certainly brake fluid.

Power steering fluid

Power steering fluid may leak from the pipe connectors on the steering rack.

Towing

When all else fails, you may find yourself having to get a tow home – or of course you may be helping somebody else. Long-distance recovery should only be done by a garage or breakdown service. For shorter distances, DIY towing using another car is easy enough, but observe the following points:

☐ Use a proper tow-rope – they are not expensive. The vehicle being towed must display an ON TOW sign in its rear window.

☐ Always turn the ignition key to the 'on' position when the vehicle is being towed, so that the steering lock is released, and that the direction indicator and brake lights will work.

☐ A rear towing eye is provided below the rear bumper. The front towing eye is provided in the vehicle tool kit, and is screwed into the front bumper after prising out the cover around the right-hand front foglight position.

☐ Before being towed, release the handbrake and select neutral on the transmission. On models with automatic transmission, special precautions apply. If in doubt, do not tow, or transmission damage may result.

☐ Note that greater-than-usual pedal pressure will be required to operate the brakes, since the vacuum servo unit is only operational with the engine running.

☐ Greater-than-usual steering effort will also be required because the steering pump only operates when the engine is running.

☐ The driver of the car being towed must keep the tow-rope taut at all times to avoid snatching.

☐ Make sure that both drivers know the route before setting off.

☐ Only drive at moderate speeds and keep the distance towed to a minimum. Drive smoothly and allow plenty of time for slowing down at junctions.

Introduction

There are some very simple checks which need only take a few minutes to carry out, but which could save you a lot of inconvenience and expense.

These *Weekly checks* require no great skill or special tools, and the small amount of time they take to perform could prove to be very well spent, for example:

☐ Keeping an eye on tyre condition and pressures, will not only help to stop them wearing out prematurely, but could also save your life.

☐ Many breakdowns are caused by electrical problems. Battery-related faults are particularly common, and a quick check on a regular basis will often prevent the majority of these.

☐ If your car develops a brake fluid leak, the first time you might know about it is when your brakes don't work properly. Checking the level regularly will give advance warning of this kind of problem.

☐ If the oil or coolant levels run low, the cost of repairing any engine damage will be far greater than fixing the leak, for example.

Underbonnet check points

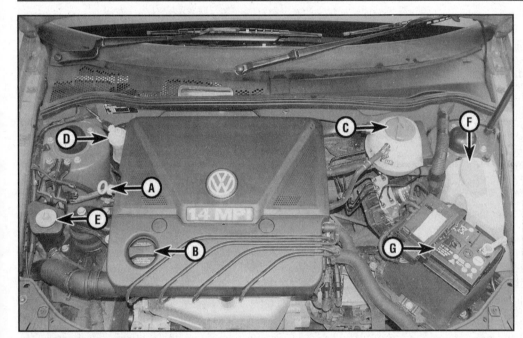

◀ **1.4 litre SOHC engine**

A *Engine oil level dipstick*

B *Engine oil filler cap*

C *Coolant expansion tank*

D *Brake fluid reservoir*

E *Power steering fluid reservoir*

F *Screen washer fluid reservoir*

G *Battery*

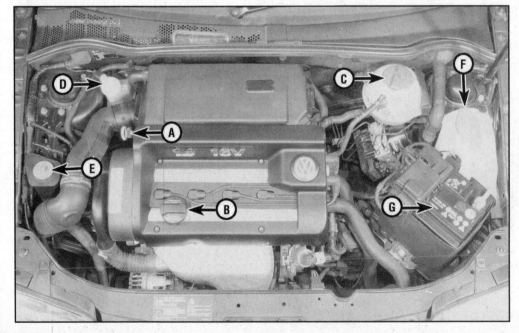

◀ **1.4 litre DOHC engine**

A *Engine oil level dipstick*

B *Engine oil filler cap*

C *Coolant expansion tank*

D *Brake fluid reservoir*

E *Power steering fluid reservoir*

F *Screen washer fluid reservoir*

G *Battery*

Engine oil level

Before you start

✔ Make sure that your car is on level ground.
✔ Check the oil level before the car is driven, or at least 5 minutes after the engine has been switched off.

HAYNES HiNT *If the oil is checked immediately after driving the car, some of the oil will remain in the upper engine components, resulting in an inaccurate reading on the dipstick.*

The correct oil

Modern engines place great demands on their oil. It is very important that the correct oil for your car is used (See *Lubricants and fluids*).

Car Care

● If you have to add oil frequently, you should check whether you have any oil leaks. Place some clean paper under the car overnight, and check for stains in the morning. If there are no leaks, the engine may be burning oil – blue smoke in the exhaust *(see Fault finding)*.

● Always maintain the level between the upper and lower dipstick marks (see photo 3). If the level is too low severe engine damage may occur. Oil seal failure may result if the engine is overfilled by adding too much oil.

1 The dipstick top is often brightly-coloured for easy identification (see *Underbonnet check points* for exact location). Withdraw the dipstick.

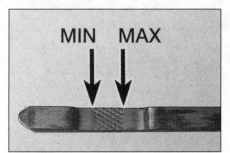
3 Note the oil level on the end of the dipstick, which should be within the hatched area marked. If the oil level is at the bottom of, or below, the hatched area, topping-up is required.

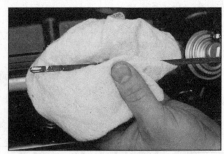
2 Using a clean rag or paper towel remove all oil from the dipstick. Insert the clean dipstick into the tube as far as it will go, then withdraw it again.

4 Oil is added through the filler cap. Unscrew the cap and top-up the level; a funnel may be useful in reducing spillage. Add the oil slowly, checking the level on the dipstick often, and allowing time for the oil to run to the sump. Add oil until the level is at the top of the hatched area on the dipstick – don't overfill (see *Car care*).

Coolant level

⚠ *Warning: DO NOT attempt to remove the expansion tank pressure cap when the engine is hot, as there is a very great risk of scalding. Do not leave open containers of coolant about, as it is poisonous.*

Car Care

● With a sealed-type cooling system, adding coolant should not be necessary on a regular basis. If frequent topping-up is required, it is likely there is a leak. Check the radiator, all hoses and joint faces for signs of staining or wetness, and rectify as necessary.

● It is important that antifreeze is used in the cooling system all year round, not just during the winter months. Don't top-up with water alone, as the antifreeze will become too diluted.

● The manufacturer states that if the coolant in the expansion tank is red in colour (VW G12 coolant), on no account should this be mixed with any other type of coolant, even the small amounts likely to be required for topping-up. Refer to your VW dealer for the latest advice.

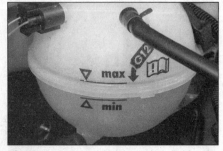
1 The coolant level varies with the temperature of the engine. When the engine is cold, the coolant level should be between the MAX and MIN marks. When the engine is hot, the level may rise slightly above the MAX mark.

2 If topping-up is necessary, **wait until the engine is cold**. Slowly unscrew the expansion tank cap, to release any pressure present in the cooling system, and remove it.

3 Add a mixture of water and antifreeze to the expansion tank, until the coolant is up to the MAX mark. Refit the cap, turning it clockwise as far as it will go until it is secure.

Brake fluid level

Warning:
● Brake fluid can harm your eyes and damage painted surfaces, so use extreme caution when handling and pouring it.
● Do not use fluid that has been standing open for some time, as it absorbs moisture from the air, which can cause a dangerous loss of braking effectiveness.

The fluid level in the reservoir will drop slightly as the brake pads wear down, but the fluid level must never be allowed to drop below the MIN mark.

Before you start
✔ Make sure that your car is on level ground.

Safety First!
● If the reservoir requires repeated topping-up this is an indication of a fluid leak somewhere in the system, which should be investigated immediately.

● If a leak is suspected, the car should not be driven until the braking system has been checked. Never take any risks where brakes are concerned.

1 The brake fluid reservoir is located on the right-hand side of the engine compartment, next to the suspension strut top mounting.

2 The MAX and MIN marks are indicated on the front of the reservoir. The fluid level must be kept between the marks at all times. If topping-up is necessary, first wipe clean the area around the filler cap to prevent dirt entering the hydraulic system.

3 Unscrew the reservoir cap and carefully lift it out of position, taking care not to damage the level switch float. Place the cap and float on a piece of clean rag. Inspect the reservoir; if the fluid is dirty, the hydraulic system should be drained and refilled (see Chapter 1).

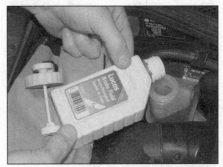

4 Carefully add fluid, taking care not to spill it onto the surrounding components. Use only the specified fluid; mixing different types can cause damage to the system. After topping-up to the correct level, securely refit the cap and wipe off any spilt fluid.

Screen washer fluid level*

* On models with a headlight washer system, the screen wash is also used to clean the headlights. The underbonnet reservoir also serves the tailgate washer.

● Screenwash additives not only keep the windscreen clean during bad weather, they also prevent the washer system freezing in cold weather – which is when you are likely to need it most. Don't top up using plain water, as the screenwash will become diluted and will freeze in cold weather. On no account use coolant antifreeze in the washer system – this could discolour or damage paintwork.

1 The screen washer fluid reservoir is located in the left-hand rear corner of the engine compartment, behind the battery.

2 The screen washer level can be seen through the reservoir body. If topping-up is necessary, open the cap. When topping-up the reservoir, add a screenwash additive in the quantities recommended on the additive bottle.

Tyre condition and pressure

It is very important that tyres are in good condition, and at the correct pressure - having a tyre failure at any speed is highly dangerous. Tyre wear is influenced by driving style - harsh braking and acceleration, or fast cornering, will all produce more rapid tyre wear. As a general rule, the front tyres wear out faster than the rears. Interchanging the tyres from front to rear ("rotating" the tyres) may result in more even wear. However, if this is completely effective, you may have the expense of replacing all four tyres at once!

Remove any nails or stones embedded in the tread before they penetrate the tyre to cause deflation. If removal of a nail does reveal that the tyre has been punctured, refit the nail so that its point of penetration is marked. Then immediately change the wheel, and have the tyre repaired by a tyre dealer.

Regularly check the tyres for damage in the form of cuts or bulges, especially in the sidewalls. Periodically remove the wheels, and clean any dirt or mud from the inside and outside surfaces. Examine the wheel rims for signs of rusting, corrosion or other damage. Light alloy wheels are easily damaged by "kerbing" whilst parking; steel wheels may also become dented or buckled. A new wheel is very often the only way to overcome severe damage.

New tyres should be balanced when they are fitted, but it may become necessary to re-balance them as they wear, or if the balance weights fitted to the wheel rim should fall off. Unbalanced tyres will wear more quickly, as will the steering and suspension components. Wheel imbalance is normally signified by vibration, particularly at a certain speed (typically around 50 mph). If this vibration is felt only through the steering, then it is likely that just the front wheels need balancing. If, however, the vibration is felt through the whole car, the rear wheels could be out of balance. Wheel balancing should be carried out by a tyre dealer or garage.

1 Tread Depth - visual check

The original tyres have tread wear safety bands (B), which will appear when the tread depth reaches approximately 1.6 mm. The band positions are indicated by a triangular mark on the tyre sidewall (A).

2 Tread Depth - manual check

Alternatively, tread wear can be monitored with a simple, inexpensive device known as a tread depth indicator gauge.

3 Tyre Pressure Check

Check the tyre pressures regularly with the tyres cold. Do not adjust the tyre pressures immediately after the vehicle has been used, or an inaccurate setting will result.

Tyre tread wear patterns

Shoulder Wear

Underinflation (wear on both sides)
Under-inflation will cause overheating of the tyre, because the tyre will flex too much, and the tread will not sit correctly on the road surface. This will cause a loss of grip and excessive wear, not to mention the danger of sudden tyre failure due to heat build-up.
Check and adjust pressures
Incorrect wheel camber (wear on one side)
Repair or renew suspension parts
Hard cornering
Reduce speed!

Centre Wear

Overinflation
Over-inflation will cause rapid wear of the centre part of the tyre tread, coupled with reduced grip, harsher ride, and the danger of shock damage occurring in the tyre casing.
Check and adjust pressures

If you sometimes have to inflate your car's tyres to the higher pressures specified for maximum load or sustained high speed, don't forget to reduce the pressures to normal afterwards.

Uneven Wear

Front tyres may wear unevenly as a result of wheel misalignment. Most tyre dealers and garages can check and adjust the wheel alignment (or "tracking") for a modest charge.
Incorrect camber or castor
Repair or renew suspension parts
Malfunctioning suspension
Repair or renew suspension parts
Unbalanced wheel
Balance tyres
Incorrect toe setting
Adjust front wheel alignment
Note: *The feathered edge of the tread which typifies toe wear is best checked by feel.*

Power steering fluid level

Before you start

✔ Park the car on level ground.
✔ Set the steering wheel straight-ahead.
✔ If the system is cold, the fluid level should be checked with the engine switched off.
✔ If the system is at operating temperature, the fluid level should be checked with the engine running.

 HAYNES HiNT *For the check to be accurate, the steering must not be turned once the engine has been stopped.*

Safety first!

● The need for frequent topping-up indicates a leak, which should be investigated immediately.

1 The reservoir is located on the right-hand side of the engine compartment.

2 Wipe clean the area around the reservoir filler neck and unscrew the filler cap/dipstick from the reservoir, using a flat-bladed screwdriver in the slot provided on the reservoir cap.

3 Wipe the fluid dipstick attached to the cap clean with a clean non-fluffy rag, then screw the cap fully back into position, hand-tight. Unscrew the cap once more, and note the reading on the dipstick. When the system is cold, the fluid level should be up to the MIN mark; when hot, it should be between the MAX and MIN marks.

4 When topping-up, use the specified type of fluid, and do not overfill the reservoir. When the level is correct, securely refit the cap.

Wiper blades

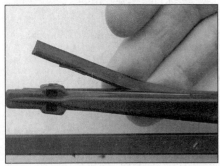

1 Check the condition of the wiper blades; if they are cracked or show any signs of deterioration, or if the glass swept area is smeared, renew them. Wiper blades should be renewed annually, regardless of their apparent condition.

2 To remove a windscreen wiper blade, pull the arm fully away from the screen until it locks. Swivel the blade through 90°, press the locking tab with your fingers and slide the blade out of the arm's hooked end.

3 Don't forget to check the tailgate wiper blade as well. To remove the blade, simply slide the blade out of the hooked end of the arm.

Battery

Caution: Before carrying out any work on the vehicle battery, read the precautions given in Safety first! at the start of this manual.

✔ Make sure that the battery tray is in good condition, and that the clamp is tight. Corrosion on the tray, retaining clamp and the battery itself can be removed with a solution of water and baking soda. Thoroughly rinse all cleaned areas with water. Any metal parts damaged by corrosion should be covered with a zinc-based primer, then painted.

✔ Periodically (approximately every three months), check the charge condition of the battery as described in Chapter 5A.

✔ On batteries which are not of the maintenance-free type, periodically (approximately every three months), check the electrolyte level in the battery – see Chapter 1.

✔ If the battery is flat, and you need to jump start your vehicle, see *Jump starting*.

HAYNES HINT

Battery corrosion can be kept to a minimum by applying a layer of petroleum jelly (not grease) to the clamps and terminals after they are reconnected.

1 The battery is located on the passenger side of the engine compartment. The exterior of the battery should be inspected periodically for damage such as a cracked case or cover.

3 If corrosion (white, fluffy deposits) is evident, remove the cables from the battery terminals, clean them with a small wire brush, then refit them. Car accessory shops sell tools for cleaning the battery post . . .

2 Check the tightness of battery clamps to ensure good electrical connections. You should not be able to move them. Also check each cable for cracks and frayed conductors.

4 . . . as well as the battery cable clamps

Electrical systems

✔ Check all external lights and the horn. Refer to the appropriate Sections of Chapter 12 for details if any of the circuits are found to be inoperative.

✔ Visually check all accessible wiring connectors, harnesses and retaining clips for security, and for signs of chafing or damage.

HAYNES HINT

If you need to check your brake lights and indicators unaided, back up to a wall or garage door and operate the lights. The reflected light should show if they are working properly.

1 If a single indicator light, stop-light or headlight has failed, it is likely that a bulb has blown and will need to be renewed. Refer to Chapter 12 for details. If both stop-lights have failed, it is possible that the switch has failed (see Chapter 9).

2 If more than one indicator light or tail light has failed, it is likely that either a fuse has blown, or that there is a fault in the circuit (see Chapter 12). The main fuses are located behind a cover panel below the steering wheel – unclip the cover for access. There may also be a small fusebox attached to the top of the battery.

3 To renew a blown fuse, simply pull it out and fit a new fuse of the correct rating (see Chapter 12). If the fuse blows again, it is important that you find out why – a complete checking procedure is given in Chapter 12.

Lubricants and fluids

Engine . . . . Multigrade engine oil, viscosity SAE 10W/40, 15W/40, or 15W/50, to VW spec 500 00, 502 00 or 501 01, or to ACEA A2/A3

Cooling system . . . . Ethylene glycol-based antifreeze with corrosion inhibitor – VW G12*

Manual transmission and final drive . . . . VW synthetic gear oil G50 or G51, SAE 75W/90**

Automatic transmission and final drive . . . . VW ATF G 052 990 A2***

Brake hydraulic system . . . . Hydraulic fluid to FMVSS 116 DOT 4

Power steering . . . . VW hydraulic oil G 002 000

Refer to Coolant renewal in Chapter 1.
** Models with the 1.4 litre DOHC (100 bhp) engine require G51 gear oil, even for topping-up.
*** The automatic transmission is regarded as 'filled for life'. Topping-up or changing the fluid can only be undertaken using special VW equipment – see Chapter 1.

Choosing your engine oil

Engines need oil, not only to lubricate moving parts and minimise wear, but also to maximise power output and to improve fuel economy.

HOW ENGINE OIL WORKS

• Beating friction

Without oil, the moving surfaces inside your engine will rub together, heat up and melt, quickly causing the engine to seize. Engine oil creates a film which separates these moving parts, preventing wear and heat build-up.

• Cooling hot-spots

Temperatures inside the engine can exceed 1000° C. The engine oil circulates and acts as a coolant, transferring heat from the hot-spots to the sump.

• Cleaning the engine internally

Good quality engine oils clean the inside of your engine, collecting and dispersing combustion deposits and controlling them until they are trapped by the oil filter or flushed out at oil change.

OIL CARE - FOLLOW THE CODE

To handle and dispose of used engine oil safely, always:

0800 66 33 66
www.oilbankline.org.uk

  • **Avoid skin contact with used engine oil. Repeated or prolonged contact can be harmful.**
  • **Dispose of used oil and empty packs in a responsible manner in an authorised disposal site. Call 0800 663366 to find the one nearest to you. Never tip oil down drains or onto the ground.**

Tyre pressures

Note: *The correct pressures are given on a sticker which is inside the fuel filler flap. Pressures apply to original-equipment tyres, and may vary if any other make of tyre is fitted; check with the tyre manufacturer or supplier for the correct pressures if necessary.*

The spare wheel may be of conventional or 'space-saver' type. A conventional spare wheel should be maintained at the highest full-load pressure for the car. The 'space-saver' spare runs at a pressure of 4.2 bar (61 psi) – this pressure should be marked on the tyre sidewall.

Chapter 1
Routine maintenance & servicing

Contents

Degrees of difficulty

Easy, suitable for novice with little experience	**Fairly easy,** suitable for beginner with some experience	**Fairly difficult,** suitable for competent DIY mechanic	**Difficult,** suitable for experienced DIY mechanic	**Very difficult,** suitable for expert DIY or professional

Lubricants and fluids

Refer to end of *Weekly checks* on page 0•17

Capacities

Engine oil (including filter)
All engines . . . .   3.2 litres

Cooling system (approximate)
All engines . . . .   5.6 litres

Transmission (approximate)
Manual transmission . . . .   2.7 litres
Automatic transmission (fluid change) . . . .   3.0 litres

Fuel tank (approximate)
All models . . . .   45 litres

Washer reservoir
Models with headlight washers . . . .   5.5 litres
Models without headlight washers . . . .   2.5 litres

Cooling system

Antifreeze mixture:
   40% antifreeze . . . .   Protection down to -25°C
   50% antifreeze . . . .   Protection down to -35°C
Note: *Refer to antifreeze manufacturer for latest recommendations.*

Ignition system

Spark plugs:	Type	Electrode gap
Bosch recommendation:		
All engines except 1.4 litre DOHC (100 bhp)	Bosch F7 HPP 222	1.0 mm
1.4 litre DOHC (100 bhp) engines*	Bosch FR 7 LD+	0.9 mm
VW recommendation:		
All SOHC engines	NGK PZFR5 D-11	1.0 mm
All DOHC (16V) engines	NGK BKUR6 ET-10	1.0 mm

*****Note:** *Refer to Chapter 2B Specifications for engine code details.*

Brakes

Brake pad minimum thickness (including backing plate) . . . .   7.0 mm
Brake shoe friction material minimum thickness . . . .   2.5 mm

Torque wrench settings

	Nm	lbf ft
Manual transmission filler/level plug	25	18
Roadwheel bolts	110	81
Spark plugs	30	22
Sump drain plug	30	22

The maintenance intervals in this manual are provided with the assumption that you, not the dealer, will be carrying out the work. These are the minimum intervals recommended for cars driven daily. If you wish to keep your car in peak condition at all times, you may wish to perform some of these procedures more often. We encourage frequent maintenance, since it enhances the efficiency, performance and resale value of your car.

When the car is new, it should be serviced by a dealer service department, in order to preserve the factory warranty.

Every 250 miles (400 km) or weekly

☐ Refer to *Weekly checks*

Every 5000 miles (7500 km)

☐ Renew the engine oil and filter (Section 3)

Note: *Frequent oil and filter changes are good for the engine. We recommend changing the oil at the mileage specified here, or at least twice a year if the mileage covered is a less.*

Every 10 000 miles (15 000 km) – OIL on interval display

In addition to the items listed in the previous service, carry out the following:

☐ Check the front brake pad thickness (Section 4)
☐ Reset the service interval display (Section 5)

Every 12 months or 20 000 miles – 01 on interval display

In addition to the items listed in the previous service, carry out the following:

☐ Check operation of all lights and horn (Section 6)
☐ Check the condition of the airbag unit(s) (Section 7)
☐ Check the operation of the washer system(s) (Section 8)
☐ Lubricate all hinges, locks and door check straps (Section 9)
☐ Check engine management and other systems for fault codes (Section 10)
☐ Check battery electrolyte level – where applicable (Section 11)
☐ Check all underbonnet components and hoses for fluid leaks (Section 12)
☐ Check the transmission and driveshaft gaiters for leaks and damage (Section 13)
☐ Check the braking system for leaks and damage (Section 14)
☐ Check the rear brake shoe/pad thickness (Section 15)
☐ Check the condition of the exhaust system and its mountings (Section 16)
☐ Check the steering and suspension components for condition and security (Section 17)
☐ Check the headlight beam adjustment (Section 18)
☐ Carry out a road test (Section 19)
☐ Reset the service interval display (Section 5)

Every 20 000 miles (30 000 km) or 2 years

Note: *If the car is covering more than 20 000 miles (30 000 km) a year, also carry out all the operations described above.*

☐ Lubricate folding fabric sunroof guide rail (Section 20)
☐ Renew the pollen filter element (Section 21)
☐ Check the condition of the auxiliary drivebelt(s), and renew if necessary (Section 22)
☐ Check the manual transmission oil level (Section 23)
☐ Check underbody protection for damage (Section 24)
☐ Reset the service interval display (Section 5)

Every 40 000 miles (60 000 km) or 4 years

In addition to the items listed in the previous services, carry out the following:

☐ Renew the spark plugs (Section 25)
☐ Renew the air filter element (Section 26)
☐ Check the automatic transmission fluid level (Section 27)
☐ Renew the fuel filter (Section 28)
☐ Renew the timing belt (Section 29)

Every 2 years (regardless of mileage)

In addition to the items listed in the previous services, carry out the following:

☐ Renew the coolant (Section 30)*
☐ Renew the brake fluid (Section 31)
☐ Check exhaust emissions (Section 32)

* Note: *This work is not included in the VW schedule and should not be required if the recommended VW G12 LongLife coolant anti-freeze/inhibitor is used.*

Underbonnet view of a 1.4 litre SOHC engine model (1.0 litre similar)

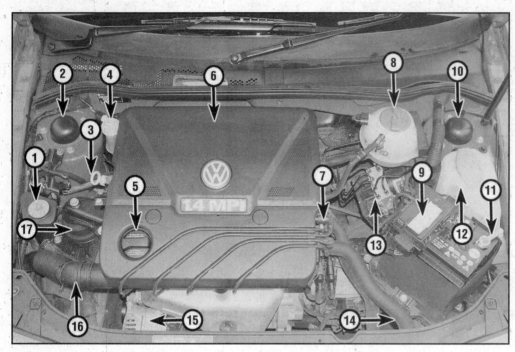

1   Power steering fluid
    reservoir
2   Suspension strut upper
    mounting (right-hand)
3   Engine oil dipstick
4   Brake fluid reservoir
5   Engine oil filler cap
6   Air cleaner housing
7   DIS module (ignition coil)
8   Coolant expansion tank
9   Engine compartment
    fusebox
10 Suspension strut upper
    mounting (left-hand)
11 Battery negative terminal
12 Washer fluid reservoir
13 ABS module
14 Radiator top hose
15 Alternator
16 Inlet air hose
17 Engine right-hand
    mounting

Underbonnet view of a 1.4 litre DOHC engine model

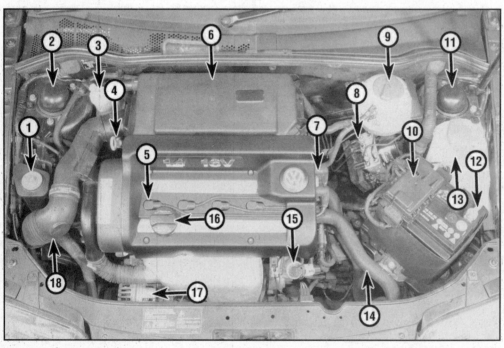

1   Power steering fluid
    reservoir
2   Suspension strut upper
    mounting (right-hand)
3   Brake fluid reservoir
4   Engine oil dipstick
5   No 1 spark plug lead
6   Air cleaner housing
7   DIS module (ignition coil)
8   ABS module
9   Coolant expansion tank
10 Engine compartment
    fusebox
11 Suspension strut upper
    mounting (left-hand)
12 Battery negative terminal
13 Washer fluid reservoir
14 Radiator top hose
15 EGR valve
16 Engine oil filler cap
17 Alternator
18 Inlet air hose

Front underbody view

1 Front brake caliper
2 Front suspension lower arm
3 Power steering pump
4 Engine oil drain plug
5 Right-hand driveshaft
6 Oil filter
7 Exhaust manifold
8 Radiator cooling fan motor
9 Radiator bottom hose
10 Horn
11 Track rod
12 Anti-roll bar
13 Engine rear mounting
14 Exhaust front mounting

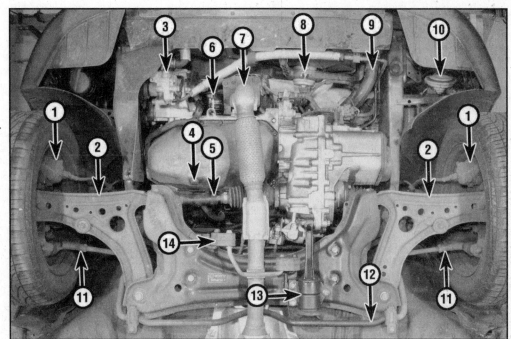

Rear underbody view

1 Handbrake cable
2 Rear shock absorber mounting
3 Exhaust mounting
4 Exhaust rear silencer
5 Rear axle
6 Fuel tank

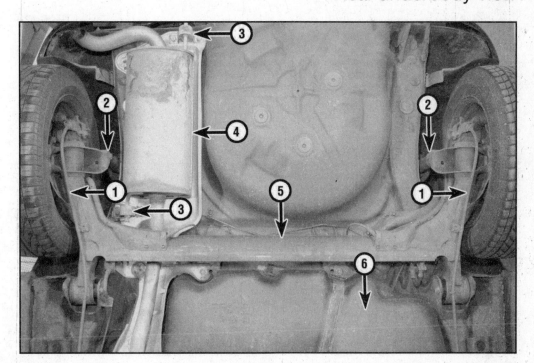

1 Introduction

General information

This Chapter is designed to help the home mechanic maintain his/her car for safety, economy, long life and peak performance.

The Chapter contains a master maintenance schedule, followed by Sections dealing specifically with each task in the schedule. Visual checks, adjustments, component renewal and other helpful items are included. Refer to the accompanying illustrations of the engine compartment and the underside of the car for the locations of the various components.

Servicing your car in accordance with the mileage/time maintenance schedule and the following Sections will provide a planned maintenance programme, which should result in a long and reliable service life. This is a comprehensive plan, so maintaining some items but not others at the specified service intervals, will not produce the same results.

As you service your car, you will discover that many of the procedures can – and should – be grouped together, because of the particular procedure being performed, or because of the proximity of two otherwise unrelated components to one another. For example, if the car is raised for any reason, the exhaust can be inspected at the same time as the suspension and steering components.

The first step in this maintenance programme is to prepare yourself before the actual work begins. Read through all the Sections relevant to the work to be carried out, then make a list and gather all the parts and tools required. If a problem is encountered, seek advice from a parts specialist, or a dealer service department.

Service interval display

All VW Polo models are equipped with a service interval display indicator in the LCD display at the base of the speedometer. Every time the engine is started, the panel will illuminate for a few seconds, providing a handy reminder of when the next service is required:

Display clear – no service required.
Display shows OIL – 10 000 mile (15 000 km): Oil change service required.
Display shows 01 – 12-monthly or 20 000 mile (30 000 km): Inspection service required.

The display should not necessarily be used as a definitive guide to the servicing needs of your Polo, but it is useful as a reminder to ensure that servicing is not accidentally overlooked. Owners of older cars, or those covering a small annual mileage, may feel inclined to service their car more often, in which case the service interval display is perhaps less relevant.

The display should be reset whenever a service is carried out, and the procedure for this is described in Section 5.

2 Regular maintenance

1 If, from the time the car is new, the routine maintenance schedule is followed closely, and frequent checks are made of fluid levels and high-wear items, as suggested throughout this manual, the engine will be kept in relatively good running condition, and the need for additional work will be minimised.

2 It is possible that there will be times when the engine is running poorly due to the lack of regular maintenance. This is even more likely if a used car, which has not received regular and frequent maintenance checks, is purchased. In such cases, additional work may need to be carried out, outside of the regular maintenance intervals.

3 If engine wear is suspected, a compression test (refer to the relevant Part of Chapter 2) will provide valuable information regarding the overall performance of the main internal components. Such a test can be used as a basis to decide on the extent of the work to be carried out. If, for example, a compression test indicates serious internal engine wear, conventional maintenance as described in this Chapter will not greatly improve the performance of the engine, and may prove a waste of time and money, unless extensive overhaul work is carried out first.

4 The following series of operations are those most often required to improve the performance of a generally poor-running engine:

Primary operations

a) *Clean, inspect and test the battery (See 'Weekly checks' and Section 11, where applicable).*
b) *Check all the engine-related fluids (See 'Weekly checks').*
c) *Check the condition and tension of the auxiliary drivebelt (Section 22).*
d) *Renew the spark plugs (Section 25).*
e) *Check the ignition HT leads (see Chapter 5B).*
f) *Check the condition of the air filter, and renew if necessary (Section 26).*
g) *Check the fuel filter (Section 28).*
h) *Check the condition of all hoses, and check for fluid leaks (Section 12).*
i) *Check the exhaust gas emissions (Section 32).*

5 If the above operations do not prove fully effective, carry out the following secondary operations:

Secondary operations

All items listed under *Primary operations*, plus the following:

a) *Check the charging system (see Chapter 5A).*
b) *Check the ignition system (see Chapter 5B).*
c) *Check the fuel system (see Chapter 4A).*
d) *Renew the ignition HT leads (see Chapter 5B)*

Every 5000 miles (7500 km)

3 Engine oil and filter renewal

1 Frequent oil and filter changes are the most important maintenance procedures which can be undertaken by the DIY owner. As engine oil ages, it becomes diluted and contaminated, which leads to premature engine wear.

2 Before starting this procedure, gather all the necessary tools and materials. Also make sure that you have plenty of clean rags and newspapers handy, to mop up any spills. Ideally, the engine oil should be warm, as it will drain better, and more built-up sludge will be removed with it. Take care, however, not to touch the exhaust or any other hot parts of the engine when working under the car. To avoid any possibility of scalding, and to protect yourself from possible skin irritants and other harmful contaminants in used engine oils, it is advisable to wear gloves when carrying out this work.

3 Access to the underside of the car will be greatly improved if it can be raised on a lift, driven onto ramps, or jacked up and supported on axle stands (see *Jacking and vehicle support*). Whichever method is chosen, make sure that the car remains level, or if it is at an angle, that the drain plug is at the lowest point. Where applicable, release the fasteners and remove the noise insulation tray from under the engine.

4 Using a socket and handle or a ring spanner, slacken the drain plug (at the rear of the sump) about half a turn **(see illustration)**.

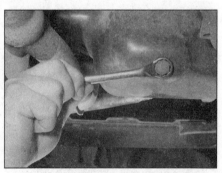

3.4 Slackening the sump drain plug

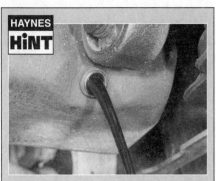

HAYNES HINT

Keep the drain plug pressed into the sump while unscrewing it by hand last couple of turns. As the plug releases, move it away sharply so the stream of oil issuing from the sump runs into the container, not up your sleeve.

Position the draining container under the drain plug, then remove the plug completely **(see Haynes Hint)**. Recover the sealing ring from the drain plug.

5 Allow some time for the old oil to drain, noting that it may be necessary to reposition the container as the oil flow slows to a trickle.

6 After all the oil has drained, wipe off the drain plug with a clean rag, and check the condition of the (attached) rubber seal. If the seal is in poor condition, a new drain plug should be fitted. Clean the area around the drain plug opening, and refit the plug. Tighten the plug securely.

7 Move the container into position under the oil filter, which is located on the front of the cylinder block.

8 Using an oil filter removal tool if necessary, slacken the filter initially, then unscrew it by hand the rest of the way **(see illustration)**. Empty the oil in the filter into the container.

9 Use a clean rag to remove all oil, dirt and sludge from the filter sealing area on the engine. Check the old filter to make sure that

3.8 Loosening the oil filter using a chain-type removal tool

the rubber sealing ring has not stuck to the engine. If it has, carefully remove it.

10 Apply a light coating of clean engine oil to the sealing ring on the new filter, then screw it into position on the engine. Tighten the filter firmly by hand only – **do not** use any tools.

11 Remove the old oil and all tools from under the car, then lower the car to the ground (if applicable).

12 Remove the dipstick, then unscrew the oil filler cap from the top of the engine. Fill the engine, using the correct grade and type of oil (see *Lubricants and fluids*). An oil can spout or funnel may help to reduce spillage. Pour in half the specified quantity of oil first, then wait a few minutes for the oil to run to the sump **(see illustrations)**. Continue adding oil a small quantity at a time until the level is up to the bottom of the hatched area on the dipstick. Adding around 0.5 litres of oil will bring the level into the hatched area on the dipstick. Add a little more oil until the level is up to the top of the hatched area on the dipstick, then refit the dipstick and the filler cap.

13 Start the engine and run it for a few minutes; check for leaks around the oil filter seal and the sump drain plug. Note that there may be a few seconds delay before the oil

3.12a Remove the oil filler cap . . .

3.12b . . . then fill the engine using the correct grade and quantity of oil

pressure warning light goes out when the engine is started, as the oil circulates through the engine oil galleries and the new oil filter before the pressure builds-up.

14 Switch off the engine, and wait a few minutes for the oil to settle in the sump once more. With the new oil circulated and the filter completely full, recheck the level on the dipstick, and add more oil as necessary. Refit the noise insulation tray to the underside of the engine, where applicable.

15 Dispose of the used engine oil safely, with reference to *General repair procedures* in the *Reference* section of this manual.

Every 10 000 miles (15 000 km)

4   Front brake pad check

1 Firmly apply the handbrake, loosen the front roadwheel bolts, then jack up the front of the car and support it securely on axle stands. Remove the front roadwheels.

2 For a comprehensive check, the brake pads should be removed and cleaned. The operation of the caliper can then also be checked, and the condition of the brake disc itself can be fully examined on both sides. Refer to Chapter 9 **(see Haynes Hint)**.

3 If any pad's friction material is worn to the specified thickness or less, *all four pads must be renewed as a set.*

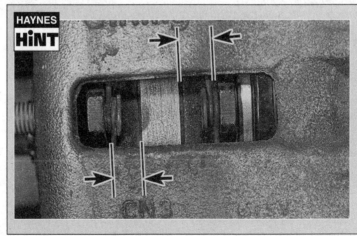

HAYNES HINT

For a quick check, the thickness of the friction material on each brake pad can be measured through the aperture in the caliper body.

5.2 Resetting the service interval display

5 Resetting service interval display

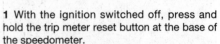

1 With the ignition switched off, press and hold the trip meter reset button at the base of the speedometer.
2 Keeping the button pressed, switch on the ignition **(see illustration)**. Hold the button pressed for about 10 seconds after switching on the ignition, and the service display will change to a row of dashes, indicating that the service display has successfully been reset.
3 Release the trip reset button, then switch the ignition off, and on again, to confirm the resetting. Switch the ignition off to complete.

6 Lights and horn operation check

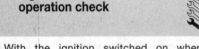

1 With the ignition switched on where necessary, check the operation of all exterior lights.
2 Check the brake lights with the help of an assistant, or by reversing close to a reflective door. Make sure that all the rear lights are capable of operating independently, without affecting any of the other lights – for example, switch on as many rear lights as possible, then try the brake lights. If any unusual results are found, this is usually due to an earth fault or other poor connection at that rear light unit.
3 Again with the help of an assistant or using a reflective surface, check as far as possible that the headlights work on both main and dipped beam.
4 Renew any defective bulbs with reference to Chapter 12.

HAYNES HiNT *Particularly on older cars, bulbs can stop working as a result of corrosion build-up on the bulb or its holder – fitting a new bulb may not cure the problem in this instance. When renewing any bulb, if you find any green or white-coloured powdery deposits, these should be cleaned off using emery cloth.*

5 Check the operation of all interior lights, including the glovebox and luggage area illumination lights. Switch on the ignition, and check that all relevant warning lights come on as expected – the car's handbook should give details of these. Now start the engine, and check that the appropriate lights go out. When you are next driving at night, check that all the instrument panel and facia lighting works correctly. If any problems are found, refer to Chapter 12.

6 Finally, choose an appropriate time of day to test the operation of the horn.

7 Airbag unit check

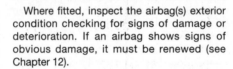

Where fitted, inspect the airbag(s) exterior condition checking for signs of damage or deterioration. If an airbag shows signs of obvious damage, it must be renewed (see Chapter 12).

8 Washer system(s) check

Check that each of the washer jet nozzles is clear, and that each nozzle provides a strong jet of washer fluid. The tailgate and headlight jets (where applicable) should be aimed to spray at a point slightly above the centre of the screen/headlight.

The windscreen washer nozzles have two jets; aim one of the jets slightly above the centre of the screen and the other just below, to ensure complete coverage of the screen. If necessary, adjust the jets using a pin.

Later models may be fitted with additional preset washer jets which only have a limited amount of adjustment. Height adjustment on these later jets is effected by turning an eccentric on the spray jet.

9 Hinge and lock lubrication

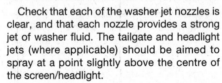

Lubricate the hinges of the bonnet, doors and tailgate with light general-purpose oil. Similarly, lubricate all latches, locks and lock strikers, and the door check straps with general-purpose oil or grease **(see illustration)**.

At the same time, check the security and operation of all the locks, adjusting them if necessary (see Chapter 11).

Lightly lubricate the bonnet release mechanism and cable with suitable grease.

Do not attempt to lubricate the steering lock.

10 Engine management system fault code check

1 This check is part of the manufacturer's maintenance schedule, and involves 'interrogating' the engine management control unit (and those for the automatic transmission and/or ABS, as applicable) using special dedicated test equipment. Such testing will allow the test equipment to read any fault codes stored in the electronic control unit memory.
2 Unless a fault is suspected, this test is not essential, although it should be noted that it is recommended by the manufacturers.
3 It is possible for quite serious faults to occur in the engine management system without the owner being aware of it. Certain engine management system faults will cause the system to enter an emergency back-up

9.1 Lubricate the door check straps

mode, which is often so sophisticated that engine performance is not apparently much affected. If a problem has caused the system to enter its back-up mode, this will usually be most apparent when starting and running from cold.

11 Battery electrolyte level check

⚠️ **Warning: The electrolyte inside a battery is diluted acid – it is a good idea to wear suitable rubber gloves. When topping-up, don't overfill the cells so that the electrolyte overflows. In the event of any spillage, rinse the electrolyte off without delay. Refit the cell covers and rinse the battery with copious quantities of clean water. Don't attempt to syphon out any excess electrolyte.**

1 Some models covered by this Manual may be fitted with a maintenance-free battery as standard equipment, or may have had one fitted. If the battery in your car is marked 'Freedom', 'Maintenance-Free' or similar, no electrolyte level checking is required (the battery is often completely sealed, preventing any topping-up).

2 Batteries which do require their electrolyte level to be checked can be recognised by the presence of removable covers over the six battery cells – the battery casing is also sometimes translucent, so that the electrolyte level can be more easily checked. Make sure you do not have a maintenance-free battery before attempting to top-up the electrolyte level.

3 Remove the cell covers and either look down inside the battery to see the level web, or check the level using any markings provided on the battery casing. The electrolyte should at least cover the battery plates. If necessary, top-up a little at a time with distilled (deionised) water until the level in all six cells is correct – don't fill the cells up to the brim. Wipe up any spillage, then refit the cell covers.

12 Hose and fluid leak check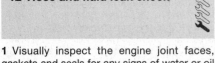

1 Visually inspect the engine joint faces, gaskets and seals for any signs of water or oil leaks. Pay particular attention to the areas around the camshaft cover, cylinder head, oil filter and sump joint faces. Bear in mind that, over a period of time, some very slight seepage from these areas is to be expected – what you are really looking for is any indication of a serious leak. Should a leak be found, renew the offending gasket or oil seal by referring to the appropriate Chapters in this manual.

2 Also check the security and condition of all

A leak in the cooling system will usually show up as white- or rust-coloured deposits on the area adjoining the leak.

the engine-related pipes and hoses. Ensure that all cable-ties or securing clips are in place and in good condition. Clips that are broken or missing can lead to chafing of the hoses, pipes or wiring, which could cause more serious problems in the future.

3 Carefully check the radiator hoses and heater hoses along their entire length. Renew any hose that is cracked, swollen or deteriorated. Cracks will show up better if the hose is squeezed. Pay close attention to the hose clips that secure the hoses to the cooling system components. Hose clips can pinch and puncture hoses, resulting in cooling system leaks.

4 Inspect all the cooling system components (hoses, joint faces etc) for leaks **(see Haynes Hint)**. Where any problems of this nature are found on system components, renew the component or gasket with reference to Chapter 3.

5 Where applicable, inspect the automatic transmission fluid cooler hoses for leaks or deterioration.

6 With the car raised, inspect the fuel tank and filler neck for punctures, cracks and other damage. The connection between the filler neck and tank is especially critical. Sometimes a rubber filler neck or connecting hose will leak due to loose retaining clamps or deteriorated rubber.

7 Carefully check all rubber hoses and metal fuel lines leading away from the fuel tank.

Check for loose connections, deteriorated hoses, crimped lines, and other damage. Pay particular attention to the vent pipes and hoses, which often loop up around the filler neck and can become blocked or crimped. Follow the lines to the front of the car, carefully inspecting them all the way. Renew damaged sections as necessary.

8 From within the engine compartment, check the security of all fuel hose attachments and pipe unions, and inspect the fuel hoses and vacuum hoses for kinks, chafing and deterioration.

9 Where applicable, check the condition of the power steering fluid hoses and pipes.

13 Transmission and driveshaft gaiter check

1 Raise the front of the car and support on axle stands. Alternatively, drive the car onto ramps.

2 Inspect around the transmission for any sign of leaks or damage. In particular, check the area around the driveshaft oil/fluid seals for leakage **(see illustration)**. Slight seepage should not be of great concern, but a serious leak should be investigated further, with reference to the relevant Part of Chapter 7.

3 Check the security and condition of the wiring and wiring plugs on the transmission housing **(see illustration)**.

4 With the car raised and securely supported on stands, turn the steering onto full lock, then slowly rotate the roadwheel. Inspect the condition of the outer constant velocity (CV) joint rubber gaiters, squeezing the gaiters to open out the folds. Check for signs of cracking, splits or deterioration of the rubber, which may allow the grease to escape, and lead to water and grit entry into the joint **(see illustration)**. Also check the security and condition of the retaining clips. Repeat these checks on the inner CV joints. If any damage or deterioration is found, the gaiters should be renewed (see Chapter 8).

5 At the same time, check the general condition of the CV joints themselves by first holding the driveshaft and attempting to

13.2 Driveshaft inner CV joint, showing driveshaft seal (arrowed)

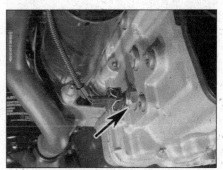

13.3 Reversing light switch (arrowed) – seen from below

13.4 Check the condition of the driveshaft gaiters (arrowed)

rotate the wheel. Repeat this check by holding the inner joint and attempting to rotate the driveshaft. Any appreciable movement indicates wear in the joints, wear in the driveshaft splines, or a loose driveshaft retaining nut.

14 Braking system check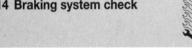

1 Starting under the bonnet, examine the brake fluid reservoir and master cylinder for leaks. When a brake fluid leak occurs, it is normal to find blistered or wrinkled paint in the area of the leak. Check the metal pipes from the master cylinder for damage, and check the brake pressure regulator, ABS unit and fluid unions for leaks.
2 With the car raised and securely supported on stands, first inspect each front brake caliper. In particular, check the flexible hose leading to the caliper for signs of damage or leaks, especially where the hose enters the metal end fitting. Make sure that the hose is not twisted or kinked, and that it cannot come into contact with any other components when the steering is on full lock.
3 From the caliper, trace the metal brake pipes back along the car. Again, look for leaks from the fluid unions or signs of damage, but additionally check the pipes for signs of corrosion. Make sure the pipes are securely located by the clips provided on the underside.

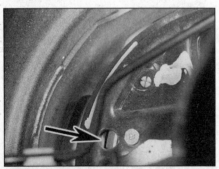

15.2 Rear brake backplate inspection hole (arrowed) for assessing brake lining wear

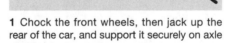

14.4 Rear brake flexible hose

4 At the rear of the car, inspect each rear brake and its flexible hose, where applicable **(see illustration)**. Examine the handbrake cable, tracing it back from each rear brake and checking for frayed cables or other damage. Lubricate the handbrake cable guides, pivots and other moving parts with general-purpose grease.
5 If any damage is found, refer to Chapter 9 for further information.

15 Rear brake shoe/pad check

1 Chock the front wheels, then jack up the rear of the car, and support it securely on axle stands.
2 For a quick check, the thickness of friction material remaining on one of the brake shoes can be observed through the holes in the trailing arm and the brake backplate. The hole in the brake backplate may be plugged with a sealing grommet, which can be prised out **(see illustration)**. If a rod of the same diameter as the specified minimum friction material thickness is placed against the shoe friction material, the amount of wear can be assessed. A torch or inspection light will probably be required, as well as a small mirror if access is difficult. If the friction material on any shoe is worn down to the specified minimum thickness or less, all four shoes must be renewed as a set.

3 For a comprehensive check, the brake drum should be removed and cleaned. This will allow the wheel cylinders to be checked, and the condition of the brake drum itself to be fully examined (see Chapter 9).
4 On models with rear disc brakes, the rear pad thickness can be checked in a similar fashion to the front pads (see Section 4).

16 Exhaust system check

1 With the engine cold (at least an hour after the car has been driven), check the complete exhaust system from the engine to the end of the tailpipe. The exhaust system is most easily checked with the car raised on a hoist, or suitably supported on axle stands, so that the exhaust components are readily visible and accessible.
2 Check the exhaust pipes and connections for evidence of leaks, severe corrosion and damage. Make sure that all brackets and mountings are in good condition, and that all relevant nuts and bolts are tight **(see illustration)**. Leakage at any of the joints or in other parts of the system will usually show up as a black sooty stain in the vicinity of the leak.
3 Rattles and other noises can often be traced to the exhaust system, especially the brackets and mountings. Try to move the pipes and silencers. If the components are able to come into contact with the body or suspension parts, secure the system with new mountings. Otherwise separate the joints (if possible) and twist the pipes as necessary to provide additional clearance.

17 Steering and suspension check

Suspension and steering

1 Raise the front of the car, and securely support it on axle stands. Where necessary for improved access, release the fasteners and remove the noise insulation tray from under the engine (where applicable).
2 Visually inspect the balljoint dust covers and the steering rack-and-pinion gaiters for splits, chafing or deterioration. Any wear of these components will cause loss of lubricant, together with dirt and water entry, resulting in rapid deterioration of the balljoints or steering gear.
3 Check the power steering fluid hoses for chafing or deterioration, and the pipe and hose unions for fluid leaks. Also check for signs of fluid leakage under pressure from the steering gear rubber gaiters, which would indicate failed fluid seals within the steering gear.

16.2 Typical exhaust system joint clamps (arrowed) – check that the nuts and bolts are tight, with no sign of leaks

17.4 Check for wear in the hub bearings by grasping the wheel and trying to rock it

4 Grasp the roadwheel at the 12 o'clock and 6 o'clock positions, and try to rock it (see illustration). Very slight free play may be felt, but if the movement is appreciable, further investigation is necessary to determine the source. Continue rocking the wheel while an assistant depresses the footbrake. If the movement is now eliminated or significantly reduced, it is likely that the hub bearings are at fault. If the free play is still evident with the footbrake depressed, then there is wear in the suspension joints or mountings. Before condemning any components, however, check that the roadwheel bolts are tightened to the specified torque.

5 Now grasp the wheel at the 9 o'clock and 3 o'clock positions, and try to rock it as before. Any movement felt now may again be caused by wear in the hub bearings or the steering track rod balljoints. If the inner or outer balljoint is worn, the visual movement will be obvious.

6 Using a large screwdriver or flat bar, check for wear in the suspension mounting bushes by levering between the relevant suspension component and its attachment point (see illustration). Some movement is to be expected as the mountings are made of rubber, but excessive wear should be obvious. Also check the condition of any visible rubber bushes, looking for splits, cracks or contamination of the rubber.

7 With the car standing on its wheels, have an assistant turn the steering wheel back-and-forth about an eighth of a turn each way. There should be very little, if any, lost movement between the steering wheel and roadwheels. If this is not the case, closely observe the joints and mountings previously described, but in addition, check the steering column universal joints for wear, and the rack-and-pinion steering gear itself.

Strut/shock absorber

8 Check for any signs of fluid leakage around the suspension strut/shock absorber body, or from the rubber gaiter around the piston rod. Should any fluid be noticed, the suspension strut/shock absorber is defective internally, and should be renewed. **Note:** *Suspension struts/shock absorbers should always be renewed in pairs on the same axle.*

9 The efficiency of the suspension strut/shock absorber may be checked by bouncing the car at each corner. Generally speaking, the body will return to its normal position and stop after being depressed. If it rises and returns on a rebound, the suspension strut/shock absorber is probably suspect. Examine also the suspension strut/shock absorber upper and lower mountings for any signs of wear.

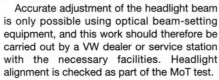

18 Headlight beam alignment check

Accurate adjustment of the headlight beam is only possible using optical beam-setting equipment, and this work should therefore be carried out by a VW dealer or service station with the necessary facilities. Headlight alignment is checked as part of the MoT test.

Basic adjustments can be carried out in an emergency, and further details are given in Chapter 12.

19 Road test

Instruments and electrical equipment

1 Check the operation of all instruments and electrical equipment.

2 Make sure that all instruments read correctly, and switch on all electrical equipment in turn, to check that it functions properly.

Steering and suspension

3 Check for any abnormalities in the steering, suspension, handling or road 'feel'.

4 Drive the car, and check that there are no unusual vibrations or noises.

5 Check that the steering feels positive, with no excessive 'sloppiness', or roughness, and check for any suspension noises when cornering and driving over bumps.

Drivetrain

6 Check the performance of the engine, clutch (where applicable), transmission and driveshafts.

7 Listen for any unusual noises from the engine, clutch and transmission.

8 Make sure the engine runs smoothly at idle, and there is no hesitation on accelerating.

9 Check that, where applicable, the clutch action is smooth and progressive, that the drive is taken up smoothly, and that the pedal travel is not excessive. Also listen for any noises when the clutch pedal is depressed.

17.6 Anti-roll bar mounting bushes (arrowed)

10 On manual transmission models, check that all gears can be engaged smoothly without noise, and that the gear lever action is smooth and not abnormally vague or 'notchy'.

11 On automatic transmission models, make sure that all gearchanges occur smoothly, without snatching, and without an increase in engine speed between changes. Check that all the gear positions can be selected with the car at rest. If any problems are found, they should be referred to a VW dealer.

12 Listen for a metallic clicking sound from the front of the car, as the car is driven slowly in a circle with the steering on full-lock. Carry out this check in both directions. If a clicking noise is heard, this indicates wear in a driveshaft joint, in which case renew the joint if necessary.

Braking system

13 Make sure that the car does not pull to one side when braking. If there is any sign of this, and one front wheel suffers a greater build-up of brake dust than the other, it is likely that the brake caliper piston on that side has seized. Fit new brake pads (on both front wheels) as described in Chapter 9.

14 Check that there is no vibration through the steering when braking.

15 Check that the handbrake operates correctly without excessive movement of the lever, and that it holds the car stationary on a slope.

16 Test the operation of the brake servo unit as follows. With the engine off, depress the footbrake four or five times to exhaust the vacuum. Hold the brake pedal depressed, then start the engine. As the engine starts, there should be a noticeable 'give' in the brake pedal as vacuum builds-up. Allow the engine to run for at least two minutes, and then switch it off. If the brake pedal is depressed now, it should be possible to detect a hiss from the servo as the pedal is depressed. After about four or five applications, no further hissing should be heard, and the pedal should feel considerably harder.

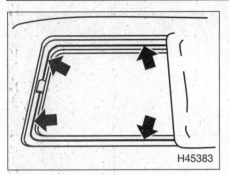

20.1 Folding fabric sunroof guide rail (arrowed)

21.2 Pull off the rubber weatherstrip from the top of the bulkhead

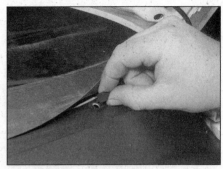

21.3 Peel back the rubber seal for access to the cowl panel retaining clips

Every 20 000 miles (30 000 km) or 2 years

20 Fabric sunroof guide rail lubrication

1 Using a clean cloth and a suitable solvent if necessary, thoroughly clean the sunroof guide rail (see illustration).
2 Apply a little general-purpose grease to the guide rail, then check the sunroof operation.

21 Pollen filter renewal

1 The pollen filter is located beneath the windscreen cowl panels; it is located on the left side on right-hand-drive models, and the right side on left-hand drive models.
2 Open the bonnet, and lift up the rubber weatherstrip from the relevant end of the top of the engine compartment bulkhead (see illustration).
3 Peel back the rubber seal at the base of the windscreen, for access to the two cowl panel retaining clips (see illustration). Take care when prising these clips out of position, as they are easily broken.
4 Remove the cowl panel from the car (see illustration).
5 Unclip the filter air deflector and remove it (see illustration).
6 Release the two clips at the front to release the frame, and lift the pollen filter and frame upwards and out from its location (see illustrations). Note which way round the frame is fitted.
7 Separate the frame from the old filter, noting how it is fitted (see illustration). Slot the new filter into the frame.
8 Wipe clean the filter housing, then fit the new filter and frame. Clip the filter securely in position and refit the air deflector and cowl panel.
9 Refit the rubber seal to the engine compartment bulkhead to complete.

22 Auxiliary drivebelt check and renewal

Checking

1 Disconnect the battery negative lead, and position the lead away from the battery (also see *Disconnecting the battery*).
2 Park the car on a level surface, apply the handbrake and chock the rear wheels. Loosen the right-hand front wheel bolts.
3 Raise the front of the car, rest it securely on axle stands and remove the right-hand front roadwheel.
4 Turn the steering to full right-hand lock. Where applicable, remove the fasteners, and lower the wheel arch liner and/or noise insulation tray for access to the drivebelt. Models with power steering may have a cover fitted over the drivebelt – if so, release the fasteners and remove it.

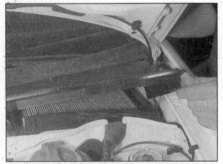

21.4 Lifting out the cowl panel

21.5 Removing the pollen filter air deflector plate

21.6a Release the retaining clips at the front ...

21.6b ... then remove the pollen filter and frame

21.7 Separating the pollen filter from the frame

5 Using a socket and wrench on the crankshaft sprocket bolt, rotate the crankshaft so that the full length of the auxiliary drivebelt can be examined. Look for cracks, splitting and fraying on the surface of the belt; check also for signs of glazing (shiny patches) and separation of the belt plies. If damage or wear is visible, the belt should be renewed. If there is any evidence of contamination by oil, grease or coolant, the reason should be investigated without delay.

6 Check the drivebelt tension by pressing on the belt at a point midway between two pulleys. Depending on the type of belt, it should move by approximately 5 to 10 mm. If the drivebelt appears excessively slack, this may indicate that a new belt is needed, or that there is a problem with the automatic tensioner (see Chapter 2A or 2B).

7 On completion, refit the wheel arch liner and noise insulation tray (as applicable), then refit the roadwheel and lower the car to the ground. Tighten the roadwheel bolts to the specified torque.

Renewal

8 For details of auxiliary drivebelt renewal, refer to the relevant part of Chapter 2A or 2B.

23 Manual transmission oil level check

1 Park the car on a level surface. The oil level must be checked before the car is driven, or at least 5 minutes after the engine has been switched off. If the oil is checked immediately after driving the car, some of the oil will remain distributed around the transmission

components, resulting in an inaccurate level reading.

2 The filler/level plug is on the front of the transmission housing, and can be accessed from above. If preferred, however, the plug can be reached from below, but note that this may mean removing the noise insulation tray (where applicable) from under the engine for access.

3 Wipe clean the area around the filler/level plug. A 17 mm hexagonal socket (or a large Allen key) will be required to remove the plug, which will probably be quite tight **(see illustration)**.

4 The oil level should reach the lower edge of the filler/level hole. A certain amount of oil will have gathered behind the filler/level plug, and will trickle out when it is removed; this does **not** necessarily indicate that the level is correct. To ensure that a true level is established, wait until the initial trickle has stopped, then add oil through the hole as necessary until a trickle of new oil can be seen emerging. The level will be correct when the flow ceases; use only good-quality oil of the specified type.

5 Filling the transmission with oil is an extremely awkward operation; above all, allow plenty of time for the oil level to settle properly before checking it. If a large amount is added to the transmission, and a large amount flows out on checking the level, refit the filler/level plug; take the car on a short journey so that the new oil is distributed fully around the transmission components, then recheck the level when it has settled again.

6 If the transmission has been overfilled so that oil flows out when the filler/level plug is removed, check that the car is completely level (front-to-rear and side-to-side), and

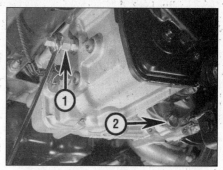

23.3 Loosening the filler/level plug (1) using a hex adapter – also shown is the transmission oil drain plug (2)

allow the surplus to drain off into a suitable container.

7 When the level is correct, refit the plug, tightening it to the specified torque, and wipe off any spilt oil.

24 Underbody protection check

Raise and support the car on axle stands. Using an electric torch or lead light, inspect the entire underside of the car, paying particular attention to the wheel arches. Look for any damage to the flexible underbody coating, which may crack or flake off with age, leading to corrosion. Also check that the wheel arch liners are securely attached with any clips provided – if they come loose, dirt may get in behind the liners and defeat their purpose. If there is any damage to the underseal, or any corrosion, it should be repaired before the damage gets too serious.

Every 40 000 miles (60 000 km) or 4 years

25 Spark plug renewal

1 The correct functioning of the spark plugs is vital for the correct running and efficiency of the engine. It is essential that the plugs fitted are appropriate for the engine (a suitable type is specified at the beginning of this Chapter). If this type is used and the engine is in good condition, the spark plugs should not need attention between scheduled renewal intervals. Spark plug cleaning is rarely necessary, and should not be attempted unless specialised equipment is available, as damage can easily be caused to the firing ends.

2 Before removing the spark plugs, allow the engine time to cool.

3 To gain access to the spark plugs, refer to Chapter 4A, and remove the air filter housing.

4 If the marks on the original-equipment

spark plug (HT) leads cannot be seen, mark the leads 1 to 4, to correspond to the cylinder the lead serves (No 1 cylinder is at the timing belt end of the engine).

5 Where metal heat shields are fitted to the lead end fittings, take care not to burn your hands if the engine is still warm. Pull the leads

25.5a Pull the HT lead end fittings off the plugs

from the plugs by gripping the end fitting, not the lead, otherwise the lead connection may be fractured – on DOHC (16V) engines, use a hook made from stiff wire to pull up on the HT lead connectors **(see illustrations)**.

6 It is advisable (if possible) to remove the dirt from the spark plug recesses using a clean

25.5b Pull on the HT lead connectors with a suitable hook . . .

25.5c ... then remove the leads together with the channels

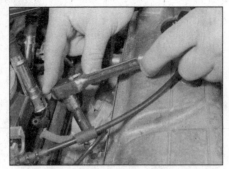

25.7a Unscrew the spark plugs using a suitable socket ...

25.7b ... and remove them from the cylinder head – note multi-earth-electrode spark plug

25.13 Adjusting a spark plug electrode gap

brush, vacuum cleaner or compressed air before removing the plugs, to prevent dirt dropping into the cylinders.

7 Unscrew the plugs using a spark plug spanner, suitable box spanner or a deep socket and extension bar **(see illustrations)**. Keep the socket aligned with the spark plug – if it is forcibly moved to one side, the ceramic insulator may be broken off. As each plug is removed, examine it as follows.

It is very often difficult to insert spark plugs into their holes without cross-threading them. To avoid this possibility, fit a short length of 5/16 inch internal diameter rubber hose over the end of the spark plug. The flexible hose acts as a universal joint to help align the plug with the plug hole. Should the plug begin to cross-thread, the hose will slip on the spark plug, preventing thread damage to the aluminium cylinder head.

8 Examination of the spark plugs will give a good indication of the condition of the engine. If the insulator nose of the spark plug is clean and white, with no deposits, this is indicative of a weak mixture or too hot a plug (a hot plug transfers heat away from the electrode slowly, a cold plug transfers heat away quickly).

9 If the tip and insulator nose are covered with hard black-looking deposits, then this is indicative that the mixture is too rich. Should the plug be black and oily, then it is likely that the engine is fairly worn, as well as the mixture being too rich.

10 If the insulator nose is covered with light tan to greyish-brown deposits, then the mixture is correct and it is likely that the engine is in good condition.

11 The spark plug electrode gap is of considerable importance as, if it is too large or too small, the size of the spark and its efficiency will be seriously impaired. Where the gap can be adjusted, it should be set to the value specified at the start of this Chapter. **Note:** *Spark plugs with multiple earth electrodes are becoming an increasingly common fitment. Unless there is clear information to the contrary, no attempt should be made to adjust the plug gap on a spark plug with more than one earth electrode.*

12 To set the gap, measure it with a feeler blade and then bend open, or closed, the outer plug electrode until the correct gap is achieved. The centre electrode should never be bent, as this may crack the insulator and cause plug failure, if nothing worse. If using feeler blades, the gap is correct when the appropriate-size blade is a firm sliding fit.

13 Special spark plug electrode gap adjusting tools are available from most motor accessory shops, or from some spark plug manufacturers **(see illustration)**.

14 Before fitting the spark plugs, check that the threaded connector sleeves are tight, and that the plug exterior surfaces and threads are clean. It's often difficult to screw in new spark plugs without cross-threading them – this can be avoided using a piece of rubber hose **(see Haynes Hint)**.

15 Remove the rubber hose (if used), and tighten the plug to the specified torque using the spark plug socket and a torque wrench. If a torque wrench is not available, tighten the plug by hand until it just seats, then tighten it by no more than a quarter of a turn further with the plug socket and handle. Refit the remaining spark plugs in the same manner.

16 Connect the HT leads securely in their correct order.

17 Refer to Chapter 4A and refit the air filter housing.

26 Air filter renewal

SOHC engines

1 Prise up the two trim caps in the air cleaner top cover, then remove the bolt under each cap. Recover the spacer sleeve for each bolt from inside the air cleaner, otherwise they may fall out when the assembly is turned over **(see illustrations)**.

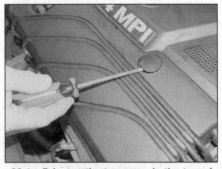

26.1a Prise up the two caps in the top of the air cleaner ...

26.1b ... to expose the 10 mm bolts underneath

26.1c Unscrew the bolts . . .

26.1d . . . and remove them together with their spacer sleeves

26.2 Unclip the HT leads from their guides in the air cleaner

26.3a Disconnect the breather hose on the right-hand side . . .

26.3b . . . and the vacuum pipe on the left

26.4a Use pliers to release the spring clip securing the air intake duct, then pull the duct off . . .

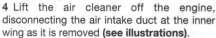

2 Unclip the HT leads from the front of the air cleaner – do not disconnect them from the DIS module **(see illustration)**.

3 Pull the crankcase breather hose off the base of the air cleaner, at the driver's side. Also pull off the vacuum pipe on the passenger side of the air cleaner **(see illustrations)**.

4 Lift the air cleaner off the engine, disconnecting the air intake duct at the inner wing as it is removed **(see illustrations)**.

5 Turn the air cleaner over, and remove the cross-head screws securing the inner cover. Separate the cover, and remove both air filter elements **(see illustrations)**.

26.4b . . . and lift the air cleaner off the engine, releasing the two mounting pegs at the rear

26.5a Remove the cross-head screws around the edge . . .

26.5b . . . then lift off the inner cover . . .

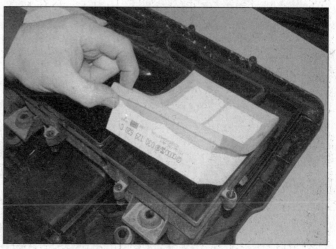

26.5c . . . and remove the two filter elements, noting how they are fitted

DOHC (16V) engines

6 Pull off the breather hose on the driver's side of the air cleaner **(see illustration)**.
7 Unscrew and remove the seven screws securing the air cleaner top cover **(see illustration)**. The screws are of different lengths, so note their locations as they are removed.
8 Turn the cover over, and lift out the filter element **(see illustration)**.

All models

9 Remove any debris that may have collected inside the air cleaner, making sure that it does not enter the engine (ideally, vacuum it out, or wipe with a damp cloth).
10 Fit the new air filter element(s) in position, noting any direction-of-fitting markings and ensuring that the edges are securely seated.
11 Reassemble/refit the air cleaner using a reversal of the removal procedure.

27 Automatic transmission fluid level check

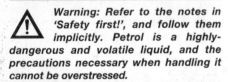

Checking the fluid level by the DIY mechanic is not advisable; no dipstick is provided. The transmission is regarded as being 'filled for life'. Fluid level checking requires the use of dedicated VW test equipment, and an involved procedure requiring accurate measurement of fluid temperature. In view of this, the car must be taken to a VW dealer for the fluid level to be checked.

28 Fuel filter renewal

⚠️ **Warning: Refer to the notes in 'Safety first!', and follow them implicitly. Petrol is a highly-dangerous and volatile liquid, and the precautions necessary when handling it cannot be overstressed.**

1 The fuel filter is situated underneath the rear of the car, to the rear of the fuel tank **(see illustration)**. To gain access to the filter, chock the front wheels, then jack up the rear of the car and support it securely on axle stands.
2 Depressurise the fuel system with reference to the relevant Part of Chapter 4.

26.6 Disconnect the breather hose on the right-hand side of the air cleaner

26.8 Lift out the filter from the inside of the cover

3 If you have them, fit hose clamps to the filter inlet and outlet hoses. These are not essential, but even with the system depressurised, there will still be an amount of petrol in the pipes (and the old filter), and this will syphon out when the pipes are disconnected. Even with hose clamps fitted, the old filter will contain some fuel, so have some rags ready to soak up any spillage.
4 Release the hose clips and detach the hoses from the filter. If crimp-type clips are used, discard them and fit proper petrol pipe clips when reassembling. Similarly, if the fuel hoses show any sign of perishing or cracking, particularly at the hose ends or where the hose enters the metal end fitting, renew the hoses.
5 Before removing the filter, note any direction-of-flow markings on the filter body, and check against the new filter – the arrow should point in the direction of fuel flow (towards the black fuel supply pipe leading to the front of the car).
6 Undo the retaining clamp screw and remove the old filter.

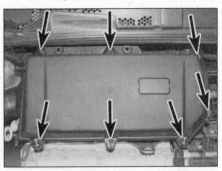

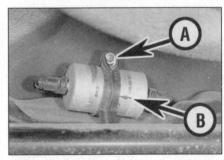

26.7 Remove the seven screws from the air cleaner top cover

28.1 Fuel filter location – note retaining clamp screw (A) and direction-of-flow arrow (B)

7 Fit the new filter into position, with the flow marking arrow correctly orientated, and secure with the retaining clamp.
8 Reconnect the fuel hoses using new clips if necessary. Ensure that no dirt is allowed to enter the hoses or filter connections. Release the hose clamps.
9 Start the engine (there may be a delay as the system repressurises and the new filter fills with fuel). Let the engine run for several minutes while you check the filter hose connections for leaks.
10 Where applicable, fit the protective undershield and secure with the retaining clips, then lower the car to the ground.

⚠️ **Warning: Dispose safely of the old filter; it will be highly flammable, and may explode if thrown on a fire.**

29 Timing belt renewal

Refer to Chapter 2A or 2B.

Every 2 years (regardless of mileage)

30 Coolant renewal

Note: This work is not included in the VW schedule and should not be required if the recommended VW G12 LongLife coolant

antifreeze/inhibitor is used. However, if standard antifreeze/inhibitor is used, the work should be carried out at the recommended interval.

⚠️ **Warning: Wait until the engine is cold before starting this procedure. Do not allow antifreeze to come in contact with**

your skin, or with the car's painted surfaces. Rinse off spills immediately with plenty of water. Never leave antifreeze lying around in an open container, or in a puddle in the driveway or on the garage floor. Children and pets are attracted by its sweet smell, but antifreeze can be fatal if ingested.

Cooling system draining

1 With the engine completely cold, cover the expansion tank cap with a wad of rag, and slowly turn the cap anti-clockwise to relieve the pressure in the cooling system (a hissing sound will normally be heard). Wait until any pressure remaining in the system is released, then continue to turn the cap until it can be removed.

2 Where necessary, release the fasteners and remove the noise insulation tray from under the engine. Position a suitable container beneath the radiator bottom hose connection, then release the retaining clip and ease the hose from the radiator stub. If the hose joint has not been disturbed for some time, it will be necessary to gently manipulate the hose to break the joint. Do not use excessive force, or the radiator stub could be damaged. Allow the coolant to drain into the container.

3 If the coolant has been drained for a reason other than renewal, then provided it is clean and less than two years old, it can be re-used, though this is not recommended (see *Antifreeze type and mixture* later in this Section).

4 Once all the coolant has drained, reconnect the hose to the radiator and secure it in position with the retaining clip.

Cooling system flushing

5 If coolant renewal has been neglected, or if the antifreeze mixture has become diluted, then in time the cooling system may gradually lose efficiency, as the coolant passages become restricted due to rust, scale deposits, and other sediment. Flushing the system clean can restore the cooling system efficiency.

6 The radiator should be flushed independently of the engine, to avoid unnecessary contamination.

Radiator flushing

7 To flush the radiator, disconnect the top and bottom hoses and any other relevant hoses from the radiator, with reference to Chapter 3.

8 Insert a garden hose into the radiator top inlet. Direct a flow of clean water through the radiator, and continue flushing until clean water emerges from the radiator bottom outlet.

9 If after a reasonable period, the water still does not run clear, the radiator can be flushed with a good proprietary cooling system cleaning agent. It is important that their manufacturer's instructions are followed carefully. If the contamination is particularly bad, insert the hose in the radiator bottom outlet, and reverse-flush the radiator.

Engine flushing

10 To flush the engine, remove the thermostat as described in Chapter 3, then temporarily refit the thermostat cover.

11 With the top and bottom hoses disconnected from the radiator, insert a garden hose into the radiator top hose. Direct a clean flow of water through the engine, and continue flushing until clean water emerges from the radiator bottom hose.

12 On completion of flushing, refit the thermostat and reconnect the hoses with reference to Chapter 3.

Cooling system filling

13 Before attempting to fill the cooling system, make sure that all hoses and clips are in good condition, and that the clips are tight. Note that an antifreeze mixture must be used all year round, to prevent corrosion of the engine components (see following sub-Section).

14 Remove the expansion tank filler cap, and fill the system by slowly pouring the coolant into the expansion tank to prevent airlocks from forming.

15 If the coolant is being renewed, begin by pouring in a couple of litres of water, followed by the correct quantity of antifreeze, then top-up with more water.

16 Once the level in the expansion tank starts to rise, squeeze the radiator top and bottom hoses to help expel any trapped air in the system. Once all the air is expelled, top-up the coolant level to the MAX mark and refit the expansion tank cap.

17 Start the engine and run it until it reaches normal operating temperature, then stop the engine and allow it to cool.

18 Check for leaks, particularly around disturbed components. Check the coolant level in the expansion tank, and top-up if necessary. Note that the system must be cold before an accurate level is indicated in the expansion tank. If the expansion tank cap is removed while the engine is still warm, cover the cap with a thick cloth, and unscrew the cap slowly to gradually relieve the system pressure (a hissing sound will normally be heard). Wait until any pressure remaining in the system is released, then continue to turn the cap until it can be removed.

Antifreeze type and mixture

19 The antifreeze should always be renewed at the specified intervals. This is necessary not only to maintain the antifreeze properties, but also to prevent corrosion which would otherwise occur as the corrosion inhibitors become progressively less effective.

20 Always use ethylene-glycol-based antifreeze suitable for use in mixed-metal cooling systems. The quantity of antifreeze and levels of protection are indicated in the Specifications.

21 When the car was new, the cooling system will have been filled with VW G12 (red colour) coolant. At the time of writing, the manufacturer's advice on coolant is as follows:

a) On no account should the red G12 coolant be mixed with any type of blue coolant, including the earlier VW G11 coolant. If the system is to be filled with blue coolant, ensure that the system is completely drained and the cylinder block flushed with clean water before refilling.

b) Engines with an aluminium cylinder block (all 1.0 litre engines) must be filled only with G12 coolant.

22 Before adding antifreeze, the cooling system should be completely drained, preferably flushed, and all hoses checked for condition and security.

23 After filling with antifreeze, a label should be attached to the expansion tank, stating the type and concentration of antifreeze used, and the date installed. Any subsequent topping-up should be made with the same type and concentration of antifreeze.

24 Do not use engine antifreeze in the washer system, as it will cause damage to the paintwork.

Airlocks

25 If, after draining and refilling the system, symptoms of overheating are found which did not occur previously, then the fault is almost certainly due to trapped air at some point in the system, causing an airlock and restricting the flow of coolant; usually, the air is trapped because the system was refilled too quickly.

26 If an airlock is suspected, first try gently squeezing all visible coolant hoses. A coolant hose which is full of air feels quite different to one full of coolant, when squeezed. After refilling the system, most airlocks will clear once the system has cooled, and been topped-up.

27 Sometimes, taking the car for a short drive will clear an airlock, but watch carefully for signs of overheating.

28 While the engine is running at operating temperature, switch on the heater and heater fan, and check for heat output. Provided there is sufficient coolant in the system, any lack of heat output could be due to an airlock in the system.

29 Airlocks can have more serious effects than simply reducing heater output – a severe airlock could reduce coolant flow around the engine. Check that the radiator top hose is hot when the engine is at operating temperature – a top hose which stays cold could be the result of an airlock (or a non-opening thermostat).

30 If the problem persists, stop the engine and allow it to cool down **completely**, before unscrewing the expansion tank filler cap or loosening the hose clips and squeezing the hoses to bleed out the trapped air. In the worst case, the system will have to be at least partially drained (this time, the coolant can be saved for re-use) and flushed to clear the problem.

31 Brake fluid renewal

Note: *VW recommend that at least 0.25 litre of brake fluid is expelled from each bleed nipple.*

 Warning: Brake hydraulic fluid can harm your eyes and damage painted surfaces, so use extreme

caution when handling and pouring it. Do not use fluid that has been standing open for some time, as it absorbs moisture from the air. Excess moisture can cause a dangerous loss of braking effectiveness.

1 The procedure is similar to that for the bleeding of the hydraulic system as described in Chapter 9. The brake fluid reservoir should be emptied by syphoning, using a clean poultry baster or similar before starting, and allowance should be made for the old fluid to be expelled when bleeding a section of the circuit.

 Old hydraulic fluid is often much darker in colour than the new, making it easy to distinguish the two.

2 Working as described in Chapter 9, open the first bleed screw in the sequence, and pump the brake pedal gently until nearly all the old fluid has been emptied from the master cylinder reservoir.

3 Top-up to the MAX level with new fluid, and continue pumping until only the new fluid remains in the reservoir, and new fluid can be seen emerging from the bleed screw. Tighten the screw, and top the reservoir level up to the MAX level line.

4 Work through all the remaining bleed screws in the sequence until new fluid can be seen at all of them. Be careful to keep the master cylinder reservoir topped-up to above the MIN level at all times, or air may enter the system and greatly increase the length of the task.

5 When the operation is complete, check that all bleed screws are securely tightened, and that their dust caps are refitted. Wash off all traces of spilt fluid, and recheck the fluid level.

6 Check the operation of the brakes before taking the car on the road.

32 Exhaust emissions check

This check is part of the manufacturer's maintenance schedule, and involves testing the exhaust emissions using an exhaust gas analyser. Unless a fault is suspected, this test is not essential, although it should be noted that it is recommended by the manufacturers. In the majority of cases, adjusting the idle speed and mixture is either not possible, or requires access to dedicated VW test equipment. Exhaust emissions testing is included as part of the MoT test.

Chapter 2 Part A:
SOHC engine in-car repair procedures

Contents

Degrees of difficulty

Easy, suitable for novice with little experience	**Fairly easy,** suitable for beginner with some experience	**Fairly difficult,** suitable for competent DIY mechanic	**Difficult,** suitable for experienced DIY mechanic	**Very difficult,** suitable for expert DIY or professional

Specifications

General

Engine codes*:
999 cc (1.0 litre), Motronic ME 7.5.10 injection, 50 bhp	AUC or ALD
1390 cc (1.4 litre), Motronic ME 7.5.10 injection, 55 bhp	AKP
1390 cc (1.4 litre), Motronic ME 7.5.10 injection, 60 bhp	AKK, ANW or AUD

* Note: See 'Vehicle identification' for the location of code marking on the engine.

Bore:
1.0 litre	67.1 mm
1.4 litre	76.5 mm

Stroke:
1.0 litre	70.6 mm
1.4 litre	75.6 mm

Compression ratio:
1.0 litre	10.5:1
1.4 litre	10.4:1

Compression pressures:
Wear limit	7.0 bar
Maximum difference between all cylinders	3.0 bar
Firing order	1 – 3 – 4 – 2
No 1 cylinder location	Timing belt end

Lubrication system

Oil pump type	Gear type, driven directly from front of crankshaft

Oil pressure (oil temperature 80°C):
At idle	1.0 bar
At 2000 rpm	2.0 bar

Torque wrench settings

	Nm	lbf ft
Alternator mounting bolts	25	18
Alternator mounting bracket-to-engine bolts	55	41
Auxiliary drivebelt tensioner pulley bolt	45	33
Auxiliary drivebelt tensioner-to-bracket bolt	25	18
Big-end bearing caps bolts/nuts*:		
Stage 1	20	15
Stage 2	Angle-tighten a further 90°	
Camshaft cover bolts*:		
Stage 1	6	4
Stage 2	Angle-tighten a further 90°	
Camshaft sprocket bolt*:		
Stage 1	20	15
Stage 2	Angle-tighten a further 90°	
Crankshaft oil seal housing bolts*	10	7
Crankshaft pulley to crankshaft sprocket (socket-head bolts)	20	15
Crankshaft sprocket bolt – oil threads*:		
Stage 1	90	66
Stage 2	Angle-tighten a further 90°	
Cylinder head bolts*:		
Stage 1	30	22
Stage 2	Angle-tighten a further 90°	
Stage 3	Angle-tighten a further 90°	
Dipstick tube bolts	10	7
Driveplate bolts*:		
Stage 1	60	44
Stage 2	Angle-tighten a further 90°	
Engine right-hand mounting-to-block bolts*:		
Stage 1	40	30
Stage 2	Angle-tighten a further 90°	
Engine/transmission mountings – oiled threads **(see illustration 12.9)***:		
A:		
Stage 1	40	30
Stage 2	Angle-tighten a further 90°	
B	50	37
C:		
Stage 1	20	15
Stage 2	Angle-tighten a further 90°	
D	25	18
E	60	44
F:		
Stage 1	60	44
Stage 2	Angle-tighten a further 90°	
G:		
Stage 1	20	15
Stage 2	Angle-tighten a further 90°	
H:		
Manual transmission	50	37
Automatic transmission	30	22
I:		
Stage 1	40	30
Stage 2	Angle-tighten a further 90°	
J:		
Stage 1	20	15
Stage 2	Angle-tighten a further 90°	
Exhaust manifold	25	18
Exhaust manifold warm-air collector plate bolts	10	7
Exhaust pipe to manifold:		
M8	25	18
M10	40	30
Flywheel bolts*:		
Stage 1	60	44
Stage 2	Angle-tighten a further 90°	
Knock sensor	20	15
Lock carrier:		
Front retaining bolts (to chassis legs)	23	17
Upper retaining bolts	5	4

Torque wrench settings (continued)

	Nm	lbf ft
Oil pressure switch	25	18
Oil pump mounting bolts*	12	9
Oil pump pick-up bracket bolts	10	7
Roadwheel bolts	110	81
Sump bolts	15	11
Sump drain plug	30	22
Timing belt guard/coolant pump mounting bolts	20	15
Timing belt inner cover-to-cylinder head bolts	10	7
Timing belt lower cover bolts*	10	7
Timing belt tensioner roller locknut	20	15
Transmission bellhousing to engine:		
M10 bolts	60	44
M12 bolts	80	59

* Use new bolts/nuts

---

1 General information

Using this Chapter

Chapter 2 is divided into three Parts; A, B and C. This Part describes repair operations that can be carried out with the engine in the car, on single overhead camshaft (SOHC or 8-valve) engines. Part B covers in-car repairs on double overhead camshaft (DOHC or 16-valve) engines, while Part C covers the removal of the engine/transmission as a unit, and describes the engine dismantling and overhaul procedures.

In Parts A and B, the assumption is made that the engine is installed in the car, with all ancillaries connected. If the engine has been removed for overhaul, the preliminary dismantling information which precedes each operation may be ignored.

Access to the engine bay can be improved by removing the bonnet and the front lock carrier assembly; for details, see Chapter 2C, Section 2.

Engine description

Throughout this Chapter, engines are identified and referred to by the manufacturer's code letters, rather than capacity. A listing of all engines covered, together with their code letters, is given in the Specifications.

The engines are water-cooled, single overhead camshaft, in-line four-cylinder units, with aluminium-alloy cylinder blocks and cylinder heads. All are mounted transversely at the front of the car, with the transmission bolted to the left-hand side of the engine.

The cylinder head carries the camshaft, which is driven by a toothed timing belt. It also houses the inlet and exhaust valves, which are closed by single coil springs, and which run in guides pressed into the cylinder head. The camshaft actuates the valves indirectly via roller rocker fingers (followers) and hydraulic tappets, mounted in the cylinder head. The cylinder head contains integral oilways which supply and lubricate the tappets.

The crankshaft is supported by five main bearings – the crankshaft must not be removed, otherwise the block will distort; the crankshaft and block must therefore be renewed as an assembly.

Engine coolant is circulated by a pump, driven by the camshaft timing belt. For details of the cooling system, refer to Chapter 3.

Lubricant is circulated under pressure by a pump, driven by the crankshaft via a chain. Oil is drawn from the sump through a strainer, and then forced through an externally-mounted, renewable screw-on filter. From there, it is distributed to the cylinder head, where it lubricates the camshaft journals and hydraulic tappets, and also to the crankcase, where it lubricates the main bearings, connecting rod big- and small-ends, gudgeon pins and cylinder bores.

Repairs with engine in car

The following operations can be performed without removing the engine:

a) Auxiliary drivebelt – removal and refitting.
b) Camshaft – removal and refitting*.
c) Camshaft oil seal – renewal.
d) Camshaft sprocket – removal and refitting.
e) Coolant pump – removal and refitting (refer to Chapter 3).
f) Crankshaft oil seals – renewal.
g) Crankshaft sprocket – removal and refitting.
h) Cylinder head – removal and refitting*.
i) Engine mountings – inspection and renewal.
j) Oil pump and pickup assembly – removal and refitting.
k) Sump – removal and refitting.
l) Timing belt, sprockets and cover – removal, inspection and refitting.

* Cylinder head dismantling procedures are detailed in Chapter 2C, with details of camshaft and hydraulic tappet removal.

Note: *It is possible to remove the pistons and connecting rods (after removing the cylinder head and sump) without removing the engine. However, this is not recommended. Work of this nature is more easily and thoroughly completed with the engine on the bench, as described in Chapter 2C.*

2 Locating TDC on No 1 cylinder

Note: *This sub-Section has been written with the assumption that the distributor, HT leads and timing belt are correctly fitted.*

General information

1 The crankshaft and camshaft sprockets are driven by the timing belt, and rotate in phase with each other. When the timing belt is removed during servicing or repair, it is possible for the shafts to rotate independently of each other, and the correct phasing is then lost.

2 The design of the engines covered in this Chapter is such that potentially damaging piston-to-valve contact may occur if the camshaft is rotated when any of the pistons are stationary at, or near, the top of its stroke.

3 For this reason, it is important that the correct phasing between the camshaft and crankshaft is preserved whilst the timing belt is off the engine. This is achieved by setting the engine in a reference condition (known as Top Dead Centre or TDC) before the timing belt is removed, and then preventing the shafts from rotating until the belt is refitted. Similarly, if the engine has been dismantled for overhaul, the engine can be set to TDC during reassembly to ensure that the correct shaft phasing is restored. **Note:** *The coolant pump is also driven by the timing belt, but the pump alignment with respect to the crankshaft and camshaft is not critical.*

4 TDC is the highest position a piston reaches within its respective cylinder – in a four-stroke engine, each piston reaches TDC twice per cycle; once on the compression stroke, and once on the exhaust stroke. In general, TDC normally refers to No 1 cylinder on the compression stroke (the cylinders are numbered 1 to 4, with No 1 being at the timing belt end of the engine).

5 The crankshaft sprocket has a notch ground away from one of its teeth which, when aligned with a reference marking on the crankshaft right-hand oil seal flange, indicates

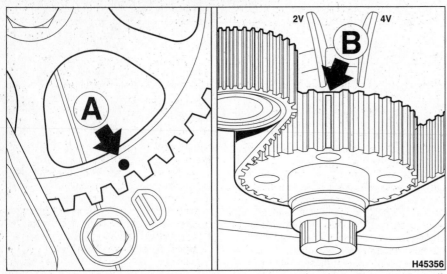

2.5 Camshaft sprocket (A) and crankshaft sprocket (B) TDC timing marks

that No 1 cylinder (and hence also No 4 cylinder) is at TDC. However, the crankshaft sprocket is only visible with the timing belt lower cover removed – there is also a notch in the crankshaft pulley, which, when aligned with a 0 mark moulded into the timing belt lower cover, indicates TDC. The camshaft sprocket is also equipped with a timing mark (a dot punched in its outer face) – when this is aligned with the raised pointer moulded into the timing belt inner cover, the engine is correctly synchronised, and the timing belt can then be refitted and tensioned **(see illustration)**.

6 The following sub-Sections describe setting the engine to TDC on No 1 cylinder.

Setting TDC on No 1 cylinder

Timing belt fitted

7 Before starting work, disconnect the battery negative lead (also see *Disconnecting the battery*).

8 Disable the ignition system by disconnecting the DIS ignition module multiplug. Prevent any vehicle movement by applying the handbrake and chocking the rear wheels. Ensure that the transmission is in neutral (manual transmission) or P (automatic transmission).

9 Remove the spark plugs as described in Chapter 1.

10 To bring any piston up to TDC, it will be necessary to rotate the crankshaft manually. This can be done by using a spanner or socket on the centre bolt that retains the crankshaft sprocket (refer to Section 5 for more detail).

11 With reference to Section 4, remove the timing belt upper cover to expose the camshaft sprocket beneath. Identify the timing marks on both the camshaft sprocket and the inner section of the timing belt cover. Continue turning the crankshaft clockwise until these marks are exactly aligned with each other **(see illustration)**.

12 At this point, identify the timing marks on the crankshaft pulley and the timing belt lower cover. The cover has a Z and a 0 mark moulded into it – when the notch in the rim of the crankshaft pulley aligns with the 0 mark, the engine is set to TDC.

13 Alternatively, check that the crankshaft sprocket and the crankshaft right-hand oil

seal flange timing marks are correctly aligned **(see illustration 2.5)**. There are two marks – 2V and 4V, or 2-valves and 4-valves per cylinder. On the engines covered in this Chapter, the first one (2V) is correct. **Note**: *The crankshaft pulley and the timing belt lower cover must be removed to expose the crankshaft sprocket timing marks.*

14 When all the above steps have been completed successfully, the engine will be set to TDC on No 1 cylinder.

Caution: If the timing belt is to be removed, ensure that the crankshaft, camshaft and intermediate shaft alignment is preserved by preventing the sprockets from rotating with respect to each other.

Timing belt removed

15 This procedure has been written with the assumption that the timing belt has been removed and that the alignment between the camshaft and crankshaft has been lost, for example following engine removal and overhaul.

16 On all the engines covered in this manual, it is possible for damage to be caused by the piston crowns striking the valve heads, if the camshaft is rotated with the timing belt removed and the crankshaft set to TDC. For this reason, the TDC setting procedure must be carried out in a particular order, as described in the following paragraphs.

17 Before the cylinder head is refitted, use a spanner or socket on the crankshaft sprocket centre bolt to turn the crankshaft in its normal direction of rotation, until all four pistons are positioned **halfway down** their bores, with No 1 piston on its upstroke – ie, around 90° before TDC.

18 With the cylinder head and camshaft sprocket fitted, identify the timing marks on both the camshaft sprocket and the inner section of the timing belt cover; refer to the illustration in *General information*.

19 Turn the camshaft sprocket in its normal direction of rotation until the timing marks on the sprocket and timing belt inner cover are exactly aligned.

20 Identify the timing marks on the crankshaft sprocket and the crankshaft right-hand oil seal flange **(see illustration)**. Using a socket and wrench on the crankshaft sprocket retaining bolt, turn the crankshaft through 90° (quarter of a turn) in its normal direction of rotation, to bring the timing marks into alignment.

21 When all the above steps have been completed successfully, the engine will be set at TDC on No 1 cylinder. The timing belt can now be fitted as described in Section 4.

Caution: Until the timing belt is fitted, ensure that the crankshaft, camshaft and intermediate shaft alignment is preserved by preventing the sprockets from rotating with respect to each other.

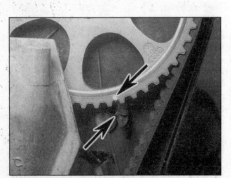

2.11 Camshaft sprocket punched mark and notch in timing belt inner cover aligned (arrowed)

2.20 Crankshaft sprocket chamfered tooth (1) and timing mark (2)

3 Cylinder compression test

1 When engine performance is down, or if misfiring occurs which cannot be attributed to the ignition or fuel systems, a compression test can provide diagnostic clues as to the engine's condition. If the test is performed regularly, it can give warning of trouble before any other symptoms become apparent.

2 The engine must be fully warmed-up to normal operating temperature, the battery must be fully-charged, and all the spark plugs must be removed (refer to Chapter 1). The aid of an assistant will also be required.

3 Disable the ignition system by disconnecting the DIS ignition module multi-plug.

4 To prevent possible damage to the catalytic converter, depressurise and disable the fuel injection system by removing the fuel pump fuse or relay (see Chapter 4A).

5 Fit a compression tester to the No 1 cylinder spark plug hole – the type of tester which screws into the plug thread is preferable.

6 Have an assistant hold the accelerator pedal in the full-throttle position, then crank the engine on the starter motor; after one or two revolutions, the compression pressure should build up to a maximum figure, and then stabilise. Record the highest reading obtained.

7 Repeat the test on the remaining cylinders, recording the pressure in each. Keep the accelerator pedal fully depressed.

8 All cylinders should produce very similar pressures; a difference of more than 2 bars between any two cylinders indicates a fault (the manufacturer quotes a maximum difference between the highest and lowest of all four readings). Note that the compression should build-up quickly in a healthy engine; low compression on the first stroke, followed by gradually-increasing pressure on successive strokes, indicates worn piston rings. A low compression reading on the first stroke, which does not build-up during successive strokes, indicates leaking valves or a blown head gasket (a cracked head could also be the cause). Deposits on the undersides of the valve heads can also cause low compression.

9 Refer to the Specifications section of this Chapter, and compare the recorded compression figures with those stated by the manufacturer.

10 If the pressure in any cylinder is low, carry out the following test to isolate the cause. Introduce a teaspoonful of clean oil into that cylinder through its spark plug hole, and repeat the test.

11 If the addition of oil temporarily improves the compression pressure, this indicates that bore or piston wear is responsible for the pressure loss. No improvement suggests that leaking or burnt valves, or a blown head gasket, may be to blame.

12 A low reading from two adjacent cylinders is almost certainly due to the head gasket having blown between them; the presence of coolant in the engine oil will confirm this.

13 If one cylinder is about 20 percent lower than the others and the engine has a slightly rough idle, a worn camshaft lobe could be the cause.

14 If the compression reading is unusually high, the combustion chambers are probably coated with carbon deposits. If this is the case, the cylinder head should be removed and decarbonised.

15 On completion of the test, refit the spark plugs and restore the ignition and fuel systems.

4 Timing belt and outer covers – removal and refitting

General information

1 The primary function of the toothed timing belt is to drive the camshaft, but it is also used to drive the coolant pump. Should the belt slip or break in service, the valve timing will be disturbed and piston-to-valve contact may occur, resulting in serious engine damage. Similarly, the coolant pump may leak coolant onto the belt, or if the pump is severely worn, the pump may seize and break the belt.

2 For this reason, it is important that the timing belt is tensioned correctly, and inspected regularly for signs of wear or deterioration.

3 Note that the removal of the *inner* section of the timing belt cover is described as part of the camshaft oil seal renewal procedure; see Section 8.

Removal

4 Before starting work, immobilise the engine and vehicle as follows:
a) Disconnect the battery negative lead, and position the lead away from the terminal (see 'Disconnecting the battery').
b) Prevent any vehicle movement by applying the handbrake and chocking the rear wheels. Ensure that the transmission is in neutral (manual transmission) or P (automatic transmission).
c) Loosen the right-hand front wheel bolts, then jack up the front of the car and support securely on axle stands (see 'Jacking and vehicle support').

5 Remove the air cleaner as described in Chapter 4A. Pull out the engine oil dipstick and place it to one side, out of the way.

6 To renew the belt, the engine right-hand mounting must first be removed. Support the weight of the engine using an engine hoist from above, or using a securely-located hydraulic jack and suitable block of wood from below. Do not jack under the sump without using a block of wood to spread the load, or the sump will be damaged. Volkswagen technicians use an engine support bar which locates in the inner wing channels.

7 With the engine securely supported, progressively loosen the engine mounting bolts and remove the engine right-hand mounting from the car (see illustrations).

8 The engine must now be lowered slightly, to allow the crankshaft pulley to be removed.

9 Remove the auxiliary drivebelt as described in Section 6.

10 Unscrew and remove the four crankshaft pulley retaining bolts – it should be possible to counterhold the pulley using a spanner or socket on the crankshaft sprocket bolt. Remove the crankshaft pulley (see illustrations).

4.7a Remove the mounting bolts . . .

4.10a Loosen the crankshaft pulley bolts, counterholding on the centre bolt . . .

4.7b . . . and lift off the engine right-hand mounting

4.10b ... and withdraw the crankshaft pulley

4.11a Release the timing belt upper cover retaining clips ...

4.11b ... then remove the timing belt upper cover

> **HAYNES HiNT**
>
> *To prevent the crankshaft drivebelt pulley from rotating whilst the bolts are being slackened, select top gear (manual transmission) and get an assistant to apply the footbrake firmly. Failing this, grip the sprocket by wrapping a length of old rubber hose or inner tube around it. If top gear is selected to help in removing the pulley, make sure the transmission is returned to neutral before proceeding.*

11 Release the retaining clips, and remove the timing belt upper cover **(see illustrations)**.

12 Unscrew and remove the three retaining bolts, release the clips, and remove the timing belt lower cover **(see illustration)**. To improve access to the front bolt, rotate the auxiliary

drivebelt tensioner clockwise and hold it out of the way using a spanner on the centre bolt. The tensioner can be removed completely, if preferred, by turning the centre bolt anti-clockwise; remove the bolt, washer and tensioner pulley.

13 Using the information in Section 2, set the engine to TDC on No 1 cylinder.

14 Examine the timing belt for manufacturer's markings that indicate the direction of rotation. If none are present, make your own using typist's correction fluid or a dab of paint – do not cut or score the belt in any way

Caution: If the belt appears to be in good condition and can be re-used, it is essential that it is refitted the same way around, otherwise accelerated wear will result, leading to premature failure.

15 Loosen the tensioner roller locknut, and allow the tensioner to rotate anti-clockwise to

relieve the tension on the belt **(see illustration)**.

16 Slide the belt off the sprockets, taking care to avoid twisting or kinking it excessively **(see illustration)**. Ensure that the sprockets remain aligned with their respective timing markings once the timing belt has been removed.

Caution: It is potentially damaging to allow the camshaft to turn with the timing belt removed and the engine set at TDC, as piston-to-valve contact may occur.

17 Examine the belt for evidence of contamination by coolant or lubricant. If this is the case, identify the source of the contamination before progressing any further. Check the belt for signs of wear or damage, particularly around the leading edges of the belt teeth. Renew the belt if its condition is in doubt; the cost of belt renewal is negligible compared with potential cost of the engine repairs, should the belt fail in service. Similarly, if the belt is known to have covered more than 30 000 miles, it is prudent to renew it regardless of condition, as a precautionary measure.

18 If the timing belt is not going to be refitted for some time, it is a wise precaution to hang a warning label on the steering wheel, to remind yourself (and others) not to attempt starting the engine. You may wish to further immobilise the engine against being started, perhaps by taping over the ignition switch.

Refitting

19 Ensure that the timing marks on the camshaft and crankshaft sprockets are correctly aligned with their corresponding TDC reference marks on the timing belt inner cover and crankshaft oil seal flange; refer to Section 2 for details.

20 Engage the timing belt teeth with the crankshaft sprocket, then manoeuvre it into position over the coolant pump and camshaft sprockets. Observe the direction of rotation markings on the belt **(see illustration)**.

21 Pass the flat side of the belt over the tensioner roller – avoid bending the belt back on itself or twisting it excessively as you do this. Ensure the 'front run' of the belt is taut – ie, all the slack should be in the section of the belt that passes over the tensioner roller.

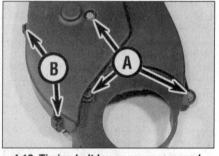

4.12 Timing belt lower cover removed, showing locations of retaining bolts (A) and clips (B)

4.15 Loosening the belt tensioner locknut

4.16 Removing the timing belt

4.20 Engaging the timing belt with the crankshaft sprocket

4.22a Turn the tensioner clockwise using an Allen key until the pointer aligns with the slot in the tensioner baseplate

4.22b When the belt tension is correctly set, tighten the tensioner locknut

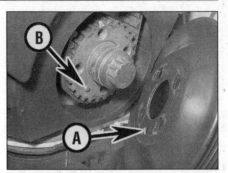

4.26 Refitting the crankshaft pulley – small hole (A) fits over peg (B) on crankshaft sprocket

22 Tension the belt as follows: tighten the tensioner locknut lightly, then insert an Allen key into the adjustment hole, and turn the eccentrically-mounted tensioner clockwise until the slack in the belt is taken up. Continue turning the tensioner until the sliding pointer lines up with the notch in the tensioner baseplate. On completion, tighten the tensioner locknut to the specified torque **(see illustrations)**.

23 Using a spanner or wrench and socket on the crankshaft sprocket bolt, rotate the crankshaft through two complete revolutions, and reset the engine to TDC on No 1 cylinder, with reference to Section 2. Recheck the alignment of the tensioner, and adjust it if necessary.

24 Refer to Section 5 and test the operation of the tensioner.

25 Refit the lower and upper sections of the timing belt outer cover, refitting the clips and tightening the retaining bolts securely. Use new bolts on the timing belt lower cover.

26 Refit the pulley for the ribbed auxiliary drivebelt to the crankshaft sprocket, noting that the small hole in the pulley fits over a peg on the crankshaft sprocket **(see illustration)**, then insert and tighten the retaining bolts to the specified torque. Counterhold the sprocket using one of the methods described in paragraph 10.

27 Working from Section 6, refit and tension the auxiliary drivebelt.

28 Raise the engine back into a position where the right-hand engine mounting can be refitted.

29 Refit the engine mounting using new bolts, and tighten the bolts to the specified torque. Note that the mounting upper and lower bolts are tightened to different torques. Lower the hoist or the jack on completion.

30 Refit the air cleaner warm-air ducting to the exhaust manifold and inner wing. Where applicable, restore ignition and fuel systems by reconnecting the coil and refitting the fuel pump fuse or relay.

31 Reconnect the battery negative lead.

---

5   Timing belt sprockets and tensioner – removal, inspection and refitting

---

1 Before starting work, immobilise the engine and vehicle as follows:

a) *Disconnect the battery negative lead, and position the lead away from the terminal (see 'Disconnecting the battery').*

b) *Prevent any vehicle movement by applying the handbrake and chocking the rear wheels. Ensure that the transmission is in neutral (manual transmission) or P (automatic transmission).*

Timing belt tensioner

Removal

2 With reference to Section 2, set the engine to TDC on No 1 cylinder.

3 Referring to Section 4, remove the right-hand engine mounting, then remove the

auxiliary drivebelt, crankshaft pulley, and the timing belt upper and lower covers.

4 Slacken the locknut at the hub of the tensioner pulley, and allow the assembly to rotate anti-clockwise, relieving the tension on the timing belt.

5 Remove the locknut and slide the tensioner off its mounting stud.

Inspection

6 Wipe the tensioner clean, but do not use solvents that may contaminate the bearings. Spin the tensioner pulley on its hub by hand. Stiff movement or excessive freeplay is an indication of severe wear; the tensioner is not a serviceable component, and it should be renewed if its condition is less than perfect.

Refitting and testing

7 Slide the tensioner pulley over the mounting stud. The U-shape in the tensioner baseplate fits over the bolt **(see illustration)**. Refit the locknut and tighten it lightly – do not fully tighten the nut at this stage.

8 With reference to Section 4, tension the timing belt.

9 The operation of the belt tensioner can be tested as follows. Apply finger pressure to the timing belt at a point mid-way between the camshaft and crankshaft sprockets. The sliding pointer that protrudes from behind the tensioner roller should slide away from the alignment notch in the tensioner baseplate as pressure is applied, and then move back as the pressure is removed **(see illustrations)**.

5.7 Slide tensioner onto its mounting stud, fitting the U-shaped baseplate over the bolt (arrowed)

5.9a Apply pressure to the belt, and the tensioner pointer (arrowed) should move away from the central position . . .

5.9b . . . then return to correct alignment as pressure is released

To make a camshaft sprocket holding tool, obtain two lengths of steel strip about 6 mm thick by 30 mm wide or similar, one 600 mm long, the other 200 mm long (all dimensions approximate). Bolt the two strips together to form a forked end, leaving the bolt slack so that the shorter strip can pivot freely. At the end of each 'prong' of the fork, secure a bolt with a nut and a locknut, to act as the fulcrums; these will engage with the cut-outs in the sprocket, and should protrude by about 30mm.

10 Any reluctance to return to the correct position indicates that the tensioner should be renewed – correct tension is critical to the operation of the belt, and the importance of the belt tensioner cannot be overstressed.

11 Referring to Section 4, refit the timing belt upper and lower covers, the crankshaft pulley, auxiliary drivebelt, and the right-hand engine mounting. Reconnect the battery negative lead.

Camshaft timing belt sprocket

Removal

12 With reference to Sections 2 and 4, remove the timing belt covers and set the engine to TDC on No 1 cylinder. Slacken the timing belt tensioner locknut and rotate it anti-clockwise to relieve the tension on the timing belt. Carefully slide the timing belt off the camshaft sprocket.

⚠️ *Warning: It is potentially damaging to allow the camshaft to turn with the timing belt*

5.19 Tighten the camshaft sprocket bolt to the specified torque, and then through the specified angle

5.14 Remove the camshaft sprocket bolt . . .

removed and the engine set at TDC, as piston-to-valve contact may occur. Take care that the camshaft sprocket is not turned as it is removed. As a precaution against damage, VW recommend that the crankshaft be turned back a few degrees, away from TDC, while the camshaft sprocket is removed/refitted. The crankshaft may then be turned back to TDC when the timing belt is to be refitted.

13 The camshaft sprocket must be held stationary whilst its retaining bolt is slackened; if access to the correct VAG special tool is not possible, a simple home-made tool using basic materials may be fabricated **(see Tool Tip)**.

14 Using the home-made tool, brace the camshaft sprocket. Slacken and remove the retaining bolt **(see illustration)**.

15 Slide the camshaft sprocket from the end of the camshaft **(see illustration)**. Where applicable, recover the Woodruff key from the keyway.

16 With the sprocket removed, look for signs of oil leaking from the camshaft oil seal. If necessary, refer to Section 8 and renew it.

17 Wipe the sprocket and camshaft mating surfaces clean.

Refitting

18 Where applicable, fit the Woodruff key into the keyway, with the plain surface facing upwards. Offer up the sprocket to the camshaft, engaging the slot in the sprocket with the Woodruff key. On engines where a key is not used, ensure that the tooth in the

5.23 Slacken the crankshaft sprocket bolt

5.15 . . . and take off the camshaft sprocket – note the alignment tooth and keyway (arrowed)

sprocket hub engages with the keyway in the end of the camshaft.

19 Counterholding the camshaft sprocket as for removal, fit and tighten the camshaft sprocket bolt to the specified torque, and then through the specified angle **(see illustration)**.

20 Working from Sections 2 and 4, check that the engine is still set to TDC on No 1 cylinder, then refit and tension the timing belt. Refit the timing belt covers and all other components removed for access, as described in Section 4. Reconnect the battery negative lead.

Crankshaft timing belt sprocket

Removal

21 With reference to Sections 2 and 4, remove the timing belt covers and set the engine to TDC on No 1 cylinder.

22 The crankshaft sprocket must be held stationary whilst its retaining bolt is slackened. If access to the correct VAG flywheel locking tool is not available, lock the crankshaft in position by removing the starter motor, as described in Chapter 5A, to expose the flywheel ring gear. Then get an assistant insert a stout lever between the gear teeth and the transmission bellhousing whilst the sprocket retaining bolt is slackened.

23 Holding the engine against rotation as described in the previous paragraph, slacken the crankshaft sprocket bolt – do not remove it yet **(see illustration)**.

24 Ensure that the engine is still set to TDC, then slacken the timing belt tensioner centre nut and rotate it anti-clockwise to relieve the tension on the timing belt. Carefully slide the timing belt off the crankshaft sprocket.

25 Withdraw the bolt and slide off the crankshaft sprocket **(see illustrations)**.

26 With the sprocket removed, examine the crankshaft oil seal for signs of leaking. If necessary, refer to Section 9 and renew it.

27 Wipe the sprocket and crankshaft mating surfaces clean.

Refitting

28 Offer up the sprocket, engaging the tooth on the inside of the sprocket with the keyway in the end of the crankshaft **(see illustration)**. Insert a new bolt, and tighten it hand-tight at

5.25a Remove the crankshaft sprocket bolt (this is a 'bi-hex' type) . . .

5.25b . . . then slide the sprocket off the crankshaft

5.28 Crankshaft sprocket alignment tooth and keyway (arrowed)

this stage. **Note:** *Due to the high torque to which the sprocket bolt must be tightened, there is a danger that the crankshaft sprocket may turn as it is tightened, particularly if the tool used to lock the flywheel ring gear slips. For this reason, it is recommended that the final tightening of the crankshaft sprocket bolt is delayed until after the timing belt has been fitted.*

29 Working from Sections 2 and 4, check that the engine is still set to TDC on No 1 cylinder, then refit and tension the timing belt.

30 Fit the new crankshaft sprocket bolt, and lightly oil the bolt threads. Tighten the bolt to the specified torque, then through the specified angle, using the method described in paragraph 22 to lock the flywheel **(see illustrations)**. If the engine is out of the car, have an assistant support the engine as the bolt is tightened – a great deal of effort will be required, and the engine may tip over.

31 Refit the timing belt covers and all other components removed for access, as described in Section 4. Reconnect the battery negative lead.

Coolant pump timing belt sprocket

32 The coolant pump sprocket is an integral part of the coolant pump assembly, and cannot be removed or renewed separately. To remove the coolant pump, refer to Chapter 3.

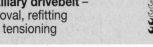

6 Auxiliary drivebelt – removal, refitting and tensioning

General information

1 Depending on the vehicle specification, the auxiliary drivebelt, which is driven from a pulley mounted on the crankshaft, will provide drive for the alternator, power steering pump and (on models with air conditioning), the refrigerant compressor.

2 The ribbed auxiliary belt may be fitted with an automatic tensioning device, depending on its run (and hence the number of components it is driving). Otherwise, the belt is tensioned by the alternator mountings, which have an in-built tensioning spring.

5.30a Tighten the bolt to the specified torque . . .

3 On refitting, the auxiliary belt must be tensioned correctly, to ensure correct operation under all conditions, and for prolonged service life.

Removal

4 Park the car on a level surface, apply the handbrake and chock the rear wheels. Loosen the right-hand front wheel bolts.

5 Raise the front of the car, rest it securely on axle stands and remove the right-hand front roadwheel.

6 Where applicable, remove the fasteners, and lower the wheel arch liner and/or noise insulation tray for access to the drivebelt **(see illustrations)**. Some models may have a cover fitted over the drivebelt – if so, release the fasteners and remove it.

7 Examine the ribbed belt for manufacturer's

6.6b . . . and washer-type fastener . . .

5.30b . . . and then through the specified angle – use an angle gauge if available, to ensure accuracy

markings, indicating the direction of rotation. If none are present, make some using typist's correction fluid or a dab of paint – do not cut or score the belt in any way.

6.6a Typical wheel arch liner retaining bolt (arrowed) . . .

6.6c . . . which can be 'unscrewed' using a suitable screwdriver in the slots

6.8 Rotate the auxiliary drivebelt tensioner clockwise to relieve the tension on the belt

With automatic tensioner

8 Fit a ring spanner to the tensioner centre nut, and rotate the assembly clockwise, against its spring tension **(see illustration)**.

Without automatic tensioner

9 Slacken the alternator upper and lower mounting bolts by between one and two turns.

10 Push the alternator down to its stop against the spring tension, so that it rotates around its uppermost mounting.

All models

11 Pull the belt off the alternator pulley, then release it from the remaining pulleys **(see illustration)**.

Refitting and tensioning

Caution: Observe the manufacturer's direction of rotation markings on the belt, when refitting.

12 Pass the ribbed belt underneath the

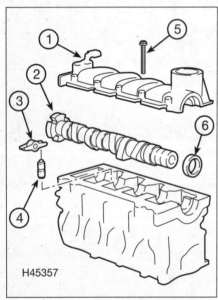

H45357

7.6 Camshaft and related components

1 *Camshaft cover*
2 *Camshaft*
3 *Follower (roller rocker finger)*
4 *Hydraulic tappet*
5 *Camshaft cover bolt*
6 *Camshaft oil seal*

6.11 Removing the auxiliary drivebelt

crankshaft pulley, ensuring that the ribs seat in the channels on the surface of the pulley.

With automatic tensioner

13 Fit a ring spanner to the tensioner centre nut, and rotate the assembly clockwise, against its spring tension.

14 Pass the flat side of the belt underneath the tensioner roller, then fit it over the pulleys. Ensure that the belt ribs engage correctly with the pulley grooves.

15 Release the spanner and allow the tensioner roller to bear against the flat side of the belt.

Without automatic tensioner

16 Repeatedly push the alternator down to its stop against the spring tension, so that it rotates around its uppermost mounting, and check that it moves back freely when released. If necessary, slacken the alternator mounting bolts by a further half a turn.

17 Keep the alternator pushed down against its stop, pass the belt over the alternator pulley, then release the alternator and allow it to tension the belt.

18 Start the engine and allow it to idle for about 10 seconds, leaving the alternator mounting bolts slackened.

19 Switch the engine off, then tighten first the lower, then the upper alternator mounting bolts to the specified torque.

All models

20 Refit the drivebelt cover, wheel arch liner and noise insulation tray, as applicable.

21 Refit the right-hand front roadwheel and lower the car to the ground. Tighten the roadwheel bolts to the specified torque.

---

7 Camshaft, followers and hydraulic tappets – removal, inspection and refitting

Removal

1 Remove the camshaft sprocket as described in Section 5. Unbolt and remove the timing belt backplate fitted behind the camshaft sprocket.

2 Disconnect the camshaft position sensor wiring plug from the top of the cover, next to the DIS ignition module.

3 Remove the DIS ignition module as described in Chapter 5B.

4 Starting at either end and working inwards, progressively loosen the camshaft cover bolts by no more than a quarter-turn each at a time, until all are loose and can be removed. New bolts should be obtained for refitting.

5 Carefully lift off the camshaft cover, noting that it is fitted using sealant, and may require some rocking to release it (take care if prising it off, not to damage the sealing surfaces).

6 Lift out the camshaft, and place it on a clean surface **(see illustration)**. Rest the shaft on clean newspaper or rags, so that the cam lobes cannot get damaged.

7 If the followers and tappets are also to be removed, it is vital that they are kept in their original fitted order, and that the tappets are not allowed to drain while they are removed. The followers can be laid out onto a marked piece of card. Obtain eight small, clean plastic containers which can be filled with oil to store the tappets in (or get a larger container, and divide it into eight, marked compartments – plastic egg trays will do).

8 Lift off the followers for No 1 cylinder (nearest the timing chain end), and lay them onto a piece of card, or into a compartmented box – ensure that the followers are not interchanged. Repeat this process for the remaining followers.

9 Lift out the hydraulic tappets for No 1 cylinder inlet and exhaust valves, and place them each in a numbered 'oil bath' to prevent them from draining fully. Repeat this process for the remaining tappets.

Inspection

10 With the camshaft, followers and hydraulic tappets removed, check each for signs of obvious wear (scoring, pitting etc) and for ovality, and renew if necessary.

11 Measure the outside diameter of each tappet – take measurements at the top and bottom of each tappet, then a second set at right-angles to the first; if any measurement is significantly different from the others, the tappet is tapered or oval (as applicable) and must be renewed.

12 Visually examine the camshaft lobes for score marks, pitting, galling (wear due to rubbing) and evidence of overheating (blue, discoloured areas). Look for flaking away of the hardened surface layer of each lobe. Renew the camshaft if any of these conditions are apparent. Examine the condition of the bearing surfaces, both on the camshaft journals and in the cylinder head/camshaft cover. If the bearing surfaces are worn excessively, the cylinder head or camshaft cover will need to be renewed.

13 Check the followers for signs of wear, and for excessive play or roughness in the rollers. If any of the followers are worn, check the corresponding lobes on the camshaft.

14 If the engine's valve components have sounded noisy, particularly if the noise persists after initial start-up from cold, there is

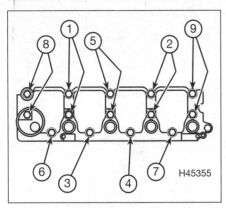

7.21 Camshaft cover bolt tightening sequence

reason to suspect a faulty hydraulic tappet. Only a good mechanic experienced in these engines can tell whether the noise level is typical, or if renewal of one or more of the tappets is warranted. If faulty tappets are diagnosed, and the engine's service history is unknown, it is always worth trying the effect of renewing the engine oil and filter (see Chapter 1), using *only* good-quality engine oil of the recommended viscosity and specification, before going to the expense of renewing any of the tappets.

Refitting

15 Clean off all traces of old sealant from the cylinder head and cover mating faces, making sure no sealant debris contaminates the head.
16 Liberally oil the cylinder head hydraulic tappet bores, and the followers. Carefully refit the tappets to their original positions in the cylinder head – some care will be required to enter the tappets squarely into their bores. Check that each tappet rotates freely, then clip on its corresponding follower – again, generously-oiled. Make sure the followers are sitting correctly on their valve ends.
17 Liberally oil the camshaft lobes, and offer it into place with the lobes for No 1 cylinder facing upwards.
18 Clean all traces of oil from the mating faces of the cylinder head and camshaft cover, ready for a coat of sealant.
19 Apply a thin coating (excess sealant would block vital oilways in the head) of suitable RTV sealant to the cylinder head and camshaft cover mating faces – VW's own sealant is AMV 154 103.
20 Offer the camshaft cover into place, aligning the locating pegs with the cylinder head holes at the front edge. Aim to fit the cover in one movement – lifting it off and retrying will reduce the effectiveness of the sealant.
21 Working in sequence **(see illustration)**, diagonally tighten the first two pairs of bolts in the sequence to the specified Stage 1 torque, to initially seat the cover and camshaft/ tappets. Next, go round in the full sequence, and tighten all the bolts to Stage 1.
22 With all the cover bolts tightened to

8.2a Remove two bolts on the end of the engine, and one at the front (arrowed) . . .

Stage 1, go round again and further tighten each bolt in the sequence through the specified Stage 2 angle. It is recommended that an angle gauge is used (these are available from good car accessory shops and motor factors) to ensure accuracy. However, 90° is a right angle, which can be assessed easily using the start and finishing positions of the socket handle.
23 Further refitting is a reversal of removal.

8 Camshaft oil seal – renewal

1 Refer to Section 5 and remove the camshaft sprocket.
2 After removing the retaining bolts, lift the timing belt inner cover away from the cylinder head – this will expose the oil seal **(see illustrations)**.
3 Remove the oil seal, using the same method as that described for the crankshaft oil seal removal, in Section 9.
4 Clean out the seal housing and sealing surface of the camshaft by wiping it with a lint-free cloth – avoid using solvents that may enter the cylinder head and affect component lubrication. Remove any swarf or burrs that may cause the seal to leak.
5 Lubricate the lip of the new oil seal with clean engine oil, and push it over the camshaft until it is positioned above its housing.
6 Using a hammer and a socket of suitable

9.4 Drill a small hole into the old seal . . .

8.2b . . . and take off the timing belt inner cover

8.2c Camshaft oil seal (arrowed)

diameter, drive the seal squarely into its housing. **Note:** *Select a socket that bears only on the hard outer surface of the seal, not the inner lip which can easily be damaged.*
7 Refit the timing belt inner cover to the cylinder head, and tighten the retaining bolts to the specified torque.
8 With reference to Section 5, refit the camshaft sprocket.

9 Crankshaft oil seals – renewal

Crankshaft right-hand oil seal

1 Drain the engine oil – see Chapter 1.
2 Refer to Section 6 and remove the auxiliary drivebelt.
3 With reference to Sections 2, 4 and 5 of this Chapter, remove the crankshaft pulley, timing belt outer covers, timing belt and crankshaft sprocket.
4 Note the depth to which the old seal has been fitted, relative to its housing. Drill a small hole into the existing oil seal **(see illustration)**. Take great care to avoid drilling through into the seal housing or the crankshaft sealing surface. It may be necessary to drill another hole, if difficulty is experienced in pulling out the old seal, but we found that one hole was sufficient.
5 Thread a self-tapping screw into the hole, and using a pair of pliers, pull on the head of the screw to extract the oil seal **(see illustrations)**.

9.5a . . . then insert a self-tapping screw . . .

9.5b . . . and pull out the seal using pliers

9.8 Offering up the new oil seal – note the insulating tape over the end of the crankshaft, used to prevent the seal catching on the keyway

9.9a Fit the old seal over the new seal . . .

9.9b . . . then fit the crankshaft sprocket and bolt, and use the sprocket to press the new seal into place

10 Cylinder head and manifolds
– removal, separation and refitting

Removal

1 Select a solid, level surface to park the car on. Give yourself enough space to move around it easily.

2 Disconnect the battery negative lead, and position it away from the terminal (see *Disconnecting the battery*).

3 Referring to Chapter 1, drain the cooling system.

4 Remove the air cleaner housing as described in Chapter 4A.

5 Also in Chapter 4A, depressurise the fuel injection system.

6 Referring to Chapter 5B, remove the DIS ignition module.

7 Referring to Chapter 3 if necessary, loosen the hose clips and disconnect the coolant hoses from the thermostat housing.

8 Disconnect the following electrical connections, labelling as necessary for refitting:

a) The main engine wiring harness plug connector (below the DIS ignition module). This plug typically has a screw fitting – note the red alignment markings **(see illustration)**. Some models have a number of more conventional plug connectors in this location – all should be labelled and disconnected. Unclip the wiring plug(s) from the mounting bracket.

b) The camshaft position sensor on top of the engine, inboard of the DIS ignition module.

c) The roadspeed sensor from the top of the transmission **(see illustration)**.

d) The oil pressure switch from the rear of the cylinder head **(see illustration)**.

e) All wiring plugs underneath the thermostat housing.

f) The injector plug(s) and wiring harness from the inlet manifold (refer to Chapter 4A). Unclip and disconnect the harness, and lay it to one side.

g) Once all the wiring plugs have been disconnected, release the wiring harness

6 Clean out the seal housing and sealing surface of the crankshaft by wiping it with a lint-free cloth – avoid using solvents that may enter the crankcase and affect component lubrication. Remove any swarf or burrs that could cause the seal to leak.

7 Tape over the end of the crankshaft, to protect the new oil seal as it is fitted.

8 Lubricate the lip of the new oil seal with clean engine oil, and position it over the housing **(see illustration)**.

9 The new seal must be fitted to the same depth as was noted for the old seal. Using a hammer and a socket of suitable diameter, drive the seal squarely into its housing. **Note:** *Select a socket that bears only on the hard outer surface of the seal, not the inner lip which can easily be damaged.* As an alternative, place the old oil seal over the new seal, then fit the sprocket and its bolt, and tighten the bolt a little at a time to press the

10.8a Disconnecting the main engine wiring harness plug connector . . .

new seal into position **(see illustrations)**. Be sure to remove the old oil seal before finally fitting and tightening the sprocket and its bolt.

10 With reference to Sections 2, 4 and 5 of this Chapter, refit the crankshaft sprocket, then refit and tension the timing belt. On completion, refit the timing belt outer covers, crankshaft pulley and other removed components.

11 The remainder of the refitting procedure is a reversal of removal, as follows:

a) With reference to Section 6, refit and tension the auxiliary drivebelt.

b) Refer to Chapter 1 and refill the engine with the correct grade and quantity of oil.

Crankshaft left-hand oil seal

12 The crankshaft left-hand oil seal is integral with the housing, and must be renewed as an assembly, complete with the crankshaft speed/position sensor wheel. The sensor wheel is attached to the oil seal/housing assembly, and is a press-fit on the crankshaft flange. VW special tool T10017 is required to fit this assembly and, in the workshop, we found that there is no means of accurately aligning the sensor wheel on the crankshaft without the tool (there is no locating key, and there are no alignment marks). If the sensor wheel is not precisely aligned on the crankshaft, the crankshaft speed/position sensor will send incorrect TDC signals to the engine management ECU, and the engine will not run correctly (the engine may not run at all). As the appropriate special tool is only available to VW dealers, there is no alternative but to have the new assembly fitted by a VW dealer.

10.8b ... roadspeed sensor wiring plug ...

10.8c ... and oil pressure switch wire

10.9a Disconnect the charcoal canister hose from the inlet manifold ...

from any retaining ties, and move it to one side.

9 Disconnect the following hoses:
a) *The inlet manifold hose leading to the charcoal canister solenoid valve on the right-hand inner wing (see illustration).*
b) *The brake servo vacuum hose from the inlet manifold.*
c) *The fuel supply and return hoses from their connections in the engine compartment, noting the direction-of-flow and colour coding markings (see illustration). Anticipate some loss of fuel. Plug or seal off the hose ends, to reduce further fuel loss and prevent the ingress of dirt.*

10 At the rear of the thermostat housing, slide out the plastic 'horseshoe clip' which joins the thermostat housing to the coolant pump supply pipe running along the back of the engine block **(see illustration).**

11 Refer to Section 6 and remove the auxiliary drivebelt.

12 With reference to Sections 2 and 4 of this Chapter, remove the crankshaft pulley and timing belt outer covers. Disengage the timing belt from the camshaft sprocket.

13 Once the timing belt has been disengaged, the engine can be raised back into its original position, and the right-hand engine mounting refitted while the cylinder head is removed.

14 To avoid any possibility of piston-to-valve contact during cylinder head removal, it is recommended that the crankshaft be turned back a few degrees away from the TDC position, to take the pistons down the bores.

15 Remove the warm-air collector plate from the top of the exhaust manifold, then disconnect the exhaust downpipe from the manifold **(see illustrations).** Recover the gasket.

16 Slacken and remove the bolt securing the engine oil dipstick tube to the rear of the cylinder head **(see illustration).** Unbolt and remove the engine lifting eye next to the oil filler.

17 Disconnect the wiring plug from the throttle body.

18 On later models where the lambda sensor is screwed into the exhaust manifold, disconnect the lambda sensor wiring plug at the connector.

10.9b ... and the fuel supply and return hoses – note direction-of-flow arrow markings

19 Remove the camshaft cover, camshaft, followers and tappets as described in Section 7.

20 Working in sequence, progressively loosen

10.15a Remove the warm air collector plate bolts ...

10.16 Remove the dipstick tube securing bolt

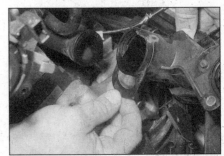

10.10 Pull out the 'horseshoe clip' from the base of the thermostat housing (removed for clarity)

the cylinder head bolts by half a turn at a time, using a suitable socket, until all bolts can be unscrewed by hand **(see illustrations).**

21 Check that nothing remains connected to

10.15b ... then lift off the plate

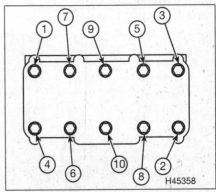

10.20a Cylinder head bolt LOOSENING sequence

H45358

10.20b Loosen the bolts by half a turn at a time, using a suitable splined socket

the cylinder head, then lift the head away from the cylinder block; seek assistance if possible, as it is a heavy assembly, especially if it is being removed complete with the manifolds. Remove the gasket from the top of the block. Do not discard the gasket yet.

22 If the cylinder head is to be dismantled for overhaul, refer to Chapter 2C.

Manifold separation

23 Inlet manifold removal and refitting is described in Chapter 4A.

24 Progressively slacken and remove the exhaust manifold retaining nuts. Lift the manifold away from the cylinder head, and recover the gaskets.

25 Ensure that the mating surfaces are completely clean, then refit the exhaust manifold, using new gaskets. Tighten the retaining nuts to the specified torque.

Preparation for refitting

26 The mating faces of the cylinder head and cylinder block/crankcase must be perfectly clean before refitting the head. Use a hard plastic or wood scraper to remove all traces of gasket and carbon; also clean the piston crowns. Take particular care during the cleaning operations, as aluminium alloy is easily damaged. Also, make sure that the carbon is not allowed to enter the oil and water passages – this is particularly important for the lubrication system, as carbon could block the oil supply to the engine's components. Using adhesive tape and paper, seal the water, oil and bolt holes in the cylinder block/crankcase.

10.32 Ensure that the gasket part number and TOP markings are face up

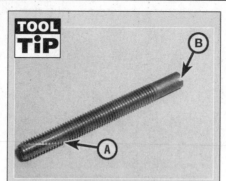

If a tap is not available, make a home-made substitute by cutting a slot (A) down the threads of one of the old cylinder head bolts. After use, the bolt head can be cut off, and the shank can then be used as an alignment dowel to assist cylinder head refitting. Cut a screwdriver slot (B) in the top of the bolt, to allow it to be unscrewed.

27 Check the mating surfaces of the cylinder block/crankcase and the cylinder head for nicks, deep scratches and other damage. If slight, they may be removed carefully with a file, but if excessive, machining may be the only alternative to renewal.

28 If warpage of the cylinder head gasket surface is suspected, use a straight-edge to check it for distortion. Refer to Part C of this Chapter if necessary.

29 Check the condition of the cylinder head bolts, and particularly their threads, whenever they are removed. Wash the bolts in suitable solvent, and wipe them dry. Check each for any sign of visible wear or damage, renewing any bolt if necessary. Measure the length of each bolt, to check for stretching (although this is not a conclusive test, if all bolts have stretched by the same amount). VW do not specify that the bolts must be renewed, however, it is strongly recommended that the bolts should be renewed as a complete set whenever they are disturbed.

30 Clean out the cylinder head bolt drillings using a suitable tap. If a tap is not available, make a home-made substitute **(see Tool Tip)**.

31 On all the engines covered in this Chapter, it is possible for the piston crowns to

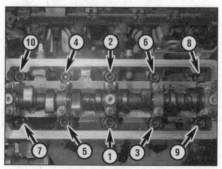

10.37 Cylinder head bolt TIGHTENING sequence

strike and damage the valve heads, if the camshaft is rotated with the timing belt removed and the crankshaft set to TDC. For this reason, the crankshaft must be set to a position other than TDC on No 1 cylinder, before the cylinder head is refitted. Set the crankshaft to TDC on No 1 cylinder, using the information in Section 2, then turn the crankshaft back by a few degrees, away from the TDC position. If preferred, for maximum safety, the pistons can be positioned halfway down their bores, with No 1 piston on its upstroke – ie, 90° before TDC.

Refitting

32 Check that the new gasket is the same type as the one which was removed. Lay the new head gasket on the cylinder block, ensuring that the manufacturer's TOP and part number markings are face up **(see illustration)**. Do not handle the gasket excessively before it is fitted, or it may become damaged.

> **HAYNES HiNT** *Because no locating dowels are fitted, it may prove difficult to accurately align the head on the block when refitting. To overcome this, two of the old cylinder head bolts can be modified to act as locating dowels. Cut the heads off two of the bolts, and then cut a slot in the top of the bolt, so that a flat-bladed screwdriver may be used to unscrew the bolts from the block once the head is placed over them. Screw the two 'dowels' into place either end of the head, then lower the head into position over them. Fit two or more of the new head bolts to locate the head, then unscrew the 'dowels' using a screwdriver.*

33 Before fitting the cylinder head, check that the camshaft sprocket timing mark is aligned with the mark on the timing belt inner cover, as described in Section 2. Try to avoid turning the camshaft sprocket as the head is refitted.

34 With the help of an assistant, place the cylinder head and manifolds centrally on the cylinder block. Check that the head gasket is correctly seated before allowing the weight the full weight of the cylinder head to rest upon it.

35 Apply a smear of grease to the threads, and to the underside of the heads, of the cylinder head bolts; use a good-quality high-melting point grease.

36 Carefully enter each bolt into its relevant hole (*do not drop them in*) and screw in, by hand only, until finger-tight.

37 Working progressively and in sequence, tighten the cylinder head bolts to their Stage 1 torque setting, using a torque wrench and suitable socket **(see illustration)**.

38 The bolts should now be angle-tightened, in the same sequence, through

11.2 Flywheel locked in position with a home-made tool

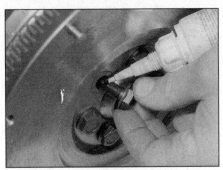

11.7 Apply locking fluid to the new flywheel bolts, if necessary

11.9 Tighten the flywheel bolts to the specified torque

the specified Stage 2 angle, using a socket and extension bar. It is recommended that an angle-measuring gauge is used during this stage of the tightening, to ensure accuracy. If a gauge is not available, use white paint to make alignment marks between the bolt head and cylinder head prior to tightening; the marks can then be used to check that the bolt has been rotated through the correct angle during tightening. Repeat the exercise for the Stage 3 setting.

39 The remainder of the refitting sequence is a reversal of the removal procedure.

11 Flywheel/driveplate – removal, inspection and refitting

Flywheel

Removal

1 Remove the manual transmission and clutch as described in Chapter 7A and Chapter 6.

2 Lock the flywheel in position using a home-made locking tool, fabricated from a piece of scrap metal **(see illustration)**. Bolt it to one of the transmission bellhousing mounting holes. Mark the position of the flywheel with respect to the crankshaft using a dab of paint.

3 Slacken and withdraw the flywheel mounting bolts, then lift off the flywheel.

Caution: Get an assistant to help, as the flywheel is extremely heavy.

Inspection

4 If the flywheel's clutch mating surface is deeply scored, cracked or otherwise damaged, the flywheel must be renewed. However, it may be possible to have it surface-ground; seek the advice of a VAG dealer or engine reconditioning specialist.

5 If the ring gear is badly worn or has missing teeth, the flywheel must be renewed.

Refitting

6 Clean the mating surfaces of the flywheel and crankshaft. Remove any remaining locking compound from the threads of the crankshaft holes, using the correct-size tap, if available.

If a suitable tap is not available, cut two slots down the threads of one of the old flywheel bolts with a hacksaw, and use the bolt to remove the locking compound from the threads.

7 If the new flywheel retaining bolts are not supplied with their threads precoated, apply a suitable thread-locking compound to the threads of each bolt **(see illustration)**.

8 Offer up the flywheel to the crankshaft, using the alignment marks made during removal, and fit the new retaining bolts.

9 Lock the flywheel using the method employed on dismantling, and tighten the retaining bolts to the specified torque and angle **(see illustration)**.

10 Refit the clutch as described in Chapter 6. Remove the locking tool, and refit the transmission as described in Chapter 7A.

Driveplate

Removal

11 Remove the automatic transmission as described in Chapter 7B.

12 Lock the driveplate in position by bolting a piece of scrap metal between the driveplate and one of the transmission bellhousing mounting holes. Mark the position of the driveplate with respect to the crankshaft using a dab of paint.

13 Slacken and withdraw the driveplate mounting bolts, then lift off the driveplate. Recover the packing plate and the shim (where applicable).

12.7 Engine right-hand mounting

Refitting

14 Refitting is a reversal of removal, using the alignment marks made during removal. Fit new mounting bolts and tighten them to the specified torque. Remove the locking tool, and refit the transmission as described in Chapter 7B.

12 Engine/transmission mountings – inspection and renewal

Inspection

1 If improved access is required, raise the front of the car and support it securely on axle stands.

2 Check the mounting rubbers to see if they are cracked, hardened or separated from the metal at any point; renew the mounting if any such damage or deterioration is evident.

3 Check that all the mounting's fasteners are securely tightened; use a torque wrench to check if possible.

4 Using a large screwdriver or a crowbar, check for wear in the mounting by carefully levering against it to check for free play. Where this is not possible, enlist the aid of an assistant to move the engine/transmission back-and-forth, or from side-to-side, while you watch the mounting. While some free play is to be expected even from new components, excessive wear should be obvious. If excessive free play is found, check first that the fasteners are correctly secured, then renew any worn components as described below.

Renewal

Right-hand mounting

5 Disconnect the battery negative lead, and position it away from the terminal (see *Disconnecting the battery*).

6 Support the weight of the engine from above using a hoist or lifting beam, or support it from below using a securely-located trolley jack and suitable block of wood underneath the sump. Do not jack directly under the sump without using a block of wood, or the sump may be damaged.

7 With the engine supported from above or

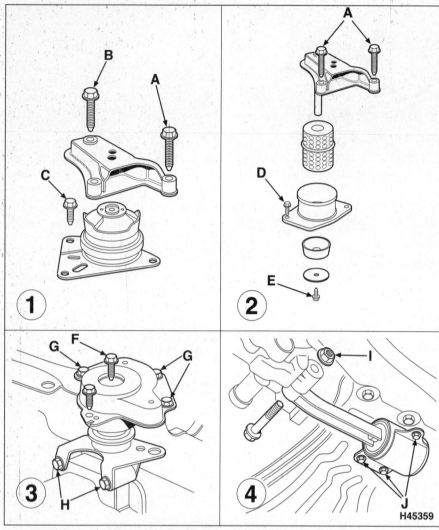

12.13a Two of the transmission left-hand mounting bolts are hidden under the wiring harness plastic guide . . .

12.13b . . . which can be unscrewed and removed

a) Use new bolts, and apply a little oil to their threads before fitting.
b) Tighten all bolts to the specified torque.
c) Note that the tightening torque for the upper and lower bolts is different.

Left-hand mounting

10 Disconnect the battery negative lead, and position it away from the terminal.

11 Support the weight of the engine/transmission from above using a hoist or lifting beam, or support it from below using a securely-located trolley jack and suitable block of wood underneath the bellhousing. Position the jack head directly underneath the engine/bellhousing mating surface. Do not jack directly under the sump without using a block of wood, or the sump may be damaged.

12 With the engine/transmission supported from above or below, loosen and withdraw the central through-bolt from the mounting on the transmission.

13 Unbolt the mounting block from the inner wing, and remove it from the engine bay. Note that two of the bolts may be hidden under the wiring harness plastic guide, which is secured by two screws (see illustrations).

14 Unbolt the mounting bracket from the end of the transmission casing.

15 Refitting is a reversal of removal, noting the following points (see illustration 12.9):
a) Use new bolts, and apply a little oil to their threads before fitting.
b) Tighten all bolts to the specified torque.

Rear mounting

16 Disconnect the battery negative lead, and

12.9 Engine/transmission mounting details – for tightening torques, see Specifications

1 Engine right-hand mounting (manual transmission models)
2 Engine right-hand mounting (automatic transmission models)
3 Transmission left-hand mounting
4 Engine/transmission rear mounting

below, slacken and withdraw the upper bolts, and separate the engine mounting **(see illustration)**.

8 The remaining bolts can now be removed, and the lower part of the mounting removed from the inner wing.

9 Refitting is a reversal of removal, noting the following points **(see illustration)**:

12.13c With the weight of the engine/transmission securely supported, unscrew the bolts (arrowed) . . .

12.13d . . . and separate the mounting

position it away from the terminal.

17 Support the weight of the engine/ transmission from above using a hoist or lifting beam, or support it from below using a securely-located trolley jack and suitable block of wood underneath the bellhousing. Position the jack head directly underneath the engine/bellhousing mating surface. Do not jack directly under the sump without using a block of wood, or the sump may be damaged.

18 With the engine/transmission supported from above or below, slacken the nut and withdraw the through-bolt from the mounting on the transmission **(see illustration)**.

19 Remove the three bolts from the subframe, and withdraw the mounting from under the car.

20 Refitting is a reversal of removal, noting the following points **(see illustration 12.9)**:

  a) *Use new bolts, and apply a little oil to their threads before fitting.*

  b) *Tighten all bolts to the specified torque.*

  c) *When tightening the through-bolt, hold the bolt and tighten the nut onto it.*

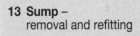

13 Sump – removal and refitting

Removal

1 Disconnect the battery negative lead, and position it away from the terminal (see *Disconnecting the battery*).

2 Refer to Chapter 1 and drain the engine oil.

3 Park the car on a level surface, apply the handbrake and chock the rear wheels.

4 Raise the front of the car, and rest it securely on axle stands or wheel ramps; refer to *Jacking and vehicle support*.

5 Where applicable, release the fasteners and remove the auxiliary drivebelt cover and the cable guide from the sump.

6 Disconnect the exhaust system downpipe from the exhaust manifold, as described in Chapter 4B. By releasing the exhaust system from its mountings, it should be possible to lower the system sufficiently to gain clearance to lower the sump.

7 Refer to Chapter 8 and disconnect the right-hand driveshaft from the transmission output flange.

8 Working around the outside of the sump, progressively slacken and withdraw the sump retaining bolts **(see illustration)**.

9 Break the joint by striking the sump with the palm of your hand, then lower the sump and withdraw it from underneath the car. If it sticks, try removing the drain plug once more, and use a tool such as a screwdriver inserted in the drain hole as a lever to prise the sump free (take care not to damage the drain hole threads). Keep the sump level as it is lowered, to prevent spillage of any remaining oil in it.

10 While the sump is removed, take the opportunity to check the oil pump pick-up/strainer for signs of clogging or

12.18 Engine/transmission rear mounting

disintegration. If necessary, remove the pump as described in Section 14, and clean or renew the strainer.

Refitting

11 Clean all traces of sealant or old gasket, as applicable, from the mating surfaces of the cylinder block/crankcase and sump, then use a clean rag to wipe out the sump.

12 Ensure that the sump and cylinder block/crankcase mating surfaces are clean and dry, then apply a 2 to 3 mm bead of suitable RTV silicone sealant to the sump mating surface. Run the bead of sealant around the inside of the bolt holes.

⚠️ *Warning: Take care not to apply excessive amounts of sealant, in the hope of obtaining a better seal – if too much is applied, the excess may enter the sump and then block the oil pump strainer, causing oil starvation.*

13 The sump should be offered into position immediately, and the retaining bolts tightened hand-tight initially.

> **HAYNES HiNT** *To make aligning the sump easier, obtain two or three M6 studs, and screw them by a few threads into opposite sides of the cylinder block/crankcase mating surface. The sump can be offered into position and fitted over the studs, then the remaining sump bolts can be fitted and hand-tightened. Remove the studs, and fit the rest of the sump bolts.*

14 Progressively tighten the sump bolts to the specified torque. Refer to the sealant manufacturer's advice on the length of time required for the sealant to set. Typically, it is advisable to wait for several hours before filling the engine with oil. If the car is to be left for some time with no oil in the sump, ensure that the battery remains disconnected, so that no attempt is made to start the engine.

15 Refit the driveshaft as described in Chapter 8, and the exhaust downpipe as described in Chapter 4B.

16 Where applicable, refit the auxiliary drivebelt cover and the cable guide to the sump.

17 Lower the car to the ground, then refer to

13.8 Removing the sump bolts (seen with engine removed and inverted, for clarity)

Chapter 1 and refill the engine with the specified grade and quantity of oil.

18 Restore the battery connection, then run the engine and check for leaks.

14 Oil pump and pickup – removal, inspection and refitting

Removal

1 Remove the timing belt as described in Section 4.

2 Turn the crankshaft a quarter-turn (90°) clockwise to reposition Nos 1 and 4 pistons at TDC. Ensure that the crankshaft sprocket tooth with the chamfered inner edge is aligned with the corresponding mark on the oil pump housing (see Section 3).

3 Turn the crankshaft to move the crankshaft sprocket three teeth anti-clockwise away from the TDC position. The third tooth to the right of the tooth with the ground-down outer edge must align with the corresponding mark on the oil pump housing. This procedure positions the crankshaft correctly to enable oil pump refitting.

4 Remove the timing belt tensioner as described in Section 5.

5 Remove the sump as described in Section 13.

6 Unscrew the securing bolts and remove the oil pick-up pipe from the oil pump and cylinder block **(see illustration)**. Recover the gasket.

7 Remove the crankshaft sprocket, noting which way round it is fitted.

14.6 Removing the oil pick-up pipe

14.8 Removing the oil pump

14.10 Lifting off the oil pump rear cover

14.11 Note that the rotors fit with the punched dots (arrowed) facing the oil pump cover

14.15 Prise the crankshaft oil seal from the oil pump

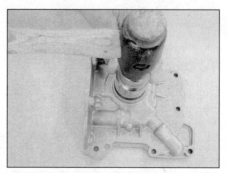

14.17 Driving a new oil seal into the oil pump using a socket

17 Press or drive a new oil seal into position in the oil pump, using a socket or tube of suitable diameter **(see illustration)**. Ensure that the seal seats squarely in the oil pump. Ensure that the socket or tube bears only on the hard outer ring of the seal, and take care not to damage the seal lips. Press or drive the seal into position until it is seated on the shoulder in the housing. Make sure that the closed end of the seal is facing outwards.

Refitting

18 Commence refitting by cleaning all traces of old gasket and sealant from the mating faces of the cylinder block and oil pump.

19 Wind a length of tape around the end of the crankshaft to protect the oil seal lips as the oil pump is slid into position.

20 Fit a new oil pump gasket over the dowels in the cylinder block **(see illustration)**.

21 Turn the inner oil pump rotor to align one of the drive cut-outs in the edge of the inner rotor with the line on the oil pump rear cover **(see illustration)**.

22 Lightly oil the four tips of the oil pump drive cam on the end of the crankshaft.

23 Coat the lips of the crankshaft oil seal with a thin film of clean engine oil.

24 Slide the oil pump into position over the end of the crankshaft until it engages with the

8 Unscrew the securing bolts, noting their locations to ensure correct refitting, and remove the oil pump **(see illustration)**. Recover the gasket.

Inspection

9 No spare parts are available for the oil pump, and if worn or faulty the complete pump must be renewed.

10 To inspect the oil pump rotors, remove the securing screws, and lift off the oil pump rear cover **(see illustration)**.

11 Note that the rotors fit with the punched dots on the edges of the rotors facing the oil pump cover **(see illustration)**.

12 Lift out the rotors, and inspect them for wear and damage. If there are any signs of wear or damage, the complete oil pump assembly must be renewed.

13 Lubricate the contact faces of the rotors with clean engine oil, then refit the rotors to the pump, ensuring that the punched dots on the edges of the rotors face the pump cover.

14 Refit the pump cover, and tighten the screws securely.

15 Using a flat-bladed screwdriver, prise the crankshaft oil seal from the oil pump, and discard it **(see illustration)**.

16 Thoroughly clean the oil seal seat in the oil pump.

14.20 Fit a new gasket over the dowels in the cylinder block

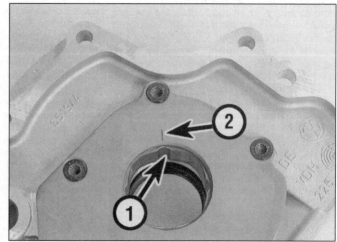

14.21 Align one of the drive cut-outs (1) in the edge of the rotor with the line (2) on the oil pump rear cover

14.24 Slide the oil pump over the end of the crankshaft. Note the tape used to protect the oil seal

14.25 Fit the new oil pump securing bolts to the locations (arrowed) noted before removal

dowels, taking care not to damage the oil seal, and ensuring that the inner rotor engages with the drive cam on the crankshaft **(see illustration)**.

25 Fit new oil pump securing bolts, to the locations noted before removal, and tighten them to the specified torque **(see illustration)**.

26 Remove the tape from the end of the crankshaft, then refit the crankshaft sprocket, noting that the pulley locating pin must be

outermost. Temporarily refit the securing bolt and washer to retain the sprocket.

27 Refit the oil pick-up pipe, using a new gasket, and tighten the securing bolts to the specified torque **(see illustration)**.

28 Refit the sump as described in Section 13.

29 Refit the timing belt tensioner as described in Section 5.

30 Refit the timing belt as described in Section 4.

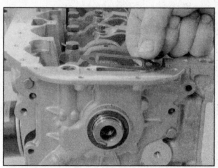

14.27 Fit a new oil pick-up pipe gasket

Chapter 2 Part B:
DOHC engine in-car repair procedures

Contents

Degrees of difficulty

| **Easy,** suitable for novice with little experience | **Fairly easy,** suitable for beginner with some experience | **Fairly difficult,** suitable for competent DIY mechanic | **Difficult,** suitable for experienced DIY mechanic | **Very difficult,** suitable for expert DIY or professional |

Specifications

General

Engine codes*:
  1390 cc (1.4 litre), Marelli 4LV injection, 75 bhp .... AHW, APE or AUA
  1390 cc (1.4 litre), Marelli 4LV injection, 100 bhp .... AFH, AFK, AQQ or AUB
* Note: *See 'Vehicle identification' for the location of code marking on the engine.*
Bore .... 76.5 mm
Stroke .... 75.6 mm
Compression ratio .... 10.5 : 1
Compression pressures:
  Minimum compression pressure .... Approximately 7.0 bar
  Maximum difference between cylinders .... Approximately 3.0 bar
Firing order .... 1 – 3 – 4 – 2
No 1 cylinder location .... Timing belt end

Camshafts

Camshaft endfloat (maximum) .... 0.40 mm
Camshaft bearing running clearance .... No figure specified
Camshaft run-out .... No figure specified

Lubrication system

Oil pump type .... Gear type, driven directly from front of crankshaft
Oil pressure (oil temperature 80°C):
  At idle .... 1.0 bar
  At 2000 rpm .... 2.0 bar

Torque wrench settings

	Nm	lbf ft
Ancillary (alternator, etc) bracket mounting bolts	50	37
Auxiliary drivebelt tensioner securing bolt:		
M8 bolt:		
Stage 1	20	15
Stage 2	Angle-tighten a further 90°	
M10 bolt	45	33
Big-end bearing caps bolts*:		
Stage 1	30	22
Stage 2	Angle-tighten a further 90°	
Camshaft carrier bolts*:		
Stage 1	10	7
Stage 2	Angle-tighten a further 90°	
Camshaft left-hand endplate bolts	10	7
Camshaft sprocket bolts*:		
Stage 1	20	15
Stage 2	Angle-tighten a further 90°	
Clutch pressure plate/driveplate mounting bolts*:		
Stage 1	60	44
Stage 2	Angle-tighten a further 90°	
Coolant pump bolts	20	15
Crankcase breather (oil separator) bolts	10	7
Crankshaft left-hand oil seal housing bolts	12	9
Crankshaft pulley/sprocket bolt*:		
Stage 1	90	66
Stage 2	Angle-tighten a further 90°	
Cylinder head bolts*:		
Stage 1	30	22
Stage 2	Angle-tighten a further 90°	
Stage 3	Angle-tighten a further 90°	
Engine-to-automatic transmission bolts:		
M12 bolts	80	59
M10 cylinder block-to-transmission bolts	60	44
M10 sump-to-transmission bolts	25	18
Engine-to-manual transmission bolts	80	59
Engine-to-manual transmission cover plate bolts	10	7
Engine mountings	See Chapter 2A Specifications	
Exhaust manifold nuts	25	18
Exhaust pipe-to-manifold nuts	40	30
Oil cooler securing nut	25	18
Oil drain plug	30	22
Oil level/temperature sensor-to-sump bolts	10	7
Oil pick-up pipe securing bolts	10	7
Oil pressure warning light switch	25	18
Oil pump securing bolts*	12	9
Sump:		
Sump-to-cylinder block bolts	13	10
Sump-to-transmission bolts	45	33
Timing belt outer cover bolts:		
Small bolts	10	7
Large bolts	20	15
Timing belt rear cover bolts:		
Small bolts	10	7
Large bolt (coolant pump bolts)	20	15
Timing belt idler pulley bolt	50	37
Timing belt tensioner:		
Main timing belt tensioner bolt	20	15
Secondary timing belt tensioner bolt	20	15

* **Note:** *Use new bolts*

---

1 General information

Using this Chapter

Chapter 2 is divided into three Parts; A, B and C. This Part describes repair operations that can be carried out with the engine in the car, on double overhead camshaft (DOHC or 16-valve) engines. Part A covers in-car repairs on single overhead camshaft (SOHC or 8-valve) engines, while Part C covers the removal of the engine/transmission as a unit, and describes the engine dismantling and overhaul procedures.

In Parts A and B, the assumption is made that the engine is installed in the car, with all ancillaries connected. If the engine has been removed for overhaul, the preliminary dismantling information which precedes each operation may be ignored.

Access to the engine bay can be improved by removing the bonnet and the front lock carrier assembly; for details, see Chapter 2C, Section 2.

Engine description

Throughout this Chapter, engines are identified and referred to by their capacity and, where necessary, by the manufacturer's code letters. A listing of all engines covered, together with their code letters, is given in the Specifications.

The engines are water-cooled, double overhead camshaft, in-line four-cylinder units, with aluminium-alloy cylinder blocks and cylinder heads. All are mounted transversely at the front of the car, with the transmission bolted to the left-hand side of the engine.

The crankshaft is of five-bearing type, and thrustwashers are fitted to the centre main bearing to control crankshaft endfloat. The crankshaft and main bearings are matched to the alloy cylinder block, and it is not possible to reassemble the crankshaft and cylinder block once the components have been separated. If the crankshaft or bearings are worn, the complete cylinder block/crankshaft assembly must be renewed.

The inlet camshaft is driven via a toothed belt from the crankshaft sprocket, and the exhaust camshaft is driven from the inlet camshaft by a second toothed belt. The camshafts are located in a camshaft carrier, which is bolted to the top of the cylinder head.

The valves are closed by coil springs, and run in guides pressed into the cylinder head; the camshafts actuate the valves via roller rockers and hydraulic tappets. There are four valves per cylinder; two inlet valves and two exhaust valves.

The oil pump is driven directly from the front of the crankshaft. Oil is drawn from the sump through a strainer, and then forced through an externally-mounted, renewable filter. From there, it is distributed to the cylinder head, where it lubricates the camshaft journals and hydraulic tappets, and also to the crankcase, where it lubricates the main bearings, connecting rod big-ends, gudgeon pins and cylinder bores. A coolant-fed oil cooler is fitted to certain engines.

On all engines, engine coolant is circulated by a pump, driven by the main timing belt. For details of the cooling system, refer to Chapter 3.

Repairs with engine in car

The following operations can be performed without removing the engine:

a) *Compression pressure – testing.*
b) *Camshaft carrier – removal and refitting.*
c) *Crankshaft pulley – removal and refitting.*
d) *Timing belt covers – removal and refitting.*
e) *Timing belt tensioner and sprockets – removal and refitting.*
f) *Inlet camshaft timing belt, sprockets and tensioner – removal and refitting.*
g) *Camshaft oil seal(s) – renewal.*
h) *Camshafts and hydraulic tappets – removal, inspection and refitting.*

i) *Cylinder head – removal and refitting*.*
j) *Sump – removal and refitting.*
k) *Oil pump – removal, overhaul and refitting.*
l) *Crankshaft oil seals – renewal.*
m) *Engine/transmission mountings – inspection and renewal.*
n) *Flywheel – removal, inspection and refitting.*

* *Cylinder head dismantling procedures are detailed in Chapter 2C, with details of camshaft and hydraulic tappet removal.*

Note: *It is possible to remove the pistons and connecting rods (after removing the cylinder head and sump) without removing the engine. However, this is not recommended. Work of this nature is more easily and thoroughly completed with the engine on the bench, as described in Chapter 2C.*

2 Compression test – description and interpretation

1 When engine performance is down, or if misfiring occurs which cannot be attributed to the ignition or fuel systems, a compression test can provide diagnostic clues as to the engine's condition. If the test is performed regularly, it can give warning of trouble before any other symptoms become apparent.

2 The engine must be fully warmed-up to normal operating temperature, the battery must be fully charged and the spark plugs must be removed. The aid of an assistant will be required.

3 Disable the ignition system by disconnecting the wiring plug from the DIS ignition module. Depressurise and disable the fuel system, as described in Chapter 4A.

4 Fit a compression tester to the No 1 cylinder spark plug hole. The type of tester that screws into the plug thread is preferred.

5 Have the assistant hold the throttle wide open and crank the engine for several seconds on the starter motor. **Note:** *The throttle will not operate until the ignition is switched on.* After one or two revolutions, the compression pressure should build up to a maximum figure and then stabilise. Record the highest reading obtained.

6 Repeat the test on the remaining cylinders, recording the pressure in each.

7 All cylinders should produce very similar pressures. Any difference greater than that specified indicates the existence of a fault. Note that the compression should build-up quickly in a healthy engine. Low compression on the first stroke, followed by gradually increasing pressure on successive strokes, indicates worn piston rings. A low compression reading on the first stroke, which does not build-up during successive strokes, indicates leaking valves or a blown head gasket (a cracked head could also be the cause). Deposits on the undersides of the valve heads can also cause low compression.

8 If the pressure in any cylinder is reduced to

the specified minimum or less, carry out the following test to isolate the cause. Introduce a teaspoonful of clean oil into that cylinder through its spark plug hole and repeat the test.

9 If the addition of oil temporarily improves the compression pressure, this indicates that bore or piston wear is responsible for the pressure loss. No improvement suggests that leaking or burnt valves, or a blown head gasket, may be to blame.

10 A low reading from two adjacent cylinders is almost certainly due to the head gasket having blown between them and the presence of coolant in the engine oil will confirm this.

11 If one cylinder is about 20 percent lower than the others and the engine has a slightly rough idle, a worn camshaft lobe could be the cause.

12 If the compression reading is unusually high, the combustion chambers are probably coated with carbon deposits. If this is the case, the cylinder head should be removed and decarbonised.

13 On completion of the test, refit the spark plugs and reconnect the DIS ignition module wiring.

3 Engine assembly and valve timing marks – general information and usage

General information

1 TDC is the highest point in the cylinder that each piston reaches as it travels up and down when the crankshaft turns. Each piston reaches TDC at the end of the compression stroke and again at the end of the exhaust stroke, but TDC generally refers to piston position on the compression stroke. No 1 piston is at the timing belt end of the engine.

2 Positioning No 1 piston at TDC is an essential part of many procedures, such as timing belt removal and camshaft removal.

3 The design of the engines covered in this Chapter is such that piston-to-valve contact may occur if the camshaft or crankshaft is turned with the timing belt removed. For this reason, it is important to ensure that the camshaft and crankshaft do not move in relation to each other once the timing belt has been removed from the engine.

4 The crankshaft pulley has a marking which, when aligned with a corresponding reference marking on the timing belt cover, indicates that No 1 piston (and hence also No 4 piston) is at TDC. Note that on some models, the crankshaft pulley timing mark is located on the outer flange of the pulley. In order to make alignment of the timing marks easier, it is advisable to remove the pulley (see Section 5) and, using a set-square, scribe a corresponding mark on the inner flange of the pulley **(see illustrations)**.

5 Note also that there is also a timing mark which can be used with the crankshaft

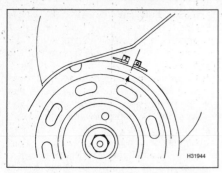

3.4a Crankshaft pulley timing mark aligned with TDC mark on timing belt cover

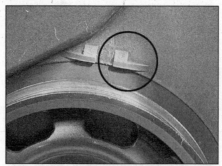

3.4b Timing mark scribed on inner flange of pulley aligned with TDC mark on timing belt cover

3.5 Crankshaft sprocket tooth with chamfered edge aligns with cast arrow on oil pump

sprocket – this is useful if the crankshaft pulley and timing belt have been removed. When No 1 piston is at TDC, the crankshaft sprocket tooth with the chamfered inner edge aligns with a cast arrow on the oil pump **(see illustration)**.

6 The camshaft sprockets are equipped with TDC positioning holes. When the positioning holes are aligned with the corresponding holes in the camshaft carrier, No 1 piston is at TDC on the compression stroke **(see illustration)**.

7 Additionally, on some models, the flywheel/driveplate has a TDC marking, which can be observed by unscrewing a protective plastic cover from the transmission bellhousing. The mark takes the form of a notch in the edge of the flywheel on manual transmission models, or an O marking on automatic transmission models. Note that it is not possible to use these marks on all models due to the limited access available to view the marks.

Setting No 1 cylinder to TDC

Note: *Suitable locking pins will be required to lock the camshaft sprockets in position during this procedure. On some engines, it may be necessary to use a small engineer's mirror to view the timing marks from under the wheel arch.*

8 Before starting work, make sure that the ignition is switched off (ideally, the battery negative lead should be disconnected).

9 Remove the air cleaner assembly as described in Chapter 4A.

10 If desired, to make the engine easier to turn, remove all of the spark plugs as described in Chapter 1.

11 Apply the handbrake, then jack up the front of the vehicle and support on axle stands (see *Jacking and vehicle support*).

12 Remove the right-hand front roadwheel, then remove the securing screws and/or clips, and remove the appropriate engine under-shields to enable access to the crankshaft pulley.

13 Remove the upper timing belt cover as described in Section 6.

14 Turn the engine clockwise, using a spanner on the crankshaft pulley bolt, until the TDC mark on the crankshaft pulley or flywheel/driveplate is aligned with the corresponding mark on the timing belt cover or transmission casing, and the locking pin holes in the camshaft sprockets are aligned with the corresponding holes in the camshaft carrier.

15 If necessary, to give sufficient clearance for the camshaft locking tool to be engaged with the camshaft sprockets, unbolt the air cleaner support bracket from the engine mounting. Similarly, if necessary, unbolt the power steering fluid reservoir and move it to one side, leaving the fluid hoses connected.

16 A suitable tool will now be required to lock the camshaft sprockets in the TDC position. A special VW tool is available for this purpose, but a suitable tool can be improvised using two M8 bolts and nuts, and a short length of steel bar. With the camshaft sprocket positioned as described in paragraph 14, measure the distance between the locking pin hole centres, and drill two corresponding 8 mm clearance holes in the length of steel bar. Slide the M8 bolts through the holes in the bar, and secure them using the nuts.

17 Slide the tool into position in the holes in the camshaft sprockets, ensuring that the pins (or bolts) engage with the holes in the camshaft carrier **(see illustration)**. The engine is now locked in position, with No 1 piston at TDC on the firing stroke.

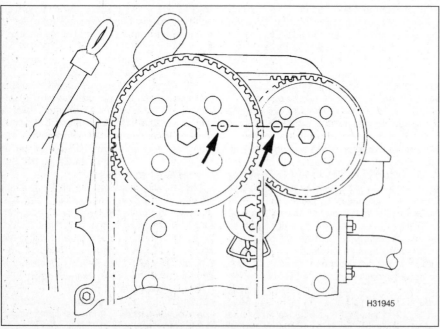

3.6 Camshaft sprocket positioning holes (arrowed) aligned with holes in camshaft carrier (No 1 piston at TDC)

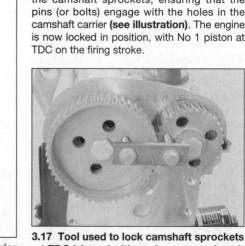

3.17 Tool used to lock camshaft sprockets at TDC (viewed with engine removed, and timing belt removed from engine)

4 Auxiliary drivebelt – removal and refitting

General information

1 Depending on the vehicle specification, the auxiliary drivebelt, which is driven from a pulley mounted on the crankshaft, will provide drive for the alternator, power steering pump and (on models with air conditioning), the refrigerant compressor.
2 The ribbed auxiliary belt is fitted with an automatic tensioning device.

Removal

3 For improved access, apply the handbrake, then jack up the front of the vehicle and support it on axle stands (see *Jacking and vehicle support*). Remove the right-hand front roadwheel, then remove the access panel from the inner wheel arch.
4 Use a spanner to turn the tensioner central bolt clockwise to release the tension on the drivebelt **(see illustration)**.
5 Note how the drivebelt is routed, then remove it from the crankshaft pulley, alternator pulley, power steering pump pulley, and air conditioning compressor pulley (where applicable).

Refitting

6 Locate the new drivebelt on the pulleys, then release the tensioner. Check that the belt is located correctly in the multi-grooves in the pulleys.
7 Refit the access panel and roadwheel, and lower the vehicle to the ground.

5 Crankshaft pulley – removal and refitting

Removal

1 Disconnect the battery negative lead (see *Disconnecting the battery*).
2 For improved access, jack up the front of the vehicle, and support securely on axle stands (see *Jacking and vehicle support*). Remove the right-hand front roadwheel.
3 Remove the securing screws and/or release the clips, and withdraw the relevant engine undershield(s) to enable access to the crankshaft pulley.
4 If necessary (for any later work to be carried out), turn the crankshaft using a socket or spanner on the crankshaft pulley bolt, until the relevant timing marks align (see Section 3).
5 Remove the auxiliary drivebelt, as described in Section 4.
6 To prevent the crankshaft from turning as the pulley bolt is slackened, a tool similar to that shown can be used. Engage the tool with two of the slots in the pulley **(see illustration)**.
7 Counterhold the pulley, and slacken the

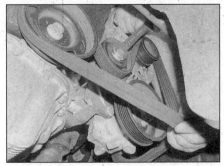

4.4 Removing the auxiliary drivebelt

pulley bolt (take care – the bolt is very tight) using a socket and a suitable extension.
8 Unscrew the bolt, and remove the pulley **(see illustration)**.
9 Refit the crankshaft pulley securing bolt, with a spacer washer positioned under its head, to retain the crankshaft sprocket.

Refitting

10 Unscrew the crankshaft pulley/sprocket bolt used to retain the sprocket, and remove the spacer washer, then refit the pulley to the sprocket. Ensure that the locating pin on the sprocket engages with the corresponding hole in the pulley.
11 Oil the threads of the new crankshaft pulley bolt. Prevent the crankshaft from turning as during removal, then fit the new pulley securing bolt, and tighten it to the specified torque, in the two stages given in the Specifications.

5.6 Counterhold the crankshaft pulley using a tool similar to that shown

6.2 Removing the upper outer timing belt cover

12 Refit the auxiliary drivebelt as described in Section 4.
13 Refit the engine undershield(s).
14 Refit the roadwheel, lower the vehicle to the ground, and reconnect the battery negative lead.

6 Timing belt covers – removal and refitting

Upper outer cover

1 Remove the air cleaner assembly as described in Chapter 4A.
2 Release the two securing clips, and lift the cover from the engine **(see illustration)**.
3 Refitting is a reversal of removal.

Lower outer cover

4 Remove the crankshaft pulley, as described in Section 5.
5 Release the two cover securing clips, located at the rear of the engine, then unscrew the two lower securing bolts, and the single bolt securing the cover to the engine mounting bracket. Withdraw the cover downwards from the engine **(see illustrations)**.
6 Refitting is a reversal of removal, but refit the crankshaft pulley with reference to Section 5.

Rear timing belt cover

Note: *As the rear timing belt cover securing bolts also secure the coolant pump, it is*

5.8 Removing the crankshaft pulley

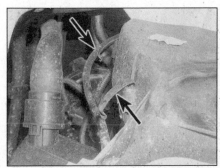

6.5a Release the two securing clips (arrowed) . . .

6.5b . . . then unscrew the two lower securing bolts (arrowed) . . .

6.5c . . . and the single bolt securing the cover to the engine mounting bracket . . .

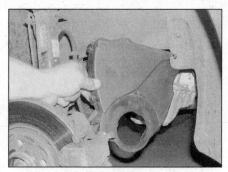

6.5d . . . and withdraw the lower timing belt cover

6.8 Removing the idler pulley/bracket assembly (viewed with engine removed)

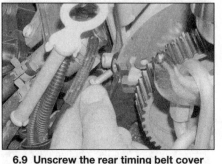

6.9 Unscrew the rear timing belt cover securing bolt located next to the right-hand engine lifting eye

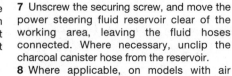

6.10 Removing the rear timing belt cover (viewed with engine removed)

advisable to drain the cooling system (see Chapter 1) before starting this procedure, and to renew the coolant pump seal/gasket (see Chapter 3) before refitting the cover. Refill the cooling system with reference to Chapter 1.

7 Remove the timing belt as described in Section 7.

8 Unbolt the timing belt idler pulley/bracket assembly **(see illustration)**.

9 Unscrew the rear timing belt cover securing bolt located next to the right-hand engine lifting eye **(see illustration)**.

10 Unscrew the two securing bolts, and remove the rear timing belt cover. Note that the bolts also secure the coolant pump **(see illustration)**.

11 Refitting is a reversal of removal, but tighten the timing belt idler pulley/bracket bolt to the specified torque, and refit the timing belt as described in Section 7.

7.13 Slacken the tensioner bolt, lever the tensioner anti-clockwise with an Allen key, then retighten the tensioner bolt

7.14 Removing the main timing belt

7 Timing belt(s) – removal and refitting

Removal

1 These engines have two timing belts; the main timing belt drives the inlet camshaft from the crankshaft, and the secondary timing belt drives the exhaust camshaft from the inlet camshaft.

Main timing belt

2 Disconnect the battery negative lead (see *Disconnecting the battery*).

3 Remove the air cleaner assembly as described in Chapter 4A.

4 Release the two securing clips and remove the upper and lower timing belt covers as described in Section 6.

5 Refit the crankshaft pulley securing bolt, with a spacer washer positioned under its head, to retain the crankshaft sprocket.

6 Turn the crankshaft to position No 1 piston at TDC on the firing stroke, and lock the camshaft sprockets in position, as described in Section 3.

7 Unscrew the securing screw, and move the power steering fluid reservoir clear of the working area, leaving the fluid hoses connected. Where necessary, unclip the charcoal canister hose from the reservoir.

8 Where applicable, on models with air conditioning, unscrew the securing bolt, and remove the auxiliary drivebelt idler pulley.

9 Attach a hoist and lifting tackle to the right-hand (timing belt end) engine lifting bracket, and raise the hoist to just take the weight of the engine.

10 Remove the complete engine right-hand mounting assembly, as described in Section 18.

11 Unscrew the four securing bolts, and remove the right-hand engine mounting bracket from the engine.

12 If either of the timing belts are to be refitted, mark their running directions to ensure correct refitting.

13 Engage a suitable Allen key with the hole in the main timing belt tensioner plate, then slacken the tensioner bolt, lever the tensioner anti-clockwise using the Allen key (to release the tension on the belt), and retighten the tensioner bolt **(see illustration)**.

14 Temporarily remove the camshaft sprocket locking tool, then slide the main timing belt from the sprockets, noting its routing **(see illustration)**. Refit the camshaft sprocket locking tool once the timing belt has been removed.

15 Turn the crankshaft a quarter-turn (90°) anti-clockwise to position Nos 1 and 4 pistons slightly down their bores from the TDC position. This will eliminate any risk of piston-to-valve contact if the crankshaft or camshaft is turned whilst the timing belt is removed.

Secondary timing belt

16 Once the main timing belt has been removed, to remove the secondary timing belt, proceed as follows.

17 Engage a suitable Allen key with the hole in the secondary timing belt tensioner plate, then slacken the tensioner bolt, and lever the tensioner clockwise using the Allen key (to release the tension on the belt). Unscrew the securing bolt, and remove the secondary timing belt tensioner **(see illustrations)**.

18 Temporarily remove the camshaft sprocket locking tool, and slide the secondary timing belt from the sprockets **(see illustration)**. Refit the sprocket locking tool once the belt has been removed.

Refitting

Secondary timing belt

19 Check that the camshaft sprockets are still locked in position by the locking pins, then turn the crankshaft a quarter-turn (90°) clockwise to reposition Nos 1 and 4 pistons at TDC. Ensure that the crankshaft sprocket tooth with the chamfered inner edge is aligned with the corresponding mark on the oil pump housing **(see illustration)**.

20 Temporarily remove the camshaft sprocket locking tool, and fit the secondary timing belt around the camshaft sprockets. Make sure that the belt is as tight as possible on its top run between the sprockets (but note that there will be some slack in the belt). If the original belt is being refitted, observe the running direction markings. Refit the camshaft

7.17a Slacken the secondary timing belt tensioner bolt, and lever the tensioner clockwise using an Allen key . . .

7.18 Removing the secondary timing belt

sprocket locking tool once the belt has been fitted to the sprockets.

21 Check that the secondary timing belt tensioner pointer is positioned on the far right of the tensioner backplate.

22 Press the secondary timing belt up using the tensioner, and fit the tensioner securing bolt (if necessary turn the tensioner with an Allen key until the bolt hole in the tensioner aligns with the bolt hole in the cylinder head). Make sure that the lug on the tensioner backplate engages with the core plug hole in the cylinder head **(see illustration)**.

23 Use the Allen key to turn the tensioner anti-

7.17b . . . then unscrew the securing bolt and remove the tensioner

7.19 Crankshaft sprocket tooth with chamfered edge aligned with cast arrow on oil pump

clockwise until the tensioner pointer aligns with the lug on the tensioner backplate, with the lug positioned against the left-hand stop in the core plug hole **(see illustration)**. Tighten the tensioner bolt to the specified torque.

Main timing belt

24 Where applicable, ensure that the secondary drivebelt has been refitted and tensioned, then again temporarily remove the camshaft sprocket locking tool, and fit the main timing belt around the sprockets. Work in an anti-clockwise direction, starting at the coolant pump, followed by the tensioner

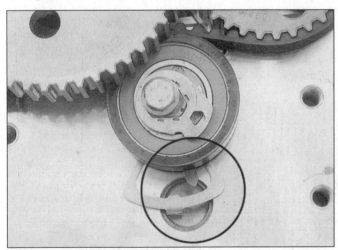

7.22 The secondary timing belt tensioner pointer should be positioned on the far right of the tensioner backplate, and the lug on the backplate should be engaged with the core plug hole

7.23 Turn the tensioner anti-clockwise until the tensioner pointer aligns with the lug on the tensioner backplate, with the lug positioned against the left-hand stop in the core plug hole

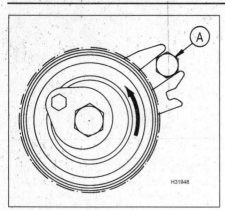

8.3 Turn the tensioner anti-clockwise to the position shown before fitting. Note that the cut-out engages with the bolt (A) on the cylinder block when fitting

8.8a Removing the smaller . . .

8.8b . . . and larger timing belt idler pulleys

roller, crankshaft sprocket, idler roller, inlet camshaft sprocket and the second idler roller. If the original belt is being refitted, observe the running direction markings. Once the belt has been refitted, refit the camshaft sprocket locking tool.

25 Ensure that the tensioner bolt is slack, then engage an Allen key with the hole in the tensioner plate, and turn the plate clockwise until the tension indicator pointer is aligned with the centre of the cut-out in the backplate. Tighten the tensioner securing bolt to the specified torque.

26 Remove the camshaft sprocket locking tool.

27 Using a spanner or socket on the crankshaft pulley bolt, turn the engine through two complete turns in the normal direction of rotation, until the crankshaft sprocket tooth with the chamfered inner edge is aligned with the corresponding mark on the oil pump housing (**refer to illustration 3.5**). Check that the locking tool can again be fitted to lock the camshaft sprockets in position – if not, one or both of the timing belts may have been incorrectly fitted.

28 With the crankshaft timing marks aligned, and the camshaft sprockets locked in position, check the tension of the timing belts. The secondary and main belt tension indicators should be positioned as described in paragraphs 23 and 25 respectively – if not, repeat the appropriate tensioning procedure, then recheck the tension.

29 When the belt tension is correct, refit the right-hand engine mounting bracket, and tighten the securing bolts to the specified torque.

30 Refit the complete right-hand engine mounting assembly, as described in Section 18.

31 Disconnect the hoist and lifting tackle from the engine lifting bracket.

32 Where applicable, refit the auxiliary drivebelt idler pulley.

33 Refit the lower outer timing belt cover, with reference to Section 6 if necessary.

34 Refit the crankshaft pulley as described in Section 5.

35 Refit the upper outer timing belt cover.

36 Refit the air cleaner assembly, and reconnect the battery negative lead.

8 Timing belt tensioner and sprockets – removal, inspection and refitting

Tensioner

Main timing belt

1 Remove the main timing belt as described in Section 7.

2 Unscrew the main timing belt tensioner bolt, and remove the tensioner from the engine.

3 Engage an Allen key with the hole in the tensioner plate, and turn the tensioner anti-clockwise to the position shown (**see illustration**).

4 Refit the tensioner to the engine, ensuring that the cut-out in the tensioner backplate engages with the bolt on the cylinder block (**refer to illustration 8.3**). Refit the tensioner securing bolt, and tighten by hand.

5 Refit and tension the main timing belt as described in Section 7.

Secondary timing belt

6 Removal and refitting of the tensioner is described as part of the timing belt removal procedure in Section 7.

Main timing belt idler pulleys

7 Remove the timing belt as described in Section 7.

8.13 Refitting the crankshaft sprocket. Pulley locating pin (arrowed) must be outermost

8 Unscrew the securing bolt and remove the relevant idler pulley. Note that the smaller pulley (the idler pulley nearest the inlet manifold side of the engine) can be removed complete with its mounting bracket (unbolt the mounting bracket bolt, leaving the pulley attached to the bracket) (**see illustrations**).

9 Refit the relevant idler pulley and tighten the securing bolt to the specified torque. Note that if the smaller idler pulley has been removed complete with its bracket, ensure that the bracket locates over the rear timing belt cover bolt on refitting.

10 Refit and tension the main timing belt as described in Section 7.

Crankshaft sprocket

11 Remove the main timing belt as described in Section 7.

12 Unscrew the crankshaft pulley, and the washer used to retain the sprocket, and withdraw the sprocket from the crankshaft.

13 Commence refitting by positioning the sprocket on the end of the crankshaft, noting that the pulley locating pin must be outermost (**see illustration**). Temporarily refit the pulley securing bolt and washer to retain the sprocket.

14 Refit the main timing belt as described in Section 7.

Camshaft sprockets

15 Remove the main and secondary timing belts as described in Section 7. Ensure that the crankshaft has been turned a quarter-turn (90°) anti-clockwise to position Nos 1 and 4 pistons slightly down their bores from the TDC position. This will eliminate any risk of piston-to-valve contact if the crankshaft or camshaft is turned whilst the timing belt is removed.

16 The relevant camshaft sprocket bolt must now be slackened. The camshaft must be prevented from turning as the sprocket bolt is unscrewed – **do not** rely solely on the sprocket locking tool for this. To hold the sprocket, make up a tool similar to that shown, and use it to hold the sprocket stationary by means of the holes in the sprocket (**refer to illustration 8.19**).

17 Unscrew the camshaft sprocket bolt, and withdraw the sprocket from the front of the camshaft, noting which way round it is fitted.

18 Commence refitting by offering the sprocket up to the camshaft, ensuring that lug on the sprocket engages with the notch in the end of the camshaft. If both camshaft sprockets have been removed, note that the double sprocket (for the main and secondary timing belts) should be fitted to the inlet camshaft, and note that the exhaust camshaft sprocket must be fitted first (see illustration).

19 Fit a new sprocket securing bolt, then use the tool to hold the sprocket stationary, as during removal, and tighten the bolt to the specified torque, in the two stages given in the Specifications (see illustration).

20 Refit the secondary and main timing belts as described in Section 7.

Coolant pump sprocket

21 The coolant pump sprocket is integral with the coolant pump. Refer to Chapter 3 for details of coolant pump removal.

9 Camshaft carrier – removal and refitting

Removal

1 Disconnect the battery negative lead (see *Disconnecting the battery*).

2 Remove the main and secondary timing belts, as described in Section 7.

3 Disconnect the HT leads from the spark plugs. Use a hooked length of stout wire to pull the connectors from the spark plugs (see illustration).

4 Release the securing lug, and disconnect the wiring plug from the DIS module, then unscrew the securing bolts, and remove the DIS module and HT leads as an assembly (see illustrations).

5 Disconnect the inlet camshaft position sensor wiring connector (see illustration).

6 Unscrew the bolt securing the exhaust gas recirculation solenoid valve to the end of the camshaft carrier (see illustration). Move the valve to one side.

7 Disconnect the wiring plug from the oil pressure warning light switch, located at the front left-hand corner of the camshaft carrier.

8.18 Refit the sprocket, ensuring that the lug (1) on the sprocket engages with the notch (2) in the end of the camshaft

9.3 Use a hooked length of wire to pull the connectors from the spark plugs

Release the wiring harness from the clip on the end of the camshaft carrier, and move the wiring to one side (see illustrations).

8 Remove the rear timing belt cover securing

9.4b . . . then remove the DIS module and HT leads

9.6 Unscrew the bolt securing the exhaust gas recirculation solenoid valve to the end of the camshaft carrier

8.19 Tighten the sprocket securing bolt using a suitable tool to hold the sprocket stationary

9.4a Unscrew the DIS module securing bolts . . .

bolt, located next to the right-hand engine lifting eye (see illustration).

9 Working progressively from the centre out, in a diagonal sequence, slacken and remove

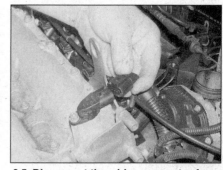

9.5 Disconnect the wiring connector from the inlet camshaft position sensor

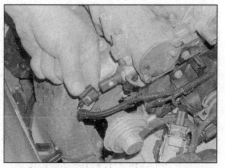

9.7a Disconnect the oil pressure warning light switch wiring plug . . .

9.7b . . . then release the wiring from the clip on the end of the camshaft carrier

9.8 Remove the rear timing belt cover securing bolt located next to the right-hand engine lifting eye

9.9 Remove the camshaft carrier securing bolts . . .

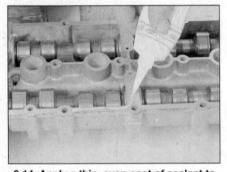

9.14 Apply a thin, even coat of sealant to the cylinder head mating face of the camshaft carrier

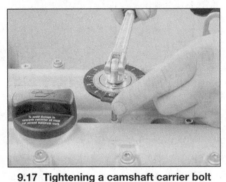

9.17 Tightening a camshaft carrier bolt through the specified Stage 2 angle

the camshaft carrier securing bolts **(see illustration)**.

10 Carefully lift the camshaft carrier from the cylinder head. The camshafts can be removed from the carrier, as described in Section 10.

Refitting

11 Commence refitting by thoroughly cleaning all traces of old sealant, and all traces of oil and grease, from the mating faces of the cylinder head and camshaft carrier. Ensure that no debris enters the cylinder head or camshaft carrier.

12 Ensure that the crankshaft is still positioned a quarter-turn (90°) anti-clockwise from the TDC position, and that the camshafts are locked in position with the locking tool, as described in Section 3.

13 Check that the valve rockers are correctly

located on the valves, and securely clipped into position on the hydraulic tappets.

14 Apply a thin, even coat of sealant (VW AMV 188 003, or equivalent) to the cylinder head mating face of the camshaft carrier **(see illustration)**. Do not apply the sealant too thickly, as excess sealant may enter and block the oilways, causing engine damage.

15 Carefully lower the camshaft carrier onto the cylinder head, until the camshafts rest on the rockers. Note that the camshaft carrier locates on dowels in the cylinder head; if desired, to make fitting easier, two guide studs can be made up as follows:

a) Cut the heads off two M6 bolts, then cut slots in the top of each bolt to enable the bolt to be unscrewed using a flat-bladed screwdriver.

b) Screw one bolt into each of the camshaft carrier bolt locations at opposite corners of the cylinder head.

c) Lower the camshaft carrier over the bolts to guide it into position on the cylinder head.

16 Fit new camshaft carrier securing bolts, and tighten them progressively, working from the centre out, in a diagonal sequence (ie, tighten all bolts through one turn, then tighten all bolts through a further turn, and so on). Ensure that the camshaft carrier sits squarely on the cylinder head as the bolts are tightened, and make sure that the carrier engages with the cylinder head dowels. Where applicable, once the camshaft carrier contacts the surface of the cylinder head, unscrew the two guide studs, and fit the two remaining new camshaft carrier securing bolts in their place.

17 Tighten the camshaft carrier securing bolts to the specified torque, in the two stages given in the Specifications **(see illustration)**.

18 Leave the camshaft carrier sealant to dry for approximately 30 minutes before carrying out any further work on the cylinder head or camshaft carrier.

19 Once the sealant has been allowed to dry, refit the rear timing belt cover bolt.

20 Reconnect the oil pressure warning light switch wiring plug, and clip the wiring into position on the end of the camshaft carrier.

21 Refit the exhaust gas recirculation solenoid valve bracket to the camshaft carrier, and tighten the securing bolt. Make sure that the lug on the camshaft carrier endplate engages with the corresponding hole in the solenoid valve bracket.

22 Reconnect the camshaft position sensor wiring connector.

23 Refit the DIS module and tighten the securing bolts, then reconnect the DIS module wiring connector, and the spark plug HT leads.

24 Refit the secondary and main timing belts, as described in Section 7.

25 Reconnect the battery negative lead.

10 Camshafts – removal, inspection and refitting

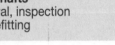

Removal

1 Remove the camshaft carrier as described in Section 9.

2 Remove the camshaft sprockets, with reference to Section 8 if necessary.

3 If the inlet camshaft is to be removed, unscrew the securing bolt, and remove the inlet camshaft position sensor **(see illustration)**.

4 Remove the relevant camshaft carrier endplate **(see illustration)**. Note that the inlet camshaft endplate is secured by the DIS module bolts, which have already been removed, and the exhaust camshaft endplate

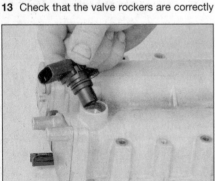

10.3 Remove the inlet camshaft position sensor

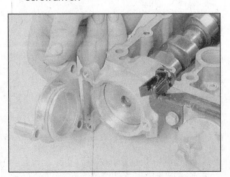

10.4 Remove the camshaft carrier endplate

is secured by three bolts, one of which also secures the exhaust gas recirculation solenoid valve.

5 Carefully withdraw the relevant camshaft from the endplate end of the camshaft carrier, taking care not to damage the bearing surfaces of the camshaft and housing as the camshaft is withdrawn **(see illustration)**.

Inspection

6 Visually inspect the camshafts for evidence of wear on the surfaces of the lobes and journals. Normally their surfaces should be smooth and have a dull shine; look for scoring, erosion or pitting and areas that appear highly polished, indicating excessive wear. Accelerated wear will occur once the hardened exterior of the camshaft has been damaged, so always renew worn items. **Note:** *If these symptoms are visible on the tips of the camshaft lobes, check the corresponding rocker, as it will probably be worn as well.*

7 If the machined surfaces of the camshaft appear discoloured or blued, it is likely that it has been overheated at some point, probably due to inadequate lubrication. This may have distorted the shaft, so check the run-out as follows: place the camshaft between two V-blocks and using a DTI gauge, measure the run-out at the centre journal. No maximum run-out figure is quoted by the manufacturers, but it should be obvious if the camshaft is excessively distorted.

8 To measure camshaft endfloat, temporarily refit the relevant camshaft to the camshaft carrier, and refit the camshaft sealing plate to the rear of the camshaft carrier. Anchor a DTI gauge to the timing belt end of the camshaft carrier and align the gauge probe with the camshaft axis. Push the camshaft to one end of the camshaft carrier as far as it will travel, then rest the DTI gauge probe on the end of the camshaft, and zero the gauge display. Push the camshaft as far as it will go to the other end of the camshaft carrier, and record the gauge reading. Verify the reading by pushing the camshaft back to its original position and checking that the gauge indicates zero again.

9 Check that the camshaft endfloat measurement is within the limit listed in the Specifications. Wear outside of this limit may be cured by renewing the relevant camshaft carrier endplate, although wear is unlikely to be confined to any one component, so renewal of the camshafts and camshaft carrier must be considered.

Refitting

10 Refitting is a reversal of removal, bearing in mind the following points:

a) *Before refitting the camshaft, renew the camshaft right-hand oil seal, with reference to Section 12.*

b) *Lubricate the bearing surfaces in the camshaft carrier, and the camshaft lobes before refitting the camshaft(s).*

c) *Renew the sealing O-ring on each*

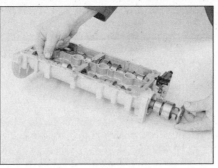

10.5 Withdraw the camshaft from the endplate end of the camshaft carrier

camshaft carrier endplate (see illustration).

d) *Refit the camshaft sprocket(s) with reference to Section 8, noting that if both sprockets have been removed, the exhaust camshaft sprocket must be fitted first.*

e) *Refit the camshaft carrier as described in Section 9.*

11 Rockers and hydraulic tappets – removal, inspection and refitting

Removal

1 Remove the camshaft carrier, as described in Section 9.

2 As the components are removed, keep them in strict order, so that they can be refitted in their original locations.

3 Unclip the rockers from the hydraulic tappets, and lift them from the cylinder head **(see illustration)**.

4 Carefully lift the tappets from their bores in the cylinder head. It is advisable to store the tappets (in order) upright in an oil bath whilst they are removed from the engine.

Inspection

5 Check the cylinder head bore contact surfaces of the tappets for signs of scoring or damage. Similarly, check the tappet bores in the cylinder head for signs of scoring or damage. If significant scoring or damage is found, it may be necessary to renew the

10.10 Renew the camshaft carrier endplate O-ring

cylinder head and the complete set of tappets.

6 Inspect the hydraulic tappets for obvious signs of wear or damage, and renew if necessary. Check that the oil holes in the tappets are free from obstructions.

7 Check the valve, tappet, and camshaft contact faces of the rockers for wear or damage, and also check the rockers for any signs of cracking. Renew any worn or damaged rockers.

8 Inspect the camshaft lobes, as described in Section 10.

Refitting

9 Oil the tappet bores in the cylinder head, and the tappets themselves, then carefully slide the tappets into their original bores **(see illustration)**.

10 Oil the rocker contact faces of the tappets, and the tops of the valve stems, then refit the rockers to their original locations, ensuring that the rockers are securely clipped onto the tappets.

11 Check the endfloat of each camshaft, as described in Section 10, then refit the camshaft carrier as described in Section 9.

12 Camshaft oil seals – renewal

Right-hand oil seals

1 Remove the main and secondary timing belts as described in Section 7.

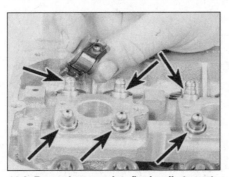

11.3 Removing a rocker (hydraulic tappets arrowed)

11.9 Oil the tappets before fitting

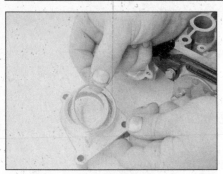

12.12 Locate the new O-ring in the groove in the endplate

2 Remove the relevant camshaft sprocket as described in Section 8.

3 Drill two small holes into the existing oil seal, diagonally opposite each other. Take great care to avoid drilling through into the seal housing or camshaft sealing surface. Thread two self-tapping screws into the holes, and using a pair of pliers, pull on the heads of the screws to extract the oil seal.

4 Clean out the seal housing and the sealing surface of the camshaft by wiping it with a lint-free cloth. Remove any swarf or burrs that may cause the seal to leak.

5 Lubricate the lip and outer edge of the new oil seal with clean engine oil, and push it over the camshaft until it is positioned above its housing. To prevent damage to the sealing lips, wrap some adhesive tape around the end of the camshaft.

6 Using a hammer and a socket of suitable diameter, drive the seal squarely into its housing. **Note:** *Select a socket that bears only on the hard outer surface of the seal, not the inner lip which can easily be damaged.*

7 Refit the relevant camshaft sprocket with reference to Section 8.

8 Refit and tension the secondary and main timing belts as described in Section 7.

Left-hand oil seals

9 The camshaft left-hand oil seals take the form of O-rings located in the grooves in the camshaft carrier endplates.

10 Unscrew the securing bolts, and remove the relevant camshaft endplate, noting that the DIS ignition module securing bolts secure the exhaust camshaft endplate.

11 Prise the old O-ring from the groove in the endplate.

12 Lightly oil the new O-ring, and carefully locate it in the groove in the endplate **(see illustration)**.

13 Refit the endplate (and the DIS module, where applicable), and tighten the securing bolts to the specified torque.

---

13 Cylinder head –
removal, inspection
and refitting

Note: *The cylinder head must be removed with the engine cold.*

Removal

1 Disconnect the battery negative lead (see *Disconnecting the battery*).

2 Drain the cooling system as described in Chapter 1.

3 Remove the main and secondary timing belts as described in Section 7.

4 As the engine is currently supported using a hoist attached to the engine lifting brackets bolted to the cylinder head, it is now necessary to attach a suitable bracket to the cylinder block, so that the engine can still be supported as the cylinder head is removed.

5 A suitable bracket can be bolted to the cylinder block using spacers, and a long bolt screwed into the hole located next to the coolant pump **(see illustration)**. Ideally, attach a second set of lifting tackle to the hoist, adjust the lifting tackle to support the engine using the bracket attached to the cylinder block, then disconnect the lifting tackle attached to the bracket on the cylinder head. Alternatively, temporarily support the engine under the sump using a jack and a block of wood, then transfer the lifting tackle from the bracket on the cylinder head to the bracket bolted to the cylinder block.

6 Release the hose clips, and disconnect the two radiator hoses from the coolant housing at the transmission end of the cylinder head **(see illustration)**. Similarly, release the hose clips and disconnect the remaining three small coolant hoses from the rear of the coolant housing.

7 Remove the air cleaner assembly, complete with the air trunking, as described in Chapter 4A.

8 Unscrew the bolt securing the oil level dipstick tube bracket to the cylinder head, then lift the dipstick tube, and turn it to one side, to clear the working area **(see illustration)**. Release the wiring harnesses from the clip on the dipstick tube bracket. Note that the dipstick tube bracket bolt also secures the inlet manifold.

9 Unscrew the two securing bolts and disconnect the exhaust gas recirculation (EGR) pipe from the throttle body. Recover the gasket **(see illustration)**.

10 Unscrew the bolt securing the EGR pipe bracket to the coolant housing.

11 Unscrew the six securing bolts (three upper and three lower) and lift the inlet manifold back from the engine **(see illustration)**. Ensure that the inlet manifold is adequately supported in the engine

13.5 Home-made engine lifting bracket screwed into the hole located next to the coolant pump

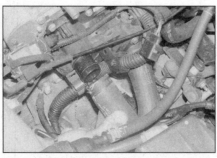

13.6 Disconnect the radiator hoses from the coolant housing at the transmission end of the cylinder head

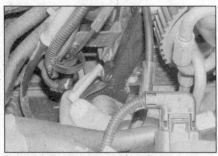

13.8 Unscrew the bolt securing the oil level dipstick tube bracket to the cylinder head

13.9 Disconnect the EGR pipe from the throttle body and recover the gasket

13.11 Lift the inlet manifold back from the engine

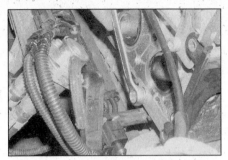

13.12 Unbolt the wiring connector bracket from the right-hand rear corner of the cylinder head

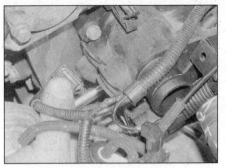

13.13a Disconnect the coolant temperature sensor wiring plug . . .

13.13b . . . then unclip the wiring harnesses and move them to one side

compartment, and take care not to strain any wires, cables or hoses. Recover the O-rings if they are loose.

12 Unbolt the wiring connector bracket from the right-hand rear corner of the cylinder head **(see illustration)**.

13 Disconnect the wiring plug from the coolant temperature sensor, located in the coolant housing at the transmission end of the cylinder head, then unclip the wiring harnesses from the coolant housing, and move them to one side **(see illustrations)**.

14 Disconnect the vacuum hose from the exhaust gas recirculation (EGR) valve **(see illustration)**.

15 Unclip the wiring from the bracket attached to the exhaust heat shield, then unscrew the securing bolts (two upper bolts and one lower bolt), and remove the heat shield **(see illustrations)**.

16 Disconnect the exhaust front section from the manifold with reference to Chapter 4B. If desired, the exhaust manifold can be removed as follows:
a) Unscrew the union nut securing the EGR pipe to the exhaust manifold, and remove the EGR pipe.
b) Unscrew the exhaust manifold securing nuts, then lift off the manifold and recover the gasket.

17 Remove the camshaft carrier, with reference to Section 9.

18 Pull out the metal clip securing the plastic coolant pipe to the coolant housing at the left-hand rear corner of the cylinder head **(see illustration)**.

19 Progressively slacken the cylinder head

bolts in order, then unscrew and remove the bolts **(see illustration)**.

20 With all the bolts removed, lift the cylinder head from the block. If the cylinder head is stuck, tap it with a soft-faced mallet to break the joint. **Do not** insert a lever into the gasket joint. As the cylinder head is lifted off, release the coolant pump pipe from the thermostat housing on the cylinder head.

21 Lift the cylinder head gasket from the block.

Inspection

22 Dismantling and inspection of the cylinder head is covered in Part C of this Chapter. Additionally, check the condition of the coolant pump pipe-to-thermostat housing O-ring, and renew if necessary.

Refitting

23 The mating faces of the cylinder head and

block must be perfectly clean before refitting the head. Use a scraper to remove all traces of gasket and carbon, also clean the tops of the pistons. Take particular care with the aluminium surfaces, as the soft metal is easily damaged. Make sure that debris is not allowed to enter the oil and water passages – this is particularly important for the oil circuit, as carbon could block the oil supply to the camshaft and crankshaft bearings. Using adhesive tape and paper, seal the water, oil and bolt holes in the cylinder block. To prevent carbon entering the gap between the pistons and bores, smear a little grease in the gap. After cleaning a piston, rotate the crankshaft to that the piston moves down the bore, then wipe out the grease and carbon with a cloth rag. Clean the other piston crowns in the same way.

24 Check the head and block for nicks, deep scratches and other damage. If slight, they

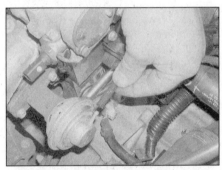

13.14 Disconnect the vacuum hose from the EGR valve

13.15a Unclip the wiring from the bracket on the exhaust heat shield . . .

13.15b . . . then remove the heat shield

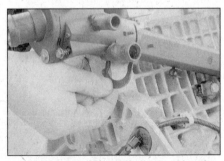

13.18 Pull out the metal clip securing the coolant pipe to the coolant housing (engine removed for clarity)

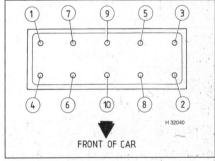

13.19 Cylinder head bolt slackening sequence

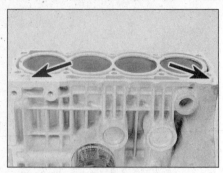

13.28a Ensure that the dowels (arrowed) are in place in the cylinder block

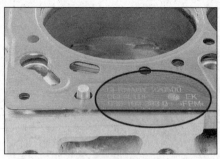

13.28b Ensure that the part number and OBEN/TOP markings on the cylinder head gasket are uppermost

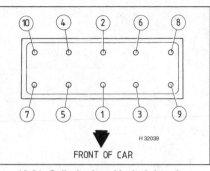

13.31 Cylinder head bolt tightening sequence

may be removed carefully with a file. More serious damage may be repaired by machining, but this is a specialist job.

25 If warpage of the cylinder head is suspected, use a straight-edge to check it for distortion, as described in Part C of this Chapter.

26 Ensure that the cylinder head bolt holes in the crankcase are clean and free of oil. Syringe or soak up any oil left in the bolt holes. This is most important in order that the correct bolt tightening torque can be applied, and to prevent the possibility of the block being cracked by hydraulic pressure when the bolts are tightened.

27 Ensure that the crankshaft has been turned to position Nos 1 and 4 pistons slightly down their bores from the TDC position (see Section 7). This will eliminate any risk of piston-to-valve contact as the cylinder head is refitted. Also ensure that the camshaft sprockets are locked in the TDC position using the locking tool, as described in Section 3.

28 Ensure that the cylinder head locating dowels are in place in the cylinder block, then fit a new cylinder head gasket over the dowels, ensuring that the part number is uppermost. Where applicable, the OBEN/TOP marking should also be uppermost **(see illustrations)**. Note that VW recommend that the gasket is only removed from its packaging immediately prior to fitting.

29 Lower the cylinder head into position on the gasket, ensuring that it engages correctly over the dowels. As the cylinder head is lowered into position, ensure that the coolant pump pipe engages with the thermostat housing (use a new O-ring if necessary).

30 Fit the new cylinder head bolts, and screw them in as far as possible by hand.

31 Working progressively, in sequence, tighten all the cylinder head bolts to the specified Stage 1 torque **(see illustration)**.

32 Again working progressively, in sequence, tighten all the cylinder head bolts through the specified Stage 2 angle.

33 Finally, tighten all the cylinder head bolts, in sequence, to the specified Stage 3 torque.

34 Reconnect the lifting tackle to the right-hand engine lifting bracket on the cylinder head, then adjust the lifting tackle to support the engine. Once the engine is adequately

supported using the cylinder head bracket, disconnect the lifting tackle from the bracket bolted to the cylinder block, and unbolt the improvised engine lifting bracket from the cylinder block. Alternatively, remove the trolley jack and block of wood from under the sump.

35 Refit the clip securing the plastic coolant pipe to the coolant housing.

36 Refit the camshaft carrier as described in Section 9.

37 Further refitting is a reversal of removal, bearing in mind the following points:

a) Refit the exhaust manifold and reconnect the EGR pipe, and/or reconnect the exhaust front section to the manifold, as described in Section 4B.

b) Refit the inlet manifold using new O-rings.

c) Reconnect the EGR pipe to the throttle body using a new gasket.

d) Refit the secondary and main timing belts as described in Section 7.

e) Ensure that all wires, pipes and hoses are correctly reconnected and routed, as noted before removal.

f) Tighten all fixings to the specified torque, where applicable.

g) On completion, refill the cooling system as described in Chapter 1.

14 Sump – removal and refitting

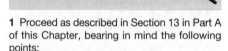

1 Proceed as described in Section 13 in Part A of this Chapter, bearing in mind the following points:

a) The exhaust front section must be removed as described in Chapter 4B, to allow clearance for removal of the sump.

b) When refitting the sump, to guide the sump into position on the cylinder block mating face, two guide studs can be improvised by cutting the heads off two M6 bolts, and cutting slots in the ends of the bolts so that they can later by unscrewed using a flat-bladed screwdriver. Screw the guide studs into two diagonally opposite sump securing bolt holes. Offer the sump into position, then fit the remaining sump bolts. Once

the sump is held securely in position, unscrew the guide studs, and refit the remaining two sump securing bolts.

15 Oil pump – removal, inspection and refitting

Refer to Chapter 2A, Section 14.

16 Flywheel/driveplate – removal, inspection and refitting

1 Removal, inspection and refitting of the driveplate is as described in Section 11 in Part A of this Chapter.

17 Crankshaft oil seals – renewal

Right-hand oil seal

1 Remove the main timing belt as described in Section 7, and the crankshaft sprocket with reference to Section 8.

2 To remove the seal without removing the oil pump, drill two small holes diagonally opposite each other, insert self-tapping screws, and pull on the heads of the screws with pliers.

3 Alternatively, the oil seal can be removed with the oil pump (see Section 15).

4 Thoroughly clean the oil seal seating in the oil pump.

5 Wind a length of tape around the end of the crankshaft to protect the oil seal lips as the seal is fitted.

6 Fit a new oil seal to the oil pump, pressing or driving it into position using a socket or tube of suitable diameter. Ensure that the socket or tube bears only on the hard outer ring of the seal, and take care not to damage the seal lips. Press or drive the seal into position until it is seated on the shoulder in the oil pump. Make sure that the closed end of the seal is facing outwards.

7 Refit the crankshaft sprocket with reference

to Section 8, and the main timing belt as described in Section 7.

Left-hand oil seal

8 The crankshaft left-hand oil seal is integral with the housing, and must be renewed as an assembly, complete with the crankshaft speed/position sensor wheel. The sensor wheel is attached to the oil seal/housing assembly, and is a press-fit on the crankshaft flange. VW special tool T10017 is required to fit this assembly and, in the workshop, we found that there is no means of accurately aligning the sensor wheel on the crankshaft without the tool (there is no locating key, and there are no alignment marks). If the sensor wheel is not precisely aligned on the crankshaft, the crankshaft speed/position sensor will send incorrect TDC signals to the engine management ECU, and the engine will not run correctly (the engine may not run at all). As the appropriate special tool is only available to VW dealers, there is no alternative but to have the new assembly fitted by a VW dealer.

18 Engine/transmission mountings – inspection and renewal

Refer to Section 12 in Part A of this Chapter.

19 Engine oil cooler – removal and refitting

Removal

1 The oil cooler is mounted above the oil filter, at the front of the cylinder block **(see illustrations)**.
2 Position a container beneath the oil filter to catch escaping oil and coolant, then remove the oil filter, with reference to Chapter 1 if necessary.
3 Clamp the oil cooler coolant hoses to minimise oil spillage, then remove the clips, and disconnect the hoses from the oil cooler. Be prepared for coolant spillage.
4 Where applicable, release the oil cooler pipes from any retaining brackets or clips.
5 Unscrew the oil cooler securing nut from the oil filter mounting threads, then slide off the oil cooler. Recover the O-ring from the top of the oil cooler.

Refitting

6 Refitting is a reversal of removal, bearing in mind the following points:
a) Use a new oil cooler O-ring.
b) Fit a new oil filter.
c) On completion, check and if necessary top up the oil and coolant levels.

20 Oil pressure relief valve – removal, inspection and refitting

The oil pressure relief valve is an integral part of the oil pump. The valve piston and spring are located to the side of the oil pump rotors and can be inspected once the oil pump has been removed from the engine and the rear cover has been removed (see Section 15). If any sign of wear or damage is found the oil pump assembly will have to be renewed; the relief valve piston and spring are not available separately.

19.1a Oil cooler location

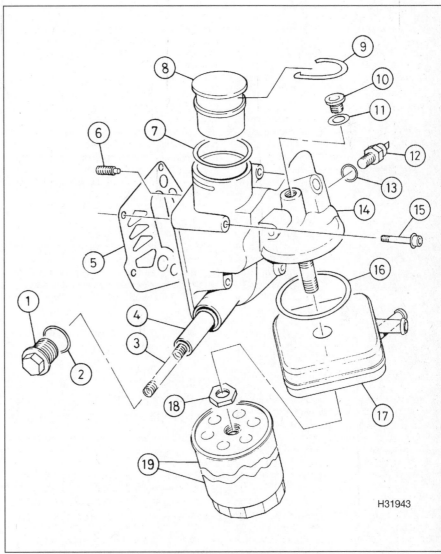

H31943

19.1b Oil cooler details

1 Oil pressure relief valve plug	6 Non-return valve	11 Seal	15 Bolt
2 Sealing ring	7 Seal	12 Oil pressure warning light switch	16 Seal
3 Spring	8 Sealing cap	13 Seal	17 Oil cooler
4 Piston	9 Retaining clip	14 Oil filter housing	18 Nut
5 Gasket	10 Sealing plug		19 Oil filter

21.2 Disconnecting the oil pressure switch wiring connector

21 Oil pressure warning light switch – removal and refitting

Removal

1 The oil pressure warning light switch is fitted to the front of the cylinder head, on its left-hand end. To gain access to the switch, remove the air cleaner as described in Chapter 4A.

2 Disconnect the wiring connector and wipe clean the area around the switch **(see illustration)**.

3 Unscrew the switch from the cylinder head and remove it along with its sealing washer. If the switch is to be left removed from the engine for any length of time, plug the hole in the cylinder head.

Refitting

4 Examine the sealing washer for signs of damage or deterioration and if necessary renew.

5 Refit the switch, complete with washer, and tighten it to the specified torque.

6 Securely reconnect the wiring connector then refit the air cleaner. Check and, if necessary, top-up the engine oil as described in *Weekly checks*.

Chapter 2 Part C:
Engine removal and overhaul procedures

Contents

Degrees of difficulty

| **Easy,** suitable for novice with little experience | 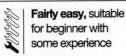 | **Fairly easy,** suitable for beginner with some experience | | **Fairly difficult,** suitable for competent DIY mechanic | | **Difficult,** suitable for experienced DIY mechanic | | **Very difficult,** suitable for expert DIY or professional | |

Specifications

Engine codes
Refer to Chapter 2A or 2B Specifications

Cylinder head

Minimum dimension – top of valve stem to top surface of cylinder head:	
SOHC engines	32.1 mm
DOHC engines	7.6 mm
Minimum cylinder head height:	
SOHC engines	135.6 mm
DOHC engines	108.25 mm
Maximum cylinder head gasket face distortion:	
SOHC engines	0.1 mm
DOHC engines	0.05 mm

Valves

	Inlet	Exhaust
Valve stem diameter	5.98 mm	5.96 mm
Valve head diameter:		
1.0 litre engines	31.0 mm	26.0 mm
1.4 litre SOHC engines	33.5 mm	28.0 mm
1.4 litre DOHC engines	29.5 mm	26.0 mm
Valve length:		
1.0 litre engines	99.0 mm	99.0 mm
1.4 litre SOHC engines	99.2 mm	99.2 mm
1.4 litre DOHC engines	100.9 mm	100.5 mm
Valve seat angle (all engines)	45°	

Camshaft

Endfloat:	
SOHC engines	0.15 mm
DOHC engines	0.40 mm

Bearing running clearances

Big-end bearings:	
New	0.020 to 0.061 mm
Wear limit	0.091 mm

Piston rings

End gaps:
Top compression ring:
  New . . . . 0.20 to 0.50 mm
  Wear limit . . . . 1.0 mm
Lower compression ring:
  New . . . . 0.40 to 0.70 mm
  Wear limit . . . . 1.0 mm
Oil scraper ring . . . . 0.40 to 1.40 mm
Ring-to-groove clearance:
Compression rings:
  New . . . . 0.04 to 0.08 mm
  Wear limit . . . . 0.15 mm
Oil scraper ring . . . . Cannot be measured

Cylinder block

Bore diameter:
1.0 litre engines:
  Standard . . . . 67.11 mm
  1st oversize . . . . 67.36 mm
  2nd oversize . . . . 67.61 mm
  3rd oversize . . . . 67.86 mm
1.4 litre engines:
  Standard . . . . 76.51 mm
  1st oversize . . . . 76.76 mm
  2nd oversize . . . . 77.01 mm
  3rd oversize . . . . 77.26 mm

Pistons

Piston diameter:
1.0 litre engines:
  Standard . . . . 67.085 mm
  1st oversize . . . . 67.335 mm
  2nd oversize . . . . 67.585 mm
  3rd oversize . . . . 67.835 mm
1.4 litre engines:
  Standard . . . . 76.475 mm
  1st oversize . . . . 76.725 mm
  2nd oversize . . . . 76.975 mm
  3rd oversize . . . . 77.225 mm

Crankshaft*

* All engines have an aluminium cylinder block, and the crankshaft on these engines must not be removed, or the block main bearings will distort. Even loosening the main bearing caps will have this effect. For this reason, if crankshaft or main bearing wear is suspected, the crankshaft and cylinder block must be renewed complete, and there are no specifications relating to crankshaft main bearing dimensions provided by the manufacturers.

Torque wrench settings

Refer to Chapter 2A or 2B Specifications

---

1 Engine and transmission removal –
preparation and precautions

If you have decided that the engine must be removed for overhaul or major repair work, several preliminary steps should be taken.

Locating a suitable place to work is extremely important. Adequate work space, along with storage space for the car, will be needed. If a workshop or garage is not available, at the very least a solid, level, clean work surface is required.

If possible, clear some shelving close to the work area, and use it to store the engine components and ancillaries as they are removed and dismantled. In this manner, the components stand a better chance of staying clean and undamaged during the overhaul. Laying out components in groups together with their fixings bolts, screws, etc, will save time and avoid confusion when the engine is refitted.

Clean the engine compartment and engine/transmission before beginning the removal procedure; this will help visibility and help to keep tools clean.

The help of an assistant should be available; there are certain instances when one person cannot safely perform all of the operations required to remove the engine from the car. Safety is of primary importance, considering the potential hazards involved in this kind of operation. A second person should always be in attendance to offer help in an emergency. If this is the first time you have removed an engine, advice and aid from someone more experienced would also be beneficial.

Plan the operation ahead of time. Before starting work, obtain (or arrange for the hire of) all of the tools and equipment you will need. Access to the following items will allow the task of removing and refitting the engine/transmission to be completed safely and with relative ease: a heavy-duty trolley jack – rated in excess of the combined weight of the engine and transmission, complete sets of spanners and sockets as described in the front of this manual, wooden blocks, and plenty of rags and cleaning solvent for mopping-up spilled oil, coolant and fuel. A selection of different-sized plastic storage bins will also prove useful for keeping dismantled components grouped together. If any of the equipment must be hired, make sure that you arrange for it in advance, and perform all of the operations possible without it beforehand; this may save you time and money.

Plan on the car being out of use for quite a while, especially if you intend to carry out an engine overhaul. Read through the whole of this Section and work out a strategy based on your own experience and the tools, time and workspace available to you. Some of the overhaul processes may have to carried out by a VAG dealer or an engineering works – these establishments often have busy schedules, so it would be prudent to consult them before removing or dismantling the engine, to get an idea of the amount of time required to carry out the work.

When removing the engine from the car, be methodical about the disconnection of external components. Labelling cables and hoses as they are removed will greatly assist the refitting process.

Always be extremely careful when lifting the engine/transmission assembly from the engine bay. Serious injury can result from careless actions. If help is required, it is better to wait until it is available rather than risk personal injury and/or damage to components by continuing alone. By planning ahead and taking your time, a job of this nature, although major, can be accomplished successfully and without incident.

On all models described in this manual, the engine and transmission are removed as a complete assembly, upwards and forwards.

This involves the removal of the lock carrier, which is the panel assembly that forms the upper front part of the engine bay. Although the lock carrier is a large assembly, its removal is not difficult, and the benefits in terms of ease of access are well worth the effort involved.

Note that the engine and transmission should ideally be removed with the car standing on all four roadwheels, but access to the driveshafts and exhaust system downpipe will be improved if the car can be temporarily raised onto axle stands.

2 Engine and transmission – removal, separation and refitting

Removal

All models

1 Select a solid, level surface to park the car upon. Give yourself enough space to move around it easily. Raise the front of the car and support it on axle stands.
2 Refer to Chapter 11 and remove the bonnet from its hinges. Also remove the noise insulation tray from under the engine (where fitted).
3 Referring to Chapter 5A, remove the battery and the battery tray.
4 With reference to Chapter 1, carry out the following:
 a) *If the engine is to be dismantled, drain the engine oil.*

 b) *Drain the cooling system.*
5 The 'lock carrier' is a panel assembly comprising the front valance and bonnet lock mechanism, radiator and grille, cooling fan, and headlight units. Its removal gives greatly-improved access to the engine and transmission, and allows them to be lifted out of the car via the front of the engine bay. To remove the lock carrier, carry out the following:
 a) *Remove the front bumper as described in Chapter 11.*
 b) *Referring to Chapter 3, disconnect the radiator top and bottom hoses from the radiator.*
 c) *Disconnect the wiring plugs from the radiator thermo-switch and cooling fan motor (see illustrations).*
 d) *Unplug the wiring harness at the multiway connector situated at the rear of the lock carrier. Cover the connector housings with a plastic bag to prevent the ingress of dirt or water.*
 e) *Detach the bonnet lock release cable at the connector on the left-hand inner wing. Unclip the plastic cover, then release the cable end fitting (see illustrations).*
 f) *On models with air conditioning, loosen the refrigerant line securing clamps.*
 g) *Remove the lock carrier fixings at the following locations: two flange screws on the uppermost edge above the headlight units, one vertical screw each side at the rear of the front valance, and six bolts (four on the left, two on the right) threaded into the ends of the chassis rails (see illustrations).*

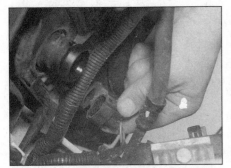

2.5a Disconnect the radiator fan thermo-switch wiring plug . . .

2.5b . . . and the radiator cooling fan motor wiring plug . . .

2.5c . . . then unclip the wiring harness from the fan frame

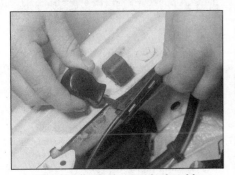

2.5d Unclip the bonnet lock cable connector plastic cover . . .

2.5e . . . then unhook the cable end fitting

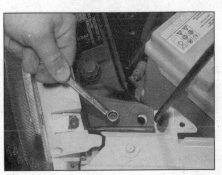

2.5f Remove the flange screws above the headlights . . .

2.5g . . . and the chassis rail bolts (arrowed)

2.5h Lock carrier assembly removed from front of car

h) Lift the lock carrier assembly away from the front of the car and rest it on a dust sheet (see illustration); tilt the assembly forward as you remove it, to avoid spilling any coolant that may remain in the radiator. Note: On models with air conditioning, the compressor remains connected to the refrigerant condenser by the supply and return hoses, and is removed together with the lock carrier assembly.

Caution: Take care to avoid kinking or straining the air conditioning refrigerant hoses.

6 Remove the auxiliary drivebelt and the drivebelt pulleys, as described in Chapter 2A or 2B.

7 Referring to Chapter 6, disconnect the clutch cable from the transmission.

8 Refer to Chapter 3 and perform the following:

a) Slacken the clips and disconnect the radiator hoses from the engine, and from the thermostat housing/coolant pump (as applicable) (see illustration).

b) Disconnect the coolant hoses from the expansion tank and heater pipes.

9 On models with air conditioning, refer to Chapter 3 and carry out the following additional operations:

a) Unbolt the air conditioning fluid reservoir from its mountings, and allow it to hang free.

b) Remove the retaining bolts from the clips securing the refrigerant condenser supply and return pipes.

c) Unbolt the air conditioning compressor from the engine, and allow it to rest on the floor. Make sure the refrigerant hoses are not under strain.

10 Refer to Chapter 10 and remove the power steering pump (see illustration).

There's no need to disconnect the fluid lines, as long as the pump is positioned so that the pipes are not under strain (or likely to be damaged during engine removal).

11 With reference to Chapter 4B, unplug the lambda sensor at the multiway connector.

12 Remove the air cleaner as described in Chapter 4A.

13 Referring to Chapter 5B, remove the DIS ignition module.

14 Refer to Chapter 9 and disconnect the brake servo vacuum hose from the port on the inlet manifold.

15 Refer to Chapter 4B and disconnect the charcoal canister emission control system hose at the connection on the inner wing. Make a careful note of the point of connection to ensure correct refitting.

16 With reference to Chapter 4A, carry out the following operations:

a) Depressurise the fuel system.

b) Remove the exhaust manifold-to-air cleaner and throttle body airbox-to-air cleaner ducting from the engine bay.

c) Disconnect the fuel supply and return hoses – observe the precautions at the start of Chapter 4A.

d) Disconnect the wiring plugs associated with the fuel and ignition system components, labelling the plugs if necessary to aid refitting.

17 Unplug the wiring harness at the multi-plugs situated at the left-hand end of the cylinder block. Note their locations for correct refitting (see illustration).

18 Cover the connector housings with a plastic bag to prevent the ingress of dirt or water. Release the harness from all the metal retaining clips.

19 Refer to Chapter 5A and disconnect the wiring from the alternator, starter motor and solenoid.

20 Remove the wiring loom support bracket from the rear of the block.

21 With reference to Chapter 5B and Chapter 4A or 4B as applicable, identify those sections of the engine, ignition and fuelling system electrical harness that remain connected to sensors and actuators on the engine. Establish which connectors must be separated to permit engine removal, labelling each connector carefully as it is disconnected, to ensure correct refitting (see illustration).

22 On manual transmission models, refer to Chapter 7A and carry out the following:

a) At the front of the transmission casing, disconnect the wiring from the reversing light switch. Also disconnect the wiring plug from the roadspeed sender on top of the transmission. Depending on model, there may be some additional wiring harness plugs at the front of the transmission – these should be disconnected, and the wiring harness released from any retaining clips (see illustration).

b) Disconnect the gear selection mechanism from the transmission.

2.8 Disconnecting a heater hose from the thermostat housing

2.10 Unbolt and remove the power steering pump

2.17 Disconnect the engine harness plugs at the left-hand end of the cylinder head

2.21 Disconnecting the wiring harness from the engine

c) On models with cable-operated gear
selection, remove the gear selector cable
support bracket from the engine block
and the bulkhead.

23 On automatic transmission models, refer
to Chapter 7B and carry out the following:
a) Select position P, then release the
selector cable from the selector lever at
the top of the transmission casing.
Remove the cable guide rail if necessary.
b) Clamp the coolant hoses leading to the
transmission fluid cooler, then release the
clips and disconnect the hoses from the
cooler ports.
c) Unplug the wiring harness from the
transmission at the connectors; label each
connector to aid refitting later.
d) Remove the torque converter cover plate
and the transmission sump cover plate.

24 Refer to Chapter 8 and separate the
driveshafts from the transmission differential
output shaft flanges. Once the driveshafts
have been separated, do not let the shafts
hang down at too steep an angle, or the outer
CV joints may be damaged. On automatic
transmission models, the left-hand driveshaft
must be removed completely.

25 With reference to Chapter 4B, remove the
heat shield, then unbolt the exhaust downpipe
from the exhaust manifold. Recover and
discard the gasket.

26 Unbolt the engine and transmission
earthing straps from the bodywork **(see
illustrations)**.

27 Connect a hoist and raise it so that the
weight of the engine and transmission are just
supported. Arrange the hoist and sling so that
the engine and transmission are kept level
when they are being withdrawn from the car.

28 Unscrew and remove the engine and
transmission mounting bolts, referring to
Chapter 2A or 2B as necessary. Where
possible, leave the bonded rubber mountings
attached to the support points; this will avoid
the need for realignment during refitting.

29 Check around the engine and transmission assembly to ensure that all associated
attachments are disconnected and positioned
out of the way. Engage the services of an
assistant to help in guiding the assembly clear
of surrounding components, especially the
exhaust downpipe and the power steering fluid
pipework, where applicable. Carefully raise the
engine/transmission assembly so that it is
clear of the mountings, and remove the
assembly from the front of the car.

30 Once the engine/transmission assembly is
clear of the car, move it to an area where it
can be cleaned and worked on.

Separation

31 Rest the engine and transmission
assembly on a firm, flat surface, and use
wooden blocks as wedges to keep the unit
steady.

Manual transmission models

32 The transmission is secured to the engine

2.22 Disconnect any additional wiring harness plugs from the front of the transmission

by a combination of machine screws and
studs, threaded into the cylinder block and
bellhousing – the total number of fixings
depends on the type of transmission and
vehicle specification.

33 Starting at the bottom, remove all the
screws and nuts, then carefully draw the
transmission away from the engine, resting it
securely on wooden blocks. Collect the
locating dowels if they are loose enough to be
extracted.

**Caution: Take care to prevent the
transmission from tilting until the input
shaft is fully disengaged from the clutch
friction disc.**

34 Refer to Chapter 6, and remove the clutch
release mechanism, pressure plate and
friction disc.

Automatic transmission models

35 Mark the position of the torque converter
with respect to the driveplate, using chalk or a
marker pen. Remove the three nuts that
secure the driveplate to the torque converter;
turn the engine over using a socket and
wrench on the crankshaft sprocket to rotate
the driveplate and expose each nut in turn.

36 The transmission is secured to the engine
by a combination of machine screws and
studs with nuts, threaded into the cylinder
block and bellhousing – the total number of
fixings depends on the type of transmission
and vehicle specification.

37 Starting at the bottom, remove all the
screws and nuts, then carefully draw the
transmission away from the engine, resting it
securely on wooden blocks. Collect the

2.26a Remove the securing nut . . .

locating dowels if they are loose enough to be
extracted.

**Caution: Take care to prevent the torque
converter from sliding off the transmission
input shaft – hold it in place as the
transmission is withdrawn.**

38 Place a length of batten across the open
face of the bellhousing, fastening it with
cable-ties, to keep the torque converter in
place in its housing.

Refitting

39 If the engine and transmission have not
been separated, go to paragraph 45.

Manual transmission models

40 Smear a little high-melting-point grease
on the splines of the transmission input shaft.
Do not use an excessive amount, as there is
the risk of contaminating the clutch friction
disc. Carefully offer up the transmission to the
cylinder block, guiding the dowels into the
mounting holes in cylinder block.

41 Refit the bellhousing bolts and nuts,
hand-tightening them to secure the
transmission in position. **Note:** *Do not tighten
them to force the engine and transmission
together.* Ensure that the bellhousing and
cylinder block mating faces will butt together
evenly without obstruction, before tightening
the bolts and nuts to their specified torque.

Automatic transmission models

42 Remove the torque converter restraint
from the face of the bellhousing. Check that
the drive lugs on the torque converter hub are
correctly engaged with the recesses in the
inner wheel of the automatic transmission
fluid pump.

43 Carefully offer up the transmission to the
cylinder block, guiding the dowels into the
mounting holes in cylinder block. Observe the
markings made during the removal, to ensure
correct alignment between the torque
converter and the driveplate.

44 Refit the bellhousing bolts and nuts,
hand-tightening them to secure the
transmission in position. **Note:** *Do not tighten
them to force the engine and transmission
together.* Ensure that the bellhousing and
cylinder block mating faces will butt together
evenly without obstruction, before tightening
the bolts and nuts to their specified torque.

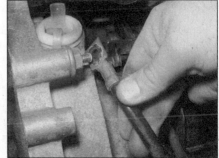
2.26b . . . and disconnect the transmission earth strap

All models

45 Attach the jib of an engine hoist to the lifting eyelets on the cylinder head, and raise the engine and transmission from the ground.

46 Wheel the hoist up to the front of the car and with the help of an assistant, guide the engine and transmission in through the front of the engine bay. Rotate the assembly slightly so that the transmission casing enters first.

47 If necessary, lower the assembly slightly, so that the transmission mounting can slide under the mounting point on the inner wing. When correctly aligned, the assembly can be raised to engage the mounting, and the through-bolt can be fitted and hand-tightened.

48 Raise the opposite side of the assembly as required, so that the engine right-hand mounting can be aligned and refitted onto the mounting on the inner wing. Insert the bolts and tighten them by hand only at this stage.

49 Align and reconnect the engine/transmission rear mounting.

50 Detach the engine hoist jib from the lifting eyelets.

51 Settle the engine and transmission assembly on its mountings by rocking it backwards and forwards, then tighten the mounting nuts and bolts to their specified torques.

52 Refer to Chapter 8 and refit/reconnect the driveshafts to the transmission.

53 The remainder of the refitting sequence is a direct reversal of the removal procedure, noting the following points:

a) *Ensure that all sections of the wiring harness follow their original routing; use new cable-ties to secure the harness in position, keeping it away from sources of heat and abrasion.*

b) *On models with manual transmission, refer to Chapter 7A and reconnect the gear selection mechanism to the transmission, then check the overall operation of the mechanism. If necessary, adjust the gear selection rod/cables.*

c) *Refer to Chapter 6 and reconnect the cable to the transmission, then check the operation of the automatic adjustment mechanism, where applicable.*

d) *On models with automatic transmission, refer to Chapter 7B and reconnect the selector cable to the transmission, then check (and if necessary adjust) the overall operation of the gear selection mechanism.*

e) *Refer to Chapter 11 and refit the lock carrier assembly to the front of the car; ensure that all wiring harness connections are remade correctly and tighten the retaining fixings to the specified torque.*

f) *Ensure that all hoses are correctly routed and are secured with the correct hose clips, where applicable. If the hose clips originally fitted were of the crimp variety, they cannot be used again; proprietary worm-drive clips must be fitted in their place, unless otherwise specified.*

g) *Refill the cooling system as described in Chapter 1.*

h) *Refill the engine with appropriate grades and quantities of oil (Chapter 1).*

54 When the engine is started for the first time, check for air, coolant, lubricant and fuel leaks from manifolds, hoses, etc. If the engine has been overhauled, read the notes in Section 11 before attempting to start it.

<hr>

3 Engine overhaul – preliminary information

Warning: All models have an aluminium cylinder block, and the crankshaft on these engines must not be removed, or the block main bearings will distort. Even loosening the main bearing caps will have this effect. For this reason, if crankshaft or main bearing wear is suspected, the crankshaft and cylinder block must be renewed complete.

It is much easier to dismantle and work on the engine if it is mounted on a portable engine stand. These stands can often be hired from a tool hire shop. Before the engine is mounted on a stand, the flywheel should be removed, so that the stand bolts can be tightened into the end of the cylinder block/crankcase.

If a stand is not available, it is possible to dismantle the engine with it blocked up on a sturdy workbench, or on the floor. Be very careful not to tip or drop the engine when working without a stand.

If you intend to obtain a reconditioned engine, all ancillaries must be removed first, to be transferred to the new engine (just as they will if you are doing a complete engine overhaul yourself). These components include the following:

a) *Power steering pump (Chapter 10).*

b) *Air conditioning compressor (Chapter 3) – where applicable.*

c) *Alternator (including mounting brackets)and starter motor (Chapter 5A).*

d) *The ignition system and HT components, including all sensors, DIS module, HT leads and spark plugs (Chapters 1 and 5B).*

e) *The fuel injection system components (Chapter 4A or 4B)*

f) *All electrical switches, actuators and sensors, and the engine wiring harness (Chapter 4A or 4B, Chapter 5B, Chapter 12).*

g) *Inlet and exhaust manifolds (Chapter 2A or 2B)*

h) *Engine oil dipstick and tube (Chapter 2A or 2B)*

i) *Engine mountings (Chapter 2A or 2B).*

j) *Flywheel/driveplate (Chapter 2A or 2B).*

k) *Clutch components (Chapter 6) – manual transmission*

Note: *When removing the external components from the engine, pay close attention to details that may be helpful or important during refitting. Note the fitted position of gaskets,*

seals, spacers, pins, washers, bolts, and other small components.

If you are obtaining a 'short' engine (the engine cylinder block/crankcase, crankshaft, pistons and connecting rods, all fully assembled), then the cylinder head, sump and baffle plate, oil pump, timing belt (together with its tensioner and covers), auxiliary belt (together with its tensioner), coolant pump, thermostat housing, coolant outlet elbows, oil filter housing and where applicable oil cooler will also have to be removed.

If you are planning a full overhaul, the engine can be dismantled in the order given below:

a) *Inlet and exhaust manifolds.*

b) *Timing belt, sprockets and tensioner.*

c) *Cylinder head.*

d) *Flywheel/driveplate.*

e) *Sump.*

f) *Oil pump.*

g) *Piston/connecting rod assemblies.*

<hr>

4 Cylinder head – dismantling, cleaning, inspection and assembly

Note: *New and reconditioned cylinder heads are available from VW, and from engine specialists. Specialist tools are required for the dismantling and inspection procedures, and new components may not be readily available. It may, therefore, be more practical for the home mechanic to buy a reconditioned head, rather than to dismantle, inspect and recondition the original head.*

Dismantling

1 Remove the cylinder head from the engine block (this includes removing the camshaft(s)), and separate the inlet and exhaust manifolds from it (Part A or B of this Chapter).

2 Unscrew the thermostat housing and oil pressure switch from the cylinder head.

3 It is important that groups of components are kept together when they are removed and, if still serviceable, refitted in the same groups. If they are refitted randomly, accelerated wear leading to early failure will occur. Stowing groups of components in plastic bags or storage bins will help to keep everything in the right order **(see illustration)**. Label parts

4.3 Keep groups of components together in labelled bags or boxes

according to their fitted location, eg, 'No 1 exhaust', 'No 2 inlet', etc – note that No 1 cylinder is nearest the timing belt end of the engine.

4 Turn the cylinder head over, and rest it on one side. Using a valve spring compressor, compress each valve spring in turn, extracting the split collets when the upper valve spring seat has been pushed far enough down the valve stem to free them **(see illustration)**. If the spring seat sticks, tap the upper jaw of the compressor with a hammer to free it.

5 Release the valve spring compressor and remove the upper spring seat and valve spring **(see illustrations)**.

6 Use a pair of pliers to extract the valve stem oil seal. Withdraw the valve itself from the head gasket side of the cylinder head **(see illustrations)**. If the valve sticks in the guide, carefully deburr the end face with fine abrasive paper. Repeat this process for the remaining valves.

Cleaning

7 Using a suitable degreasing agent, remove all traces of oil deposits from the cylinder head, paying particular attention to the journal bearings, hydraulic tappet bores, valve guides and oilways. Scrape off any traces of old gasket from the mating surfaces, taking care not to score or gouge them. If using emery paper, do not use a grade of less than 100. Turn the head over and using a blunt blade, scrape any carbon deposits from the combustion chambers and ports.
Caution: Do not erode the sealing surface of the valve seat. Finally, wash the entire head casting with a suitable solvent to remove the remaining debris.

8 Clean the valve heads and stems using a fine wire brush. If the valve is heavily coked, scrape off the majority of the deposits with a blunt blade first, then use the wire brush.
Caution: Do not erode the sealing surface of the valve face.

9 Thoroughly clean the remainder of the components using solvent and allow them to dry completely. Discard the oil seals, as new items must be fitted when the cylinder head is reassembled.

Inspection

Cylinder head casting

10 Examine the head casting closely to identify any damage sustained or cracks that may have developed. Pay particular attention to the areas around the mounting holes, valve seats and spark plug holes. If cracking is discovered between the valve seats, Volkswagen state that the cylinder head may be re-used, provided the cracks are no larger than 0.3 mm wide **(see illustration)**. More serious damage will mean the renewal of the cylinder head casting.

11 Moderately pitted and scorched valve seats can be repaired by lapping the valves in during reassembly, as described later in this

Chapter. Badly worn or damaged valve seats may be restored by recutting, however the maximum permissible reworking dimension **must** not be exceeded, which will only allow minimal reworking. To calculate the maximum

permissible reworking dimension, proceed as follows **(see illustration)**:

a) If a new valve is to be fitted, use the new valve for the following calculation.

b) Insert the valve into its guide in the

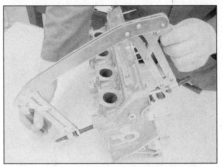

4.4 **Compressing a valve spring with a compressor tool**

4.5a **Removing the spring cap . . .**

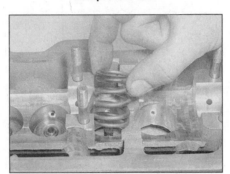

4.5b **. . . and valve spring – SOHC engine**

4.6a **Using a removal tool . . .**

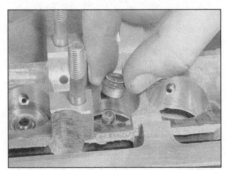

4.6b **. . . to remove the valve stem oil seals – SOHC engine**

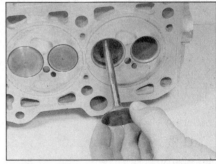

4.6c **Removing a valve – SOHC engine**

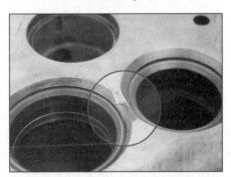

4.10 **Look for cracking between the valve seats**

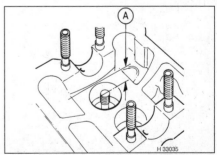

4.11 **Measure the distance (A) between the top face of the valve stem and the top surface of the cylinder head**

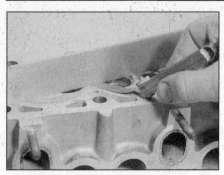

4.12 Measuring the distortion of the cylinder head gasket surface

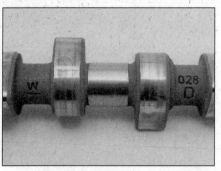

4.14 Camshaft identification markings

cylinder head, and push the valve firmly on to its seat.

c) *Using a flat edge placed across the top surface of the cylinder head, measure the distance between the top face of the valve stem, and the top surface of the cylinder head. Record the measurement obtained.*

d) *Consult the Specifications, and look up the value for the minimum permissible dimension between the top face of the valve stem and the top surface of the cylinder head.*

e) *Now take the measured distance and subtract the minimum permissible dimension, to give the maximum permissible reworking dimension, eg, Measured distance (34.4 mm) minus Minimum permissible dimension (34.0 mm) = Maximum permissible reworking dimension (0.4 mm).*

12 Measure any distortion of the gasketed surfaces using a straight-edge and a set of feeler blades. Take one measurement longitudinally on both the inlet and exhaust manifold mating surfaces. Take several measurements across the head gasket surface, to assess the level of distortion in all planes **(see illustration)**. Compare the measurements with the figures in the Specifications. If the head is distorted out of specification, it may be possible to repair it by smoothing down any high-spots on the surface with fine abrasive paper.

13 Minimum cylinder head heights (measured between the cylinder head gasket surface and the cylinder head cover gasket

surface), where quoted by the manufacturer, are listed in Specifications. If the cylinder head is to be professionally machined, bear in mind the following:

a) *The minimum cylinder head height dimension (where specified) must be adhered to.*

b) *The valve seats will need to be recut to suit the new height of the cylinder head, otherwise valve-to-piston crown contact may occur.*

c) *Before the valve seats can be recut, check that there is enough material left on the cylinder head to allow repair; if too much material is removed, the valve stem may protrude too far above the top of the valve guide, and this would prevent the hydraulic tappets from operating correctly. Refer to a professional head rebuilder or machine shop for advice.*

Note: *Depending on engine type, it may be possible to obtain new valves with shorter valve stems – refer to your VAG dealer for advice.*

Camshaft(s)

14 The camshaft is identified by means of markings stamped onto the side of the shaft, between the inlet and exhaust lobes **(see illustration)**. Refer to your VW dealer or engine overhaul specialist for an explanation of the markings.

15 Visually inspect the camshaft for evidence of wear on the surfaces of the lobes and journals. Normally their surfaces should be smooth and have a dull shine; look for scoring, erosion or pitting and areas that

appear highly polished – these are signs that wear has begun to occur. Accelerated wear will occur once the hardened exterior of the camshaft has been damaged, so always renew worn items. **Note:** *If these symptoms are visible on the tips of the camshaft lobes, check the corresponding tappet, as it will probably be worn as well.*

16 If the machined surfaces of the camshaft appear discoloured or 'blued', it is likely that it has been overheated at some point, probably due to inadequate lubrication. This may have distorted the shaft, so have the run-out checked at an engineering works. If it is excessive, camshaft renewal should be considered.

17 To measure the camshaft endfloat, temporarily refit the camshaft to the cylinder head, then fit the first and last bearing caps and tighten the retaining nuts to the specified first stage torque setting – refer to *Reassembly* for details. Anchor a DTI gauge to the timing pulley end of the cylinder head, and align the gauge probe with the camshaft axis **(see illustration)**. Push the camshaft to one end of the cylinder head as far as it will travel, then rest the DTI gauge probe on the end of the camshaft, and zero the gauge display. Push the camshaft as far as it will go to the other end of the cylinder head, and record the gauge reading. Verify the reading by pushing the camshaft back to its original position and checking that the gauge indicates zero again. **Note:** *The hydraulic tappets must **not** be fitted whilst this measurement is being taken.*

18 Check that the camshaft endfloat measurement is within the limit listed in the Specifications. Wear outside of this limit is unlikely to be confined to any one component, so renewal of the camshaft, cylinder head and bearing caps must be considered; seek the advice of a cylinder head rebuilding specialist.

Valves and associated components

Note: *On all engines, the valve heads cannot be recut (although they may be lapped in); new or exchange units must be obtained.*

19 Examine each valve closely for signs of wear. Inspect the valve stems for wear ridges, scoring or variations in diameter; measure their diameters at several points along their lengths with a micrometer **(see illustration)**.

20 The valve heads should not be cracked, badly pitted or charred. Note that light pitting of the valve head can be rectified by grinding-in the valves during reassembly, as described later in this Section.

21 Place the valves in a V-block and using a DTI gauge, measure the run-out at the valve head. A maximum figure is not quoted by the manufacturer, but the valve should be renewed if the run-out appears excessive.

22 Using vernier calipers, measure the free length of each of the valve springs **(see illustration)**. As a manufacturer's figure is not quoted, the only way to check the length of the springs is by comparison with a new component. Note that valve springs are

4.17 Checking camshaft endfloat using a DTI gauge

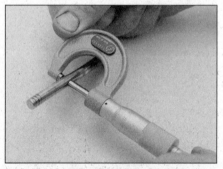

4.19 Measure the diameter of a valve stem with a micrometer

4.22 Measure the free length of each of the valve springs

4.23 Checking the squareness of a valve spring

4.25 Grinding-in a valve

usually renewed during a major engine overhaul.

23 Stand each spring on its end on a flat surface, against an engineer's square **(see illustration)**. Check the squareness of the spring visually; if it appears distorted, renew the spring. No squareness limits are specified by the manufacturers.

Reassembly

Caution: Unless all new components are to be used, maintain groups when refitting valve train components – do not mix components between cylinders, and ensure that components are refitted in their original positions.

24 To achieve a gas-tight seal between the valves and their seats, it will be necessary to grind, or 'lap', the valves in. To complete this process, you will need a quantity of fine/coarse grinding paste and a grinding tool – this can either be of the dowel and rubber sucker type, or the automatic type which are driven by a rotary power tool.

25 Smear a small quantity of *fine* grinding paste on the sealing face of the valve head. Turn the cylinder head over so that the combustion chambers are facing upwards, and insert the valve into the correct guide. Attach the grinding tool to the valve head and using a backward/forward rotary action, grind the valve head into its seat **(see illustration)**. Periodically lift the valve and rotate it to redistribute the grinding paste.

26 Continue this process until the contact between valve and seat produces an unbroken, matt grey ring of uniform width on

both faces. Repeat the operation for the remaining valves.

27 If the valves and seats are so badly pitted that coarse grinding paste must be used, check first that there is enough material left on both components to make this operation worthwhile – if too little material is left remaining, the valve stems may protrude too far above their guides, impeding the correct operation of the followers and hydraulic tappets (see paragraph 11). Refer to a machine shop or cylinder head rebuilding specialist for advice.

28 Assuming the repair is feasible, work as described in the previous paragraph but use the coarse grinding paste initially, to achieve a dull finish on the valve face and seat. Then, wash off coarse paste with solvent and repeat the process using fine grinding paste to obtain the correct finish.

29 When all the valves have been ground in, remove all traces of grinding paste from the

cylinder head and valves with solvent, and allow them to dry completely.

30 Turn the head over and place it on a stand, or wooden blocks.

31 Working on one valve at a time, lubricate the valve stem with clean engine oil, and insert it into the guide. Fit one of the protective plastic sleeves supplied with the new valve stem oil seals over the valve end face – this will protect the oil seal whilst it is being fitted **(see illustrations)**.

32 Dip a new valve stem seal in clean engine oil, and carefully push it over the valve and onto the top of the valve guide – take care not to damage the stem seal as it passes over the valve end face. Use a suitable long-reach socket (or if available, a special valve stem oil seal fitting tool) to press it firmly into position **(see illustrations)**.

33 Locate the valve spring over the valve stem **(see illustration)**.

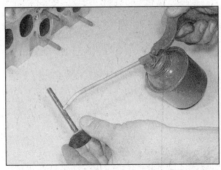

4.31a Lubricate the valve stem with clean engine oil – SOHC engine

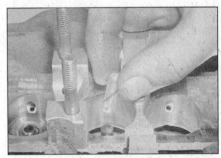

4.31b Fitting a protective sleeve over the valve stem before fitting the stem seal – SOHC engine

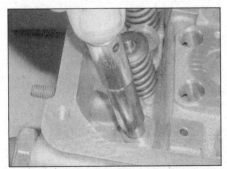

4.32a Using a long-reach socket to fit a valve stem oil seal – DOHC engine

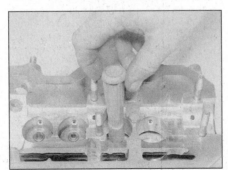

4.32b Using a special installer to fit a valve stem oil seal – SOHC engine

4.33 Fitting a valve spring – SOHC engine

4.34a Fitting the upper spring seat – SOHC engine

4.34b Use grease to hold the split collets in the groove – SOHC engine

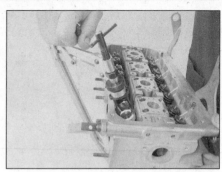

4.34c Compressing a valve spring using a compressor tool – DOHC engine

34 Fit the upper seat over the top of the springs, then using a valve spring compressor, compress the springs until the upper seat is pushed beyond the collet grooves in the valve stem. Refit the split collet, using a dab of grease to hold the two halves in the grooves (**see illustrations**). Gradually release the spring compressor, checking that the collet remains correctly seated as the spring extends. When correctly seated, the upper seat should force the two halves of the collet together, and hold them securely in the grooves in the end of the valve.
35 Repeat this process for the remaining sets of valve components. To settle the components after installation, strike the end of each valve stem with a mallet, using a block of wood to protect the stem from damage. Check before progressing any further that the spilt collets remain firmly held in the end of the valve stem by the upper spring seat.

5 Pistons and connecting rods – removal and inspection

> ⚠ *Warning: All models have an aluminium cylinder block, and the crankshaft on these engines must not be removed, or the block main bearings will distort. Even loosening the main bearing caps will have this effect. Take care, therefore, that only the big-end cap bolts are loosened during the following procedures.*

Removal

1 Refer to Part A or B of this Chapter and remove the cylinder head, flywheel, sump and baffle plate, oil pump and pick-up, as applicable.
2 With the pistons sitting halfway down their bores, carefully feel around the tops of the cylinder bores. Any wear ridges found at the point where the pistons reach top dead centre must be removed, otherwise the pistons may be damaged when they are pushed out of their bores. This can be accomplished with a scraper or ridge reamer.
3 Scribe the number of each piston on its crown, to allow identification later; note that No 1 is at the timing belt end of the engine.
4 Rotate the crankshaft until pistons Nos 1 and 4 are at bottom dead centre. Unless they are already identified, mark the big-end bearing caps and connecting rods with their respective piston numbers, using a centre-punch or a scribe (**see illustration**). Note the orientation of the bearing caps in relation to the connecting rod; it may be difficult to see the manufacturer's markings at this stage, so scribe alignment arrows on them both to ensure correct reassembly. **Note:** *The caps will only fit the correct way round on the correct connecting rod, as the caps are cracked off the rods during production. It is still advisable to mark the caps and rods for location and orientation, however, to save time when reassembling.*
5 Note the fitted orientation of the connecting rods and caps in relation to the timing belt end of the engine. Depending on engine code,

there will be some form of marking on the side of rod and cap which faces the timing belt end – this may be a punch mark, cut-out, raised dot or a different profile in the casting. Make your own marks on the timing belt side of the rod and cap if the manufacturer's marks are unclear.
6 Unbolt the bearing cap bolts, half a turn at a time, until they can be removed by hand (**see illustrations**). Recover the bottom shell bearing, and tape it to the cap for safe-keeping. Note that if the shell bearings are to be re-used, they must be refitted to the same connecting rod.
7 Drive the pistons out of the top of their bores by pushing on the underside of the piston crown with a piece of dowel or a hammer handle. As the piston and connecting rod emerge, recover the top shell bearing and tape it to the connecting rod for safe-keeping.
8 Turn the crankshaft through half a turn and working as described above, remove Nos 2 and 3 pistons and connecting rods. Remember to maintain the components in their cylinder groups, whilst they are in a dismantled state.
9 If required, insert a small flat-bladed screwdriver into the removal slot, and prise the gudgeon pin circlips from each piston. Push out the gudgeon pin, and separate the piston and connecting rod (**see illustrations**). Discard the circlips, as new items **must** be fitted on reassembly. If the pin proves difficult to remove, heat the piston to 60°C with hot water – the resulting expansion will then allow the two components to be separated.

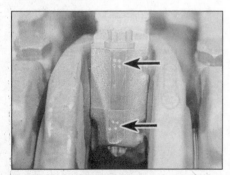

5.4 Mark the big-end caps and connecting rods with their cylinder numbers (arrowed)

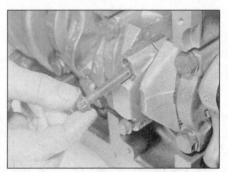

5.6a Unscrew the big-end bearing cap bolts . . .

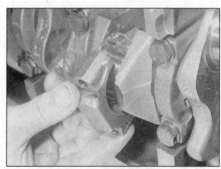

5.6b . . . and remove the cap

5.9a Insert a small screwdriver into the slot and prise off the gudgeon pin circlips

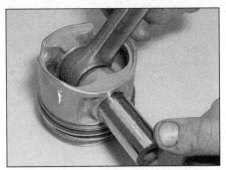

5.9b Push out the gudgeon pin and separate the piston and connecting rod

5.10 Piston rings can be removed using an old feeler blade

Inspection

10 Before an inspection of the pistons can be carried out, the existing piston rings must be removed, using a removal/installation tool, or an old feeler blade if such a tool is not available **(see illustration)**. Always remove the upper piston rings first, expanding them to clear the piston crown. The rings are very brittle and will snap if they are stretched too much – sharp edges are produced when this happens, so protect your eyes and hands. Discard the rings on removal, as new items must be fitted when the engine is reassembled.

11 Use a section of old piston ring to scrape the carbon deposits out of the ring grooves, taking care not to score or gouge the edges of the groove.

12 Carefully scrape away all traces of carbon from the top of the piston. A hand-held wire brush (or a piece of fine emery cloth) can be used, once the majority of the deposits have been scraped away. Be careful not to remove any metal from the piston, as it is relatively soft. **Note:** *Take care to preserve the piston number markings that were made during removal.*

13 Once the deposits have been removed, clean the pistons and connecting rods with paraffin or a suitable solvent, and dry thoroughly. Make sure that the oil return holes in the ring grooves are clear.

14 Examine the piston for signs of terminal wear or damage. Some normal wear will be apparent, in the form of a vertical 'grain' on the piston thrust surfaces and a slight looseness of the top compression ring in its groove. Abnormal wear should be carefully examined, to assess whether the component is still serviceable and what the cause of the wear might be.

15 Scuffing or scoring of the piston skirt may indicate that the engine has been overheating, through inadequate cooling, lubrication or abnormal combustion temperatures. Scorch marks on the skirt indicate that blow – by has occurred, perhaps caused by worn bores or piston rings. Burnt areas on the piston crown are usually an indication of pre-ignition, pinking or detonation. In extreme cases, the piston crown may be melted by operating under these conditions. Corrosion pit marks in

the piston crown indicate that coolant has seeped into the combustion chamber and/or the crankcase. The faults causing these symptoms must be corrected before the engine is brought back into service, or the same damage will recur.

16 Check the pistons, connecting rods, gudgeon pins and bearing caps for cracks. Lay the connecting rods on a flat surface, and look along the length to see if it appears bent or twisted. If you have doubts about their condition, get them measured at an engineering workshop. Inspect the small-end bush bearing for signs of wear or cracking.

17 Using a micrometer, measure the diameter of all four pistons at a point 10 mm from the bottom of the skirt, at right-angles to the gudgeon pin axis **(see illustration)**. Compare the measurements with those listed in the Specifications. **Note:** *If the cylinder block was rebored during a previous overhaul, oversize pistons may have been fitted.* Record the measurements and use them to check the piston clearances when the cylinder bores are measured, later in this Chapter.

18 Hold a new piston ring in the appropriate groove and measure the ring-to-groove clearance using a feeler blade **(see illustration)**. Note that the rings are of different widths, so use the correct ring for the groove. Compare the measurements with those listed; if the clearances are outside of the tolerance band, then the piston must be renewed. Confirm this by checking the width of the piston ring with a micrometer.

19 The orientation of the piston with respect

to the connecting rod must be correct when the two are reassembled. The piston crown is marked with an arrow (which may be obscured by carbon deposits); this must point towards the timing belt end of the engine when the piston is installed. The connecting rod and its bearing cap both have recesses machined into them, close to their mating surfaces – these recesses must both face the same way as the arrow on the piston crown (ie towards the timing belt end of the engine) when correctly installed. Reassemble the two components to satisfy this requirement.

20 Lubricate the gudgeon pin and small-end bush with clean engine oil. Slide the pin into the piston, engaging the connecting rod small-end. Fit two **new** circlips to the piston at either end of the gudgeon pin, such that their open ends are facing 180° away from the removal slot in the piston. Repeat this operation for the remaining pistons.

6 Cylinder block/ crankcase casting – cleaning and inspection

Cleaning

Note: *Before starting any major cleaning operations, consider the fact that the crank-shaft must remain fitted, and the potential damage to the main bearings that could result from allowing dirt to contaminate them.*

1 Remove all external components and electrical switches/sensors from the block.

5.17 Using a micrometer, measure the diameter of all four pistons

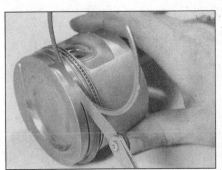

5.18 Measuring the piston ring-to-groove clearance using a feeler blade

6.6 To clean the cylinder block threads, run a correct-size tap into the holes

For complete cleaning, the core plugs should ideally be removed. Drill a small hole in the plugs, then insert a self-tapping screw into the hole. Extract the plugs by pulling on the screw with a pair of grips, or by using a slide hammer.

2 Scrape all traces of gasket and sealant from the cylinder block/crankcase, taking care not to damage the sealing surfaces.

3 Remove all oil gallery plugs (where fitted). The plugs are usually very tight – they may have to be drilled out, and the holes retapped. Use new plugs when the engine is reassembled.

4 If the casting is extremely dirty, it should be steam-cleaned. After this, clean all oil holes and galleries one more time. Flush all internal passages with warm water until the water runs clear. Dry thoroughly, and apply a light film of oil to all mating surfaces and cylinder bores, to prevent rusting. If you have access to compressed air, use it to speed up the drying process, and to blow out all the oil holes and galleries.

⚠ **Warning: Wear eye protection when using compressed air.**

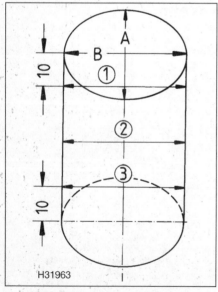

H31963

6.12 Bore measurement points

5 If the castings are not very dirty, you can do an adequate cleaning job with hot, soapy water and a stiff brush. Take plenty of time, and do a thorough job. Regardless of the cleaning method used, be sure to clean all oil holes and galleries very thoroughly, and to dry all components well. Protect the cylinder bores as described above, to prevent rusting.

6 All threaded holes must be clean, to ensure accurate torque readings during reassembly. To clean the threads, run the correct-size tap into each of the holes to remove rust, corrosion, thread sealant or sludge, and to restore damaged threads **(see illustration)**. If possible, use compressed air to clear the holes of debris produced by this operation. **Note:** *Take extra care to exclude all cleaning liquid from blind tapped holes, as the casting may be cracked by hydraulic action if a bolt is threaded into a hole containing liquid.*

7 Apply suitable sealant to the new oil gallery plugs, and insert them into the holes in the block. Tighten them securely.

8 If the engine is not going to be reassembled immediately, cover it with a large plastic bag to keep it clean; protect all mating surfaces and the cylinder bores as described above, to prevent rusting.

Inspection

9 Visually check the casting for cracks and corrosion. Look for stripped threads in the threaded holes. If there has been any history of internal water leakage, it may be worthwhile having an engine overhaul specialist check the cylinder block/crankcase with professional equipment. If defects are found, have them repaired if possible; if not, a new block will be required.

10 Check the cylinder bores for scuffing or scoring. Any evidence of this kind of damage should be cross-checked with an inspection of the pistons: see Section 5 of this Chapter. If the damage is in its early stages, it may be possible to repair the block by reboring it. Seek the advice of an engineering workshop before you progress.

11 To allow an accurate assessment of the

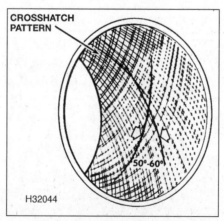

H32044

6.17 Cylinder bore honing pattern

wear in the cylinder bores to be made, their diameter must be measured at a number of points, as follows. Insert a bore gauge into bore No 1, and take three measurements in line with the crankshaft axis; one at the top of the bore, roughly 10 mm below the bottom of the wear ridge, one halfway down the bore and one at a point roughly 10 mm the bottom of the bore. **Note:** *Stand the cylinder block squarely on a workbench during this procedure, inaccurate results may be obtained if the measurements are taken when the engine mounted on a stand.*

12 Rotate the bore gauge through 90°, so that it is at right-angles to the crankshaft axis and repeat the measurements detailed in paragraph 11 **(see illustration)**. Record all six measurements, and compare them with the data listed in the Specifications. If any one cylinder exceeds its maximum bore diameter, then *all four* cylinders will have to be rebored and oversize pistons will have to be fitted. Note that the imbalances produced by not reboring all the cylinders together would render the engine unusable.

13 Use the piston diameter measurements recorded earlier (see Section 5) to calculate the piston-to-bore clearances. Figures are not available from the manufacturer, so seek the advice of your VAG dealer or engine reconditioning specialist.

14 Place the cylinder block on a level work surface, crankcase downwards. Use a straight-edge and a set of feeler blades to measure the distortion of the cylinder head mating surface in both planes. Repair may be possible by machining – consult your dealer for advice.

15 Before the engine can be reassembled, the cylinder bores must be honed. This process involves using an abrasive tool to produce a fine, cross-hatch pattern on the inner surface of the bore. This has the effect of seating the piston rings, resulting in a good seal between the piston and cylinder. There are two types of honing tool available to the home mechanic, both are driven by a rotary power tool, such as a drill. The 'bottle brush' hone is a stiff, cylindrical brush with abrasive stones bonded to its bristles. The more conventional surfacing hone has abrasive stones mounted on spring-loaded legs. For the inexperienced home mechanic, satisfactory results will be achieved more easily using the bottle brush hone. **Note:** *If you are unwilling to tackle cylinder bore honing, an engineering workshop will be able to carry out the job for you at a reasonable cost.*

16 Carry out the honing as follows; you will need one of the honing tools described above, a power drill/air wrench, a supply of clean rags, some honing oil and a pair of safety glasses.

17 Fit the honing tool in the drill chuck. Lubricate the cylinder bores with honing oil and insert the honing tool into the first bore, compressing the stones to allow it to fit. Turn on the drill and as the tool rotates, move it up-and-down in the bore at a rate that produces a fine cross-hatch pattern on the surface. The lines of the pattern should ideally cross at about 50 to 60°, although some piston ring manufacturer's may quote a different angle; check the literature supplied with the new rings **(see illustration)**.

⚠️ **Warning: Wear safety glasses to protect your eyes from debris flying off the honing tool.**

18 Use plenty of oil during the honing process. Do not remove any more material than is necessary to produce the required finish. When removing the hone tool from the bore, do not pull it out whilst it is still rotating; maintain the up/down movement until the chuck has stopped, then withdraw the tool whilst rotating the chuck by hand, in the normal direction of rotation.

19 Wipe out the oil and swarf with a rag and proceed to the next bore. When all four bores have been honed, thoroughly clean the whole cylinder block in hot soapy water to remove all traces of honing oil and debris. The block is clean when a clean rag, moistened with new engine oil does not pick up any grey residue when wiped along the bore.

20 Apply a light coating of engine oil to the mating surfaces and cylinder bores to prevent rust forming. Wrap the block in a plastic bag until reassembly.

7 Big-end bearings – inspection and selection

Inspection

1 Even though the big-end bearings should be renewed during the engine overhaul, the old bearings should be retained for close examination, as they may reveal valuable information about the condition of the engine **(see illustration)**.

2 Bearing failure can occur due to lack of lubrication, the presence of dirt or other foreign particles, overloading the engine, or corrosion. Regardless of the cause of bearing failure, the cause must be corrected before the engine is reassembled, to prevent it from happening again.

3 When examining the bearing shells, remove them from the connecting rods and big-end bearing caps. Lay them out on a clean surface in the same general position as their location in the engine. This will enable you to match any bearing problems with the corresponding crankshaft journal. *Do not* touch any shell's internal bearing surface with your fingers while checking it, or the delicate surface may be scratched.

4 Dirt and other foreign matter gets into the engine in a variety of ways. It may be left in the engine during assembly, or it may pass through filters or the crankcase ventilation system. It may get into the oil, and from there

into the bearings. Metal chips from machining operations and normal engine wear are often present. Abrasives are sometimes left in engine components after reconditioning, especially when parts are not thoroughly cleaned using the proper cleaning methods. Whatever the source, these foreign objects often end up embedded in the soft bearing material, and are easily recognised. Large particles will not embed in the bearing, but will score or gouge the bearing and journal. The best prevention for this cause of bearing failure is to clean all parts thoroughly, and keep everything spotlessly-clean during engine assembly. Frequent and regular engine oil and filter changes are also recommended.

5 Lack of lubrication (or lubrication breakdown) has a number of interrelated causes. Excessive heat (which thins the oil), overloading (which squeezes the oil from the bearing face) and oil leakage (from excessive bearing clearances, worn oil pump or high engine speeds) all contribute to lubrication breakdown. Blocked oil passages, which usually are the result of misaligned oil holes in a bearing shell, will also oil-starve a bearing, and destroy it. When lack of lubrication is the cause of bearing failure, the bearing material is wiped or extruded from the steel backing of the bearing. Temperatures may increase to the point where the steel backing turns blue from overheating.

6 Driving habits can have a definite effect on bearing life. Full-throttle, low-speed operation (labouring the engine) puts very high loads on bearings, tending to squeeze out the oil film. These loads cause the bearings to flex, which produces fine cracks in the bearing face (fatigue failure). Eventually, the bearing material will loosen in pieces, and tear away from the steel backing.

7 Short-distance driving leads to corrosion of

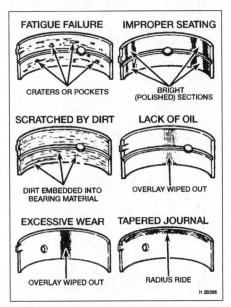

7.1 Typical bearing failures

bearings, because insufficient engine heat is produced to drive off the condensed water and corrosive gases. These products collect in the engine oil, forming acid and sludge. As the oil is carried to the engine bearings, the acid attacks and corrodes the bearing material.

8 Incorrect bearing installation during engine assembly will lead to bearing failure as well. Tight-fitting bearings leave insufficient bearing running clearance, and will result in oil starvation. Dirt or foreign particles trapped behind a bearing shell result in high spots on the bearing, which lead to failure.

9 *Do not* touch any shell's internal bearing surface with your fingers during reassembly; there is a risk of scratching the delicate surface, or of depositing particles of dirt on it.

10 As mentioned at the beginning of this Section, the bearing shells should be renewed as a matter of course during engine overhaul; to do otherwise is false economy.

Selection

11 If anything other than standard-size shells are required, leave the bearing selection to an engine overhaul specialist – the running clearances will need to be checked, which requires specialist techniques.

8 Engine overhaul – reassembly sequence

1 Before reassembly begins, ensure that all new parts have been obtained, and that all necessary tools are available. Read through the entire procedure to familiarise yourself with the work involved, and to ensure that all items necessary for reassembly of the engine are at hand. In addition to all normal tools and materials, thread-locking compound will be needed. A suitable tube of liquid sealant will also be required for the joint faces that are without gaskets. It is recommended that the manufacturer's own products are used, which are specially formulated for this purpose; the relevant product names are quoted in the text of each Section where they are required.

2 In order to save time and avoid problems, engine reassembly should ideally be carried out in the following order:

a) *Piston/connecting rod assemblies.*
b) *Oil pump (see Chapter 2A or 2B).*
c) *Sump (see Chapter 2A or 2B).*
d) *Flywheel/driveplate (see Chapter 2A or 2B).*
e) *Cylinder head and gasket (see Chapter 2A or 2B).*
f) *Tappets, followers and camshaft(s) (see Chapter 2A or 2B).*
g) *Timing belt tensioner, sprockets and timing belt (see Chapter 2A or 2B).*
h) *Engine external components and ancillaries.*
i) *Auxiliary drivebelts, pulleys and tensioners (see Chapter 2A or 2B).*

9.5 Checking a piston ring end gap using a feeler blade

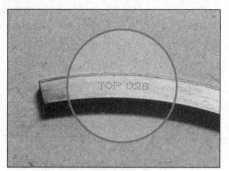

9.7 Piston ring TOP marking

2 Lubricate the cylinder bores, the pistons, and piston rings with clean engine oil. Lay out each piston/connecting rod assembly in order on a work surface.

3 Start with piston/connecting rod assembly No 1. Make sure that the piston rings are still spaced as described in Section 9, then clamp them with a piston ring compressor.

4 Insert the piston/connecting rod assembly into the top of cylinder No 1. Lower the big-end in first, guiding it to protect the cylinder bores.

5 Ensure that the orientation of the piston in its cylinder is correct – the piston crown, connecting rods and big-end bearing caps have markings, which must point towards the timing belt end of the engine when the piston is installed in the bore – refer to Section 5 for details.

6 Using a block of wood or hammer handle against the piston crown, tap the assembly through the piston ring compressor into the cylinder until the piston crown is flush with the top of the cylinder **(see illustration)**.

7 Ensure that the bearing shell is still correctly installed. Liberally lubricate the crankpin and both bearing shells with clean engine oil. Taking care not to mark the cylinder bores, tap the piston/connecting rod assembly down the bore and onto the crankpin. Refit the big-end bearing cap, tightening its new retaining nuts/bolts finger-tight at first. Note that the orientation of the bearing cap with respect to the connecting rod must be correct when the two components are reassembled (it will only fit properly one way).

8 Oil the threads and contact faces of the new retaining bolts with clean engine oil. Tighten the bolts half a turn at a time to the specified Stage 1 torque **(see illustration)**.

9 Now tighten the nuts/bolts further to the specified Stage 2 angle. Use an angle-measuring gauge, if available, to ensure accuracy **(see illustration)**.

10 Refit the remaining three piston/connecting rod assemblies in the same way.

11 Rotate the crankshaft by hand. Check that it turns freely; some stiffness is to be expected if new parts have been fitted, but there should be no binding or tight spots.

3 At this stage, all engine components should be absolutely clean and dry, with all faults repaired. The components should be laid out (or in individual containers) on a completely clean work surface.

9 Pistons and piston rings – assembly

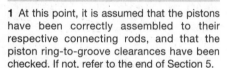

1 At this point, it is assumed that the pistons have been correctly assembled to their respective connecting rods, and that the piston ring-to-groove clearances have been checked. If not, refer to the end of Section 5.

2 Before the rings can be fitted to the pistons, the end gaps must be checked with the rings fitted into the cylinder bores.

3 Lay out the piston assemblies and the new ring sets on a clean work surface so that the components are kept together in their groups during and after end gap checking. Place the crankcase on the work surface on its side, allowing access to the top and bottom of the bores.

4 Take the No 1 piston top ring and insert it into the top of the bore. Using the No 1 piston as a ram, push the ring close to the bottom of the bore, at the lowest point of the piston travel. Ensure that it is perfectly square in the bore by pushing firmly against the piston crown.

5 Use a set of feeler blades to measure the gap between the ends of the piston ring; the correct blade will just pass through the gap with a minimal amount of resistance **(see**

illustration). Compare this measurement with the wear limit listed in the Specifications. Check that you have the correct ring before deciding that a gap is incorrect. Repeat the operation for all rings.

6 If new rings are being fitted, it is unlikely that the end gaps will be too small. If a measurement is found to be undersize, it must be corrected or there is the risk that the ends of the ring may contact each other during operation, possibly resulting in engine damage. Ensure that the ring has been fitted in its correct location, and consult your parts supplier if the ring end gap is still too small.

7 When all the piston ring end gaps have been verified, they can be fitted to the pistons. Work from the lowest ring groove (oil control ring) upwards. Note that the oil control ring comprises two side rails separated by an expander ring. Note also that the two compression rings are different in cross-section, and so must be fitted in the correct groove and the right way up, using a piston ring fitting tool. Both of the compression rings have marks stamped on one side to indicate the top facing surface **(see illustration)**. Ensure that these marks face up when the rings are fitted.

8 Distribute the end gaps around the piston, spaced at 120° intervals to the each other.

Note: *If the piston ring manufacturer supplies specific fitting instructions with the rings, follow these exclusively.*

10 Piston and connecting rod assemblies – refitting

Big-end running clearance check

1 A running clearance must exist between the big-end crankpin and its bearing shells to allow oil to circulate. As the crankshaft cannot be removed from these engines, this precludes the possibility of any regrinding work, and if standard shells have therefore been used, the running clearance should automatically be correct. If the running clearance must be checked for any reason, entrust this work to an engine overhaul specialist.

10.6 Using a hammer handle to tap the piston into its bore

10.8 Tighten the big-end bearing cap bolts/nuts to the specified torque . . .

10.9 . . . then through the specified angle

11 Engine –
initial start-up after overhaul
and reassembly

1 Refit the remainder of the engine components in the order listed in Section 8, referring to Part A or B where necessary. Refit the engine (and transmission) to the car as described in Section 2. Double-check the engine oil and coolant levels and make a final check that everything has been reconnected. Make sure that there are no tools or rags left in the engine compartment.

2 Remove the spark plugs, referring to Chapter 1 for details.

3 The engine must be immobilised such that it can be turned over using the starter motor, without starting. Disable the fuel pump by removing the fuel pump fuse, and disconnect the wiring plug from the DIS ignition module.

4 Turn the engine using the starter motor until the oil pressure warning light goes out. If the light fails to extinguish after several seconds of cranking, check the engine oil level and that the oil filter is secure. Assuming these are correct, check the security of the oil pressure switch wiring – do not progress any further until you are satisfied that oil is being pumped around the engine at sufficient pressure.

5 Refit the spark plugs, refit the fuel pump fuse and reconnect the DIS module.

6 Start the engine, but be aware that as fuel system components have been disturbed, the cranking time may be a little longer than usual.

7 While the engine is idling, check for fuel, water and oil leaks. Don't be alarmed if there are some odd smells and the occasional plume of smoke as components heat up and burn off oil deposits.

8 The hydraulic tappets may initially run noisily, but the engine should quieten down after a few seconds' running.

9 Assuming all is well, keep the engine idling until hot water is felt circulating through the top hose.

10 After a few minutes, recheck the oil and coolant levels, and top-up as necessary.

11 On all the engines described in this Chapter, there is no need to retighten the cylinder head bolts once the engine has been run following reassembly.

12 If new pistons, rings or big-end bearings have been fitted, the engine must be treated as new, and run-in for the first 600 miles (1000 km). *Do not* operate the engine at full-throttle, or allow it to labour at low engine speeds in any gear. It is recommended that the engine oil and filter are changed at the end of this period.

Notes

Chapter 3
Cooling, heating and ventilation systems

Contents

Degrees of difficulty

Easy, suitable for novice with little experience		**Fairly easy,** suitable for beginner with some experience		**Fairly difficult,** suitable for competent DIY mechanic		**Difficult,** suitable for experienced DIY mechanic		**Very difficult,** suitable for expert DIY or professional	

Specifications

General
Expansion tank cap opening pressure .... 1.4 to 1.6 bars

Thermostat
Opening temperatures:
  Starts to open .... 84°C
  Fully open .... 98°C

Electric cooling fan(s)
Cooling fan(s) cut in:
  Stage 1 speed:
    Switches on .... 92 to 97°C
    Switches off .... 84 to 91°C
  Stage 2 speed:
    Switches on .... 99 to 105°C
    Switches off .... 91 to 98°C

Torque wrench settings	Nm	lbf ft
Radiator cooling fan bracket bolts	10	7
Radiator cooling fan retaining nuts	10	7
Radiator cooling fan thermostatic switch	35	26
Radiator mounting bolts	10	7
Thermostat housing bolts	10	7
Water pump mounting bolts	20	15

1 General information and precautions

General information

The cooling system is of pressurised type, comprising a pump, an aluminium crossflow radiator, an electric cooling fan, and a thermostat. The system functions as follows. Cold coolant from the radiator passes through the hose to the water pump, where it is pumped around the cylinder block and head passages. After cooling the cylinder bores, combustion surfaces and valve seats, the coolant reaches the underside of the thermostat, which is initially closed. The coolant passes through the heater and is returned through the cylinder block to the water pump.

When the engine is cold, the coolant circulates only through the cylinder block, cylinder head, expansion tank and heater. When the coolant reaches a predetermined temperature, the thermostat opens and the coolant passes through to the radiator. As the coolant circulates through the radiator it is cooled by the inrush of air when the car is in forward motion. Airflow is supplemented by the action of the electric cooling fan when necessary. Upon reaching the radiator, the coolant is now cooled and the cycle is repeated.

The water pump is driven by the timing belt (main timing belt on DOHC engines), which is removed as described in Chapter 2A or 2B.

Coolant temperature information for the gauge mounted in the instrument panel, and for the fuel system, is provided by a single temperature sensor, mounted in the

2.3 Disconnecting the bottom hose from the thermostat housing

thermostat housing. A coolant level switch is fitted to the expansion tank.

The electric cooling fan mounted on the rear of the radiator is controlled by a thermostatic switch. At a preset coolant temperature, the switch actuates the fan.

Refer to Section 11 for information on the air conditioning system.

Precautions

⚠️ **Warning: Do not attempt to remove the expansion tank filler cap or disturb any part of the cooling system while the engine is hot, as there is a high risk of scalding. If the expansion tank filler cap must be removed before the engine and radiator have fully cooled (even though this is NOT recommended) the pressure in the cooling system must first be relieved. Cover the cap with a thick layer of cloth, to avoid scalding, and slowly unscrew the filler cap until a hissing sound can be heard. When the hissing has stopped, indicating that the pressure has reduced, slowly unscrew the filler cap until it can be removed; if more hissing sounds are heard, wait until they have stopped before unscrewing the cap completely. At all times keep well away from the filler cap opening. Be aware that, in certain circumstances, removing the filler cap with the system hot can result in a sudden rush of hot coolant (not just steam) emerging from the system.**

• **Do not allow antifreeze to come into contact with skin or painted surfaces of the vehicle. Rinse off spills immediately with plenty of water. Never leave antifreeze lying around in an open container or in a puddle in the driveway or on the garage floor. Children and pets are attracted by its sweet smell. Antifreeze can be fatal if ingested.**

• **If the engine is hot, the electric cooling fan may start rotating even if the engine is not running, so be careful to keep hands, hair and loose clothing well clear when working in the engine compartment.**

• **Refer to Section 11 for precautions to be observed when working on models with air conditioning.**

2 Cooling system hoses – disconnection and renewal

Note: *Refer to the warnings given in Section 1 of this Chapter before proceeding.*

1 If the checks described in Chapter 1 reveal a faulty hose, it must be renewed as follows.
2 First drain the cooling system (see Chapter 1). If the coolant is not due for renewal, it may be re-used if it is collected in a clean container.
3 To disconnect a hose, release its retaining clips, then move them along the hose, clear of the relevant inlet/outlet union. Carefully work the hose free **(see illustration)**. While the hoses can be removed with relative ease when new or hot, **do not** attempt to disconnect any part of the system while it is still hot.
4 Note that the radiator inlet and outlet unions are fragile; do not use excessive force when attempting to remove the hoses. If a hose proves to be difficult to remove, try to release it by rotating the hose ends before attempting to free it.

> **HAYNES HINT** *If all else fails, cut the hose with a sharp knife, then slit it so that it can be peeled off in two pieces. Although this may prove expensive if the hose is otherwise undamaged, it is preferable to buying a new radiator.*

5 When fitting a hose, first slide the clips onto the hose, then work the hose into position. If clamp type clips were originally fitted, it is a good idea to use screw type clips when refitting the hose. If the hose is stiff, use a little soapy water as a lubricant, or soften the hose by soaking it in hot water.
6 Work the hose into position, checking that it is correctly routed, then slide each clip along the hose until it passes over the flared end of the relevant inlet/outlet union, before securing it in position with the retaining clip.
7 Refill the cooling system (see Chapter 1).
8 Check thoroughly for leaks as soon as possible after disturbing any part of the cooling system.

3 Radiator – removal, inspection and refitting

Removal

1 Disconnect the battery negative lead (see *Disconnecting the battery*).
2 Drain the cooling system (see Chapter 1).
3 Remove the radiator grille.
4 Release the retaining clips and disconnect the coolant hoses from the radiator **(see illustration)**.
5 Disconnect the wiring connector from the cooling fan switch on the left-hand end of the radiator **(see illustration)**.
6 Unbolt and remove the support arm for the bonnet lock **(see illustrations)**.
7 On models equipped with air conditioning, in order to gain the clearance required to remove the radiator carry out the following.

3.4 Disconnecting the radiator top hose

3.5 Disconnecting the radiator cooling fan switch wiring plug

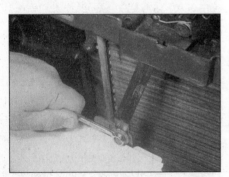

3.6a Remove the bonnet lock support arm securing bolt . . .

3.6b . . . then unhook the arm from the lock carrier, and remove it

Referring to Chapter 11, remove the front bumper and lower skirt where necessary for access to the condenser lower mounting bolts. Release the refrigerant lines from all the relevant retaining clips, then undo the retaining bolts and move the condenser forwards as far as possible, taking great care not to place any excess strain on the refrigerant lines. **Do not** disconnect the refrigerant lines from the condenser (refer to the warnings given in Section 11). Once the radiator has been removed, secure or support the condenser so that the refrigerant lines are not under strain.

8 On all models, slacken and remove the four retaining bolts from the rear of the radiator, then manoeuvre the radiator out from the front of the vehicle **(see illustrations)**.

Inspection

9 If the radiator has been removed due to suspected blockage, reverse-flush it as described in Chapter 1. Clean dirt and debris from the radiator fins, using an air line (in which case, wear eye protection) or a soft brush. Be careful, as the fins are sharp and easily damaged.

10 If necessary, a radiator specialist can perform a 'flow test' on the radiator, to establish whether an internal blockage exists.

11 A leaking radiator must be referred to a specialist for permanent repair. Do not attempt to weld or solder a leaking radiator, as damage may result.

 HAYNES HiNT *If leakage is the reason for wanting to remove the radiator, bear in mind that minor leaks can often be cured using a radiator sealant which is added to the coolant with the radiator in situ.*

12 If the radiator is to be sent for repair or renewed, remove the cooling fan switch from its left-hand end.

Refitting

13 Manoeuvre the radiator into position and refit its retaining bolts, tightening them to the specified torque setting.

14 On models with air conditioning, seat the condenser in position and securely tighten its retaining bolts. Refit the front bumper and skirt (where removed), and ensure that all refrigerant lines are retained by all the relevant clips.

15 The remainder of refitting is a reversal of removal. On completion, refer to Chapter 1 and refill the cooling system.

4 Thermostat – removal, testing and refitting

1 As the thermostat ages, it will become slower to react to changes in water tempera-

3.8a Loosen and remove the radiator retaining bolts . . .

ture ('lazy'). Ultimately, the unit may stick in the open or closed position, and this causes problems. A thermostat which is stuck open will result in a very slow warm-up; a thermostat which is stuck shut will lead to rapid overheating.

2 Before assuming the thermostat is to blame for a cooling system problem, check the coolant level. If the system is draining due to a leak, or has not been properly filled, there may be an airlock in the system (refer to the coolant renewal procedure in Chapter 1).

3 If the engine seems to be taking a long time to warm-up (based on heater output), the thermostat could be stuck open. Don't necessarily believe the temperature gauge reading – some gauges never seem to register very high in normal driving.

4 A lengthy warm-up period might suggest that the thermostat is missing – it may have been removed or inadvertently omitted by a previous owner or mechanic. Don't drive the car without a thermostat – the engine management system's ECU will then stay in warm-up mode for longer than necessary, causing emissions and fuel economy to suffer.

5 If the engine runs hot, use your hand to check the temperature of the radiator top hose. If the hose isn't hot, but the engine clearly is, the thermostat is probably stuck closed, preventing the coolant inside the engine from escaping to the radiator – renew the thermostat. Again, this problem may also be due to an airlock (refer to the coolant renewal procedure in Chapter 1).

6 If the radiator top hose is hot, it means that

4.14a Using a suitable pair of pliers, compress and release the hose clip . . .

3.8b . . . then withdraw the radiator from the front

the coolant is flowing (at least as far as the radiator) and the thermostat is open. Consult the *Fault diagnosis* section at the end of this manual to assist in tracing possible cooling system faults, but a lack of heater output would now definitely suggest an airlock or a blockage.

7 To gain a rough idea of whether the thermostat is working properly when the engine is warming up, without dismantling the system, proceed as follows.

8 With the engine completely cold, start the engine and let it idle, while checking the temperature of the radiator top hose. Periodically check the temperature indicated on the coolant temperature gauge – if overheating is indicated, switch the engine off immediately.

9 The top hose should feel cold for some time as the engine warms-up, and should then get warm quite quickly as the thermostat opens.

10 The above is not a precise or definitive test of thermostat operation, but if the system does not perform as described, remove and test the thermostat as described below.

Removal

11 Disconnect the battery negative lead (see *Disconnecting the battery*).

12 Drain the cooling system (see Chapter 1).

13 The thermostat housing is on the left-hand end of the cylinder head.

14 Release the retaining clip and disconnect the coolant hose from the thermostat housing **(see illustrations)**.

15 Slacken and remove the two bolts and

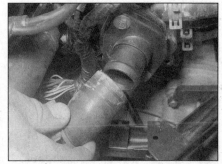

4.14b . . . and disconnect the hose from the thermostat housing

4.15a Loosen and remove the thermostat cover bolts . . .

4.15b . . . and carefully remove the thermostat cover

4.16a Withdraw the thermostat from the housing

4.16b The thermostat can be separated from its spring housing

remove the thermostat housing cover **(see illustrations)**. Take care that the thermostat does not fall out.

16 Recover the sealing ring and withdraw the thermostat, noting its fitted position. The thermostat is unusual in that the operating unit can be separated from the spring housing – note which way round it is fitted **(see illustrations)**. The thermostat appears only to be available as an assembled unit, however. Discard the sealing ring; a new one should be used on refitting.

Testing

17 If the thermostat remains in the open position at room temperature, it is faulty, and must be renewed as a matter of course.

18 Check to see if there's an opening temperature marking stamped on the thermostat.

19 Using a thermometer and container of

water, heat the water until the temperature corresponds with the temperature marking stamped on the thermostat. If no marking is found, start the test with the water hot, and heat slowly until it boils.

20 Suspend the (closed) thermostat on a length of string in the water, and check that maximum opening occurs within two minutes, or before the water boils.

21 Remove the thermostat and allow it to cool down; check that it closes fully.

22 If the thermostat does not open and close as described, or if it sticks in either position, it must be renewed. Frankly, if there is any question about the operation of the thermostat, renew it – they are not expensive items.

Refitting

23 Refitting is a reversal of removal, bearing in mind the following points:

5.5 Disconnect the cooling fan motor wiring connector

5.6a Unscrew the mounting nuts . . .

a) Ensure that the thermostat is correctly located in the housing.
b) Fit a new sealing ring, then fit the thermostat cover and tighten the bolts securely.
c) On completion refill the cooling system as described in Chapter 1.

5 Electric cooling fan – testing, removal and refitting

Testing

1 The cooling fan is supplied with current through the ignition switch, cooling fan control unit (mounted on the left-hand inner wing), the relay(s) and fuses/fusible link (see Chapter 12). The circuit is completed by the cooling fan thermostatic switch, which is mounted in the left-hand end of the radiator. The cooling fan has two speed settings; the thermostatic switch actually contains two switches, one for the stage 1 fan speed setting and another for the stage 2 fan speed setting. Testing of the cooling fan circuit is as follows, noting that the following check should be carried out on both the stage 1 speed circuit and stage 2 speed circuit (refer to the wiring diagrams at the end of Chapter 12).

2 If the fan does not appear to work, first check the fuses/fusible links. If they are good, run the engine until normal operating temperature is reached, then allow it to idle. If the fan does not cut in within a few minutes, or before the temperature gauge approaches the '110' mark or the red end of the scale, switch off the ignition and disconnect the wiring plug from the cooling fan switch. Bridge the relevant two contacts in the wiring plug using a length of spare wire, and switch on the ignition. If the fan now operates, the switch is probably faulty and should be renewed.

3 If the switch appears to work, the motor can be checked by disconnecting the motor wiring connector and connecting a 12 volt supply directly to the motor terminals. If the motor is faulty, it must be renewed, as no spares are available.

4 If the fan still fails to operate, check that the cooling fan circuit wiring (Chapter 12). Check each wire for continuity, and ensure all connections are clean and free of corrosion.

Removal

5 Disconnect the wiring connector from the cooling fan motor, and unclip the wiring harness from the fan mounting bracket **(see illustration)**.

6 Unscrew and remove the three nuts securing the cooling fan motor mounting bracket, and remove the cooling fan assembly to the rear **(see illustrations)**. No spare parts are available for the motor, and if the unit is faulty, it must be renewed.

5.6b . . . then remove the fan motor and its mounting bracket from the rear of the radiator

Refitting

7 Refitting is a reversal of removal, tightening the cooling fan retaining nuts to the specified torque.

8 Start the engine and run it until it reaches normal operating temperature. Continue to run the engine and check that the cooling fan cuts in and functions correctly.

6 Cooling system electrical switches – testing, removal and refitting

Radiator fan switch

Testing

1 Testing of the switch is described in Section 5, as part of the electric cooling fan test procedure.

Removal

2 The switch is located in the left-hand side of the radiator. The engine and radiator should be cold before removing the switch.

3 Disconnect the battery negative lead (see *Disconnecting the battery*).

4 Either drain the cooling system to below the level of the switch (as described in Chapter 1), or have ready a suitable plug which can be used to plug the switch aperture in the radiator whilst the switch is removed. If a plug is used, take great care not to damage the radiator, and do not use anything which will allow foreign matter to enter the radiator.

5 Disconnect the wiring plug from the switch.

6 Carefully unscrew the switch from the radiator.

Refitting

7 Refitting is a reversal of removal, applying a smear of suitable sealant to the threads of the switch and tightening it to the specified torque setting. On completion, refill the cooling system as described in Chapter 1, or top-up as described in *Weekly checks*.

8 Start the engine and run it until it reaches normal operating temperature, then continue to run the engine and check that the cooling fan cuts in and functions correctly.

Coolant temperature sensor

Testing

9 The coolant temperature gauge, mounted in the instrument panel, is fed with a stabilised voltage supply from the instrument panel feed (through the ignition switch and a fuse), and its earth is controlled by the sensor.

10 The sensor unit is clipped into the base of the thermostat housing **(see illustration)**. The sensor contains a thermistor, which consists of an electronic component whose electrical resistance decreases at a predetermined rate as its temperature rises. When the coolant is cold, the sensor resistance is high, current flow through the gauge is reduced, and the gauge needle points towards the 'cold' end of the scale. If the sensor is faulty, it must be renewed.

11 If the gauge develops a fault, first check the other instruments; if they do not work at all, check the instrument panel electrical feed. If the readings are erratic, there may be a fault in the instrument panel assembly. If the fault lies in the temperature gauge alone, check it as follows.

12 If the gauge needle remains at the 'cold' end of the scale, disconnect the wiring connector from the sensor unit, and earth the temperature gauge wire (see the wiring diagrams in Chapter 12 for details) to the cylinder head. If the needle then deflects when the ignition is switched on, the sensor unit is proved faulty, and should be renewed. If the needle still does not move, remove the instrument panel (Chapter 12) and check the continuity of the wiring between the sensor unit and the gauge, and the feed to the gauge unit. If continuity is shown, and the fault still

exists, then the gauge is faulty and should be renewed.

13 If the gauge needle remains at the 'hot' end of the scale, disconnect the sensor wire. If the needle then returns to the 'cold' end of the scale when the ignition is switched on, the sensor unit is proved faulty and should be renewed. If the needle still does not move, check the remainder of the circuit as described previously.

Removal

14 Either partially drain the cooling system to just below the level of the sensor (as described in Chapter 1), or have ready a suitable plug which can be used to plug the sensor aperture whilst it is removed. If a plug is used, take great care not to damage the sensor unit aperture, and do not use anything which will allow foreign matter to enter the cooling system.

15 Disconnect the battery negative lead (see *Disconnecting the battery*).

16 Disconnect the wiring from the sensor.

17 Depress the sensor unit and slide out its retaining clip. Withdraw the sensor from the coolant elbow and recover its sealing ring.

Refitting

18 Fit a new sealing ring to the sensor unit. Push the sensor fully into position and secure it in place with the retaining clip.

19 Reconnect the wiring connector, then refill the cooling system as described in Chapter 1 or top-up as described in *Weekly checks*.

Fuel system temperature sensor

20 On all models, the sensor is combined with the coolant temperature gauge sensor (see above). Testing of the sensor should be entrusted to a VW dealer.

Coolant level switch

21 The switch is incorporated into the expansion tank, and cannot be renewed separately.

22 To remove the expansion tank, disconnect the wiring plug for the level switch at the top of the tank **(see illustration)**.

23 Either drain the cooling system as described in Chapter 1, or use pipe clamps to seal off the coolant hoses to the tank before disconnecting them **(see illustration)**.

6.10 Coolant temperature sensor (arrowed)

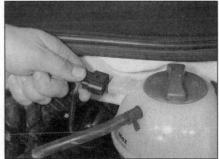

6.22 Disconnect the wiring plug from the coolant level sensor

6.23 Release the securing clips using a suitable pair of pliers, then disconnect the expansion tank hoses

6.24 Unclip the plastic cover next to the expansion tank, for access to the mounting nuts (arrowed)

24 Pull off the plastic cover **(see illustration)**, then remove the two mounting nuts and lift the tank away, noting the locating lug on its base.

25 Refitting is a reversal of removal.

7 Water pump – removal and refitting

Removal

1 Drain the cooling system as described in Chapter 1.

2 Remove the timing belt as described in Chapter 2A, or the main timing belt as described in Chapter 2B.

3 Unscrew the two bolts securing the water pump and its timing belt guard, and withdraw

the water pump and guard from the cylinder block **(see illustrations)**.

4 Discard the sealing ring – a new one should be used on refitting. Note it is not possible to overhaul the pump. If it is faulty, the unit must be renewed.

Refitting

5 Fit a new sealing ring to the rear of the pump **(see illustration)**, then locate the pump in the cylinder block.

6 Fit the timing belt guard in place, then insert the guard/pump mounting bolts and tighten them to the specified torque.

7 Refit and tension the timing belt as described in Chapter 2A or 2B.

8 On completion, refill the cooling system as described in Chapter 1.

8 Heating and ventilation system – general information

1 The heating/ventilation system consists of a four-speed blower motor (housed in the passenger compartment), face-level vents in the centre and at each end of the facia, and air ducts to the front and rear footwells.

2 The control unit is located in the facia, and the controls operate flap valves to deflect and mix the air flowing through the various parts of the heating/ventilation system. The flap valves are contained in the air distribution housing, which acts as a central distribution unit, passing air to the various ducts and vents.

3 Cold air enters the system through the grille at the rear of the engine compartment. A pollen filter is fitted to the ventilation inlet to filter out dust, soot, pollen and spores from the air entering the vehicle.

4 The airflow, which can be boosted by the blower, then flows through the various ducts, according to the settings of the controls. Stale air is expelled through at the rear of the car. If warm air is required, the cold air is passed through the heater matrix, which is supplied with coolant from the engine cooling system.

5 If necessary, the outside air supply can be closed off, allowing the air inside the vehicle to be recirculated. This can be useful to prevent unpleasant odours entering from outside the vehicle, but should only be used briefly, as the recirculated air inside the vehicle will soon deteriorate.

6 Models for certain export markets may be fitted with heated front seats. The heat is produced by electrically-heated mats in the seat and backrest cushions (see Chapter 12). The temperature is regulated automatically by a thermostat, and cannot be adjusted.

9 Heater/ventilation components – removal and refitting

Models without air conditioning

Heater/ventilation control panel

Note: *The panel illumination bulb can be removed as described in Chapter 12, Section 8.*

1 Disconnect the battery negative lead (see *Disconnecting the battery*).

2 Press down on the base of the storage box above the heater control panel to unclip and pull it out **(see illustration)**.

3 Unclip the control surround panel at the top, and remove it from around the control knobs **(see illustration)**.

4 Remove a total of six screws (three each side) and withdraw the control panel from the facia **(see illustration)**.

5 Disconnect the wiring plug at the top of the panel **(see illustration)**.

6 Release the retaining clips and disconnect the each outer cable from the panel, and each

7.3a Remove the two bolts (arrowed) . . .

7.3b . . . and remove the timing belt plastic guard . . .

7.3c . . . and the coolant pump

7.5 Fit a new O-ring to the coolant pump

9.2 Remove the storage box above the heater controls

9.3 Unclip and remove the surround panel

9.4 Remove the three screws each side, and withdraw the heater panel

9.5 Disconnect the wiring plug from the back of the panel

inner cable from its operating lever, noting their fitted positions **(see illustrations)**.

7 Refitting is a reversal of removal. Ensure that the control cables and/or the illumination bulb are operating correctly before refitting the control panel.

Heater/ventilation control cables

8 Remove the heater/ventilation control panel from the facia as described above in paragraphs 1 to 6, detaching the relevant cable from the control unit.

9 Remove the driver's side lower facia panel and the centre console as described in Chapter 11.

10 Trace the relevant cable from the control panel to the side of the heater unit, unclipping it as necessary. Release the end fitting at the heater by prising back the retaining tag and sliding the cable end out.

11 The cables are colour-coded as follows:
Footwell/defrost flap – Black.
Central flap – Grey.
Temperature flap – White.

12 Fit the new cable, ensuring that it is correctly routed and free from kinks and obstructions.

13 Connect the cable to the control unit and air distribution/blower motor housing, making sure the outer cable is clipped securely in position.

14 Check the operation of the control knob, then refit the control panel as described previously in this Section. Finally refit the cover below the air distribution/blower motor housing.

Heater matrix

15 Remove the facia panel as described in Chapter 11.

9.6a Use a small screwdriver to release the outer cable clip . . .

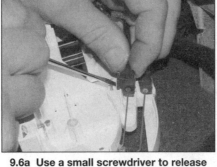

9.6b . . . then unhook the inner cable end fitting

16 Unscrew the expansion tank cap (referring to the Warning note in Section 1) to release any pressure present in the cooling system, then securely refit the cap.

17 Clamp both heater hoses as close to the bulkhead as possible to minimise coolant loss. Alternatively, drain the cooling system as described in Chapter 1.

18 Release the retaining clips and disconnect both hoses from the heater matrix unions which are located in the centre of the engine compartment bulkhead **(see illustration)**.

19 Also on the engine compartment bulkhead, remove the three nuts securing the heater unit **(see illustration)**.

20 Inside the car, carefully withdraw the heater assembly backwards from the bulkhead, noting that it is mounted on a locating peg on the passenger side.

21 Remove the two screws on top of the

heater unit, and lift up the heater matrix to remove it.

22 Refitting is a reversal of removal, bearing in mind the following points:

a) *Before offering the heater assembly into position, check the condition of the bulkhead seal at the front, and renew it if necessary.*

b) *When refitting the heater assembly, make sure the locating peg engages correctly.*

c) *On completion, refill the cooling system as described in Chapter 1.*

Heater blower motor

23 Disconnect the battery negative lead (see *Disconnecting the battery*).

24 Remove the centre console and glovebox as described in Chapter 11.

25 Remove the clips and screws, and pull down the foam cover panel underneath the heater assembly **(see illustration)**.

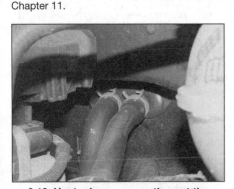

9.18 Heater hose connections at the engine compartment bulkhead

9.19 One of the heater unit mounting nuts on the bulkhead

9.25 Pull down the foam cover under the passenger side of the facia

9.26a Disconnect the wiring plug ...

9.26b ... then remove the screws and take down the blower motor resistor

9.27a Disconnect the heater blower motor wiring plug ...

9.27b ... then slide the blower motor out

26 Disconnect the wiring plug, then remove two screws and take down the blower motor resistor from below the motor itself **(see illustrations)**.
27 Disconnect the wiring plug at the top, then slide the motor downwards and out from under the facia **(see illustrations)**.
28 Refitting is a reversal of the removal procedure.

10.2 Remove the screw behind the lighting switch

10.3 Unclip the vent housing from the facia

10.4 Disconnect the headlight adjuster switch

10.7 Removing the storage box

Heater blower motor resistor

29 Carry out the operations described in paragraphs 23 to 26.
30 Refitting is the reverse of removal.

Models with air conditioning

Heater control unit

31 Refer to the information given in paragraphs 1 to 6. As the control panel is removed, the wiring plug for the air conditioning switch must also be disconnected. The switch is released from the control panel by depressing four retaining tabs.

Heater matrix

32 On models equipped with air conditioning, it is not possible to remove the heater matrix without opening the refrigerant circuit (see Section 11). Therefore this task must be entrusted to a VW dealer.

Heater blower motor

33 Refer to the information given in paragraphs 23 to 28.

Heater blower motor resistor

34 Carry out the operations described in paragraphs 23 to 26.

10 Heater/ventilation vents and housings – removal and refitting

Driver's side facia vent

1 Remove the lighting switch as described in Chapter 12.
2 Remove the single screw inside the switch location **(see illustration)**.
3 Carefully lift the whole vent panel upwards, and unclip it from the facia (two clips either side) **(see illustration)**.
4 Disconnect the wiring plug from the headlight adjuster switch, and remove the panel **(see illustration)**. Do not try to remove the vent grille from its housing, as it is a one-piece unit.
5 Refitting is the reverse of removal.

Centre vent panel

6 To remove the vent panel, first remove the radio as described in Chapter 12.
7 Carefully prise the storage box below the radio at either side, and pull it out of the facia **(see illustration)**.
8 Remove three Torx screws (one either side, and one in the centre), and pull the whole panel out from the facia **(see illustrations)**.
9 Reach inside and disconnect the wiring plug from the back of the hazard warning light switch, and the panel is free to be removed **(see illustration)**.
10 Refitting is a reversal of removal.

Passenger's side facia vent

11 Taking care not to mark the panel, prise

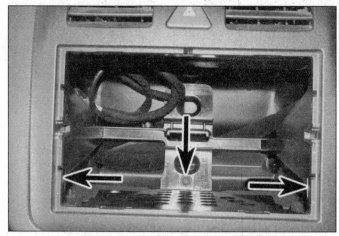

10.8a Centre vent panel securing screws (arrowed)

10.8b Remove the screws . . .

10.8c . . . and withdraw the panel from the facia

10.9 Disconnect the hazard warning light switch wiring plug

out and unclip the vent housing from the facia (two clips either side) **(see illustrations)**.
12 Do not try to remove the vent grille from its housing, as it is a one-piece unit.
13 Refitting is the reverse of removal.

11 Air conditioning system –
general information
and precautions

General information

An air conditioning system is available on certain models. It enables the temperature of incoming air to be lowered, and dehumidifies the air, which makes for rapid demisting and increased comfort.

The cooling side of the system works in the same way as a domestic refrigerator. Refrigerant gas is drawn into a belt-driven compressor and passes into a condenser mounted in front of the radiator, where it loses heat and becomes liquid. The liquid passes through an expansion valve to an evaporator,

10.11a Carefully prise the vent housing with a wide-bladed tool . . .

10.11b . . . to release the clips, and remove it from the facia

where it changes from liquid under high pressure to gas under low pressure. This change is accompanied by a drop in temperature, which cools the evaporator. The refrigerant returns to the compressor and the cycle begins again.

Air blown through the evaporator passes to the air distribution unit, where it is mixed with hot air blown through the heater matrix to

achieve the desired temperature in the passenger compartment.

The heating side of the system works in the same way as on models without air conditioning (see Section 8).

The operation of the system is controlled electronically by coolant temperature switches (see Section 5), and pressure switches which are screwed into the compressor high-pressure line. Any problems with the system should be referred to a VW dealer.

Precautions

 Warning: The refrigeration circuit contains a liquid refrigerant and it is therefore dangerous to disconnect any part of the system without specialised knowledge and equipment. The refrigerant is potentially dangerous and should only be handled by qualified persons. If it is splashed onto the skin it can cause frostbite. It is not itself poisonous, but in the presence of a naked flame (including a cigarette) it forms a poisonous gas. Uncontrolled discharging of the refrigerant is dangerous and potentially damaging to the environment.

• **Do not operate the air conditioning system if it is known to be short of refrigerant, as this may damage the compressor.**

When an air conditioning system is fitted, it is necessary to observe special precautions whenever dealing with any part of the system, its associated components and any items which require disconnection of the system. If for any reason the system must be disconnected, entrust this task to your VW dealer or a refrigeration engineer.

12 Air conditioning system components – removal and refitting

 Warning: Do not attempt to open the refrigerant circuit. Refer to the precautions given in Section 11.

1 The only operation which can be carried out easily without discharging the refrigerant is the renewal of the compressor drivebelt, which is covered in Chapter 2A or 2B. All other operations must be referred to a VW dealer or an air conditioning specialist.

2 If necessary the compressor can be unbolted and moved aside, without disconnecting its flexible hoses, after removing the drivebelt.

Many car accessory shops sell one-shot air conditioning recharge aerosols. These generally contain refrigerant, compressor oil, leak sealer and system conditioner. Some also have a dye to help pinpoint leaks.

Warning: These products must only be used as directed by the manufacturer, and do not remove the need for regular maintenance.

Chapter 4 Part A:
Fuel systems

Contents

Degrees of difficulty

Easy, suitable for novice with little experience		Fairly easy, suitable for beginner with some experience		Fairly difficult, suitable for competent DIY mechanic		Difficult, suitable for experienced DIY mechanic		Very difficult, suitable for expert DIY or professional	

Specifications

System type
SOHC engines .... Bosch Motronic ME 7.5.10
DOHC engines .... Magneti Marelli 4LV or 4CV

Fuel system data
Fuel pump type .... Electric, immersed in fuel tank
Regulated fuel pressure .... 2.5 bar
Engine idle speed (non-adjustable, electronically controlled) .... 600 to 800 rpm
Idle CO content (non-adjustable, electronically controlled) .... 0.5 % max
Injector electrical resistance .... 12 to 17 ohms

Recommended fuel
Minimum octane rating (all models) .... 95 RON unleaded

Torque wrench settings

	Nm	lbf ft
ECU mounting bracket nuts	10	7
Fuel rail mounting bolts	10	7
Inlet manifold to cylinder head	20	15
Lambda sensor	55	41

---

1 General information and precautions

General information

The Bosch Motronic and Magneti-Marelli systems are self-contained engine management systems, which control both the fuel injection and ignition. This Chapter deals with the fuel system components only – see Chapter 5B for details of the ignition system.

The fuel injection system comprises a fuel tank, an electric fuel pump, a fuel filter, fuel supply and return lines, a throttle body, a fuel rail, a fuel pressure regulator, four electronic fuel injectors, and an Electronic Control Unit (ECU) together with its associated sensors, actuators and wiring. The two systems used are essentially very similar, with only a few detail differences in certain components.

The fuel pump delivers a constant supply of fuel through a cartridge filter to the fuel rail, at a slightly higher pressure than required – the fuel pressure regulator maintains a constant fuel pressure to the fuel injectors, and returns excess fuel to the tank via the return line. This constant flow system also helps to reduce fuel temperature, and prevents vaporisation.

The fuel injectors are opened and closed by an Electronic Control Unit (ECU), which calculates the injection timing and duration according to engine speed, crankshaft position, throttle position and rate of opening, inlet manifold depression, inlet air temperature, coolant temperature, roadspeed and exhaust gas oxygen content information, received from sensors mounted on and around the engine.

Inlet air is drawn into the engine through the air cleaner, which contains a renewable paper filter element. The inlet air temperature is regulated by a valve mounted in the air cleaner inlet trunking, which blends air at ambient temperature with hot air, drawn from over the exhaust manifold.

The temperature of the air entering the throttle body is measured by a sensor mounted on the right-hand side of the inlet manifold. This sensor also monitors the pressure in the inlet manifold. This information is used by the ECU to fine-tune the fuelling requirements for different operating conditions.

The new Polo features a throttle which is electronically-controlled ('fly-by-wire') – an accelerator cable is not fitted. Instead, a throttle position sensor fitted to the accelerator pedal provides the ECU with the throttle opening signal, and this is relayed to a motor-driven throttle valve, attached to the throttle body. This system also enables the ECU to control the engine idle speed, varying the throttle opening as required by changes in engine temperature and load. As a result, manual adjustment of the engine idle speed is not necessary or possible.

The exhaust gas oxygen content is constantly monitored by the ECU via the lambda sensor, which is mounted in the exhaust pipe. The ECU then uses this information to modify the injection timing and duration to maintain the optimum air/fuel ratio – a result of this is that manual adjustment of the idle exhaust CO content is not necessary or possible. All models are fitted with a catalytic converter – see Chapter 4B.

Where fitted, the ECU controls the operation of the activated charcoal filter evaporative loss system – refer to Chapter 4B for further details.

It should be noted that fault diagnosis of all the engine management systems described in this Chapter is only possible with dedicated electronic test equipment. Problems with the systems operation should therefore be referred to a VW dealer for assessment. Once the fault has been identified, the removal/refitting sequences detailed in the following Sections will then allow the appropriate component(s) to be renewed as required.

Precautions

⚠️ *Warning: Petrol is extremely flammable – great care must be taken when working on any part of the fuel system.*

• *Do not smoke, or allow any naked flames or uncovered light bulbs near the work area. Note that gas-fired domestic appliances with pilot flames, such as heaters, boilers, etc, also present a fire hazard – bear this in mind if you are working in an area where such appliances are present. Always keep a suitable fire extinguisher close to the work area, and familiarise yourself with its operation before starting work. Wear eye protection when working on fuel systems, and wash off any fuel spilt on bare skin immediately with soap and water. Note that fuel vapour is just as dangerous as liquid fuel – possibly more so; a vessel that has been emptied of liquid fuel will still contain vapour, and can be potentially explosive.*

• *Many of the operations described in this Chapter involve the disconnection of fuel lines, which may cause an amount of fuel spillage. Before commencing work, refer to the above Warning and the information in 'Safety first!' at the beginning of this manual.*

• *Residual fuel pressure always remain in the fuel system, long after the engine has been switched off. This pressure must be relieved in a controlled manner before work can commence on any component in the fuel system – refer to Section 9 for details.*

• *When working with fuel system components, pay particular attention to cleanliness – dirt entering the fuel system may cause blockages, which will lead to poor running.*

• *In the interests of personal safety and equipment protection, many of the procedures in this Chapter suggest that the negative lead be removed from the battery terminal. This firstly eliminates the possibility of accidental short-circuits being caused as the car is being worked upon, and secondly prevents damage to electronic components (eg, sensors, actuators, ECUs) which are particularly sensitive to the power surges caused by disconnection or reconnection of the wiring harness whilst they are still 'live'.*

• *It should be noted, however, that the engine management systems described in this Chapter (and Chapter 5B) have a 'learning' capability, that allows the system to adapt to the engine's running characteristics as it wears with use. This 'learnt' information is lost when the battery is disconnected, and the system will then take a short period of time to 're-learn' the engine's characteristics – this may be manifested (temporarily) as rough idling, reduced throttle response and possibly a slight increase in fuel consumption, until the system re-adapts. The re-adaptation time will depend on how often the car is used and the driving conditions encountered.*

2 Air cleaner – removal and refitting

Removal

SOHC engines

1 Refer to Chapter 1, Section 26.

DOHC engines

2 Remove the four screws, and lift the top cover from the engine **(see illustrations)**.
3 Disconnect the breather pipe from the right-hand side of the air cleaner **(see illustration)**.
4 Prise out the rectangular cover from the top of the air cleaner, and remove the securing screw beneath **(see illustrations)**.
5 Unscrew the central screw at the front of the air cleaner **(see illustration)**.
6 Pull the air cleaner up to release it, then

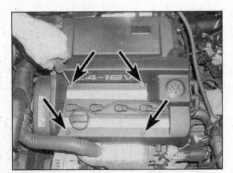

2.2a Unscrew the fasteners (arrowed) . . .

2.2b . . . and remove the engine top cover

2.3 Disconnect the breather hose from the air cleaner

remove the screw securing the air inlet spout to the hot-air hose, and lift the assembly from the engine **(see illustration)**. Recover the seal which fits over the throttle housing air inlet, and check its condition – renew if it is split or otherwise damaged.

Refitting

7 Refit the air cleaner by following the removal procedure in reverse. The air cleaner housing must be correctly mounted on the throttle body, to ensure there is no air leakage.

2.4a Prise out and remove the rectangular cover . . .

2.4b . . . and remove the screw beneath it

3 Inlet air temperature control system – general information

1 The inlet air temperature control system consists of a temperature-controlled flap valve, mounted in its own housing in the air cleaner inlet trunking, and a duct to the warm-air collector plate over the exhaust manifold.
2 The temperature sensor in the flap valve housing senses the temperature of the inlet air, and opens the valve when a preset lower limit is reached. As the flap valve opens, warm air drawn from around the exhaust manifold blends with the inlet air.
3 As the temperature of the inlet air rises, the sensor closes the flap progressively, until the warm-air supply from the exhaust manifold is completely closed off, and only air at ambient temperature is admitted to the air cleaner.
4 With the ducting removed from the temperature control flap valve housing, the sensor is visible. If a hairdryer and suitable freeze spray is available, the action of the sensor can be tested.

4 Accelerator cable – general

These models do not have an accelerator cable, and instead have an electronically-controlled arrangement known variously as Electronic Power Control (EPC), E-Gas, or alternatively, a 'fly-by-wire' throttle. The throttle

2.5 Remove the screw at the front of the air cleaner

position sensor at the top of the accelerator pedal is linked via the ECU to a throttle control motor (positioner) on the throttle body which opens and closes the throttle valve.

5 Fuel system components – removal and refitting

Note: *Observe the precautions in Section 1 before working on any component in the fuel system.*

Throttle body

Removal

1 Remove the air cleaner housing as described in Section 2.
2 Disconnect the battery negative lead, and

2.6 Removing the air cleaner assembly

position it away from the terminal (see *Disconnecting the battery*).
3 Unplug the wiring connector from the throttle control motor **(see illustration)**.
4 On SOHC engines, disconnect the hose for the charcoal canister from the port on the throttle body **(see illustration)**, and the vacuum pipe at the base.
5 Slacken and withdraw the through-bolts. On SOHC engines, the bolts also secure a mounting bracket for the crankcase breather vacuum valve, which should be lifted off and placed to one side. Lift the throttle body away from the inlet manifold – recover and discard the throttle body gasket **(see illustrations)**.
6 On DOHC engines, the throttle body sits on a separate flange for the EGR system – if required, the EGR pipe can be unbolted, and the flange removed from the manifold, together with its gaskets.

5.3 Disconnect the wiring plug from the throttle housing

5.4 Disconnect the charcoal canister hose from the throttle body

5.5a Remove the through-bolts, then lift away the throttle body . . .

5.5b . . . and recover the base gasket

5.12 Fuel supply and return connections at the fuel rail – note direction-of-flow arrows and colour-coding

seals as they emerge from the manifold **(see illustrations)**.

14 The injectors can be removed individually from the fuel rail by extracting the relevant metal clip and easing the injector out of the rail. Recover the injector upper O-ring seals **(see illustrations)**.

15 If required, remove the fuel pressure regulator, referring to the relevant sub-Section for guidance.

16 Check the electrical resistance of the injector using a multimeter and compare it with the Specifications.

Refitting

17 Refit the injectors and fuel rail by following the removal procedure in reverse, noting the following points:
  a) Renew the injector O-ring seals if they appear worn or damaged.
  b) Ensure that the injector retaining clips are securely seated.
  c) Check that the fuel supply and return hoses are reconnected correctly – refer to the colour coding described in 'Removal'.
  d) Check that all vacuum and electrical connections are remade correctly and securely.
  e) On completion, check exhaustively for fuel leaks before bringing the car back into service.

5.13a Lift out the fuel rail . . .

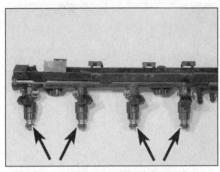

5.13b . . . and recover the injector lower O-ring seals (arrowed)

Fuel pressure regulator

Removal

18 Disconnect the battery negative lead, and position it away from the terminal (see *Disconnecting the battery*).

19 Refer to Section 9 and depressurise the fuel system.

20 Disconnect the vacuum hose from the port on the fuel pressure regulator.

21 Release the spring clip and temporarily disconnect the fuel supply hose from the fuel rail. This will allow the majority of fuel in the regulator to drain out. Be prepared for an amount of fuel loss – position a small container and some old rags underneath the fuel regulator housing. Reconnect the hose once the fuel has drained. **Note:** *The supply hose is marked with a black or white arrow.*

22 On SOHC engines, extract the retaining clip from the top of the regulator housing and

Refitting

7 Refitting is a reversal of removal, noting the following:
  a) Use new gaskets.
  b) Tighten the throttle body through-bolts securely, to prevent air leaks. A tightening torque for these bolts is not specified by the manufacturers.
  c) Ensure that all hoses and electrical connectors are refitted securely.

Fuel injectors and fuel rail

Note: *If a faulty injector is suspected, before removing the injectors, it is worth trying the effect of one of the proprietary injector-cleaning treatments. These can be added to the petrol in the tank, and are intended to clean the injectors as you drive.*

Removal

8 Disconnect the battery negative lead, and

position it away from the terminal (see *Disconnecting the battery*).

9 Unplug the injector harness connectors, labelling them to aid correct refitting later. Unclip the wiring harness clips from the top of the fuel rail, and lay the harness to one side.

10 Refer to Section 9 and depressurise the fuel system.

11 Disconnect the vacuum hose from the port on the fuel pressure regulator.

12 Slacken the clips and disconnect the fuel supply and return hoses from the end of the fuel rail. *Carefully* note the fitted positions of the hoses – the supply hose is marked with a black or white arrow, and the return hose is marked with a blue arrow **(see illustration)**.

13 Slacken and withdraw the fuel rail mounting bolts, then carefully lift the rail away from the inlet manifold, together with the injectors. Recover the injector lower O-ring

5.14a Using a suitable screwdriver, prise out the injector securing clip . . .

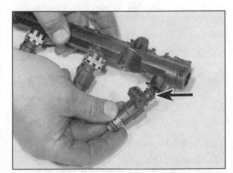

5.14b . . . and remove it from the fuel rail

5.14c Ease out the injector, and recover the upper O-ring seal (arrowed)

5.22 Fuel pressure regulator retaining clip – SOHC engines

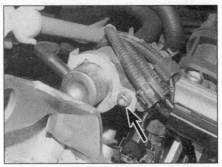

5.23 Fuel pressure regulator retaining plate securing screw – DOHC engines

5.27 Disconnect the inlet manifold pressure sensor wiring connector (viewed from underneath)

lift out the regulator body, recovering the O-ring seals **(see illustration)**.

23 On DOHC engines, the regulator is secured by a retaining plate, which has a single screw **(see illustration)**. Remove the screw, lift off the plate, and withdraw the regulator. Recover the O-ring seals.

Refitting

24 Refit the fuel pressure regulator by following the removal procedure in reverse, noting the following points:
a) *Renew the O-ring seals if they appear worn or damaged.*
b) *Ensure that the regulator retaining clip/plate is securely seated.*
c) *Refit the regulator vacuum hose securely.*

Inlet air temperature/ pressure sensor

Removal

25 The sensor is attached to the right-hand side of the inlet manifold (right as seen from the driver's seat) **(see illustration 10.6)**.
26 Disconnect the battery negative lead, and position it away from the terminal (see *Disconnecting the battery*).
27 Disconnect the wiring plug from the sensor **(see illustration)**. Remove the securing screw(s), and pull the sensor from the manifold. Recover the O-ring seal(s), and, on DOHC engines only, the guide plate.

Refitting

28 Refitting is a reversal of removal, renewing the O-ring seal(s) if necessary, and tightening the securing screw(s) securely.

Roadspeed sensor

29 The roadspeed sensor is mounted on the transmission, next to the gearchange linkage – refer to Chapter 7A. Do not confuse the sensor with the reversing light switch, which has a smaller wiring connector.

Coolant temperature sensor

30 Refer to Chapter 3, Section 6.

Lambda sensor(s)

Removal

31 The lambda sensor may be threaded into the exhaust downpipe, ahead of the catalytic

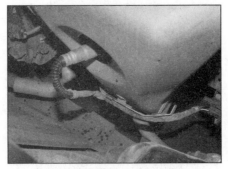

5.31a Lambda sensor location – SOHC engine

5.36 The fuel injection ECU is situated under the windscreen cowl panels

converter, or fitted between the branches of the exhaust manifold (on models with a precatalyst) **(see illustrations)**. Most models also have a second sensor, fitted after the second converter, to monitor the converter's performance. Refer to Chapter 4B for more details.

32 Disconnect the battery negative lead and position it away from the terminal (see *Disconnecting the battery*). Unplug the wiring harness from the lambda sensor at the connector, usually located down in front of the engine, at the transmission end.

33 To access the precatalyst sensor, detach the warm-air hose and remove the three bolts from the exhaust manifold heat shield (where necessary, also unclip the sensor wiring, or unbolt the wiring support bracket from the heat shield). Access to the other sensors is improved by jacking up the front of the car, and supporting on axle stands (see *Jacking*

5.31b Lambda sensor location – DOHC engine

and vehicle support). Slacken and withdraw the sensor, taking care to avoid damaging the sensor probe as it is removed. **Note:** *As a flying lead remains connected to the sensor after is has been disconnected, if the correct-size spanner is not available, a slotted socket will be required to remove the sensor.*

Refitting

34 Apply a little anti-seize grease to the sensor threads – avoid contaminating the probe tip.
35 Refit the sensor to its housing, tightening it to the correct torque. Restore the harness connection.

Electronic control unit (ECU)

Note: *The unit is coded, and should not be removed without consulting a VW dealer, otherwise it may not function correctly when the multi-plug is reconnected.*
36 The ECU is located centrally behind the engine compartment bulkhead, under one of the windscreen cowl panels **(see illustration)**. Remove the cowl panel as described in Chapter 12, Section 13.

Camshaft position sensor

Removal

37 The sensor is fitted on top of the engine, at the transmission end. On DOHC engines, the sensor is fitted to the rear (inlet) camshaft.
38 On SOHC engines, remove the air cleaner as described in Chapter 1, Section 26.
39 On DOHC engines, remove the four screws and lift off the engine top cover, releasing any wiring or hoses attached.

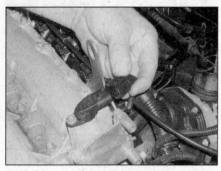

5.40 Disconnecting the camshaft position sensor

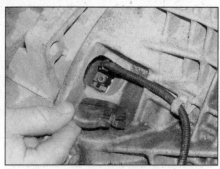

5.44 Prise out the rubber bung for access to the speed sensor

40 Pull the wiring connector off the sensor **(see illustration)**.
41 Unscrew the sensor mounting bolt, and pull the sensor out.

Refitting

42 Refitting is a reversal of removal.

EGR system components

43 Refer to Chapter 4B.

Engine speed sensor

Removal

44 The engine speed sensor is mounted at the left-hand rear of the cylinder block, next to the transmission bellhousing, and access is very difficult. Prise out the rubber bung for access to the sensor **(see illustration)**.
45 Trace the wiring back from the sensor, and unplug the harness connector.
46 Unscrew the retaining bolt and withdraw the sensor from the cylinder block.

Refitting

47 Refitting is a reversal of removal.

Throttle position sensor

48 The sensor is integral with the accelerator pedal. The pedal assembly can be removed (once access has been gained by removing the driver's lower facia panel – see Chapter 11) by disconnecting the sensor wiring plug and unscrewing the nuts securing the pedal to its mounting bracket **(see illustration)**.

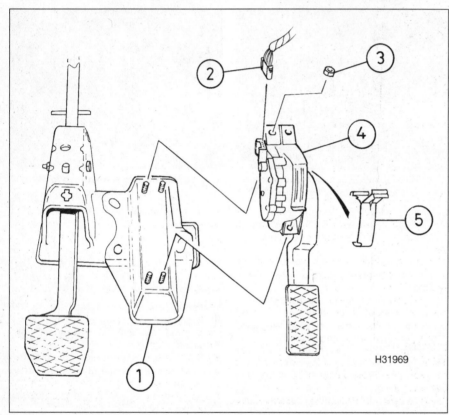

5.48 Accelerator pedal and throttle position sensor

1 Bracket	3 Mounting nuts
2 Position sensor wiring connector	4 Position sensor
	5 Retainer for footwell cover

H31969

---

6 Fuel filter –
  renewal

Refer to Chapter 1, Section 28.

---

7 Fuel pump and gauge sender unit –
  removal and refitting

Note: *Observe the precautions in Section 1 before working on any component in the fuel system.*

⚠ *Warning: Avoid direct skin contact with fuel – wear protective clothing and gloves when handling fuel system components. Ensure that the work area is well-ventilated to prevent the build-up of fuel vapour.*

General information

1 The fuel pump and gauge sender unit are combined in one assembly, which is mounted on the top of the fuel tank. Access is via a hatch provided in the load space floor. The unit protrudes into the fuel tank, and its removal involves exposing the contents of the tank to the atmosphere.

Removal

2 Depressurise the fuel system (Section 9).
3 Ensure that the car is parked on a level

7.5a Loosen and remove the screws . . .

7.5b . . . then lift out the access hatch

7.6 Unplug the pump/sender unit wiring connector

7.7 Disconnecting the fuel supply hose

7.8 Unscrew and remove the securing ring

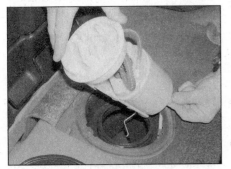

7.9 Lift out the unit, and let the fuel drain into the tank

7.12 If not removed with the unit, recover the rubber seal and check its condition

7.14 Arrow markings on pump/sender unit and access aperture aligned

surface, then disconnect the battery negative lead and position it away from the terminal (see *Disconnecting the battery*).

4 Fold the rear seat forwards, and remove the trim from the load space floor.

5 Slacken and withdraw the access hatch screws, and lift the hatch away from the floorpan **(see illustrations opposite)**.

6 Unplug the wiring harness connector from the pump/sender unit **(see illustration)**.

7 Pad the area around the supply and return fuel hoses with rags to absorb any spilt fuel, then squeeze the quick-release fittings and remove them from the ports at the sender unit **(see illustration)**. Observe the supply and return arrows markings on the ports – label the fuel hoses accordingly to ensure correct refitting later.

8 Unscrew the plastic securing ring and lift it out. Use a pair of water pump pliers to grip and rotate the plastic securing ring. Recover the flange and seal **(see illustration)**.

9 Turn the pump/sender unit to the left to release it from its bayonet fitting and lift it out, holding it above the level of the fuel in the tank until the excess fuel has drained out **(see illustration)**.

10 Remove the pump/sender unit from the car and lay it on an absorbent card or rag. Inspect the float at the end of the sender unit swinging arm for punctures and fuel ingress – renew the unit if it appears damaged.

11 The fuel pick-up incorporated in the assembly is spring-loaded to ensure that it always draws fuel from the lowest part of the

tank. Check that the pick-up is free to move under spring tension with respect to the sender unit body.

12 Inspect the rubber seal from the fuel tank aperture for signs of fatigue – renew it if necessary **(see illustration)**.

13 Inspect the sender unit wiper and track; clean off any dirt and debris that may have accumulated, and look for breaks in the track.

Refitting

14 Refit the sender unit by following the removal procedure in reverse, noting the following points:

a) *Take care not to bend the float arm as the unit is refitted.*

b) *When correctly installed, the pump/sender unit float arm must point towards the fuel filler pipe.*

c) *Smear the tank aperture rubber seal with clean fuel before fitting it in position.*

d) *The arrow markings on the sender unit body and the fuel tank must be aligned* **(see illustration)**.

e) *Reconnect the fuel hoses to the correct ports – observe the direction-of-flow arrow markings.*

8 Fuel tank – removal and refitting

Note: *Observe the precautions in Section 1 before working on any component in the fuel system.*

Removal

1 Before the tank can be removed, it must be drained of as much fuel as possible. As no drain plug is provided, it is preferable to carry out this operation with the tank almost empty.

2 Disconnect the battery negative lead and position it away from the terminal (see *Disconnecting the battery*). Using a hand pump or syphon, remove any remaining fuel from the bottom of the tank.

3 Gain access to the top of the fuel pump/sender unit as described in Section 7, and disconnect the wiring harness from the top of the pump sender unit at the multiway connector.

4 Disconnect the fuel return hose (colour-coded blue) from the pump/sender unit, along with the fuel supply and breather pipes. Label the pipes to ensure accurate refitting.

5 Loosen the right-hand rear wheel bolts, then jack up the rear of the car and remove the right-hand rear wheel.

6 Position a trolley jack under the centre of the tank. Insert a block of wood between the jack head and the tank to prevent damage to the tank surface. Raise the jack until it just takes the weight of the tank.

7 Loosen and remove the two retaining nuts, then detach the tank support bracket from the body. Note that this bracket doubles as an exhaust support – be ready to support the exhaust system as the nuts are removed. If wished, the remaining two nuts can also be removed, and the bracket removed completely.

8 Unhook all the rear exhaust mountings from the body, then lower the exhaust system sufficiently to allow the fuel tank to be lowered. Do not allow the exhaust to hang down unsupported – tie it loosely to the body with wire, or position suitable supports underneath it, to just take its weight.

9 Working inside the rear right-hand wheel arch, slacken and withdraw the screws that secure the tank filler neck inside of the wheel arch. Open the fuel filler flap and peel the rubber sealing flange away from the bodywork.

10 Loosen and remove the retaining bolts at the front edge and around the tank, keeping one hand on the tank to steady it as it is released from its mountings.

11 Lower the jack and tank away from the underside of the car; detach the filler pipes and the outlet pipe from the fuel filter as the tank is lowered. Disconnect the charcoal canister vent pipe from the port on the filler neck as it is exposed. Locate the earthing strap and disconnect it from the terminal at the filler neck.

12 If the tank is contaminated with sediment or water, remove the fuel pump/sender unit (see Section 7) and swill the tank out with clean fuel. The tank is injection-moulded from a synthetic material, and if damaged, it should be renewed. However, in certain cases it may be possible to have small leaks or minor damage repaired. Seek the advice of a suitable specialist before attempting to repair the fuel tank.

Refitting

13 Refitting is the reverse of the removal procedure, noting the following points:

a) *When lifting the tank back into position, make sure the mounting rubbers are correctly positioned, and take care to ensure none of the hoses get trapped between the tank and vehicle body.*

b) *Ensure that all pipes and hoses are correctly routed, are not kinked, and are securely held in position with their retaining clips.*

c) *Reconnect the earth strap to its terminal on the filler neck.*

d) *Tighten the tank retaining bolts securely.*

e) *On completion, refill the tank with fuel, and exhaustively check for signs of leakage prior to taking the car out on the road.*

9 Fuel injection system – depressurisation

Warning: The following procedure will merely relieve the pressure in the fuel system – remember that fuel will still be present in the system components and take precautions accordingly before disconnecting any of them.

Note: *Observe the precautions in Section 1 before working on any component in the fuel system.*

1 The fuel system referred to in this Section is defined as the tank-mounted fuel pump, the fuel filter, the fuel injector, the throttle body-mounted fuel pressure regulator, and the metal pipes and flexible hoses of the fuel lines between these components. All these contain fuel, which will be under pressure while the engine is running and/or while the ignition is switched on. The pressure will remain for some time after the ignition has been switched off, and must be relieved before any of these components are disturbed for servicing work. Ideally, the engine should be allowed to cool completely before work commences.

2 Referring to Chapter 12, locate and remove the fuel pump relay. Alternatively, identify and remove the fuel pump fuse from the fusebox.

3 With the fuel pump disabled, crank the engine for about ten seconds. The engine may fire and run for a while, but let it continue running until it stops. The fuel injector should have opened enough times during cranking to considerably reduce the line fuel pressure, and reduce the risk of fuel spraying out when a fuel line is disturbed.

4 Disconnect the battery negative terminal (see *Disconnecting the battery*).

5 Place a suitable container beneath the relevant connection/union to be disconnected, and have a large rag ready to soak up any escaping fuel not being caught by the container.

6 Slowly loosen the connection or union nut (as applicable) to avoid a sudden release of pressure, and position the rag around the connection to catch any fuel spray which may be expelled. Once the pressure has been released, disconnect the fuel line. Insert plugs to minimise fuel loss and prevent the entry of dirt into the fuel system.

10 Inlet manifold – removal and refitting

Note: *Observe the precautions in Section 1 before working on any component in the fuel system.*

Removal

1 Refer to Section 9 and depressurise the fuel system, then disconnect the battery negative lead and position it away from the terminal (see *Disconnecting the battery*).

2 Refer to Section 2 and remove the air cleaner housing.

3 Refer to Section 5 and remove the throttle body from the inlet manifold.

4 Unplug the wiring harness from the inlet air temperature/pressure sensor (see Section 5).

5 Disconnect the brake servo vacuum hose from the port on the side of the inlet manifold.

6 Refer to Section 5 and remove the fuel rail and fuel injectors **(see illustration). Note:** *The fuel rail may be moved to one side, leaving the fuel lines connected to it, but take care to avoid straining them.*

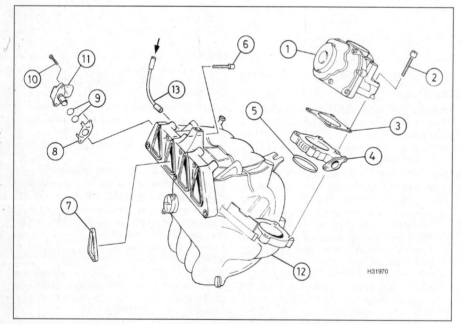

H31970

10.6 Inlet manifold details

1	*Throttle housing*	*6*	*Inlet manifold bolt*	*11 Inlet air temperature/pressure sensor*
2	*Throttle housing bolt*	*7*	*Manifold seal*	
3	*Gasket*	*8*	*Guide plate*	*12 Inlet manifold*
4	*EGR pipe flange*	*9*	*O-rings*	*13 Fuel pressure regulator vacuum hose*
5	*Seal*	*10*	*Screw*	

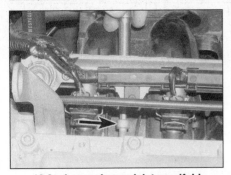

10.8a Loosening an inlet manifold mounting bolt (arrowed)

10.8b Removing the inlet manifold from the cylinder head – DOHC engine

10.9 Unclip the fuel hoses from the base of the manifold, and remove the manifold from the engine compartment

10.10 When refitting the inlet manifold, use new O-ring seals

11.2a Unclip and remove the ashtray . . .

11.2b . . . for access to the diagnostic connector

7 On engine code AUC, remove the two bolts securing the EGR pipe to the base of the manifold. When the manifold is removed, recover the gasket – a new one should be used when refitting.

8 Progressively slacken and remove the inlet manifold-to-cylinder head bolts. Move the manifold away from the head, and recover the O-ring seals **(see illustrations)**.

9 Where necessary, unclip the fuel supply and return hoses from underneath the manifold **(see illustration)**. If the hoses are disconnected, note their locations and colour-coding identification for refitting. The manifold can now be removed from the engine compartment.

Refitting

10 Refit the inlet manifold by following the removal procedure in reverse, noting the following points:

  a) Use new manifold O-ring seals **(see illustration)**.
  b) Tighten the manifold-to-cylinder head bolts to the specified torque.
  c) Check that all vacuum, electrical and fuel system connections are remade correctly and securely.

  d) On completion, check exhaustively for fuel leaks before bringing the car back into service.

11 Fuel injection system – testing and adjustment

1 If a fault appears in the fuel injection system, first ensure that all the system wiring connectors are securely connected and free of corrosion. Then ensure that the fault is not due to poor maintenance; ie, check that the air cleaner filter element is clean, the spark plugs are in good condition and correctly gapped, the cylinder compression pressures are correct, the ignition timing is correct and the engine breather hoses are clear and undamaged, referring to Chapter 1A, Chapter 2A and Chapter 5B.

2 If these checks fail to reveal the cause of the problem, the car should be taken to a suitably-equipped VW dealer for testing. A diagnostic connector is incorporated in the engine management system wiring harness (located underneath the ashtray in the centre console), into which a dedicated electronic test equipment can be plugged **(see illustrations)**. The test equipment is capable of 'interrogating' the engine management system ECU electronically and accessing its internal fault log. In this manner, faults can be pinpointed quickly and simply, even if their occurrence is intermittent. Testing all the system components individually in an attempt to locate the fault by elimination is a time-consuming operation that is unlikely to be fruitful (particularly if the fault occurs dynamically), and carries high risk of damage to the ECU's internal components.

3 Experienced home mechanics equipped with an accurate tachometer and a carefully-calibrated exhaust gas analyser may be able to check the exhaust gas CO content and the engine idle speed; if these are found to be out of specification, then the car must be taken to a suitably-equipped VW dealer for assessment. Neither the air/fuel mixture (exhaust gas CO content) nor the engine idle speed are manually adjustable; incorrect test results indicate a fault within the fuel injection system.

Notes

Chapter 4 Part B:
Emission control and exhaust systems

Contents

Degrees of difficulty

Easy, suitable for novice with little experience	**Fairly easy,** suitable for beginner with some experience	**Fairly difficult,** suitable for competent DIY mechanic	**Difficult,** suitable for experienced DIY mechanic	**Very difficult,** suitable for expert DIY or professional

Specifications

Torque wrench settings	Nm	lbf ft
EGR pipe flange bolts	8	6
EGR valve adapter bolts	20	15
EGR valve mounting bolts	8	6
EGR valve mounting nuts	20	15
Exhaust clamp nuts	40	30
Exhaust manifold nuts*	25	18
Exhaust manifold support bracket to engine	25	18
Exhaust manifold-to-downpipe nuts*	40	30
Exhaust mounting bracket nuts and bolts	25	18
Lambda (oxygen) sensor	50	37

*Use new nuts

1 General information

Emission control systems

All petrol models are designed to use unleaded petrol, and are controlled by engine management systems that are programmed to give the best compromise between driveability, fuel consumption and exhaust emission production. In addition, a number of systems are fitted that help to minimise other harmful emissions. A crankcase emission control system is fitted, which reduces the release of pollutants from the engine's lubrication system, and a catalytic converter is fitted which reduces exhaust gas pollutant. An evaporative loss emission control system is fitted which reduces the release of gaseous hydrocarbons from the fuel tank.

Crankcase emission control

To reduce the emission of unburned hydrocarbons from the crankcase into the atmosphere, the engine is sealed and the blow-by gases and oil vapour are drawn from inside the crankcase, through a wire-mesh oil separator, into the inlet tract to be burned by the engine during normal combustion.

Under conditions of high manifold depression, the gases will be sucked positively out of the crankcase. Under conditions of low manifold depression, the gases are forced out of the crankcase by the (relatively) higher crankcase pressure. If the engine is worn, the raised crankcase pressure (due to increased blow-by) will cause some of the flow to return under all manifold conditions.

Exhaust emission control

To minimise the amount of pollutants which escape into the atmosphere, all petrol models are fitted with a three-way catalytic converter in the exhaust system. The fuelling system is of the closed-loop type, in which an oxygen (lambda) sensor in the exhaust system provides the engine management system ECU with constant feedback, enabling the ECU to adjust the air/fuel mixture to optimise combustion.

Most models have two catalysts – a precatalyst built into the exhaust manifold (which can be identified by having the (first) oxygen sensor screwed into the manifold), and a second catalyst fitted further down under the car.

The lambda (oxygen) sensor has a built-in heating element, controlled by the ECU through the oxygen sensor relay, to quickly bring the sensor's tip to its optimum operating temperature. The sensor's tip is sensitive to

oxygen, and sends a voltage signal to the ECU that varies according on the amount of oxygen in the exhaust gas. If the inlet air/fuel mixture is too rich, the exhaust gases are low in oxygen so the sensor sends a low-voltage signal, the voltage rising as the mixture weakens and the amount of oxygen rises in the exhaust gases. Peak conversion efficiency of all major pollutants occurs if the inlet air/fuel mixture is maintained at the chemically-correct ratio for the complete combustion of petrol of 14.7 parts (by weight) of air to 1 part of fuel (the stoichiometric ratio). The sensor output voltage alters in a large step at this point, the ECU using the signal change as a reference point and correcting the inlet air/fuel mixture accordingly by altering the fuel injector pulse width.

Models with two catalysts have two sensors – one before the precatalyst and one after the main catalytic converter. This enables more efficient monitoring of the exhaust gas, allowing a faster response time. The overall efficiency of the converters can also be checked. Details of the oxygen sensor removal and refitting are given in Chapter 4A, Section 5.

An Exhaust Gas Recirculation (EGR) system is also fitted to several models. This reduces the level of nitrogen oxides produced during combustion by introducing a proportion of the

2.3 Charcoal canister purge valve wiring connector (arrowed)

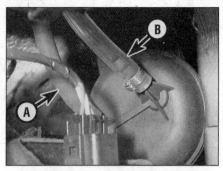

2.7 Charcoal canister pipe to purge valve (A) and pipe to fuel tank (B)

exhaust gas back into the inlet manifold, under certain engine operating conditions, via a plunger valve. The system is controlled electronically by the engine management ECU.

Evaporative emission control

To minimise the escape of unburned hydrocarbons into the atmosphere, an evaporative loss emission control system is fitted to all petrol models. The fuel tank filler cap is sealed, and a charcoal canister is mounted underneath the right-hand wing to collect the petrol vapours released from the fuel contained in the fuel tank. It stores them until they can be drawn from the canister (under the control of the fuel injection/ignition system ECU) via the purge valve(s) into the inlet tract, where they are then burned by the engine during normal combustion.

To ensure that the engine runs correctly when it is cold and/or idling, and to protect the catalytic converter from the effects of an over-rich mixture, the purge control valve(s) are not opened by the ECU until the engine has warmed-up, and the engine is under load; the valve solenoid is then modulated on and off to allow the stored vapour to pass into the inlet tract.

Exhaust systems

The exhaust system comprises the exhaust manifold (with precatalyst and oxygen sensor on most models), front pipe, catalytic converter (with second oxygen sensor on most models), intermediate pipe and silencer, and tailpipe and silencer.

The system is supported by various metal

brackets screwed to the vehicle floor, with rubber vibration dampers fitted to suppress noise.

2 Evaporative loss emission control system – information and component renewal

1 The evaporative loss emission control system consists of the purge valve, the activated charcoal filter canister and a series of connecting vacuum hoses.
2 The purge valve is located on the right-hand inner wing, while the canister is mounted in the space between the right-hand wheel arch liner and the bumper.

Purge valve

3 Ensure that the ignition is switched off, then unplug the wiring harness from the purge valve at the connector **(see illustration)**.
4 Slacken the clips and pull the hoses off the purge valve ports. Make a note of their orientation to aid refitting later.
5 Slide the purge valve out of its retaining ring, and remove it from the engine bay.
6 Refitting is a reversal of removal.

Charcoal canister

7 For improved access to the canister, remove the front bumper as described in Chapter 11. Disconnect the hoses from it, noting which ports they connect to **(see illustration)**. Release the securing lug and lift the canister out of the wheel housing.
8 Refitting is a reversal of removal.

3 Crankcase emission system – general information

1 The crankcase emission control system consists of a series of hoses that connect the crankcase vent to the camshaft cover vent (where applicable) and the air cleaner.
2 An oil separator unit may be fitted on some models. This is a large plastic housing, bolted to the rear of the engine block, and sealed to the block openings by two O-ring seals **(see illustrations)**. If the unit has become blocked, it may be worth trying to clean it out using a suitable solvent before renewing the complete unit. The unit cannot be dismantled for servicing.
3 The system requires no attention other than to check at regular intervals that the hose(s) are free of blockages and undamaged.

4 Exhaust Gas Recirculation (EGR) system – component removal

1 The EGR system consists of the EGR valve, which has an integral modulator (solenoid) valve, which is mounted on a flange joint at the exhaust manifold and is connected to a second flange joint at the throttle housing (or the base of the inlet manifold) by a metal pipe.
2 To improve access, remove the air cleaner (SOHC engines) or the engine's plastic top cover (DOHC engines).

EGR valve

Except engine code AUC

3 Disconnect the wiring plug and the vacuum hose from the valve.
4 Support the EGR valve, then unscrew and remove the two nuts which secure the EGR pipe flange and the valve **(see illustrations)**. Withdraw the valve, and recover the gaskets fitted either side of it.
5 If required, unscrew the two bolts securing the adapter elbow to the cylinder head **(see illustration)**. Withdraw the adapter, and recover the gasket.

3.2a Oil separator unit retaining bolts (seen with engine removed, for clarity)

3.2b Oil separator unit removed, showing O-ring seals (arrowed)

4.4a EGR valve front mounting nuts

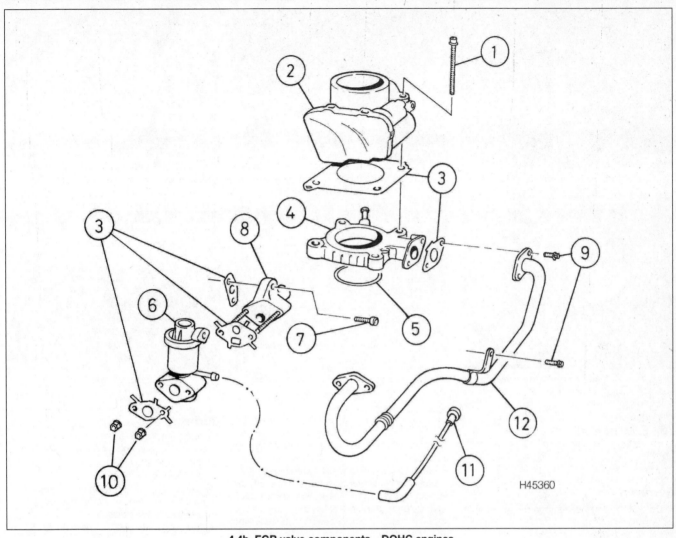

4.4b EGR valve components – DOHC engines

1 Throttle housing bolt	4 Mounting flange	7 Adaptor elbow bolt	10 Mounting nuts
2 Throttle housing	5 Seal	8 Adaptor elbow	11 Vacuum hose
3 Gasket	6 EGR valve	9 EGR pipe bolts	12 EGR pipe

6 The EGR pipe can be removed completely if required, after removing the two bolts from the elbow at the base of the throttle body **(see illustration)**. Recover the gaskets.

7 Refitting is a reversal of removal. Use new gaskets, and tighten the nuts/bolts to the specified torque. On completion, run the engine and check for signs of gas leakage.

Engine code AUC

8 The EGR valve is located on the front of the exhaust manifold, on the right-hand side (right as seen from the driver's seat). To further improve access to the valve, remove the exhaust manifold heat shield (it may be necessary ultimately to remove the exhaust manifold entirely).

9 Disconnect the wiring plug and the vacuum hose from the solenoid valve.

10 Remove the two bolts securing the pipe flange to the front of the valve. When the valve

is removed, recover the pipe flange gasket – a new one should be used when refitting.

11 Unscrew the three valve mounting bolts, and withdraw the valve together with its gasket.

12 Refitting is a reversal of removal. Use new gaskets, and tighten the bolts to the specified torque. On completion, run the engine and check for signs of gas leakage.

4.5 EGR valve adapter elbow bolts

4.6 EGR pipe bolts at the throttle body

5.3 Pull off the warm-air hose

5.4 Unclip the oxygen sensor wiring from the tubular bracket

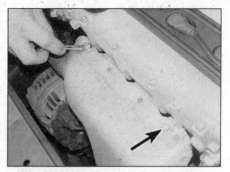

5.5a Unscrew the heat shield bolts . . .

5.5b . . . and remove the shield

5.8 Two of the manifold-to-exhaust downpipe nuts

5.10a Exhaust manifold nuts

5 Exhaust manifold – removal and refitting

Removal

1 On SOHC engines, remove the air cleaner as described in Chapter 1. On DOHC engines, remove the engine top cover, which is secured by four Allen screws.
2 Apply the handbrake, then jack up the front of the car and support it on axle stands (see *Jacking and vehicle support*).
3 Pull off the warm-air hose (for the air cleaner) from the heat shield over the manifold, and place the hose end to one side **(see illustration)**.
4 Where applicable, unscrew and remove the two bolts at the front of the manifold heat shield which secure a small tubular wiring bracket. Access to these bolts may be easier from below. Take off the bracket, unclipping the oxygen sensor wiring from it **(see illustration)**.
5 Unscrew the three bolts securing the heat shield to the manifold, unclip the oxygen sensor wiring (if not already done), and remove it from the engine compartment **(see illustrations)**.
6 On models with an oxygen sensor screwed into the manifold, trace the wiring from the sensor around the front of the engine to the connector plug. Disconnect the wiring plug, and free the wiring from any retaining clips or ties. It is preferable to remove the manifold

with the sensor in place, but care must be taken not to damage the sensor if this is done.
7 Remove the EGR valve as described in Section 4.
8 Working from below, unscrew and remove the four nuts securing the manifold to the front section of the exhaust **(see illustration)**. Use a wire brush and plenty of penetrating oil if the studs are rusty. If a nut appears to be sticking, do not try to force it; tighten the nut back half a turn, apply some more penetrating oil to the stud threads, wait several seconds for it to soak in, then gradually unscrew the nut by one turn. Repeat this process until the nut is free.
9 Separate the front pipe from the manifold, and recover the gasket (a new gasket must be used on reassembly). Once this is done, it is advisable to support the front pipe on an axle stand, to avoid placing strain on the exhaust system or second oxygen sensor wiring (for preference, remove the exhaust front section entirely, as described in Section 6).
10 Unscrew and remove the manifold retaining nuts, noting the advice given in paragraph 8 **(see illustrations)**. In some cases, the manifold studs will come out with the nuts – this poses no great problem, and the studs can be refitted if they are in good condition. For preference, however, a complete set of manifold studs and nuts (and manifold-to-front pipe nuts) should be obtained as required, as the old ones are likely to be in less-than-perfect condition.
11 Withdraw the manifold from the cylinder head, and recover the gasket from the studs.

Refitting

12 Refitting is a reversal of the removal procedure, noting the following points:
 a) *Always fit new gaskets and seals, as applicable.*
 b) *If any studs were broken when removing, drill out the remains of the stud, and fit new studs and nuts.*
 c) *It is recommended that new studs and nuts are used as a matter of course – even if the old ones came off without difficulty, they may not stand being retightened. New components will be much easier to remove in future, should this be necessary.*
 d) *If the old studs are re-used, clean the threads thoroughly to remove all traces of rust.*
 e) *Tighten the manifold securing nuts to the specified torque.*

6 Exhaust system – component renewal

Warning: Allow ample time for the exhaust system to cool before starting work. In particular, note that the catalytic converter runs at very high temperatures. If there is any chance that the system may still be hot, wear suitable gloves. When removing the exhaust front section, take care not to damage the oxygen sensor(s) if they are not removed from their locations.

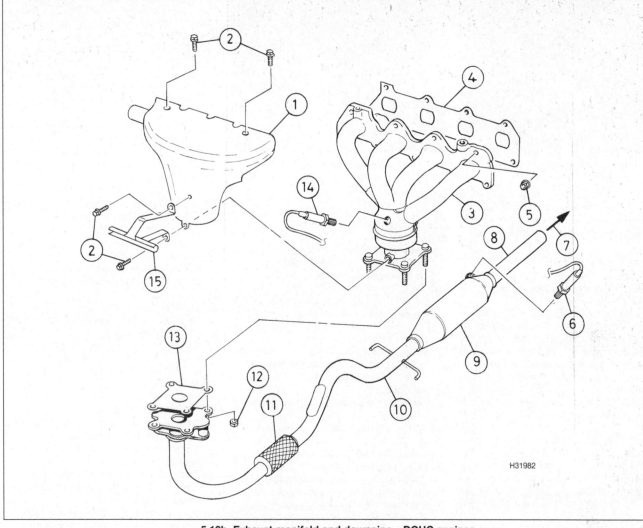

5.10b Exhaust manifold and downpipe – DOHC engines

1 Heat shield	5 Manifold mounting	8 Clamp position marking	12 Manifold-to-downpipe nut
2 Heat shield bolts	nut	9 Catalytic converter	13 Downpipe gasket
3 Exhaust manifold	6 Oxygen sensor 2	10 Front pipe	14 Oxygen sensor 1
4 Manifold gasket	7 To centre silencer	11 Flexible section	15 Wiring harness guide tube

Removal

1 The original VW system fitted in the factory is in two sections. The front section includes the catalytic converter, and can be removed complete. The centre and rear silencers can be removed and renewed separately.

2 To remove part of the system, first jack up the front or rear of the car and support it on axle stands (see *Jacking and vehicle support*). Alternatively, position the car over an inspection pit or on car ramps.

Front pipe and catalytic converter

Note: *Where applicable, handle the flexible, braided section of the front pipe carefully, and do not bend it excessively.*

3 Trace the wiring back from the oxygen sensor, and disconnect the wiring connector. On some models, the sensor wiring disappears behind an access panel behind the right-hand driveshaft, and it will be necessary to remove the cover fitted over the right-hand inner CV joint (or even the complete driveshaft, as described in Chapter 8) for access.

6.6 Exhaust downpipe-to-intermediate pipe clamp bolts (arrowed)

4 Unclip the oxygen sensor wiring from any clips or brackets, noting how it is routed for refitting.

5 If a new front section and catalyst are being fitted, unscrew the oxygen sensor(s) from the pipe.

6 Loosen the two nuts on the clamp behind the catalyst, and free the clamp so that it can be moved relative to the front and rear pipes **(see illustration)**.

7 Loosen and remove the nuts securing the front flange to the exhaust manifold. On some models, the shield over the right-hand driveshaft inner CV joint must be removed to improve access. Separate the front joint, and move it down sufficiently to clear the mounting studs.

8 Support the front of the pipe, then slide the clamp behind the catalyst either forwards or backwards to separate the joint. Twist the

6.10 Exhaust system rubber mounting at rear of front silencer

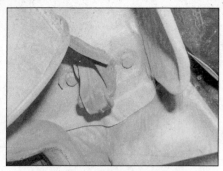

6.12 Rear silencer mounting

front pipe slightly from side-to-side, while pulling towards the front to release it from the rear section. When the pipe is free, lower it to the ground and remove it from under the car.

Rear pipe and silencers

9 Loosen the nuts securing the clamp between the silencers so that the clamp can be moved.

10 To remove the centre silencer, first loosen the nuts on the clamp behind the catalyst. To improve access, also remove the nuts securing the cradle and front mounting to the underside of the car, unhook the mounting and lower the cradle completely **(see illustration)**.

11 Slide the clamps at either end of the silencer section to release the pipe ends, and lower the silencer out of position.

12 Depending on model, the rear silencer is supported either just at the very back, or in front and behind, by a rubber mounting which is bolted to the underside of the car **(see illustration)**. The silencer is attached to these mountings by metal pegs which push into the rubber section of each mounting.

13 Unscrew the bolts, and release the mounting(s) from the underside of the car. On models with two silencer mountings, it may prove sufficient to unbolt only one, and to prise the silencer from the remaining mounting, but for preference, both should be removed, where applicable.

14 Where applicable, slide the clamp at the front end of the silencer section to release the pipe ends, and lower the silencer out of position.

Refitting

15 Each section is refitted by a reversal of the removal sequence, noting the following points:

a) *Ensure that all traces of corrosion have been removed from the flanges or pipe ends, and renew all necessary gaskets.*

b) *The design of the clamps used between the exhaust sections means that they play a greater role in ensuring a gas-tight seal – fit new clamps if they are in less than perfect condition.*

c) *When fitting the clamps, use the markings on the pipes as a guide to the clamp's correct fitted position.*

d) *Inspect the mountings for signs of damage or deterioration, and renew as necessary.*

e) *If using exhaust assembly paste, make sure this is only applied to joints downstream of the catalyst.*

f) *Prior to tightening the exhaust system mountings and clamps, ensure that all rubber mountings are correctly located and that there is adequate clearance between the exhaust system and vehicle underbody. Try to ensure that no unnecessary twisting stresses are applied to the pipes – move the pipes relative to each other at the clamps to relieve this.*

7 Catalytic converter – general information and precautions

1 The catalytic converter is a reliable and simple device which needs no maintenance in itself, but there are some facts of which an owner should be aware if the converter is to function properly for its full service life:

a) *DO NOT use leaded (4-star) or lead-replacement petrol (LRP) in a car equipped with a catalytic converter – the lead (or other additives) will coat the precious metals, reducing their converting efficiency and will eventually destroy the converter.*

b) *Always keep the ignition and fuel systems well-maintained in accordance with the manufacturer's schedule (see Chapter 1).*

c) *If the engine develops a misfire, do not drive the car at all (or at least as little as possible) until the fault is cured.*

d) *DO NOT push- or tow-start the car – this will soak the catalytic converter in unburned fuel, causing it to overheat when the engine does start.*

e) *DO NOT switch off the ignition at high engine speeds – ie, do not 'blip' the throttle immediately before switching off the engine.*

f) *DO NOT use fuel or engine oil additives – these may contain substances harmful to the catalytic converter.*

g) *DO NOT continue to use the car if the engine burns oil to the extent of leaving a visible trail of blue smoke.*

h) *Remember that the catalytic converter operates at very high temperatures. DO NOT, therefore, park the car in dry undergrowth, over long grass or piles of dead leaves after a long run.*

i) *Remember that the catalytic converter is FRAGILE – do not strike it with tools during servicing work, and take care handling it when removing it from the car for any reason.*

j) *In some cases, a sulphurous smell (like that of rotten eggs) may be noticed from the exhaust. This is common to many catalytic converter-equipped cars, and has more to do with the sulphur content of the brand of fuel being used than the converter itself.*

k) *The catalytic converter, used on a well-maintained and well-driven car, should last for between 50 000 and 100 000 miles – if the converter is no longer effective, it must be renewed.*

Chapter 5 Part A:
Starting and charging systems

Contents

Degrees of difficulty

Easy, suitable for novice with little experience	**Fairly easy,** suitable for beginner with some experience	**Fairly difficult,** suitable for competent DIY mechanic	**Difficult,** suitable for experienced DIY mechanic	**Very difficult,** suitable for expert DIY or professional

Specifications

General
System type . . . . 12 volt, negative-earth

Starter motor
Rating . . . . 12V, 0.9 kW

Battery
Ratings . . . . 36 to 110 Ah (depending on model and market)

Alternator
Minimum brush length . . . . 5 mm (tolerance +1mm, -0 mm)

Torque wrench settings	Nm	lbf ft
Alternator belt tensioner (spring type)	25	18
Alternator mounting bolts	25	18
Alternator mounting bracket-to-block bolts	55	41
Battery clamping plate bolt	22	16
Battery terminal bolts	6	4
Starter motor mounting bolts:		
Lower bolt (M8x160)	45	33
Upper bolts/nut (M8x70)	60	44

1 General information and precautions

General information

The engine electrical system consists mainly of the charging and starting systems. Because of their engine-related functions, these are covered separately from the body electrical devices such as the lights, instruments, etc (which are covered in Chapter 12). Refer to Part B of this Chapter for information on the ignition system.

The electrical system is of the 12 volt negative-earth type.

The battery may be of the low maintenance or 'maintenance-free' (sealed for life) type and is charged by the alternator, which is belt-driven from the crankshaft pulley.

The starter motor is of the pre-engaged type, with an integral solenoid. On starting, the solenoid moves the drive pinion into engagement with the flywheel ring gear before the starter motor is energised. Once the engine has started, a one-way clutch prevents the motor armature being driven by the engine until the pinion disengages from the flywheel.

Further details of the various systems are given in the relevant Sections of this Chapter. While some repair procedures are given, the usual course of action is to renew the component concerned. The owner whose interest extends beyond mere component renewal should obtain a copy of the *Automotive Electrical & Electronic Systems Manual*, available from the publishers of this manual.

Precautions

It is necessary to take extra care when working on the electrical system to avoid damage to semi-conductor devices (diodes and transistors), and to avoid the risk of personal injury. In addition to the precautions given in *Safety first!* at the beginning of this manual, observe the following when working on the system:

• *Always remove rings, watches, etc, before working on the electrical system.* Even with the battery disconnected, capacitive discharge could occur if a component's live terminal is earthed through a metal object. This could cause a shock or nasty burn.

• *Do not reverse the battery connections.* Components such as the alternator, electronic control units, or any other components having semi-conductor circuitry could be irreparably damaged.

• If the engine is being started using jump leads and a slave battery, connect the batteries *positive-to-positive* and *negative-to-negative* (see *Jump starting*). This also applies when connecting a battery charger.

• Never disconnect the battery terminals, the alternator, any electrical wiring or any test instruments when the engine is running.

• Do not allow the engine to turn the alternator when the alternator is not connected.

• Never 'test' for alternator output by 'flashing' the output lead to earth.

• Never use an ohmmeter of the type incorporating a hand-cranked generator for circuit or continuity testing.

• Always ensure that the battery negative lead is disconnected when working on the electrical system.

• Before using electric-arc welding equipment on the car, disconnect the battery, alternator and components such as the fuel injection/ignition electronic control unit to protect them from the risk of damage.

Battery disconnection

• Refer to the precautions listed in *Disconnecting the battery*, in the Reference section of this manual.

2 Battery – testing and charging

Testing

Standard and low-maintenance battery

1 If the car covers a small annual mileage, it is worthwhile checking the specific gravity of the electrolyte every three months to determine the state of charge of the battery. Use a hydrometer to make the check and compare the results with the following table. Note that the specific gravity readings assume an electrolyte temperature of 15°C (60°F); for every 10°C (18°F) below 15°C (60°F) subtract 0.007. For every 10°C (18°F) above 15°C (60°F) add 0.007.

	Ambient temperature	
	Above 25°C	Below 25°C
Fully-charged	1.210 to 1.230	1.270 to 1.290
70% charged	1.170 to 1.190	1.230 to 1.250
Discharged	1.050 to 1.070	1.110 to 1.130

2 If the battery condition is suspect, first check the specific gravity of electrolyte in each cell. A variation of 0.040 or more between any cells indicates loss of electrolyte or deterioration of the internal plates.

3 If the specific gravity variation is 0.040 or more, the battery should be renewed. If the cell variation is satisfactory but the battery is discharged, it should be charged as described later in this Section.

Maintenance-free battery

4 In cases where a 'sealed for life' maintenance-free battery is fitted, topping-up and testing of the electrolyte in each cell is not possible. The condition of the battery can therefore only be tested using a battery condition indicator or a voltmeter.

All battery types

5 If testing the battery using a voltmeter, connect the voltmeter across the battery. The test is only accurate if the battery has not been subjected to any kind of charge for the previous six hours. If this is not the case, switch on the headlights for 30 seconds, then wait four to five minutes before testing the battery after switching off the headlights. All other electrical circuits must be switched off, so check that the doors and tailgate/boot lid are fully shut when making the test.

6 If the voltage reading is less than 12.0 volts, then the battery is discharged.

7 If the battery is to be charged, remove it from the car (Section 3) and charge it as described later in this Section.

Charging

Note: *The following is intended as a guide only. Always refer to the manufacturer's recommendations (often printed on a label attached to the battery), and always disconnect both terminal leads before charging a battery.*

Standard and low-maintenance battery

8 Charge the battery at a rate of 3.5 to 4 amps and continue to charge the battery at this rate until no further rise in specific gravity is noted over a four hour period.

9 Alternatively, a trickle charger charging at the rate of 1.5 amps can safely be used overnight.

10 Specially rapid 'boost' charges which are claimed to restore the power of the battery in 1 to 2 hours are not recommended, as they can cause serious damage to the battery plates through overheating.

11 While charging the battery, note that the temperature of the electrolyte should never exceed 37.8°C (100°F).

Maintenance-free battery

12 This battery type takes considerably longer to fully recharge than the standard type, the time taken being dependent on the extent of discharge, but it can take anything up to three days.

13 A constant voltage type charger is required, to be set, when connected, to 13.9 to 14.9 volts with a charger current below 25 amps. Using this method, the battery should be usable within three hours, giving a voltage reading of 12.5 volts, but this is for a partially-discharged battery and, as mentioned, full charging can take considerably longer.

14 If the battery is to be charged from a fully-discharged state (condition reading less than 12.2 volts), have it recharged by your VW dealer or local automotive electrician, as the charge rate is higher and constant supervision during charging is necessary.

3 Battery – removal and refitting

Removal

1 Refer to *Disconnecting the battery* in the Reference section of this manual before proceeding.

2 Slacken the clamp nut and disconnect the battery negative lead from the terminal **(see illustration)**.
3 Squeeze the retaining tabs together and open the fuse cover fitted to the top of the battery **(see illustration)**.
4 Unscrew the nut(s) securing the holder to the battery positive terminal clamp **(see illustration)**.
5 Unscrew the nuts and disconnect the wiring from the fusible links.
6 Disconnect the wiring connector from the side of the fuse holder.
7 Press down on the fuse holder at the positive terminal end, and unclip the fuse holder from the top of the battery **(see illustration)**.
8 At the base of the battery, slacken and withdraw the clamp bolt, then lift off the clamping plate **(see illustration)**.
9 Where applicable, disconnect the vent pipe from the top of the battery, and remove the battery from the engine bay
10 If required, the battery tray can be unbolted and removed **(see illustration)**.

Refitting

11 Refit the battery by following the removal procedure in reverse. Where applicable, make sure the lug at the base of the battery locates in the recess in the battery tray. Tighten the clamp plate bolt to the correct torque.

4 Alternator/charging system – testing in car

Note: *Refer to 'Safety first!' and Section 1 of this Chapter before starting work.*
1 If the charge warning light fails to illuminate when the ignition is switched on, first check the alternator wiring connections for security. If satisfactory, check that the warning light bulb has not blown, and that the bulbholder is secure in its location in the instrument panel. If the light still fails to illuminate, check the continuity of the warning light feed wire from the alternator to the bulbholder. If all is satisfactory, the alternator is at fault and should be renewed or taken to an auto-electrician for testing and repair.
2 Similarly, if the charge warning light comes on with the ignition, but is then slow to go out when the engine is started, this may indicate an impending alternator problem. Check all the items listed in the preceding paragraph, and refer to an auto-electrical specialist if no obvious faults are found.
3 If the charge warning light illuminates when the engine is running, stop the engine and check that the drivebelt is correctly tensioned (see Chapter 2A or 2B) and that the alternator connections are secure. If all is so far satisfactory, check the alternator brushes and slip-rings as described in Section 6. If the fault persists, the alternator should be renewed, or

3.2 Loosen the clamp nut and disconnect the battery negative lead

3.4 . . . for access to the battery positive connection and fusible link nuts

taken to an auto-electrician for testing and repair.
4 If the alternator output is suspect even though the warning light functions correctly, the regulated voltage may be checked as follows.
5 Connect a voltmeter across the battery terminals, and start the engine.
6 Increase the engine speed until the voltmeter reading remains steady; the reading should be approximately 12 to 13 volts, and no more than 14 volts.
7 Switch on as many electrical accessories (eg, the headlights, heated rear window and heater blower) as possible, and check that the alternator maintains the regulated voltage at around 13 to 14 volts.
8 If the regulated voltage is not as stated, this may be due to worn brushes, weak brush springs, a faulty voltage regulator, a faulty diode, a severed phase winding or worn or

3.8 Unscrew the clamp bolt

3.3 Open up the fuse cover . . .

3.7 Unclip the bracket

damaged slip-rings. The brushes and slip-rings may be checked (see Section 6), but if the fault persists, the alternator should be renewed or taken to an auto-electrician.

5 Alternator – removal and refitting

Removal

1 Disconnect the battery negative lead, and position it away from the terminal (see *Disconnecting the battery*).
2 Remove the auxiliary drivebelt from the alternator pulley (see Chapter 2A or 2B).
3 Unplug the sense cable from the alternator at the connector **(see illustration)**. **Note:** *Connection details may vary according to model (some may have a single multi-plug) –*

3.10 Battery tray retaining bolts

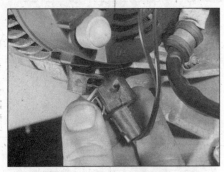

5.3 Unplug the sense cable from the alternator at the connector

5.4a Remove the protective cap . . .

5.4b . . . remove the nut and washers, then disconnect the power cable

5.4c Where applicable, unbolt and remove the cable guide

5.5a Undo the mounting bolts (arrowed)

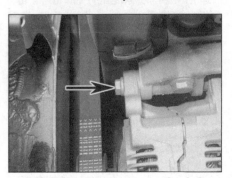

5.5b Alternator upper mounting bolt

the important thing is to disconnect all the wiring, noting how it is fitted.
4 Remove the protective cap, slacken and withdraw the nut and washers, then disconnect the power cable from the

alternator at the screw terminal post. Where applicable, unbolt and remove the cable guide **(see illustrations)**.
5 Slacken and remove the lower, then the upper bolts **(see illustrations)**, then lift the

alternator away from its bracket. Where applicable, pivot the tensioner roller out of the way to gain access to the lower mounting bolt.
6 Refer to Section 6 if the removal of the brush holder/voltage regulator module is required.

Refitting

7 Refitting is a reversal of removal. Refer to Chapter 2A or 2B as applicable for details of refitting and tensioning the auxiliary drivebelt.
8 On completion, tighten the alternator mounting bolts to the specified torque.

6.3a Where applicable, remove the retaining screws (arrowed). . .

6.3b . . . then prise open the clips . . .

---

6   Alternator –
brush holder/regulator
module renewal

1 Remove the alternator, as described in Section 5.
2 Place the alternator on a clean work surface, with the pulley facing down.
3 Remove the retaining screws, then prise open the clips and lift the plastic cover from the rear of the alternator **(see illustrations)**.
4 Slacken and withdraw the brush holder/voltage regulator module screws, then lift the module away from the alternator **(see illustrations)**.
5 Measure the free length of the brush contacts – where applicable, take the measurement from the manufacturer's emblem etched on the side of the brush contact, to the shallowest part of the curved end face of the brush **(see illustration)**.

6.3c . . . and lift the plastic cover from the rear of the alternator

6.4a Remove the brush holder/voltage regulator module screws . . .

6.4b . . . then lift the module away from the alternator

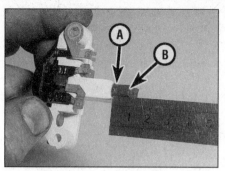

6.5 Measuring the alternator brush length – for A and B, see text

6.6 Inspect the surfaces of the slip-rings (arrowed), at the end of the alternator shaft

Check the measurement with the Specifications; renew the module if the brushes are worn below the minimum limit.

6 Inspect the surfaces of the slip-rings, at the end of the alternator shaft **(see illustration)**. If they appear excessively worn, burnt or pitted, then renewal must be considered; refer to an automobile electrical system specialist for further guidance.

7 Reassemble the alternator by following the dismantling procedure in reverse. On completion, refer to Section 5 and refit the alternator.

7 Starting system – testing

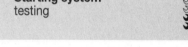

Note: *Refer to the precautions given in 'Safety first!' and in Section 1 of this Chapter before starting work.*

1 If the starter motor fails to operate when the ignition key is turned to the appropriate position, the following possible causes may be to blame:

   a) *The battery is faulty.*
   b) *The electrical connections between the switch, solenoid, battery and starter motor are somewhere failing to pass the necessary current from the battery through the starter to earth.*
   c) *The solenoid is faulty.*
   d) *The starter motor is mechanically or electrically defective.*

2 To check the battery, switch on the headlights. If they dim after a few seconds, this indicates that the battery is discharged – recharge (see Section 2) or renew the battery. If the headlights glow brightly, operate the ignition switch and observe the lights. If they dim, then this indicates that current is reaching the starter motor, therefore the fault must lie in the starter motor. If the lights continue to glow brightly (and no clicking sound can be heard from the starter motor solenoid), this indicates that there is a fault in the circuit or solenoid – see following paragraphs. If the starter motor turns slowly when operated, but the battery is in good condition, then this indicates that either the starter motor is faulty, or there is considerable resistance somewhere in the circuit.

3 If a fault in the circuit is suspected, disconnect the battery leads (including the earth connection to the body), the starter/solenoid wiring and the engine/transmission earth strap. Thoroughly clean the connections, and reconnect the leads and wiring, then use a voltmeter or test light to check that full battery voltage is available at the battery positive lead connection to the solenoid, and that the earth is sound. Smear petroleum jelly (not grease) around the battery terminals to prevent corrosion – corroded connections are amongst the most frequent causes of electrical system faults.

4 If the battery and all connections are in good condition, check the circuit by disconnecting the wire from the solenoid blade terminal. Connect a voltmeter or test light between the wire end and a good earth (such as the battery negative terminal), and check that the wire is live when the ignition switch is turned to the 'start' position. If it is, then the circuit is sound – if not the circuit wiring can be checked as described in Chapter 12.

5 The solenoid contacts can be checked by connecting a voltmeter or test light between the battery positive feed connection on the starter side of the solenoid, and earth. When the ignition switch is turned to the 'start' position, there should be a reading or lighted bulb, as applicable. If there is no reading or lighted bulb, the solenoid is faulty and should be renewed.

6 If the circuit and solenoid are proved sound, the fault must lie in the starter motor.

Begin checking the starter motor by removing it (see Section 8), and checking the brushes. If the fault does not lie in the brushes, the motor windings must be faulty. In this event, it may be possible to have the starter motor overhauled by a specialist, but check on the availability and cost of spares before proceeding, as it may prove more economical to obtain a new or exchange motor.

8 Starter motor – removal and refitting

Note: *Access to the starter motor is difficult from above or below. For clarity, the accompanying photographs were taken after removing the inlet manifold. Whilst this is not essential, it does make the job of removing the starter motor much easier – see the Chapter 4A for inlet manifold removal details.*

Removal

1 Disconnect the battery negative lead and position it away from the terminal.

2 Pull off the black plastic cap (where fitted), then disconnect the wiring from the starter solenoid **(see illustration)**.

3 Disconnect the remaining wiring from the starter motor, removing the retaining nuts and washers as necessary **(see illustrations)**.

4 Remove the longer lower through-bolt, then the two upper bolts; one of the upper bolts is 'captive', and the other has a nut. Release the starter motor from the bellhousing, and guide

8.2 Disconnect the wiring plug . . .

8.3a . . . then loosen and remove the nut . . .

8.3b . . . and disconnect the remaining wiring

8.4a Loosening one of the starter motor mounting bolts

8.4b Removing the starter motor

it out of the engine compartment **(see illustrations)**.

Refitting

5 Refit the starter motor by following the removal procedure in reverse. Tighten the mounting bolts to the specified torque.

9 Starter motor – testing and overhaul

If the starter motor is thought to be defective, it should be removed from the car and taken to an auto-electrician for assessment. In the majority of cases, new starter motor brushes can be fitted at a reasonable cost. However, check the cost of repairs first, as it may prove more economical to purchase a new or exchange motor.

Chapter 5 Part B:
Ignition system

Contents

Degrees of difficulty

Easy, suitable for novice with little experience	**Fairly easy,** suitable for beginner with some experience	**Fairly difficult,** suitable for competent DIY mechanic	**Difficult,** suitable for experienced DIY mechanic	**Very difficult,** suitable for expert DIY or professional

Specifications

System type
See Chapter 4A Specifications

Ignition coil
Type	Single DIS coil with four HT lead outputs
Primary winding resistance	N/A
Secondary resistance	4000 to 6000 ohms

Spark plugs
See Chapter 1 Specifications

Torque wrench settings	Nm	lbf ft
Ignition coil mounting bolts	10	7
Knock sensor mounting bolt	20	15
Spark plugs	30	22

1 General information

The Bosch Motronic and Magneti-Marelli systems are self-contained engine management systems, which control both the fuel injection and ignition. This Chapter deals with the ignition system components only – refer to Chapter 4A for details of the fuel system components.

The ignition system fitted to all models is of the increasingly popular 'distributorless' (DIS – Distributorless Ignition System) or 'static' type (there are no moving parts). All models have a single ignition coil unit with four HT lead terminals; therefore, these systems have no distributor cap or rotor arm, resulting in a simpler, more reliable system requiring even less maintenance.

Because there is no distributor to adjust, the ignition timing cannot be adjusted by conventional means, and the advance and retard functions are carried out by the Electronic Control Unit (ECU).

The ignition system comprises the spark plugs, HT leads, electronic ignition coil unit (or DIS module), and the ECU together with its associated sensors and wiring.

The ECU supplies a voltage to the input stage of the ignition coil, which causes the primary windings in the coil to be energised. The supply voltage is periodically interrupted by the ECU and this results in the collapse of primary magnetic field, which then induces a much larger voltage in the secondary coil, called the HT voltage. This voltage is directed (via the HT leads) to the spark plug in the cylinder currently on its ignition stroke. The spark plug electrodes form a gap small enough for the HT voltage to arc across, and the resulting spark ignites the fuel/air mixture in the cylinder. The timing of this sequence of events is critical, and is regulated solely by the ECU.

The ECU calculates and controls the ignition timing primarily according to engine speed, crankshaft position, camshaft position, and inlet airflow rate information, received from sensors mounted on and around the engine. Other parameters that affect ignition timing are throttle position and rate of opening, inlet air temperature, coolant temperature and engine knock, monitored via sensors mounted on the engine. Note that most of these sensors have a dual role, in that the information they provide is equally useful in determining the fuelling requirements as in deciding the optimum ignition or firing point – therefore, removal of some of the sensors mentioned below are described in Chapter 4A.

The ECU computes engine speed and crankshaft position from toothed impulse rotor attached to the engine flywheel, with an engine speed sensor whose inductive head runs just above rotor. As the crankshaft (and flywheel) rotate, the rotor 'teeth' pass the engine speed sensor, which transmits a pulse to the ECU every time a tooth passes it. At the top dead centre (TDC) position, there is one missing tooth in the rotor periphery, which results in a longer pause between signals from the sensor. The ECU recognises the absence of a pulse from the engine speed sensor at this point, and uses it to establish the TDC position for No 1 piston. The time interval between pulses, and the location of the missing pulse, allow the ECU to accurately determine the position of the crankshaft and its speed. The camshaft position sensor enhances this information by detecting whether a particular piston is on an inlet or an exhaust cycle.

Information on engine load is supplied to the ECU via the inlet manifold pressure sensor, and from the throttle position sensor. The engine load is determined by computation based on the quantity of air being drawn into the engine. Further engine load information is sent to the ECU from the knock sensor(s). These sensors are sensitive to vibration, and detect the knocking which occurs when the engine starts to 'pink' (pre-ignite). If pre-ignition occurs, the ECU retards the ignition timing of the cylinder that is pre-igniting in steps until the pre-ignition ceases. The ECU then advances the ignition timing of that cylinder in steps until it is restored to normal, or until pre-ignition occurs again.

Sensors monitoring coolant temperature, throttle position, roadspeed, and (where applicable) automatic transmission gear position and air conditioning system operation, provide additional input signals to the ECU on vehicle operating conditions. From all this constantly-changing data, the ECU selects, and if necessary modifies, a particular ignition advance setting from a map of ignition characteristics stored in its memory.

The ECU also uses the ignition timing to finely adjust the engine idle speed, in response to signals from the power steering switch or air conditioning switch (to prevent stalling), or if the alternator output voltage falls too low.

In the event of a fault in the system due to loss of a signal from one of the sensors, the ECU reverts to an emergency ('limp-home') program. This will allow the car to be driven, although engine operation and performance will be limited. A warning light on the instrument panel will illuminate if the fault is likely to cause an increase in harmful exhaust emissions.

It should be noted that comprehensive fault diagnosis of all the engine management systems described in this Chapter is only possible with dedicated electronic test equipment. In the event of a sensor failing or other fault occurring, a fault code will be stored in the ECU's fault log, which can only be extracted from the ECU using a dedicated fault code reader. A VW dealer will obviously have such a reader, but they are also available from other suppliers. It is unlikely to be cost-effective for the private owner to purchase a fault code reader, but a well-equipped local garage or auto-electrical specialist will have one. Once the fault has been identified, the removal/refitting sequences detailed in the following Sections will then allow the appropriate component(s) to be renewed as required.

DIS module

The ignition coil unit (DIS module) operates on the 'wasted spark' principle. The unit in fact contains two separate coils – one for cylinders 1 and 4, the other for cylinders 2 and 3. Each of the two coils produces an HT voltage at both outputs every time its primary coil voltage is interrupted – ie, cylinders 1 and 4 always 'fire' together, then 2 and 3 'fire' together. When this happens, one of the two cylinders concerned will be on the com-pression stroke (and will ignite the fuel/air mixture), while the other one is on the exhaust stroke – because the spark on the exhaust stroke has no effect, it is effectively wasted, hence the term 'wasted spark'.

2 Ignition system – testing

Warning: Extreme care must be taken when working on the system with the ignition switched on; it is possible to get a substantial electric shock from a vehicle's ignition system. Persons with cardiac pacemaker devices should keep well clear of the ignition circuits, components and test equipment. Always switch off the ignition before disconnecting or connecting any component and when using a multimeter to check resistances.

1 If a fault appears in the engine management (fuel injection/ignition) system which is thought to be ignition-related, first ensure that the fault is not due to a poor electrical connection or poor maintenance; ie, check that the air cleaner filter element is clean, the spark plugs are in good condition and correctly gapped, that the engine breather hoses are clear and undamaged, referring to Chapter 1 for further information. If the engine is running very roughly, check the compression pressures as described in Chapter 2A or 2B (as applicable).

2 The only other likely cause of ignition trouble is the HT leads, linking the DIS module to the spark plugs. Check the leads as follows. Never disconnect more than one HT lead at a time to avoid possible confusion.

3 Pull the first lead from the plug by gripping the end fitting, not the lead, otherwise the lead connection may be fractured. Check inside the end fitting for signs of corrosion, which will

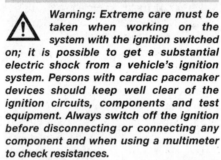

3.1 The DIS module is mounted on the top/end of the engine

look like a white crusty powder. Push the end fitting back onto the spark plug, ensuring that it is a tight fit on the plug. If not, remove the lead again and use pliers to carefully crimp the metal connector inside the end fitting until it fits securely on the end of the spark plug.

4 Using a clean rag, wipe the entire length of the lead to remove any built-up dirt and grease. Once the lead is clean, check for burns, cracks and other damage. Do not bend the lead excessively, nor pull the lead lengthwise – the conductor inside is quite fragile, and might break.

5 Disconnect the other end of the lead from the DIS module. Again, pull only on the end fitting. Check for corrosion and a tight fit in the same manner as the spark plug end.

6 If an ohmmeter is available, check for continuity between the HT lead terminals. If there is no continuity the lead is faulty and must be renewed (as a guide, the resistance of each lead should be in the region of 4 to 8 kilohms).

7 Refit the lead securely on completion, then check the remaining leads one at a time, in the same way. If there is any doubt about the condition of any HT leads, renew them as a complete set.

8 If these checks fail to reveal the cause of the problem, the car should be taken to a suitably-equipped VW dealer for testing. A diagnostic connector is incorporated in the engine management circuit (under the ashtray in the centre console) into which a special electronic diagnostic tester can be plugged (see Chapter 4A). The tester will locate the fault quickly and simply, alleviating the need to test all the system components individually which is a time consuming operation that carries a high risk of damaging the ECU.

9 The only ignition system checks which can be carried out by the home mechanic are those described in Chapter 1, relating to the spark plugs. If necessary, the system wiring and wiring connectors can be checked as described in Chapter 12 ensuring that the ECU wiring connector(s) have first been disconnected.

3 DIS module – removal and refitting

Removal

1 The DIS module (ignition coil unit) is mounted on top of the engine, at the transmission end **(see illustration)**.

2 Make sure the ignition is switched off (take out the key).

3 On SOHC engines, remove the air cleaner as described in Chapter 1; on DOHC engines, remove the engine top cover, which is secured by four Allen bolts.

4 Unplug the module wiring plug (LT connector) at the rear of the module **(see illustration)**.

3.4 Disconnect the LT wiring plug from the module

3.6a Note their positions, then disconnect the HT leads . . .

3.6b . . . unscrew the three Allen bolts, and remove the module

5 The original HT leads should be marked from 1 to 4, corresponding to the cylinder/spark plug they serve (No 1 is at the timing belt end of the engine). Some leads are also marked from A to D, and corresponding markings are found on the ignition coil HT terminals – in this case, cylinder A corresponds to No 1, B to No 2, and so on. If there are no markings present, label the HT leads before disconnecting, and either paint a marking on the ignition coil terminals, take a digital photo, or make a sketch of the lead positions for use when reconnecting.

6 Disconnect the HT leads from the ignition coil terminals, then unscrew the three mounting bolts and remove the coil unit from the engine **(see illustrations)**.

Refitting

7 Refitting is a reversal of the relevant removal procedure, noting the following points:
- a) *Tighten the coil mounting bolts to the specified torque.*
- b) *Use the marks noted before disconnecting when refitting the HT leads – if wished, spray a little water-dispersant (such as WD-40) onto each connector as it is refitted (this can also be used on the LT wiring connector).*

4 Ignition timing – general

The ignition timing is under the control of the engine management system ECU, and is not manually adjustable without access to dedicated electronic test equipment. A basic setting cannot be quoted because the ignition timing is constantly being altered to control engine idle speed (see Section 1 for details).

The car must be taken to a VW dealer if the timing requires checking or adjustment.

5 Knock sensor – removal and refitting

Removal

1 The knock sensor is located on the inlet manifold side of the cylinder block.

2 Access to the knock sensor is very awkward, but it can only be improved by removing the inlet manifold (see Chapter 4A).

3 Alternatively, firmly apply the handbrake, then jack up the front of the car and support it on axle stands (see *Jacking and vehicle support*). Undo the retaining screws and

5.4 Knock sensor and mounting bolt (seen with engine removed)

remove any engine undershield(s) as necessary so access to the knock sensor can be gained form underneath.

4 Disconnect the wiring connector from the sensor, unscrew the mounting bolt, and remove the sensor from the cylinder block **(see illustration)**.

Refitting

5 Refitting is the reverse of removal, noting the following points:
- a) *Ensure the mating surfaces of the sensor and cylinder block are clean and dry.*
- b) *The sensor mounting bolt must be tightened to the specified torque to ensure correct operation.*

Chapter 6
Clutch

Contents

Degrees of difficulty

Easy, suitable for novice with little experience	**Fairly easy,** suitable for beginner with some experience	**Fairly difficult,** suitable for competent DIY mechanic	**Difficult,** suitable for experienced DIY mechanic	**Very difficult,** suitable for expert DIY or professional

Specifications

General

Type	Single dry plate, diaphragm spring with spring-loaded hub
Operation:	
Right-hand-drive models	Cable with manual adjustment
Left-hand-drive models	Cable with automatic adjustment mechanism
Clutch disc diameter	190 mm

Torque wrench settings

	Nm	lbf ft
Pedal mounting bracket bolts	25	18
Pedal pivot pin nut	25	18
Pressure plate-to-flywheel bolts	20	15

---

1 General information

Manual transmission models are fitted with a pedal-operated single dry plate clutch system. When the clutch pedal is depressed, effort is transmitted to the clutch release mechanism mechanically, by means of a cable. The release mechanism transfers effort to the pressure plate diaphragm spring, which withdraws from the flywheel and releases the driven plate.

The flywheel is mounted on the crankshaft, with the pressure plate bolted to it. Removal of the flywheel is described in Chapter 2A.
Note: *Problems with the clutch failing to disengage may be due to distortion or partial collapse of the clutch and brake pedal bracket (also known as the pedal box). Removal of this bracket is described in Chapter 9, Section 14.*

2 Clutch cable – removal, refitting and adjustment

Note: *Left-hand-drive models were fitted with an automatic adjuster system, while right-hand-drive (eg, UK market) models have a manually-adjusted cable. Refer to the relevant sections below, according to your particular model.*

Manual adjuster

Removal

1 At the clutch release lever, loosen the cable adjuster locknut and adjuster nut, then press the cable sideways out of the release lever **(see illustration)**.
2 Pull the cable end fitting upwards from the gearbox mounting **(see illustration)**.
3 Working in the driver's footwell, remove the driver's side lower trim panel as described in Chapter 11, Section 26, for access to the foot pedals.

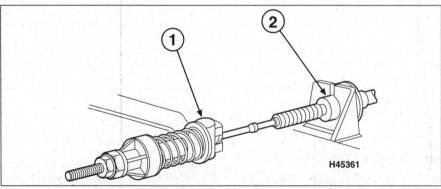

2.1 Clutch cable attachment at transmission (1) and release lever (2)

2.2 Pull the cable upwards to release it from the gearbox mounting

4 Remove the clutch pedal cover from the pedal mounting bracket, then unhook the cable end fitting from the top of the clutch pedal, and withdraw the cable into the engine compartment.

5 Release the cable from its mountings in the engine compartment, and remove the cable from the car.

Refitting

6 Refitting is a reversal of removal of removal, noting the following points:
   a) Lubricate all pivot points with a multi-purpose grease.
   b) Take care that the cable is not kinked as it is fitted.
   c) Adjust the cable as described below.

Adjustment

7 At the release lever, loosen the adjuster locknut, and turn the adjuster nut to give 15 to 20 mm of free travel at the clutch pedal. Some trial-and-error may be involved before satisfactory clutch operation is achieved. With the handbrake firmly applied, start the engine and select a gear to assess the clutch 'bite point'.

8 When adjustment is complete, tighten the locknut securely, while ensuring the adjuster nut does not move.

Automatic adjustment system

Removal

9 Depress the clutch pedal several times, to settle the automatic adjustment mechanism.

10 Working in the engine bay, slide the

3.4 Home-made flywheel locking tool in use

2.12 Compressing the adjustment mechanism using the locking strap

locking strap down to the top of the adjustment mechanism protective boot.

11 Pull the release lever approximately 10 mm towards the front of the car – this will compress the adjuster mechanism.

12 While the mechanism is compressed, hook the ends of the locking strap over the lugs protruding from the side of the adjustment mechanism **(see illustration)**. It may be necessary to enlist the help of an assistant for this. **Note:** *If the locking strap is no longer attached to the clutch cable, a home-made strap can be fabricated using cable-ties or a length of electrical cable.*

13 Press the cable outer sideways to release the mounting rubber from the clutch release arm.

14 Pull the inner cable end fitting from the gearbox mounting.

15 Remove the driver's side lower trim panel as described in Chapter 11, Section 26, for access to the foot pedals.

16 Remove the clutch pedal cover from the pedal mounting bracket, then unhook the cable end fitting from the top of the clutch pedal, and withdraw the cable into the engine compartment.

17 Release the cable from its mountings in the engine compartment, and remove the cable from the car.

Refitting

18 Refitting is a reversal of removal of removal, noting the following points:
   a) Lubricate all pivot points with a multi-purpose grease.
   b) Take care that the cable is not kinked as it is fitted.
   c) Once the cable is attached to the release arm, gearbox mounting and pedal, unhook the locking strap from the adjustment mechanism.
   d) Check the operation of the adjuster, by pulling the release lever approximately 10 mm in the opposite direction to its normal direction of travel (ie, towards the front of the car). The release lever should move freely.

All models

19 On completion, assess the feel of the clutch pedal before bringing the car back into service. If it exhibits any stiffness or shows

signs of binding, check the routing of the cable and ensure that there are no sharp bends or kinks along its length.

20 Finally, road test the car and check the operation of the clutch whilst changing up and down through the gears, whilst pulling away from a standstill and from a hill start.

---

3 Clutch assembly – removal, inspection and refitting

⚠ *Warning: Dust created by clutch wear and deposited on the clutch components may contain asbestos, which is a health hazard. DO NOT blow it out with compressed air or inhale any of it. DO NOT use petrol or petroleum-based solvents to clean off the dust. Brake system cleaner or methylated spirit should be used to flush the dust into a suitable receptacle. After the clutch components are wiped clean with clean rags, dispose of the contaminated rags and cleaner in a sealed, marked container.* **Note**: *Some friction materials may no longer contain asbestos, but it is safest to assume they DO, and to take precautions accordingly.*

Removal

1 Access to the clutch is gained by removing the engine and transmission combined, and then separating the two units as described in Chapter 2C, or by removing the transmission as described in Chapter 7A. Unless it is wished to also carry out repairs to the engine, it is preferable to gain access by removing the transmission only.

2 Unclip the release bearing from the release lever, and examine it for signs of terminal wear or damage. Spin it by hand and listen to the bearings; if the bearing sticks or is unduly noisy, it should be renewed.

3 With the transmission separated from the engine, mark the pressure plate and flywheel in relation to each other as a guide for refitting.

4 The flywheel must be held stationary while the pressure plate bolts are loosened – use a screwdriver or home-made tool engaged in the flywheel ring gear for this **(see illustration)**. Progressively slacken the pressure plate bolts in diagonal sequence. With the bolts unscrewed two or three turns, check that the cover is not binding on the dowel pins. If necessary, use a screwdriver to release the cover.

5 Remove all the bolts, then lift the pressure plate and friction disc from the flywheel.

Inspection

Note: *Given the amount of dismantling work required to gain access to the clutch components, it is not advisable to refit any components unless they are known to have been recently fitted, or are obviously in as-new condition. Further, it is common practice*

3.15a Friction disc orientation

3.15b Fitting the clutch friction disc and pressure plate

3.17 Use a centralising tool to align the friction disc

when servicing the clutch to buy a complete kit (friction disc, pressure plate and release bearing) rather than just a new friction disc.

6 Clean the cover, disc, and flywheel. *Do not inhale the dust, as it may contain asbestos which is dangerous to health.*

7 Examine the fingers of the diaphragm spring for wear or scoring. If the depth of any scoring exceeds the figure specified at the start of this Chapter, a new cover assembly must be fitted.

8 Examine the pressure plate for scoring, cracking and discoloration. Light scoring is acceptable, but if excessive, a new cover assembly must be fitted.

9 Examine the friction disc linings for wear, cracking, and for contamination with oil or grease. The linings are worn excessively if they are worn down to, or near, the rivets. Check the disc hub and splines for wear, by temporarily fitting it on the transmission input shaft. Renew the friction disc as necessary. If possible, check that the lateral run-out of the friction disc measured 2.5 mm from its outer edge does not exceed the specified amount.

10 If there is any evidence of contamination by oil or grease, the source of the leak should be traced and rectified before fitting new clutch components, otherwise the new parts will quickly go the same way. There is no satisfactory way to degrease the friction disc, once contaminated.

11 Examine the flywheel friction surface for scoring, cracking, and discoloration (caused by overheating). If excessive, it may be possible to have the flywheel machined by an engineering works, otherwise it should be renewed.

12 Before refitting the clutch, it is advisable to inspect the condition of the release bearing and lever. Spin the release bearing by hand, and check it for any signs of roughness (it is usually considered good practice to renew the bearing at the same time as the friction disc). If the release lever bushes are excessively worn, they can be drifted out and renewed. Lubricate the release lever shaft pivots and release bearing guide sleeve sparingly with high-temperature grease.

Refitting

13 Ensure that all parts are clean, and free of oil or grease, before reassembling. Apply just a small amount of high melting-point grease to the splines of the friction disc hub. Note that new pressure plates may be supplied coated with protective grease. It is only permissible to clean the grease away from the friction disc lining contact area. Removal of the grease from other areas will shorten the service life of the clutch.

14 Study the relevant illustration to ensure that the clutch friction disc is fitted the correct way round.

15 Locate the friction disc into position, then fit the pressure plate on the disc, engaging it onto the location dowels **(see illustrations)**. Hold the disc as central as possible while doing this. If refitting the original cover, make sure that the previously-made marks are aligned.

16 Insert the bolts finger-tight to hold the cover in position, but to allow movement of the friction disc.

17 The friction disc must now be centralised, to ensure correct alignment of the transmission input shaft with the clutch components and the spigot bearing in the crankshaft. To do this, a proprietary tool may be used, or alternatively, use a wooden mandrel can be made to suit. Insert the tool through the friction disc into the spigot bearing, and make sure that it is central **(see illustration)**. Failure to centralise the friction disc will mean that the transmission input shaft will not be able to pass through the clutch components, making reconnecting the engine and transmission impossible. Time spent getting the centralisation correct is time well-spent.

18 Tighten the pressure plate bolts progressively and in diagonal sequence, until the specified torque setting is reached, then remove the centralising tool.

19 Refit the engine and/or transmission with reference to Chapter 2C or 7A, as applicable.

Chapter 7 Part A:
Manual transmission

Contents

Degrees of difficulty

Easy, suitable for novice with little experience	**Fairly easy,** suitable for beginner with some experience	**Fairly difficult,** suitable for competent DIY mechanic	**Difficult,** suitable for experienced DIY mechanic	**Very difficult,** suitable for expert DIY or professional

Specifications

General

Description	Transverse-mounted, front-wheel-drive layout with integral transaxle differential/final drive. Five forward speeds, one reverse speed
Transmission type number	085
Gear selection	Rod or cable operation, depending on model

Torque wrench settings

	Nm	lbf ft
Angle piece bolts	15	11
Cable mounting bracket bolts	25	18
Cable mounting bracket-to-angle piece bolt	20	15
Cable support bracket nut	20	15
Gate selector finger bolt	20	15
Gate selector rod-to-finger nut	20	15
Gear selector cable-to-selector lever bolt	20	15
Rod-type gear selector finger bolt*	20	15
Transmission bellhousing-to-engine bolts:		
M7 bolt	15	11
M8 bolts	20	15
M12 bolts	80	59
Transmission support cable pin	20	15

* Use new bolt, with thread-locking fluid

1 General information

The manual transmission is mounted transversely in the engine bay, bolted directly to the engine. This layout has the advantage of providing the shortest possible drive path to the front wheels, as well as locating the transmission in the airflow through engine bay, optimising cooling. The unit is cased in aluminium alloy.

Drive from the crankshaft is transmitted via the clutch to the gearbox input shaft, which is splined to accept the clutch friction disc.

All forward gears are fitted with syncromeshes. When a gear is selected, the movement of the cabin floor-mounted gear lever is communicated to the gearbox either by a selector rod, or gate and gear selector cables, depending on the transmission type. This in turn actuates a series of selector forks inside the gearbox, which are slotted onto the synchromesh sleeves. The sleeves, which are locked to the gearbox shafts but can slide axially by means of splined hubs, press baulk rings into contact with the respective gear/pinion. The coned surfaces between the baulk rings and the pinion/gear act as a friction clutch, that progressively matches the speed of the synchromesh sleeve (and hence the gearbox shaft) with that of the gear/pinion. The dog teeth on the outside of the baulk ring prevent the synchromesh sleeve ring from meshing with the gear/pinion until their speeds are exactly matched; this allows gear changes to be carried out smoothly, and greatly reduces the noise and mechanical wear caused by rapid gearchanges.

Drive is transmitted to the differential crownwheel, which rotates the differential case and planetary gears, thus driving the sun gears and driveshafts. The rotation of the planetary gears on their shaft allows the inner roadwheel to rotate at a slower speed than the outer roadwheel during cornering.

All models, regardless of whether a rod-type or cable gear linkage is fitted, have a transmission support cable fitted between the transmission and the gear lever housing. The cable, which is under tension, is intended to absorb any movement from the transmission, which would otherwise be transmitted through the gear lever.

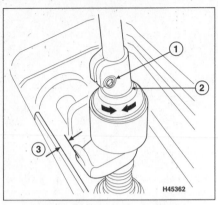

**2.4 Gearchange lever adjustment –
models with rod-type linkage**

1 Clamp bolt
2 Adjustment collar
3 Clearance less
   than 1.5 mm

2 Gearchange linkage – adjustment

Rod-type linkage

1 If the gearchange quality proves unsatisfactory following transmission refitting, proceed as described in the following paragraphs.

2 Unclip the gaiter from around the gear lever, to expose the adjustment collar.

3 Select first gear, then take up the play in the gearchange mechanism by gently pressing the gear lever to the left.

4 Measure the clearance between the gear lever stop and the side of the lever housing **(see illustration)**.

5 If the clearance is not between 1 and 2 mm, slacken the adjustment collar clamping bolt and rotate the collar until the correct clearance is achieved **(see illustration 2.4)**.

6 On completion, tighten the clamping bolt. Refit the gear lever gaiter and knob.

Cable linkage

7 To accurately adjust the operation of the gate and gear selector cables, precisely-machined jigs are required to set the gear lever in a reference position. It is recommended, therefore, that this operation be entrusted to a VW dealer.

3.7a Remove the securing nut . . .

3 Manual transmission – removal and refitting

Removal

1 Select a solid, level surface to park the car upon. Give yourself enough space to move around it easily. Apply the handbrake and chock the rear wheels.

2 Loosen the front wheel bolts, then raise the front of the car and rest it securely on axle stands (see *Jacking and vehicle support*). Remove the front wheels.

3 Refer to Chapter 11 and remove the bonnet from its hinges.

4 Disconnect the battery negative lead and position it away from the terminal (see *Disconnecting the battery*).

5 The 'lock carrier' is a panel assembly comprising the front valance and bonnet lock mechanism, radiator and grille, cooling fan, and headlight units. Its removal gives greatly-improved access to the engine and transmission, and allows them to be lifted out of the car via the front of the engine bay. Its removal is described at the beginning of the engine removal procedure – refer to Chapter 2C for details.

6 Disconnect the clutch cable from the transmission release lever (see Chapter 6).

7 Unbolt the earth strap from the transmission **(see illustrations)**.

8 Referring to Sections 5 and 6, disconnect the wiring plugs from the reversing light

3.7b . . . and disconnect the transmission earth strap

switch and roadspeed sensor. Where applicable, disconnect any additional wiring plugs at the front of the transmission, and release the wiring harness from any securing clips **(see illustration)**.

9 Referring to Chapter 8, disconnect both driveshafts from the flanges on the transmission – tie both driveshafts up out of the way, with the left-hand driveshaft up as high as possible. Turn the steering wheel to full left lock.

Models with rod-type gear linkage

10 Loosen the selector finger bolt, and remove the selector finger from below the transmission. Discard the bolt – a new one must be used on refitting.

11 Prise off the retaining circlip, and lever off the transmission support cable (where fitted) from the transmission housing. Recover the bush from the cable end fitting, and discard it – a new bush must be used on refitting.

Models with cable gear linkage

12 Unscrew the through-bolt and disconnect the gear selector cable from the selector lever. Remove the spring clip and detach the gate selector cable from the relay lever. Remove the retaining circlips and detach the cables from the cable support bracket **(see illustrations)**.

13 Remove the two angle-piece bolts at the rear, and the nut at the front, and lift off the cable support bracket from the top of the transmission. It may be necessary to push the exhaust system over slightly, to give sufficient clearance to remove the support bracket.

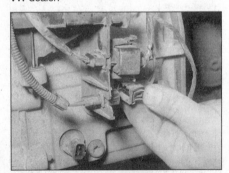

3.8 Disconnect any wiring harness multiplugs at the front of the gearbox

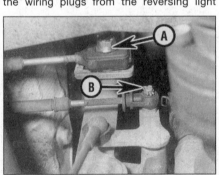

3.12a Gear selector cable through-bolt (A) and gate selector cable spring clip (B)

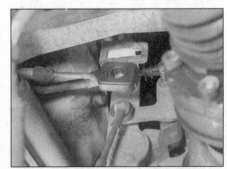

3.12b Gear selector and gate selector cables disconnected

14 Prise off the retaining circlip, and lever off the transmission support cable (where fitted) from the transmission housing. Recover the bush from the cable end fitting, and discard it – a new bush must be used on refitting **(see illustration)**.

All models

15 Unbolt the flywheel shield plate from the underside of the transmission bellhousing.
16 Position a trolley jack underneath the transmission, and raise it to just take the weight of the unit.
17 Unscrew and remove the upper bolts securing the transmission bellhousing to the engine, noting the locations of the bolts, as they are of different sizes and lengths.
18 Referring to Chapter 2A or 2B as applicable, unbolt and remove the engine/transmission rear mounting.
19 Where applicable, unbolt and remove the inlet manifold support bracket.
20 Refer to Chapter 5A and remove the starter motor.
21 Ensure that the weight of the engine and transmission is adequately supported, then unscrew and remove the two bolts securing the transmission to the left-hand mounting (refer to Chapter 2A or 2B, as applicable).
22 Carefully tilt the engine and transmission assembly down at the transmission end, making sure the weight of the transmission is still adequately supported. Check that nothing remains attached to the transmission housing which would prevent its removal.
23 Unscrew and remove the lower bolts securing the transmission bellhousing to the engine, again noting the bolt locations, as they are of different sizes and lengths.
24 Carefully prise the transmission off its locating dowels, and move it to the side, to clear the clutch components.

⚠️ *Warning: Support the transmission to ensure that it remains steady on the jack head. Keep the transmission level until the input shaft is fully withdrawn from the clutch friction disc.*

25 When all the locating dowels are clear of their mounting holes, lower the transmission out of the engine bay using the jack.

Refitting

26 Refitting the transmission is essentially a reversal of the removal procedure, but note the following points:
 a) *Apply a smear of high-melting-point grease to the clutch friction disc splines; take care to avoid contaminating the friction surfaces.*
 b) *Tighten the bellhousing bolts to the specified torque.*
 c) *Refer to Chapter 2A or 2B (as applicable) and tighten the engine and transmission mounting bolts to the correct torque.*
 d) *On models with the rod-type gear linkage, when refitting the selector finger, clean its threaded hole with an M8 tap, and fit a*

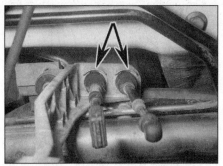

3.12c Cable retaining circlips (arrowed) at the cable support bracket

new bolt using thread-locking fluid. The finger should be assembled so that the bolt fits into the forward recess in the inner finger.
 e) *When refitting the transmission support cable, renew the cable bush at the transmission end.*
 f) *Refer to Chapter 6 when refitting the clutch cable.*
 g) *On completion, refer to Section 2 and check the gearchange linkage adjustment.*

4 Manual transmission overhaul – general information

The overhaul of a manual transmission is a complex (and often expensive) engineering task for the DIY home mechanic to undertake, which requires access to specialist equipment. It involves dismantling and reassembly of many small components, measuring clearances precisely and if necessary, adjusting them by the selection shims and spacers. Internal transmission components are also often difficult to obtain and in many instances, extremely expensive. Because of this, if the transmission develops a fault or becomes noisy, the best course of action is to have the unit overhauled by a specialist repairer or to obtain an exchange reconditioned unit.

Nevertheless, it is not impossible for the more experienced mechanic to overhaul the

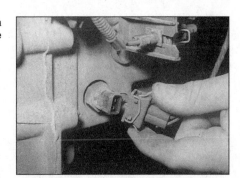

5.2 Disconnecting the reversing light switch

3.14 Prise off the circlip, and lever off the transmission support cable – renew bush in cable end fitting (arrowed)

transmission if the special tools are available and the job is carried out in a deliberate step-by-step manner, to ensure that nothing is overlooked.

The tools necessary for an overhaul include internal and external circlip pliers, bearing pullers, a slide hammer, a set of pin punches, a dial test indicator, and possibly a hydraulic press. In addition, a large, sturdy workbench and a vice will be required.

During dismantling of the transmission, make careful notes of how each component is fitted to make reassembly easier and accurate.

Before dismantling the transmission, it will help if you have some idea of where the problem lies. Certain problems can be closely related to specific areas in the transmission which can make component examination and renewal easier. Refer to *Fault diagnosis* in the Reference section of this manual for more information.

5 Reversing light switch – testing, removal and refitting

Testing

1 Ensure that the ignition is turned off (take out the key).
2 Unplug the wiring harness from the reversing light switch at the connector **(see illustration)**. The switch is located on the front of the transmission casing, with the harness clipped into a retaining bracket above.
3 Connect the probes of a continuity tester, or multimeter set to the resistance measurement function, across the terminals of the reversing light switch.
4 The switch contacts are normally open, so with any gear other than reverse selected, the tester/meter should indicate an open circuit. When reverse gear is then selected, the switch contacts should close, causing the tester/meter to indicate a short circuit.
5 If the switch appears to be constantly open or short circuit, or is intermittent in its operation, it should be renewed.

6.3 Disconnecting the roadspeed sensor connector on top of the transmission

Removal

6 Ensure that the ignition is turned off (take out the key).

7 Unplug the wiring harness from the reversing light switch at the connector.

8 Slacken the switch body using a ring spanner and withdraw it from the transmission casing. Recover the sealing ring, where fitted.

Refitting

9 Refit the switch by reversing the removal procedure.

---

6 Roadspeed sensor/ speedometer drive – removal and refitting

General information

1 All transmissions are fitted with an electronic roadspeed sensor. This device measures the rotational speed of the transmission final drive, and converts the information into an electronic signal, which is then sent to the speedometer module in the instrument panel. On most models, the signal is also used as an input by the engine management system ECU.

Removal

2 Ensure that the ignition is turned off (take out the key).

3 Locate the speed sensor, at the top of the transmission casing. Unplug the wiring harness from the sensor, at the connector **(see illustration)**.

4 Unscrew the transducer using a suitable spanner, and withdraw the unit from the transmission casing.

5 Recover the sealing ring, where fitted.

Refitting

6 Refit the sensor by following the removal procedure in reverse.

Chapter 7 Part B:
Automatic transmission

Contents

Degrees of difficulty

Easy, suitable for novice with little experience	Fairly easy, suitable for beginner with some experience	Fairly difficult, suitable for competent DIY mechanic	Difficult, suitable for experienced DIY mechanic	Very difficult, suitable for expert DIY or professional 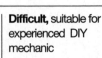

Specifications

General

Transmission type number 001
Application . . . . 1.4 litre engine models
Description . . . . Electro-hydraulically controlled planetary gearbox providing four forward speeds and one reverse speed. Drive transmitted through hydrokinetic torque converter. Lock-up clutch on top two speeds, electronic control unit (ECU). Two driving modes, selected automatically by ECU

Ratios (typical)

1st 2.875:1
2nd 1.512:1
3rd 1.000:1
4th 0.726:1
Reverse 2.656:1

Torque wrench settings

	Nm	lbf ft
Driveshaft-to-swivel hub bolt	110	81
Fluid pan bolts	8	6
Fluid temperature sender unit	8	6
Roadspeed sensor mounting bolt	6	4
Selector cable-to-selector lever locking bolt	23	17
Selector shaft lever nut	13	10
Series resistance mounting bolt	6	4
Torque converter shield plate nuts	15	11
Torque converter-to-driveplate bolts	60	44
Transmission bellhousing-to-engine bolts:		
M10 bolts	60	44
M12 bolts	80	59
Transmission speed sensor mounting bolt	6	4

1 General information

The VW type 001 automatic transmission has four forward speeds (and one reverse). The automatic gearchanges are electronically controlled, rather than hydraulically as with previous conventional types. The advantage of electronic management is to provide a faster gearchange response. A kickdown facility is also provided, to enable a faster acceleration response when required.

The transmission consists of three main assemblies, these being the torque converter, which is directly coupled to the engine; the final drive unit, which incorporates the differential unit; and the planetary gearbox, with its multi-disc clutches and brake bands. The transmission is lubricated with automatic transmission fluid (ATF), and is regarded by the manufacturers as being filled for life, with no requirement for the fluid to be changed at regular intervals. No provision is made for DIY checking of the fluid level, either – this must be carried out by a VW dealer, using special equipment capable of monitoring the fluid temperature.

The torque converter incorporates an automatic lock-up feature, which eliminates any possibility of converter slip in the top two gears; this aids performance and economy. In addition to the normal alternative of manual change, two further modes are available – sport or economy mode. In sport mode, upshifts are delayed longer, to make full use of engine power, while in economy mode, upshifts are taken as soon as possible, to permit optimum economy. The decision as to which operating mode to use is determined by the ECU, based on throttle position and its rate of change (this information is derived from the throttle potentiometer signal). In this way,

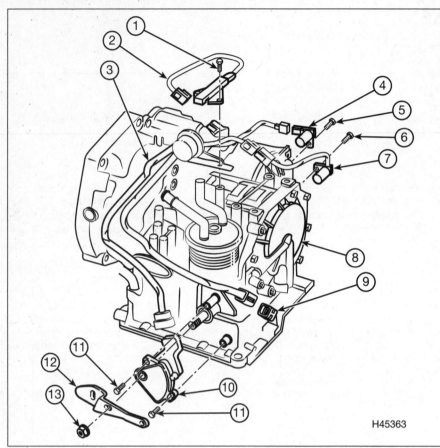

2.9 External components on the 001 automatic transmission

1 Bolt
2 Series resistance
3 Wiring harness
4 Roadspeed sensor
5 Bolt
6 Bolt
7 Transmission speed sender

8 Transmission
9 Solenoid valve wiring harness
10 Multi-function switch
11 Bolt
12 Selector shaft lever
13 Nut

H45363

gearchanges can be economy-orientated, but full acceleration is always available on demand.

Another feature of this transmission is the selector lever lock, with which the selector lever can be set in the P or N position when the engine is running, below about 3 mph. Under these conditions, selection from P or N can only be made by depressing the brake pedal. Correct functioning of the brake stop-light switch is therefore vital for this system to work correctly – see Chapter 9.

The transmission kickdown switch, which acts to select a lower gear (where possible) on full-throttle acceleration, is incorporated into the throttle position sensor (see Chapter 4A).

A starter inhibitor relay is fitted, to prevent starter motor operation unless the transmission is in P or N. The relay is located above the main fuse/relay panel (see Chapter 12), and is typically marked with the number 53.

Some models also feature a security/safety device which locks the transmission in P when the ignition key is removed (see Section 5).

The transmission is fitted with an electronic

roadspeed sensor **(see illustration 2.9)**. This device measures the rotational speed of the transmission final drive, and converts the information into an electronic signal, which is then sent to the speedometer module in the instrument panel. The signal is also used as an input by the engine management system ECU.

A fault diagnosis system is integrated into the control unit, but analysis can only be undertaken with specialised equipment. If a malfunction should occur in the transmission electrical system, automatic gear selection will continue, but the changes will be noticeably jerky. There is also an emergency running mode, in which 4th gear will not be selected. In the event of automatic selection failure, the selection of gears can be made manually. In any event, it is important that any transmission fault is identified and rectified at the earliest possible opportunity. Delay in doing so will only cause further problems. A VW dealer can interrogate the ECU fault memory for stored fault codes, enabling him

to pinpoint the fault quickly. Once the fault has been corrected and any fault codes have been cleared, normal transmission operation should be restored.

Because of the need for special test equipment, the complexity of some of the parts, and the need for scrupulous cleanliness when servicing automatic transmissions, the amount which the owner can do is limited. Repairs to the final drive differential are also not recommended. Most major repairs and overhaul operations should be left to a VW dealer, who will be equipped with the necessary equipment for fault diagnosis and repair. The information in this Chapter is therefore limited to a description of the removal and refitting of the transmission as a complete unit. The removal, refitting and adjustment of the selector cable is also described.

In the event of a transmission problem occurring, consult a VW dealer or transmission specialist before removing the transmission from the car, since the majority of fault diagnosis is carried out with the transmission in situ.

2 Automatic transmission – removal and refitting

Removal

1 Select a solid, level surface to park the car on. Give yourself enough space to move around it easily. Apply the handbrake and chock the rear wheels.

2 Loosen the front wheel bolts, and the left-hand driveshaft hub nut/bolt, then raise the front of the car and rest it securely on axle stands (see Jacking and vehicle support). Remove the front wheels. Allow a suitable working clearance underneath for the eventual withdrawal of the transmission.

3 Refer to Chapter 11 and remove the bonnet from its hinges.

4 The 'lock carrier' is a panel assembly comprising the front valance and bonnet lock mechanism, radiator and grille, cooling fan, and headlight units. Its removal gives greatly-improved access to the engine and transmission, and allows them to be lifted out of the car via the front of the engine bay. Its removal is described at the beginning of the engine removal procedure – refer to Chapter 2C for details.

5 Disconnect the battery negative lead and position It away from the terminal (see Disconnecting the battery).

6 Remove the battery as described in Chapter 5A, then remove the battery tray and the cable guide rail beneath.

7 Trace the wiring harness back from the radiator cooling fan motor, and remove the radiator fan control unit.

8 Referring to Chapter 4A, remove the air cleaner housing and air inlet trunking.

9 Disconnect all the wiring connections from

the transmission, labelling them if required for refitting **(see illustration opposite)**.

10 Using hose clamps, clamp off the fluid hoses at the fluid cooler, and disconnect the hoses.

11 Referring to Chapter 4B, remove the exhaust front downpipe and catalytic converter.

12 Referring to Chapter 8, disconnect both driveshafts from the flanges on the transmission – tie the right-hand shaft up out of the way. Remove the left-hand driveshaft completely.

13 Refer to Chapter 5A and remove the starter motor.

14 Remove three nuts and take off the torque converter shield plate from the underside of the transmission bellhousing.

15 Where fitted, remove the transmission sump guard from under the transmission.

16 Position the selector lever in P, then detach the selector cable from the lever on the transmission by unscrewing the shouldered retaining bolt; recover the serrated washer. Detach the cable retaining clip, and move the cable out of the way. The serrated washer should be discarded, and a new one fitted on reassembly.

17 Where applicable, detach the power steering pump fluid pipes from the radiator – there is no need to disconnect the fluid unions.

18 Remove the radiator cooling fan as described in Chapter 3.

19 The weight of the engine must now be supported while the engine/transmission mountings are removed. To do this, attach a lift sling to the engine, and raise it with an engine crane just enough to support the weight of the engine, or support the engine securely from below, taking care not to damage the sump. Alternatively, use an engine support beam which fits across the engine bay.

20 In order to create sufficient room for the transmission to be separated and removed, the auxiliary drivebelt and its crankshaft pulley must be removed as described in Chapter 2A or 2B.

21 Position a trolley jack underneath the transmission, and raise it to just take the weight of the unit.

22 Referring to Chapter 2A or 2B, disconnect the engine/transmission rear mounting, and remove the transmission left-hand mounting completely.

23 Unscrew and remove the upper bolts securing the transmission bellhousing to the engine, noting the locations of the bolts, as they are of different sizes and lengths.

24 Lower the engine support bar, hoist or jack (as applicable) as far as possible, ensuring that the weight of the engine is still supported.

25 Unscrew and remove the lower bolts securing the transmission bellhousing to the engine, again noting the bolt locations, as they are of different sizes and lengths.

26 Check that all fixings and attachments are clear of the transmission. Enlist the aid of an assistant to help in guiding and supporting the transmission during its removal.

27 The transmission is located on engine alignment dowels, and if stuck on them, it may be necessary to carefully tap and prise the transmission free of the dowels to allow separation. Once the transmission is disconnected from the location dowels, swivel the unit out and lower it out of the car.

⚠ *Warning: Support the transmission to ensure that it remains steady on the jack head. Ensure that the torque converter remains in position on its shaft in the torque converter housing.*

28 With the transmission removed, bolt a suitable bar and spacer across the front face of the torque converter housing, to retain the torque converter in position.

Refitting

29 Refitting is a reversal of the removal procedure, but note the following special points:

a) *When reconnecting the transmission to the engine, ensure that the location dowels are in position, and that the transmission is correctly aligned with them before pushing it fully into engagement with the engine. As the torque converter is refitted, ensure that the drive pins at the centre of the torque converter hub engage with the recesses in the automatic transmission fluid pump inner wheel.*

b) *Tighten all retaining bolts to their specified torque wrench settings.*

c) *Reconnect and adjust the selector cable, as described in Section 4.*

d) *On completion, have the transmission fluid level checked by a VW dealer. If a new transmission unit has been fitted, it may be necessary to have the transmission ECU 'matched' to the engine management ECU electronically, to ensure correct operation – seek the advice of your VW dealer.*

3 Automatic transmission overhaul – general information

In the event of a fault occurring, it will be necessary to establish whether the fault is electrical, mechanical or hydraulic in nature, before repair work can be contemplated. Diagnosis requires detailed knowledge of the transmission's operation and construction, as well as access to specialised test equipment, and so is deemed to be beyond the scope of this manual. It is therefore essential that problems with the automatic transmission are referred to a VW dealer for assessment.

Note that a faulty transmission should not be removed before the car has been assessed by a dealer, as fault diagnosis is carried out with the transmission *in situ*.

4 Selector cable – removal, refitting and adjustment

Removal

1 Disconnect the battery negative lead and position It away from the terminal (see *Disconnecting the battery*).

2 Raise and support the car at the front end on axle stands (see *Jacking and vehicle support*). Allow a suitable working clearance underneath the car.

3 Move the selector lever to the P position.

4 Undo the screw under the detent button on the lever handle, and lift the handle from the lever **(see illustration overleaf)**.

5 Detach and lift the selector cover up from the centre console.

6 Prise free the circlip and detach the cable from the shift mechanism.

7 Referring to Chapter 4B, remove the exhaust system front downpipe and catalytic converter. Where applicable, detach and remove the sections of exhaust heat shield necessary to gain access to the selector cable.

8 Withdraw the cable from the selector lever housing, and remove the protective sleeve. If the sleeve is no longer a tight fit in its selector housing aperture, or is in any way damaged, discard it and fit a new one on reassembly. Working along its length, release the cable from the securing clips. Note the cable routing carefully for refitting.

9 At the transmission end of the cable, undo the locking bolt and detach the cable from the transmission selector shaft. Recover the serrated washer, and discard it – a new one must be used on refitting.

Refitting

10 Refit the selector cable by reversing the removal procedure, noting the following points:

a) *Use a new serrated washer when reconnecting the cable to the selector lever, but do not tighten the locking bolt until the cable has been adjusted, as described below.*

b) *Ensure that the cable is correctly routed, as noted on removal, and that it is securely held by its retaining clips.*

c) *Fit the protective sleeve to the selector housing before passing through the selector cable.*

d) *When fitting the cable to the selector lever, use a new circlip.*

e) *Adjust the selector cable as described below.*

Adjustment

11 Inside the car, move the selector lever to the P position.

12 At the transmission, slacken the cable locking bolt on the side of the selector shaft lever (if not already done). Push the selector shaft up against its end stop, corresponding

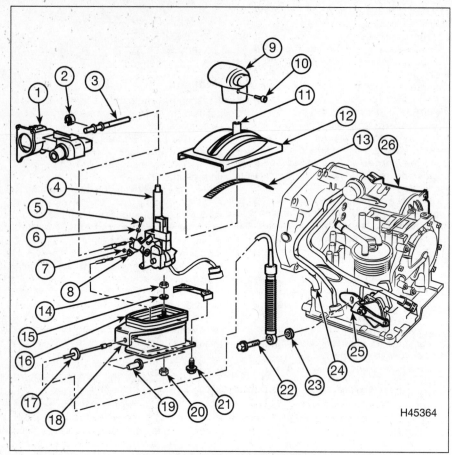

4.4 Selector lever and cable details

1 Ignition switch	8 Seal	14 Nut	20 Nut
2 Clip	9 Selector lever	15 Distance piece	21 Screw
3 Park locking	handle	16 Gasket	22 Locking bolt
cable	10 Screw	17 Selector cable	23 Washer
4 Selector lever	11 Selector lever	18 Selector lever	24 Serrated washer
5 Bolt	sleeve	housing	25 Selector shaft
6 Washer	12 Selector cover	19 Protective	lever
7 Circlip	13 Cover strip	sleeve	26 Transmission

to the P position, then tighten the locking bolt to the specified torque. If a new cable has not been fitted, check the condition of the serrated washer on the locking bolt, and renew it if it appears to be in less-than-perfect condition.

13 Verify the operation of the selector lever

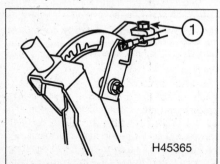

5.5 Park Lock cable clamp screw (1) at selector lever

by shifting through all gear positions and checking that every gear can be selected smoothly and without delay.

---

5 Ignition key Park Lock system – description, cable renewal and adjustment

Description

1 This system is a security/safety device, intended to prevent the car from being left with the transmission in any position other than P. The ignition key cannot be removed from the lock unless P is selected, and once the key has been removed, no other position than P can be selected.

2 This function is provided by means of a cable fitted to the selector linkage at the selector lever, and to the ignition switch assembly **(see illustration 4.4)**.

Lock cable

Removal

3 With reference to Section 4, remove the selector lever handle and cover.

4 Referring to Chapter 11, remove the centre console for access to the cable run.

5 At the selector lever, loosen the clamp screw and disconnect the cable outer **(see illustration)**. Unhook the cable eye from the peg on the operating lever.

6 Referring to Chapter 10, remove the steering wheel and the upper and lower steering column shrouds for access to the ignition switch.

7 Press the lock cable clip out of its mounting bracket, and prise the cable end fitting off its ball-stud.

8 The lock cable is now free to be removed from the car. Take careful note of the cable routing, and remove any further trim as necessary to facilitate removal of the cable.

Refitting

9 Refitting is a reversal of removal. Check the cable adjustment as described below.

Adjustment

10 If not already done, refer to paragraphs 3 and 4 to gain access to the cable at the selector lever. Loosen the cable clamp screw at the selector lever.

11 Apply the handbrake firmly. Place the selector lever in position 1.

12 Turn the ignition key to the start position, and release it.

13 Adjust the clearance between the operating lever and the locking pin by moving the cable outer in its clamp **(see illustration)**.

14 When the clearance is correct, move the selector lever to P and turn the ignition key to the off position. It should be possible to remove the ignition key – if not, repeat the adjustment procedure, and check the cable for stiffness or kinking. When the system is working correctly, it should only be possible to remove the key with the selector in P, and once the key is removed, it should not be possible to move the lever out of P.

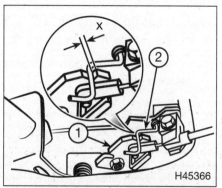

5.13 Park Lock cable adjustment

1 Operating   2 Locking pin
   lever   x = 0.7 mm

Chapter 8
Driveshafts

Contents

Degrees of difficulty

Easy, suitable for novice with little experience		Fairly easy, suitable for beginner with some experience		Fairly difficult, suitable for competent DIY mechanic		Difficult, suitable for experienced DIY mechanic	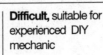	Very difficult, suitable for expert DIY or professional	

Specifications

Type . . . . Steel shafts with ball-and-cage type constant velocity joint at each end (certain models have a tripod type inner joint)

Torque wrench settings	Nm	lbf ft
Driveshaft retaining bolt (automatic transmission models)	110	81
Driveshaft retaining nut (12-point type):		
Stage 1	200	148
Slacken the nut by one turn, then:		
Stage 2	50	37
Stage 3	Angle-tighten a further 30°	
Inner CV joint-to-drive flange bolts:		
Driveshaft with tripod type inner joint (M8 bolt)	40	30
All other driveshafts	45	33
Lower arm balljoint retaining bolts	35	26
Roadwheel bolts	110	81

1 General information

Drive is transmitted from the differential to the front wheels by means of two driveshafts of unequal length. The right-hand driveshaft is longer than the left-hand, due to the position of the transmission. Depending on engine size and transmission type, there are several different types of driveshaft which may be fitted:

1) Solid-steel left-hand shaft, tubular right-hand shaft, with ball-and-cage CV joints.
2) Solid-steel shafts, ball-and-cage outer CV joint, triple-roller (tripod-type) inner CV joint, driveshafts secured to wheel hub with nut.
3) Solid-steel shafts, ball-and-cage outer CV joint, triple-roller (tripod-type) inner CV joint, driveshafts secured to wheel hub with bolt (automatic transmission models).

Both driveshafts are splined at their outer ends to accept the wheel hubs, and are threaded so that each hub can be fastened by a large nut or bolt. The inner end of each driveshaft is bolted to the transmission drive flanges.

Constant velocity (CV) joints are fitted to each end of the driveshafts, to ensure the smooth and efficient transmission of drive at all the angles possible as the roadwheels move up-and-down with the suspension, and as they turn from side-to-side under steering. As mentioned above, the constant velocity joints are either of the ball-and-cage type or tripod type.

2.1 Remove the trim/hub cap and slacken the driveshaft retaining nut

2.7a Inner CV joint splined bolts and retaining plates

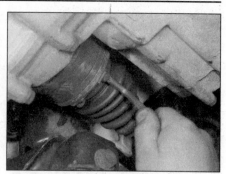

2.7b Using a suitable key or socket, slacken the splined bolts . . .

2 Driveshaft – removal and refitting

Removal

1 Remove the wheel trim/hub cap (as applicable) and slacken the driveshaft retaining nut/bolt with the car resting on its wheels **(see illustration)**. Also slacken the wheel bolts.

2 Chock the rear wheels of the car, firmly apply the handbrake, then jack up the front of the car and support it on axle stands. Remove the relevant front roadwheel.

3 Remove the CV joint protector plate from the suspension lower arm.

4 If the right-hand driveshaft is being removed, unbolt and remove the retaining clip for the lambda sensor wiring harness, where applicable. Ensure that the harness is kept clear as the driveshaft is removed/refitted.

5 Using a suitable marker pen, draw around the end of the suspension lower arm, marking the correct fitted position of the balljoint. Unscrew the balljoint retaining bolts and remove the retaining plate from the top of the lower arm.

6 Unscrew and remove the driveshaft retaining nut/bolt and (where fitted) remove its washer.

7 Slacken and remove the splined bolts securing the inner driveshaft joint to the transmission flange and, where necessary, recover the retaining plates from underneath the bolts **(see illustrations)**. Support the

2.7c . . . and recover the retaining plates

driveshaft by suspending it with wire or string – do not allow it to hang under its weight, or the joint may be damaged.

8 Carefully pull the swivel hub assembly outwards, and withdraw the driveshaft outer constant velocity joint from the hub assembly. The shaft will probably be a very tight fit in the hub; tap the joint out of the hub using a soft-faced mallet. If this fails to free it from the hub, the joint will have to be pressed out using a suitable tool which is bolted to the hub.

9 Manoeuvre the driveshaft out from underneath the car and (where fitted) recover the gasket from the end of the inner constant velocity joint. Discard the gasket – a new one should be used on refitting.

10 *Do not allow the car to rest on its wheels with one or both driveshaft(s) removed, as damage to the wheel bearing(s) may result.* If moving the car is unavoidable, temporarily insert the outer end of the driveshaft(s) in the hub(s), and tighten the driveshaft retaining nut/bolt(s) to 50 Nm/37 lbf ft; in this case, the inner end(s) of the driveshaft(s) must be supported, for example by suspending with string from the car underbody. *Do not allow the driveshaft to hang down under its weight, or the joint may be damaged.*

Refitting

11 Ensure that the transmission flange and inner joint mating surfaces are clean and dry. Where necessary, fit a new gasket to the joint by peeling off its backing foil and sticking it in position.

12 Ensure that the outer joint and hub splines are clean and dry.

13 Manoeuvre the driveshaft into position, and engage the outer joint with the hub. Ensure that the threads are clean, and apply a smear of oil to the contact face of the driveshaft retaining nut/bolt. Although VW do not specifically require that a new nut or bolt be used, it is advisable to consider fitting one, particularly in view of the high torque applied. Fit the washer (where fitted) and the nut/bolt, and draw the joint fully into position. Do not try to fully tighten the driveshaft nut/bolt until the car is resting on its wheels.

14 Refit the suspension lower arm balljoint retaining bolts, and tighten them to the specified torque setting, using the marks

made on removal to ensure that the balljoint is correctly positioned.

15 Align the driveshaft inner joint with the transmission flange, and refit the retaining plates (where applicable) and the bolts. Tighten the retaining bolts to the specified torque.

16 Refit the CV joint protector plate to the lower arm. Where removed, refit the lambda sensor wiring harness retaining clip, ensuring that the harness is securely clipped back into place.

17 Ensure that the outer joint is drawn fully into position, then refit the roadwheel and lower the car to the ground.

18 Tighten the driveshaft nut/bolt to the specified torque setting **(see Haynes Hint)**.

19 Once the driveshaft nut/bolt is correctly tightened, tighten the wheel bolts to the specified torque and refit the wheel trim/hub cap.

3 Driveshaft rubber gaiters – renewal

Outer CV joint gaiter

1 Remove the driveshaft as described in Section 2.

Where a 12-point nut is fitted, the angle between each driveshaft retaining nut flat point is 30°. If an angle-tightening gauge is not available, the angle can be accurately measured by making marks on the hub and the nearest nut flat point and tightening the nut so its mark moves by the correct number of points.

2 Secure the driveshaft in a vice equipped with soft jaws, and release the two outer joint gaiter retaining clips. If necessary, the retaining clips can be cut to release them.

3 Slide the rubber gaiter down the shaft to expose the constant velocity joint, and scoop out excess grease.

4 Using a soft-faced mallet, tap the joint off the end of the driveshaft.

5 Remove the circlip from the driveshaft groove, and slide off the thrustwasher and dished washer, noting which way around it is fitted.

6 Slide the rubber gaiter off the driveshaft and discard it.

7 Thoroughly clean the constant velocity joint(s) using paraffin, or a suitable solvent, and dry thoroughly. Carry out a visual inspection as follows.

8 Move the inner splined driving member from side-to-side to expose each ball in turn at the top of its track. Examine the balls for cracks, flat spots or signs of surface pitting.

9 Inspect the ball tracks on the inner and outer members. If the tracks have widened, the balls will no longer be a tight fit. At the same time, check the ball cage windows for wear or cracking between the windows. If, when carrying out the road test as described in Chapter 1, any noise from the driveshaft joints was apparent, inspect the joints carefully to determine the cause. Repacking the joint with grease and fitting a new gaiter is unlikely to effect a reduction in noise.

10 If on inspection any of the constant velocity joint components are found to be worn or damaged, it will be necessary to renew the complete joint assembly. If the joint is in satisfactory condition, obtain a new gaiter and retaining clips, a constant velocity joint circlip and the correct type of grease. Grease is often supplied with the joint repair kit – if not, use a good-quality molybdenum disulphide grease.

11 Tape over the splines on the end of the driveshaft, to protect the new gaiter as it is slid into place.

12 Slide the new gaiter onto the end of the driveshaft, then remove the protective tape from the driveshaft splines.

13 Slide on the dished washer, making sure its convex side is innermost, followed by the thrustwasher.

14 Fit a new circlip to the driveshaft, then tap the joint onto the driveshaft until the circlip engages in its groove. Make sure that the joint is securely retained by the circlip.

15 Pack the joint with the specified type of grease. Work the grease well into the bearing tracks whilst twisting the joint, and fill the rubber gaiter with any excess.

16 Ease the gaiter over the joint, and ensure that the gaiter lips are correctly located on both the driveshaft and constant velocity joint. Lift the outer sealing lip of the gaiter, to equalise air pressure within the gaiter.

17 Fit the large metal retaining clip to the gaiter. Pull the clip as tight as possible, and locate the hooks on the clip in their slots. Remove any slack in the gaiter retaining clip by carefully compressing the raised section of the clip. In the absence of the special tool, a pair of side-cutters may be used, taking care not to cut the clip. Secure the small retaining clip using the same procedure. Some CV gaiter kits now include plastic cable-ties to secure the gaiters – while not as effective as the metal clips, they are adequate for the task. Ensure the ties are pulled as tight as possible, and that the excess is trimmed off.

18 Check the constant velocity joint moves freely in all directions, then refit the driveshaft to the car, as described in Section 2.

Inner CV joint gaiter

19 A hydraulic press and several special tools are required to remove and refit the inner CV joint. Therefore it is recommended that gaiter renewal is entrusted to a VW dealer.

4 Driveshaft overhaul – general information

1 If any of the checks described in Chapter 1 reveal wear in any driveshaft joint, first remove the roadwheel trim or centre cap (as appropriate) and check that the driveshaft retaining nut/bolt is tight.

2 If the nut/bolt is tight, refit the centre cap or trim. Repeat this check on the remaining driveshaft nut/bolt.

3 Road test the car, and listen for a metallic clicking from the front as the car is driven slowly in a circle on full lock. This test should be performed in both directions. If a clicking noise is heard, this indicates wear in the outer constant velocity joint. This means that the joint must be renewed; reconditioning is not possible.

4 If vibration, consistent with roadspeed, is felt through the car when accelerating, there is a possibility of wear in the inner constant velocity joints.

5 To check the joints for wear, the driveshaft must be dismantled. The outer constant velocity joint can be removed and checked, but work on the inner joint should be entrusted to a VW dealer (see Section 3); if any wear or free play is found, the affected joint must be renewed.

Chapter 9
Braking system

Contents

Degrees of difficulty

Easy, suitable for novice with little experience	Fairly easy, suitable for beginner with some experience	Fairly difficult, suitable for competent DIY mechanic 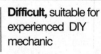	Difficult, suitable for experienced DIY mechanic	Very difficult, suitable for expert DIY or professional

Specifications

System type	Front disc brakes, rear drums or discs (DOHC engine models). Dual-circuit, diagonally-split hydraulic system with vacuum servo assistance. Cable-operated handbrake to rear wheels. Anti-lock Braking System (ABS) on all models

Front brakes

Disc diameter:	
SOHC models	239 mm
DOHC models	256 mm
Disc thickness (new):	
SOHC models	18 mm
DOHC models	20 mm
Disc thickness (minimum):	
SOHC models	16 mm
DOHC models	18 mm
Maximum disc run-out	0.1 mm
Brake pad thickness (all models, including backplate):	
New	11 to 12 mm
Minimum	7 mm

Rear drum brakes

Drum diameter:	
New	200 mm
Wear limit	201.5 mm
Maximum drum out-of-round	0.1 mm
Brake shoe friction material minimum thickness	2.5 mm

Rear disc brakes

Disc diameter	226 mm
Disc thickness:	
New	10 mm
Minimum	8 mm
Maximum disc run-out	0.1 mm
Brake pad thickness (including backplate):	
New	12 mm
Minimum	7 mm

Torque wrench settings

	Nm	lbf ft
ABS wheel sensor retaining bolt	10	7
Brake disc splash plate bolts	10	7
Brake fluid hose union	15	11
Brake pedal shaft nut	25	18
Front brake caliper:		
SOHC models:		
Mounting bolts	25	18
DOHC models:		
Guide pin bolt*	35	26
Mounting bracket bolt	125	92
Front caliper splash plate bolts	10	7
Handbrake lever mounting nuts	25	18
Master cylinder mounting nuts	25	18
Pedal bracket mounting bolts	25	18
Rear brake backplate bolts	60	44
Rear brake caliper:		
Guide pin bolt*	35	26
Mounting bracket bolt	65	48
Rear hub nut – later models*	175	129
Rear wheel cylinder bolts	10	7
Roadwheel bolts	110	81
Servo unit mounting nuts	20	15

* Use new nut/bolts

1 General information

The braking system is of the servo-assisted, dual-circuit hydraulic type. The arrangement of the hydraulic system is such that each circuit operates one front and one rear brake from a tandem master cylinder. Under normal circumstances, both circuits operate in unison. However, if there is hydraulic failure in one circuit, full braking force will still be available at two wheels.

All models are fitted with front disc brakes, with rear drum brakes on all except DOHC engine models, which have rear discs. An anti-lock braking system (ABS) is fitted to all models in the range – refer to Section 21 for further information.

The front and rear disc brakes have single-piston sliding type calipers, which ensure that equal pressure is applied to each disc pad.

The rear drum brakes incorporate leading and trailing shoes, which are actuated by twin-piston wheel cylinders. A self-adjust mechanism is incorporated, to compensate for brake shoe wear.

The handbrake provides an independent mechanical means of rear brake application.

Precautions

The car's braking system is one of its most important safety features. When working on the brakes, there are a number of points to be aware of, to ensure that your health (or even your life) is not being put at risk.

• *When servicing any part of the system, work carefully and methodically – do not take short-cuts; also observe scrupulous cleanliness when overhauling any part of the hydraulic system.*

• *Always renew components in axle sets, where applicable – this means renewing brake pads, shoes, etc, on BOTH sides, even if only one set of pads is worn, or one wheel cylinder is leaking (for example). In the instance of uneven brake wear, the cause should be investigated and fixed (on front brakes, sticking caliper pistons is a likely problem).*

• *Use only genuine VW parts, or at least those of known good quality.*

• *Although genuine VW brake pads and shoes are asbestos-free, the dust created by wear of non-genuine parts may contain asbestos, which is a health hazard. Never blow it out with compressed air, and don't inhale any of it.*

• *DO NOT use petroleum-based solvents to clean brake parts; use brake cleaner or methylated spirit only.*

• *DO NOT allow any brake fluid, oil or grease to contact the brake pads or disc.*

Warning: Brake fluid is poisonous. Take care to keep it off bare skin, and in particular not to get splashes in your eyes. The fluid also attacks paintwork and plastics – wash off spillages immediately with cold water. Finally, brake fluid is highly inflammable, and should be handled with the same care as petrol.

2 Hydraulic system – bleeding

Note: *Refer to the precautions in Section 1 before proceeding.*
Note: *VW recommend that at least 0.25 litre of hydraulic fluid is expelled from each bleed screw.*

General

1 The correct operation of any hydraulic system is only possible after removing all air from the components and circuit; this is achieved by bleeding the system.

2 During the bleeding procedure, add only clean, unused fluid of the recommended type; never re-use fluid that has already been bled from the system. Ensure that sufficient fluid is available before starting work.

3 If there is any possibility of incorrect fluid being already in the system, the brake components and circuit must be flushed completely with uncontaminated, correct fluid, and new seals should be fitted to the various components.

4 If hydraulic fluid has been lost from the system, or air has entered because of a leak, ensure that the fault is cured before continuing further.

5 Park the car on level ground, switch off the engine and select first or reverse gear.

6 Check that all pipes and hoses are secure, unions tight and bleed screws closed. Clean any dirt from around the bleed screws.

7 Unscrew the master cylinder reservoir cap, and top the master cylinder reservoir up to the MAX level line; refit the cap loosely, and remember to maintain the fluid level at least above the MIN level line throughout the procedure, or there is a risk of further air entering the system.

8 There is a number of one-man, do-it-yourself brake bleeding kits currently available from motor accessory shops. It is recommended that one of these kits is used whenever possible, as they greatly simplify the bleeding operation, and reduce the risk of expelled air and fluid being drawn back into the system. If such a kit is not available, the basic (two-man) method must be used, which is described in detail below.

9 If a kit is to be used, prepare the car as described previously, and follow the kit manufacturer's instructions, as the procedure may vary slightly according to the type being used; generally, they are as outlined below in the relevant sub-section.

10 Whichever method is used, the same sequence must be followed (paragraphs 11 and 12) to ensure the removal of all air from the system.

Bleeding sequence

11 If the system has been only partially disconnected, and suitable precautions were taken to minimise fluid loss, it should be necessary only to bleed that part of the system (ie, the primary or secondary circuit).

12 If the complete system is to be bled, then it should be done in the following sequence:
a) Right-hand rear brake.
b) Left-hand rear brake.
c) Right-hand front brake.
d) Left-hand front brake.

Warning: Under no circumstances should the bleed screws on the ABS hydraulic unit be opened.

Bleeding

Basic (two-man) method

13 Collect together a clean glass jar of reasonable size, a suitable length of plastic or rubber tubing which is a tight fit over the bleed screw, and a ring spanner to fit the screw. The help of an assistant will also be required.

14 Remove the dust cap from the first screw in the sequence **(see illustration)**. Fit the spanner and tube to the screw, place the other end of the tube in the jar, and pour in sufficient fluid to cover the end of the tube.

15 Ensure that the master cylinder reservoir fluid level is maintained at least above the MIN level line throughout the procedure.

16 Have the assistant fully depress the brake pedal several times to build-up pressure, then maintain it on the final downstroke.

17 While pedal pressure is maintained, unscrew the bleed screw (approximately one turn) and allow the compressed fluid and air to flow into the jar. The assistant should maintain pedal pressure, following it down to the floor if necessary, and should not release it until instructed to do so. When the flow stops, tighten the bleed screw again, have the assistant release the pedal slowly, and recheck the reservoir fluid level.

18 Repeat the steps given in paragraphs 16 and 17 until the fluid emerging from the bleed screw is free from air bubbles. If the master cylinder has been drained and refilled, and air is being bled from the first screw in the sequence, allow approximately five seconds between cycles for the master cylinder passages to refill.

19 When no more air bubbles appear, tighten the bleed screw securely, remove the tube and spanner, and refit the dust cap. Do not overtighten the bleed screw.

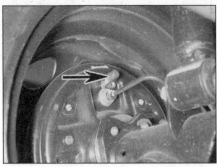

2.14 Dust cap (arrowed) over bleed screw on rear brake wheel cylinder

20 Repeat the procedure on the remaining screws in the sequence, until all air is removed from the system and the brake pedal feels firm again.

Using a one-way valve kit

21 As their name implies, these kits consist of a length of tubing with a one-way valve fitted, to prevent expelled air and fluid being drawn back into the system; some kits include a translucent container, which can be positioned so that the air bubbles can be more easily seen flowing from the end of the tube.

22 The kit is connected to the bleed screw, which is then opened **(see illustration)**. The user returns to the driver's seat, depresses the brake pedal with a smooth, steady stroke, and slowly releases it; this is repeated until the expelled fluid is clear of air bubbles.

23 Note that these kits simplify work so much that it is easy to forget the master cylinder reservoir fluid level; ensure that this is maintained at least above the MIN level line at all times.

Using a pressure-bleeding kit

24 These kits are usually operated by the reservoir of pressurised air contained in the spare tyre. However, note that it will probably be necessary to reduce the pressure to a lower level than normal; refer to the instructions supplied with the kit.

25 By connecting a pressurised, fluid-filled container to the master cylinder reservoir, bleeding can be carried out simply by opening each screw in turn (in the specified sequence), and allowing the fluid to flow out until no more air bubbles can be seen in the expelled fluid.

26 This method has the advantage that the large reservoir of fluid provides an additional safeguard against air being drawn into the system during bleeding.

27 Pressure-bleeding is particularly effective when bleeding 'difficult' systems, or when bleeding the complete system at the time of routine fluid renewal.

All methods

28 When bleeding is complete, and firm pedal feel is restored, wash off any spilt fluid, tighten the bleed screws securely, and refit their dust caps.

2.22 Bleeding front brake caliper using a one-way valve brake bleeder kit

29 Check the hydraulic fluid level in the master cylinder reservoir, and top-up if necessary (see Weekly checks).

30 Discard any hydraulic fluid that has been bled from the system; it will not be fit for re-use.

31 Check the feel of the brake pedal. If it feels at all spongy, air must still be present in the system, and further bleeding is required. Failure to bleed satisfactorily after a reasonable repetition of the bleeding procedure may be due to worn master cylinder seals.

3 Hydraulic pipes and hoses – renewal

Note: Refer to the precautions in Section 1 before proceeding.

1 If any pipe or hose is to be renewed, minimise fluid loss by first removing the master cylinder reservoir cap, then tightening it down onto a piece of polythene to obtain an airtight seal. Alternatively, flexible hoses can be sealed, if required, using a proprietary brake hose clamp; metal brake pipe unions can be plugged (if care is taken not to allow dirt into the system) or capped immediately they are disconnected. Place a wad of rag under any union that is to be disconnected, to catch any spilt fluid.

2 If a flexible hose is to be disconnected, unscrew the brake pipe union nut before removing the spring clip which secures the hose to its mounting bracket **(see illustration)**.

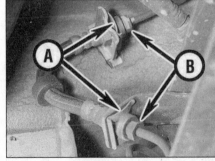

3.2 Rear brake flexible hose unions showing spring clips (A) and union nuts (B)

4.3a Loosen the caliper mounting bolts using an Allen key or socket . . .

4.3b . . . and remove the bolts from the caliper

3 To unscrew the union nuts, it is preferable to obtain a brake pipe spanner of the correct size; these are available from most large motor accessory shops. Failing this, a close-fitting open-ended spanner will be required, though if the nuts are tight or corroded, their flats may be rounded-off if the spanner slips. In such a case, a self-locking wrench is often the only way to unscrew a stubborn union, but it follows that the pipe and the damaged nuts must be renewed on reassembly. Always clean a union and surrounding area before disconnecting it. If disconnecting a component with more than one union, make a careful note of the connections before disturbing any of them.

4 If a brake pipe is to be renewed, it can be obtained, cut to length and with the union nuts and end flares in place, from VW dealers. All that is then necessary is to bend it to shape, following the line of the original, before fitting it to the car. Alternatively, most motor accessory shops can make up brake pipes from kits, but this requires very careful measurement of the original, to ensure that the new one is of the correct length. The safest answer is usually to take the original to the shop as a pattern.

5 On refitting, do not overtighten the union nuts. It is not necessary to exercise brute force to obtain a sound joint.

6 Ensure that the pipes and hoses are correctly routed, with no kinks, and that they are secured in the clips or brackets provided. After fitting, remove the polythene from the reservoir, and bleed the hydraulic system as described in Section 2. Wash off any spilt fluid, and check carefully for fluid leaks.

4 Front brake pads – renewal

Note: *Refer to the precautions in Section 1 before proceeding.*

1 Apply the handbrake, loosen the front wheel bolts, then jack up the front of the car and support it on axle stands. Remove the front roadwheels.

2 Two different types of calipers and front brake pads are fitted to the Polo range. Models with DOHC engines have a Lucas/Girling caliper, while the rest have a VW 'type II' unit. Proceed as described under the relevant sub-heading below.

VW type II caliper

3 Using a suitable Allen key or Allen socket, slacken and remove the two caliper mounting bolts **(see illustrations)**.

4 Lift the caliper and pads away from the hub **(see illustration)**. While the caliper is removed, make sure it is supported at all times, and that the flexible brake hose is not strained or unduly twisted – if the caliper must be left unattended, do not allow it to hang unsupported on the flexible brake hose.

5 Using a flat-bladed screwdriver if necessary, prise the pads out of their locations in the caliper – note that the pad with the larger friction surface is fitted to the outer side of the caliper **(see illustrations)**.

6 First measure the thickness of each brake pad (including the backing plate). If either pad is

worn at any point to the specified minimum thickness or less, all four pads must be renewed. Also, the pads should be renewed if any are fouled with oil or grease; there is no satisfactory way of degreasing friction material, once contaminated. If any of the brake pads are worn unevenly, or are fouled with oil or grease, trace and rectify the cause before reassembly.

7 If the brake pads are still serviceable, carefully clean them using a clean, fine wire brush or similar, paying particular attention to the sides and back of the metal backing. If the pads are 'glazed' (have a shiny appearance) it may be helpful to roughen the surface of the friction material in order to restore the pads' braking effectiveness. Clean out the grooves in the friction material (where applicable), and pick out any large embedded particles of dirt or debris. Carefully clean the pad locations in the caliper body/mounting bracket.

8 Prior to fitting the pads, check that the spacers are free to slide easily in the caliper body bushes, and are a reasonably tight fit. Brush the dust and dirt from the caliper and piston, but *do not* inhale it, as it is injurious to health. Inspect the dust seal around the piston for damage, and the piston for evidence of fluid leaks, corrosion or damage. If attention to any of these components is necessary, refer to Section 10.

9 If new brake pads are to be fitted, the caliper piston must be pushed back into the cylinder to make room for them. Either use a G-clamp or similar tool, or use suitable pieces of wood as levers. Provided that the master cylinder reservoir has not been overfilled with hydraulic fluid, there should be no spillage, but keep a careful watch on the fluid level while retracting the piston. If the fluid level rises above the MAX level line at any time, the surplus should be syphoned off or ejected through a plastic tube connected to the bleed screw (see Section 2). **Note:** *Do not syphon the fluid by mouth, as it is poisonous; use a syringe or an old poultry baster.*

10 Press the pads into their locations in the caliper. The inner pad can be pressed in sideways, but the outer pad must be pressed in downwards, as shown **(see illustration)**.

11 Position the caliper and pads over the disc, and press into position sufficiently until it is possible to install caliper mounting bolts.

4.4 Withdraw the caliper and brake pads from the brake disc

4.5a Prise out the smaller inner pad . . .

4.5b . . . and the larger outer brake pad from the caliper

4.10 Outer brake pad spring clip is most easily engaged in the caliper by pressing in downwards

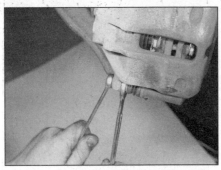

4.12 Remove the lower guide pin bolt, holding the pin as shown

4.13a Pivot the caliper upwards . . .

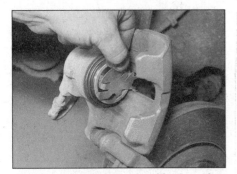

4.13b . . . then recover the shim from the caliper piston . . .

4.14 . . . and remove the pads from the caliper mounting bracket

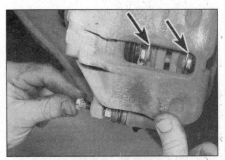

4.17 Ensure the anti-rattle springs (arrowed) are in place, then fit the new guide pin bolt

Tighten the mounting bolts to the specified torque setting.

Lucas/Girling caliper

12 Slacken and remove the lower caliper guide pin bolt, using a slim open-ended spanner to prevent the guide pin itself from rotating (see illustration). Discard the guide pin bolt – a new bolt must be used on refitting.
13 With the lower guide pin bolt removed, pivot the caliper upwards until it is clear of the brake pads and mounting bracket. If it is loose, recover the shim from the caliper piston (see illustrations).
14 Withdraw the two brake pads from the caliper mounting bracket (see illustration).
15 Examine the pads and prepare the caliper as described above in paragraphs 6 to 9, substituting 'guide pins' for references to spacers and bushes.
16 Install the pads in the caliper mounting bracket, ensuring that the friction material of each pad is against the brake disc. Note the pad with the wear sensor wiring should be installed as the inner pad.
17 If removed, refit the shim to the caliper piston. Pivot the caliper down into position, and pass the pad warning sensor wiring through the caliper aperture. If the threads of the new guide pin bolt are not already precoated with locking compound, apply a suitable thread-locking compound to them. Press the caliper into position whilst ensuring that the pad anti-rattle springs locate correctly with the caliper. Install the guide pin bolt, tightening it to the specified torque setting

while retaining the guide pin with an open-ended spanner (see illustration).

All calipers

18 Depress the brake pedal repeatedly, until the pads are pressed into firm contact with the brake disc, and normal (non-assisted) pedal pressure is restored.
19 Repeat the relevant procedure above on the remaining front brake caliper.
20 Refit the roadwheels, then lower the car to the ground and tighten the roadwheel bolts to the specified torque.
21 New pads will not give full braking efficiency until they have bedded-in. Be prepared for this, and avoid hard braking as far as possible for the first hundred miles or so after pad renewal.
22 Check the hydraulic fluid level as described in Weekly checks.

5 Rear brake shoes – renewal

Note: Refer to the precautions in Section 1 before proceeding.
1 Remove the brake drum (see Section 8).
2 Working carefully, and taking the necessary precautions, remove all traces of brake dust from the brake drum, backplate and shoes.
3 Measure the thickness of the friction material of each brake shoe at several points; if either shoe is worn at any point to the specified minimum thickness or less, **all four**

shoes must be renewed as a set. The shoes should also be renewed if any are fouled with oil or grease; there is no way of degreasing friction material, once contaminated.
4 If any of the brake shoes are worn unevenly, or fouled with oil or grease, trace and rectify the cause before reassembly.
5 If all is well, refit the brake drum as described in Section 8. To renew the brake shoes, continue as follows.
6 Note the position of the brake shoes and springs, and mark the webs of the shoes, if necessary, to aid refitting. **Note:** One of the project cars seen in the workshop had a slightly different self-adjusting spring arrangement fitted – this should be noted when following the accompanying illustrations in this Section (see illustration).
7 Using a pair of pliers, remove the shoe retainer spring cups by depressing and

5.6 Self-adjusting mechanism spring may be attached as shown (arrowed) on some models

5.7a Using pliers, remove the spring cup . . .

5.7b . . . then lift off the spring . . .

5.7c . . . and withdraw the retainer pin from the rear of the backplate

5.8 Unhook the shoes from the lower pivot point, and remove the lower return spring

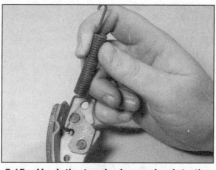

5.9a Free the shoes from the wheel cylinder. Note elastic band (arrowed) used to retain pistons . . .

5.9b . . . then detach the handbrake cable and remove the shoe assembly

turning them through 90°. With the cups removed, lift off the springs and withdraw the retainer pins **(see illustrations)**.

8 Ease the shoes out one at a time from the lower pivot point, to release the tension of the

return spring, then disconnect the lower return spring from both shoes **(see illustration)**.

9 Ease the upper end of both shoes out from their wheel cylinder locations, taking care not to damage the wheel cylinder seals, and

disconnect the handbrake cable from the trailing shoe. The brake shoe assembly can then be manoeuvred out of position and away from the backplate. Do not depress the brake pedal until the brakes are reassembled; wrap a strong elastic band around the wheel cylinder pistons to retain them **(see illustrations)**.

10 Make a note of the correct fitted positions of all components (refer to the Note in paragraph 6, and to illustration 5.6), then unhook the upper return spring, and disengage the wedge key spring **(see illustration)**.

11 Unhook the tensioning spring, and remove the pushrod from the trailing shoe, together with the wedge key.

12 Examine all components for signs of wear or damage, and renew as necessary. All return springs should be renewed, regardless of their apparent condition. Although linings are available separately (without shoes) from VW dealers, renewal of the shoes complete with linings is to be preferred, unless the necessary skills and equipment are available to fit new linings to the old shoes.

13 Peel back the rubber protective caps, and check the wheel cylinder for fluid leaks or other damage; check that both cylinder pistons are free to move easily. Refer to Section 12, if necessary, for information on wheel cylinder overhaul.

14 Apply a little brake grease to the contact areas of the pushrod and handbrake lever.

15 Hook the tensioning spring into the trailing shoe. Engage the pushrod with the opposite end of the spring, and pivot the pushrod into position on the trailing shoe **(see illustrations)**.

5.10 Prior to dismantling, note the correct fitted location of the shoe components

5.15a Hook the tensioning spring into the trailing shoe . . .

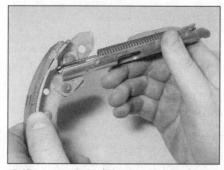

5.15b . . . then engage the pushrod with the opposite end of the spring . . .

5.15c . . . and pivot the strut into position on the shoe

16 Fit the wedge key between the trailing shoe and pushrod, making sure it is fitted the correct way around **(see illustration)**.

17 Locate the handbrake lever on the leading shoe in the pushrod, and fit the upper return spring using a pair of pliers **(see illustrations)**.

18 Fit the spring to the wedge key, and hook it onto the trailing shoe **(see illustration)**.

19 Prior to installation, clean the backplate, and apply a thin smear of high-temperature brake grease or anti-seize compound to all those surfaces of the backplate which bear on the shoes, particularly the wheel cylinder pistons and lower pivot point. Do not allow the lubricant to foul the friction material.

20 Remove the elastic band fitted to the wheel cylinder, and offer up the shoe assembly.

21 Connect the handbrake cable to the handbrake lever, and locate the top of the shoes in the wheel cylinder piston slots.

22 Fit the lower return spring to the shoes, then lever the bottom of the shoes onto the bottom anchor.

23 Tap the shoes to centralise them with the backplate, then refit the shoe retainer pins and springs, and secure them in position with the spring cups.

24 Refit the brake drum as described in Section 8.

25 Repeat the above procedure on the remaining rear brake.

26 Once both sets of rear shoes have been renewed, adjust the lining-to-drum clearance by repeatedly depressing the brake pedal until normally (non-assisted) pedal pressure returns.

27 Check and, if necessary, adjust the handbrake as described in Section 17.

28 On completion, check the hydraulic fluid level as described in *Weekly checks*.

29 New shoes will not give full braking efficiency until they have bedded-in. Be prepared for this, and avoid hard braking as far as possible for the first hundred miles or so after shoe renewal.

6 Rear brake pads – renewal

Note: *Refer to the precautions in Section 1 before proceeding.*

1 Chock the front wheels, engage 1st gear (or P), then jack up the rear of the car and support it on axle stands. Remove the rear wheels.

2 Slacken the handbrake cable and detach it from the caliper as described in Section 19.

3 Slacken and remove the caliper guide pin bolts, using a slim open-ended spanner to prevent the guide pins from rotating **(see illustration)**. Discard the guide pin bolts – new bolts must be used on refitting.

4 Lift the caliper away from the brake pads, and tie it up using a suitable piece of wire **(see**

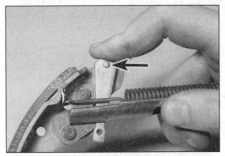

5.16 Slot the wedge key into position. Ensure raised dot (arrowed) is facing away from the shoe

5.17b . . . and hook the upper return spring into the leading shoe and pushrod (arrows)

illustration). Do not allow the caliper to hang unsupported on the flexible brake hose.

5 Withdraw the two brake pads from the caliper mounting bracket and recover the anti-rattle springs from the mounting bracket,

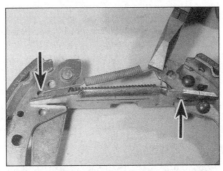

6.3 Hold the guide pin and unscrew the rear caliper guide pin bolts

6.5a . . . and remove the pads . . .

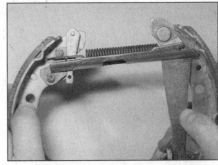

5.17a Locate the leading shoe in the pushrod . . .

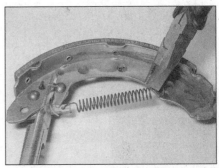

5.18 Fit the spring to the wedge key, and hook it onto the trailing shoe

noting their correct fitted locations **(see illustrations)**.

6 First measure the thickness of each brake pad (including the backing plate). If either pad is worn at any point to the specified minimum

6.4 Lift the caliper upwards and away . . .

6.5b . . . and anti-rattle springs from the caliper mounting bracket

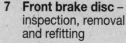

In the absence of the special tool, the piston can be screwed back into the caliper using a pair of circlip pliers.

thickness or less, **all four** pads must be renewed. Also, the pads should be renewed if any are fouled with oil or grease; there is no satisfactory way of degreasing friction material, once contaminated. If any of the brake pads are worn unevenly, or fouled with oil or grease, trace and rectify the cause before reassembly. New brake pads are available from VW dealers.

7 If one of the brake pads is significantly more worn than the other, it is quite likely that the caliper is partially seized. With the brake pads removed, the caliper body should be free to slide on the guide sleeves. If the action is suspect, dismantle and clean the caliper with reference to Section 11.

8 If the brake pads are still serviceable, carefully clean them using a clean, fine wire brush or similar, paying particular attention to the sides and back of the metal backing. Clean out the grooves in the friction material (where applicable), and pick out any large embedded particles of dirt or debris. Carefully clean the pad locations in the caliper body/mounting bracket.

9 Prior to fitting the pads, check that the guide pins are free to slide easily in the caliper bracket, and check that the rubber guide pin gaiters are undamaged. Brush the dust and dirt from the caliper and piston, but **do not** inhale it, as it is a health hazard. Inspect the dust seal around the piston for damage, and the piston for evidence of fluid leaks,

corrosion or damage. If attention to any of these components is necessary, refer to Section 11.

10 If new brake pads are to be fitted, it will be necessary to retract the piston fully into the caliper bore, by rotating it in a clockwise direction **(see Tool Tip)**. Provided that the master cylinder reservoir has not been overfilled with hydraulic fluid, there should be no spillage, but keep a careful watch on the fluid level while retracting the piston. If the fluid level rises above the MAX level line at any time, the surplus should be syphoned off, or ejected through a plastic tube connected to the bleed screw (see Section 2). **Note:** *Do not syphon the fluid by mouth, as it is poisonous; use a syringe or an old poultry baster.*

11 Fit the anti-rattle springs to the caliper mounting bracket, ensuring that they are correctly located. Install the pads in the mounting bracket, ensuring that each pad's friction material is against the brake disc.

12 Slide the caliper back into position over the pads.

13 If the threads of the new guide pin bolts are not already precoated with locking compound, apply a suitable thread-locking compound to them. Press the caliper into position, then install the bolts, tightening them to the specified torque setting while retaining the guide pin with an open-ended spanner.

14 Depress the brake pedal repeatedly, until the pads are pressed into firm contact with the brake disc, and normal (non-assisted) pedal pressure is restored.

15 Repeat the above procedure on the remaining rear brake caliper.

16 Reconnect the handbrake cables to the calipers, and adjust the handbrake as described in Section 17.

17 Refit the roadwheels, then lower the vehicle to the ground and tighten the roadwheel bolts to the specified torque setting.

18 Check the hydraulic fluid level as described in *Weekly checks*.

19 New pads will not give full braking efficiency until they have bedded-in. Be prepared for this, and avoid hard braking as far as possible for the first hundred miles or so after pad renewal.

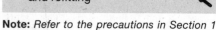

7 Front brake disc – inspection, removal and refitting

Note: *Refer to the precautions in Section 1 before proceeding.*

Inspection

Note: *If either disc requires renewal, BOTH should be renewed at the same time, to ensure even and consistent braking. New brake pads should also be fitted.*

1 Apply the handbrake, loosen the front wheel bolts, then jack up the front of the car and support it on axle stands. Remove the appropriate front roadwheel.

2 Slowly rotate the brake disc so that the full area of both sides can be checked; remove the brake pads if better access is required to the inboard surface. Light scoring is normal in the area swept by the brake pads, but if heavy scoring or cracks are found, the disc must be renewed.

3 It is normal to find a lip of rust and brake dust around the disc's perimeter; this can be scraped off if required. If, however, a lip has formed due to excessive wear of the brake pad swept area, then the disc's thickness must be measured using a micrometer **(see illustration)**. Take measurements at several places around the disc, at the inside and outside of the pad swept area; if the disc has worn at any point to the specified minimum thickness or less, the disc must be renewed.

4 If the disc is thought to be warped, it can be checked for run-out. Either use a dial gauge mounted on any convenient fixed point, while the disc is slowly rotated, or use feeler blades to measure (at several points all around the disc) the clearance between the disc and a fixed point, such as the caliper mounting bracket. If the measurements obtained are at the specified maximum or beyond, the disc is excessively warped, and must be renewed; however, it is worth checking first that the hub bearing is in good condition (Chapters 1 and/or 10). If the run-out is excessive, the disc must be renewed.

5 Check the disc for cracks, especially around the wheel bolt holes, and any other wear or damage, and renew if necessary.

Removal

6 On models with VW type II calipers, unbolt the caliper as described in Section 4, and remove it with the pads. Tie the caliper up to the front suspension coil spring using a piece of wire or string, so that the flexible brake hose is not twisted or strained.

7 On models with Lucas/Girling front brake calipers, unscrew the two bolts securing the brake caliper mounting bracket to the swivel hub, then slide the caliper assembly off the disc. Using a piece of wire or string, tie the caliper to the front suspension coil spring, to avoid placing any strain on the brake hose.

8 Use chalk or paint to mark the relationship of the disc to the hub, then remove the screw

7.3 Measuring brake disc thickness with a micrometer

7.8a Remove the disc securing screw . . .

7.8b . . . and withdraw the brake disc from the hub

securing the brake disc to the hub, and remove the disc **(see illustrations)**. If it is tight, tap its rear face with a hide or plastic mallet.

Refitting

9 Refitting is the reverse of the removal procedure, noting the following points:

a) Ensure that the mating surfaces of the disc and hub are clean and flat.

b) Align (if applicable) the marks made on removal, and securely tighten the disc retaining screw.

c) If a new disc has been fitted, use a suitable solvent to wipe any preservative coating from the disc, before refitting the caliper.

d) On models with type II brake calipers, refit the caliper and pads as described in Section 4.

e) On models with Lucas/Girling brake calipers, slide the caliper into position over the disc, making sure the pads pass

either side of the disc. Tighten the caliper bracket mounting bolts to the specified torque setting.

f) Refit the roadwheel, then lower the car to the ground and tighten the roadwheel bolts to the specified torque. On completion, repeatedly depress the brake pedal until normal (non-assisted) pedal pressure returns.

8 Rear brake drum – removal, inspection and refitting

Note: Refer to the precautions in Section 1.

Removal

1 Chock the front wheels and engage 1st gear (or P). Loosen the rear wheel bolts, then jack up the rear of the car and support it on axle stands. Remove the appropriate rear wheel.

2 Using a large flat-bladed screwdriver, carefully prise the cap out of the brake drum **(see illustration)**. It is recommended that a new cap is fitted on reassembly.

Early models

3 Extract the split pin from the hub nut, and remove the locking ring **(see illustration)**. Discard the split pin; a new one must be used on refitting.

4 Unscrew the rear hub nut, then slide off the toothed washer and remove the outer bearing from the centre of the drum **(see illustration)**.

Later models

5 Unscrew and remove the 12-point hub nut – make sure the car is well-supported, and that good-quality, close-fitting tools are used, as this nut is very tight **(see illustration)**. Discard the nut – a new one should be fitted on reassembly.

6 Slacken and remove the rear drum securing screw. If this has suffered from corrosion, it may be quite tight – ensure that a close-fitting tool is used to remove it, or the screw head may suffer damage.

All models

7 It should now be possible to withdraw the brake drum assembly from the stub axle by hand. It may be difficult to remove the drum, due to the brake shoes binding on the inside. If so, first check that the handbrake is fully released, then continue as follows.

8 Referring to Section 17, fully slacken the handbrake adjustment, to obtain maximum free play in the cable.

9 Insert a screwdriver through one of the wheel bolt holes in the brake drum, and lever up the wedge key in order to allow the brake shoes to retract fully – see Section 5 **(see illustrations)**. The brake drum can now be withdrawn.

Inspection

Note: If either drum requires renewal, BOTH should be renewed at the same time. New brake shoes should also be fitted.

10 Remove all brake dust from the drum, without inhaling it.

11 Clean the outside of the drum, and check

8.2 Lever out the cap from the centre of the brake drum

8.3 Remove the split pin and locking cap . . .

8.4 . . . then unscrew the retaining nut and remove the toothed washer

8.5 Loosening the hub nut – later models

8.9a Release the brake shoes by inserting a screwdriver through the drum hole . . .

8.9b . . . and levering the wedge key (arrowed) upwards

it for obvious signs of wear or damage, such as cracks around the roadwheel bolt holes; renew the drum if necessary.

12 Examine carefully the inside of the drum. Light scoring of the friction surface is normal, but if heavy scoring is found, the drum must be renewed. It is usual to find a lip on the drum's inboard edge which should be scraped away, to leave a smooth surface. If, however, the lip is due to the friction surface being recessed by wear, then the drum must be renewed.

13 If the drum is thought to be excessively worn, or oval, its internal diameter must be measured at several points using an internal micrometer. Take measurements in pairs, the second at right-angles to the first, and compare the two, to check for signs of ovality. Noting the specified maximum diameter, both drums could be refinished by skimming or grinding; if this is not possible, the drums on both sides must be renewed.

Refitting

14 If a new brake drum is to be installed, use a suitable solvent to remove any preservative coating inside. On early models, if necessary install the bearing races, inner bearing and oil seal as described in Chapter 10, and thoroughly grease the outer bearing.

15 Prior to refitting, fully retract the brakes shoes by lifting up the wedge key.

Early models

16 Apply a smear of grease to the drum oil seal, and carefully slide the assembly onto the stub axle.

17 Fit the outer bearing and toothed thrustwasher, ensuring its tooth is correctly engaged in the axle slot.

18 Refit the hub nut, tightening it to the point where it just contacts the washer whilst rotating the brake drum to settle the hub bearings in position. Gradually slacken the hub nut until the position is found where it is just possible to move the toothed washer from side-to-side using a screwdriver. **Note:** *Only a small amount of force should be needed to move the washer.* When the hub nut is correctly positioned, refit the locking cap and secure the nut in position with a new split pin.

Later models

19 Ensure that the ABS reluctor ring is clean, then slide on the hub/bearing. Set the hole for the drum securing screw at the top, to make alignment easier.

20 Check that the drum interior is clean, and free of any trace of oil or grease, then carefully slide it over the shoes and stub axle. Align the drum securing screw hole at the top with the one in the hub flange, then insert the screw and tighten securely.

 HAYNES HiNT *With the hub flange and drum almost aligned, temporarily insert two of the wheel bolts to align the drum securing screw hole exactly.*

21 Fit the new hub nut, and tighten it to the specified torque, noting the points made in paragraph 5.

All models

22 Fit the cap to the centre of the brake drum, driving it fully into position.

23 Depress the footbrake several times to operate the self-adjusting mechanism.

24 Repeat the above procedure on the remaining rear brake assembly (where necessary), then check and, if necessary, adjust the handbrake cable (see Section 17).

25 On completion, refit the roadwheel(s), then lower the car to the ground and tighten the wheel bolts to the specified torque.

---

9 Rear brake disc - inspection, removal and refitting

Note: *Refer to the precautions in Section 1 before proceeding.*

Inspection

Note: *If either disc requires renewal, BOTH should be renewed at the same time, to ensure even and consistent braking. New brake pads should be fitted also.*

1 Firmly chock the front wheels, engage 1st gear (or P), then jack up the rear of the car and support it on axle stands. Remove the appropriate rear roadwheel.

2 Inspect the disc as described in Section 7.

Removal

3 Unscrew the two bolts securing the brake caliper mounting bracket in position, then slide the caliper assembly off the disc. Using a piece of wire or string, tie the caliper to the rear suspension coil spring, to avoid placing any strain on the hydraulic brake hose.

4 Using a hammer and a large flat-bladed screwdriver, carefully tap and prise the cap out of the centre of the brake disc. It is recommended that a new cap is fitted on reassembly.

Early models

5 Extract the split pin from the hub nut, and remove the locking ring. Discard the split pin; a new one must be used on refitting.

6 Slacken and remove the rear hub nut, then slide off the toothed washer and remove the outer bearing from the centre of the disc.

Later models

7 Unscrew and remove the 12-point hub nut – make sure the car is well-supported, and that good-quality, close-fitting tools are used, as this nut is very tight. Discard the nut – a new one should be fitted on reassembly.

8 Slacken and remove the rear disc securing screw. If this has suffered from corrosion, it may be quite tight – ensure that a close-fitting tool is used to remove it, or the screw head may suffer damage.

All models

9 The disc can now be slid off the hub/stub axle.

Refitting

10 If a new disc is been fitted, use a suitable solvent to wipe any preservative coating from the disc. On early models, if necessary install the bearing races, inner bearing and oil seal as described in Chapter 10, and thoroughly grease the outer bearing.

Early models

11 Apply a smear of grease to the disc oil seal, and slide the disc assembly onto the stub axle.

12 Fit the outer bearing and toothed thrustwasher, ensuring its tooth is correctly engaged in the axle slot.

13 Refit the hub nut, tightening it to the point where it just contacts the washer whilst rotating the brake disc to settle the hub bearings in position. Gradually slacken the hub nut until the position is found where it is just possible to move the toothed washer from side-to-side using a screwdriver. **Note:** *Only a small amount of force should be needed to move the washer.* When the hub nut is correctly positioned, secure it in position with a new split pin.

Later models

14 Turn the hub to set the hole for the disc securing screw at the top, to make alignment easier.

15 Slide the disc over the stub axle and hub. Align the disc securing screw hole at the top with the one in the hub flange, then insert the screw and tighten securely.

 HAYNES HiNT *With the hub flange and disc almost aligned, temporarily insert two of the wheel bolts to align the disc securing screw hole exactly.*

16 Fit the new hub nut, and tighten it to the specified torque, noting the points made in paragraph 7.

All models

17 Fit the cap to the centre of the brake disc, driving it fully into position.

18 Before refitting the brake caliper, make sure that both sides of the disc are completely clean. Slide the caliper into position over the disc, making sure the pads pass either side of the disc. Tighten the caliper mounting bolts to the specified torque setting.

19 Refit the roadwheel, then lower the vehicle to the ground and tighten the wheel bolts to the specified torque setting.

---

10 Front brake caliper – removal, overhaul and refitting

Note: *Refer to the precautions in Section 1 before proceeding.*

Removal

1 Apply the handbrake, loosen the front wheel bolts, then jack up the front of the car and support it on axle stands. Remove the appropriate roadwheel.

2 Minimise fluid loss by first removing the master cylinder reservoir cap, and then tightening it down onto a piece of polythene, to obtain an airtight seal. Alternatively, use a brake hose clamp, a G-clamp or a similar tool to clamp the flexible hose.

3 Clean the area around the union, then loosen the brake hose union nut.

4 Remove the brake pads as described in Section 4.

5 On models with the Lucas/Girling caliper, unscrew the upper guide pin bolt as well as the lower one, and lift the caliper off completely.

6 Unscrew the caliper from the end of the brake hose, and remove it from the car.

Overhaul

7 With the caliper on the bench, wipe away all traces of dust and dirt, but *avoid inhaling the dust, as it is a health hazard.*

8 Withdraw the partially-ejected piston from the caliper body, and remove the dust seal.

HAYNES HINT *If the piston cannot be withdrawn by hand, it can be pushed out by applying compressed air to the brake hose union hole. Only low pressure should be required, such as is generated by a foot pump. As the piston is expelled, take great care not to trap your fingers between the piston and caliper.*

9 Using a small screwdriver, extract the piston hydraulic seal, taking great care not to damage the caliper bore **(see illustration)**.

10 Thoroughly clean all components, using only methylated spirit, isopropyl alcohol or clean hydraulic fluid as a cleaning medium. Never use mineral-based solvents such as petrol or paraffin, as they will attack the hydraulic system's rubber components. Dry the components immediately, using compressed air or a clean, lint-free cloth. Use compressed air to blow clear the fluid passages.

11 On VW calipers, withdraw the spacers from the caliper body bushes.

12 On Lucas/Girling calipers, withdraw the guide pins from the caliper mounting bracket, and remove the rubber gaiters.

13 Check all components, and renew any that are worn or damaged. Check particularly the cylinder bore and piston; these should be renewed (note that this means the renewal of the complete body assembly) if they are scratched, worn or corroded in any way. Similarly check the condition of the spacers/guide pins and their bushes/bores (as applicable); both spacers/pins should be undamaged and (when cleaned) a reasonably tight sliding fit in their bores. If there is any doubt about the condition of any component, renew it.

14 If the assembly is fit for further use, obtain the appropriate repair kit; the components are available from VW dealers in various combinations.

15 Renew all rubber seals, dust covers and caps disturbed on dismantling as a matter of course; these should never be re-used.

16 On reassembly, ensure that all components are clean and dry.

17 Soak the piston and the new piston (fluid) seal in clean hydraulic fluid. Smear clean fluid on the cylinder bore surface.

18 Fit the new piston (fluid) seal, using only your fingers (no tools) to manipulate it into the cylinder bore groove. Fit the new dust seal to the piston, and refit the piston to the cylinder bore using a twisting motion; ensure that the piston enters squarely into the bore. Press the piston fully into the bore, then press the dust seal into the caliper body.

19 On VW calipers, apply the grease supplied in the repair kit (or a copper-based high-temperature brake grease or anti-seize compound) to the spacers, and insert them into their bushes.

20 On Lucas/Girling calipers, apply the grease supplied in the repair kit (or a copper-based high-temperature brake grease or anti-seize compound) to the guide pins, and fit the new gaiters. Fit the guide pins to the caliper mounting bracket, ensuring that the gaiters are correctly located in the grooves on both the sleeve and mounting bracket.

Refitting

21 Screw the caliper fully onto the flexible hose union.

22 Refit the brake pads (see Section 4).

23 Securely tighten the brake pipe union nut.

24 Remove the brake hose clamp or polythene, as applicable, and bleed the hydraulic system as described in Section 2. Note that, providing the precautions described were taken to minimise brake fluid loss, it should only be necessary to bleed the relevant front brake.

25 Refit the roadwheel, then lower the car to the ground and tighten the roadwheel bolts to the specified torque.

11 Rear brake caliper – removal, overhaul and refitting

Note: *Refer to the precautions in Section 1 before proceeding.*

Removal

1 Chock the front wheels, engage 1st gear (or P), then jack up the rear of the car and support on axle stands. Remove the relevant rear wheel.

2 Minimise fluid loss by first removing the master cylinder reservoir cap, and then tightening it down onto a piece of polythene, to obtain an airtight seal. Alternatively, use a brake hose clamp, a G-clamp or a similar tool

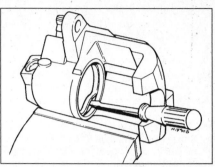

10.9 Extracting the piston seal – take care not to scratch the surface of the bore

to clamp the flexible hose.

3 Referring to Section 19, disconnect the handbrake inner and outer cables from the caliper lever and caliper bracket respectively.

4 Remove the brake pads as described in Section 6.

5 Clean the area around the union, then loosen the brake hose union nut. Unscrew the caliper from the end of the flexible hose and remove it from the car.

Overhaul

Note: *It is not possible to overhaul the brake caliper handbrake mechanism. If the mechanism is faulty, or fluid is leaking from the handbrake lever seal, the caliper assembly must be renewed.*

6 With the caliper on the bench, wipe away all traces of dust and dirt, but avoid inhaling the dust, as it is a health hazard.

7 Using a small screwdriver, carefully prise out the dust seal from the caliper bore, taking care not to damage the piston.

8 Remove the piston from the caliper bore by rotating it in an anti-clockwise direction. This can be achieved using a suitable pair of circlip pliers engaged in the caliper piston slots. Once the piston turns freely but does not come out any further, the piston can be withdrawn by hand.

HAYNES HINT *If the piston cannot be withdrawn by hand, it can be pushed out by applying compressed air to the brake hose union hole. Only low pressure should be required, such as is generated by a foot pump. As the piston is expelled, take care not to trap your fingers between the piston and caliper.*

9 Using a small screwdriver, extract the piston hydraulic seal(s), taking care not to damage the caliper bore.

10 Withdraw the guide pins from the caliper mounting bracket, and remove the guide sleeve gaiters.

11 Thoroughly clean all components, using only methylated spirit, isopropyl alcohol or clean hydraulic fluid as a cleaning medium. Never use mineral-based solvents such as petrol or paraffin, as they will attack the hydraulic system's rubber components. Dry the components immediately, using compressed air or a clean, lint-free cloth. Use compressed air to blow clear the fluid passages.

12 Inspect all the caliper components as described in Section 10, paragraphs 13 to 16, and renew as necessary, noting that the handbrake mechanism must **not** be dismantled.

13 Soak the piston and the new piston (fluid) seal in clean hydraulic fluid. Smear clean fluid on the cylinder bore surface. Fit the new piston (fluid) seal(s), using only the fingers (no tools) to manipulate into the cylinder bore groove(s).

14 Fit the new dust seal to the piston groove, then refit the piston assembly. Turn the piston in a clockwise direction, using the method employed on dismantling, until it is fully retracted into the caliper bore. Press the dust seal into position in the caliper housing.

15 Apply the grease supplied in the repair kit (or a copper-based high-temperature brake grease or anti-seize compound) to the guide pins. Fit the new gaiters to the guide pins and fit the pins to the caliper mounting bracket, ensuring that the gaiters are correctly located in the grooves on both the pins and caliper bracket.

16 Prior to refitting, fill the caliper with fresh hydraulic fluid by slackening the bleed screw and pumping the fluid through the caliper until bubble-free fluid is expelled from the union hole.

Refitting

17 Screw the caliper fully onto the flexible hose union.

18 Refit the brake pads as described in paragraphs 10 to 12 of Section 6.

19 Securely tighten the brake pipe union nut.

20 Remove the brake hose clamp or polythene, as applicable, and bleed the hydraulic system as described in Section 2. Note that, providing the precautions described were taken to minimise brake fluid loss, it should only be necessary to bleed the relevant rear brake.

21 Connect the handbrake cable to the caliper, and adjust the handbrake as described in Section 17.

22 Refit the roadwheel, then lower the car to the ground and tighten the roadwheel bolts to the specified torque. On completion, check the hydraulic fluid level as described in *Weekly checks*.

12 Rear wheel cylinder – removal, overhaul and refitting

Note: *Refer to the precautions in Section 1 before proceeding.*

Removal

1 Remove the brake drum (see Section 8).

2 Using pliers, carefully unhook the upper brake shoe return spring, and remove it from both brake shoes. Pull the upper ends of the shoes away from the wheel cylinder to disengage them from the pistons.

3 Minimise fluid loss by first removing the master cylinder reservoir cap, and then tightening it down onto a piece of polythene, to obtain an airtight seal. Alternatively, use a brake hose clamp, a G-clamp or a similar tool to clamp the flexible hose at the nearest convenient point to the wheel cylinder.

4 Wipe away all traces of dirt around the brake pipe union at the rear of the wheel cylinder, and unscrew the union nut. Carefully ease the pipe out of the wheel cylinder, and plug or tape over its end to prevent dirt entry. Wipe off any spilt immediately.

5 Unscrew the two wheel cylinder retaining bolts from the rear of the backplate, and remove the cylinder, taking great care not to allow surplus hydraulic fluid to contaminate the brake shoe linings. Later models may be fitted with an aluminium wheel cylinder, which only has one retaining bolt.

Overhaul

6 Brush the dirt and dust from the wheel cylinder, but take care not to inhale it.

7 Pull the rubber dust seals from the ends of the cylinder body **(see illustration)**.

8 The pistons will normally be ejected by the pressure of the coil spring, but if they are not, tap the end of the cylinder body on a piece of wood, or apply low air pressure – eg, from a foot pump – to the hydraulic fluid union hole to eject the pistons from their bores.

9 Inspect the surfaces of the pistons and their bores in the cylinder body for scoring, or evidence of metal-to-metal contact. If evident, renew the complete wheel cylinder assembly. The later aluminium wheel cylinder may be fitted instead of the earlier cylinder, if wished – VW state that it is permissible to mix the two types.

10 If the pistons and bores are in good condition, discard the seals and obtain a repair kit, which will contain all the necessary renewable items.

11 Remove the seals from the pistons, noting their correct fitted orientation. Lubricate the new piston seals with clean brake fluid, and fit them onto the pistons with their larger diameters innermost.

12 Dip the pistons in clean brake fluid, then fit the spring to the cylinder.

13 Insert the pistons into the cylinder bores using a twisting motion.

14 Fit the dust seals, and check that the pistons can move freely in their bores.

Refitting

15 Ensure that the backplate and wheel cylinder mating surfaces are clean, then spread the brake shoes and manoeuvre the wheel cylinder into position.

16 Engage the brake pipe, and screw in the union nut two or three turns to ensure that the thread has started.

17 Insert the two wheel cylinder retaining bolts (or the single bolt), and tighten to the specified torque. Now fully tighten the brake pipe union nut.

18 Remove the clamp from the flexible brake hose, or the polythene from the master cylinder reservoir (as applicable).

19 Ensure that the brake shoes are correctly located in the cylinder pistons, then refit the brake shoe upper return spring, using a screwdriver to stretch the spring into position.

20 Refit the brake drum (see Section 8).

21 Bleed the brake hydraulic system as described in Section 2. Providing suitable precautions were taken to minimise loss of fluid, it should only be necessary to bleed the relevant rear brake.

13 Master cylinder – removal, overhaul and refitting

Note: *Refer to the precautions in Section 1 before proceeding.*

Removal

1 Disconnect the battery negative terminal (see *Disconnecting the battery*).

2 To improve access to the master cylinder,

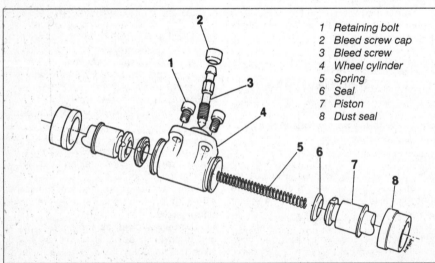

1 Retaining bolt
2 Bleed screw cap
3 Bleed screw
4 Wheel cylinder
5 Spring
6 Seal
7 Piston
8 Dust seal

12.7 Rear wheel cylinder components

remove the air cleaner and air inlet trunking as described in Chapter 4A.

3 Remove the brake fluid reservoir cap, and syphon the hydraulic fluid from the reservoir. **Note:** *Do not syphon the fluid by mouth, as it is poisonous; use a syringe or an old poultry baster.* Alternatively, open any convenient bleed screw in the system, and gently pump the brake pedal to expel the fluid through a plastic tube connected to the screw (see Section 2). Disconnect the wiring plug from the brake fluid level sender unit.

4 Wipe clean the area around the brake pipe unions on the side of the master cylinder, and place absorbent rags beneath the pipe unions to catch any surplus fluid. Make a note of the correct fitted positions of the unions, then unscrew the union nuts and carefully withdraw the pipes. Plug or tape over the pipe ends and master cylinder orifices, to minimise the loss of brake fluid, and to prevent the entry of dirt into the system. Wash off any spilt fluid immediately with cold water.

5 Slacken and remove the two nuts (and washers, where applicable) securing the master cylinder to the vacuum servo unit, then withdraw the unit from the engine compartment. Remove the O-ring from the rear of the master cylinder, and discard it.

Overhaul

6 If the master cylinder is faulty, it must be renewed. Repair kits are not available from VW dealer, so the cylinder must be treated as a sealed unit.

7 The only items which can be renewed are the mounting seals for the fluid reservoir; if these show signs of deterioration, pull off the reservoir and remove the old seals. Lubricate the new seals with clean brake fluid, and press them into the master cylinder ports. Ease the fluid reservoir into position, and push it fully home.

Refitting

8 Remove all traces of dirt from the master cylinder and servo unit mating surfaces, and fit a new O-ring to the groove on the master cylinder body.

9 Fit the master cylinder to the servo unit, ensuring that the servo unit pushrod enters the master cylinder bore centrally. Refit the master cylinder mounting nuts (and washers, where fitted) and tighten them to the specified torque.

10 Wipe clean the brake pipe unions, then refit them to the master cylinder ports and tighten them securely.

11 Refill the master cylinder reservoir with new fluid, and bleed the complete hydraulic system as described in Section 2.

14 Brake pedal – removal and refitting

Removal

1 Disconnect the battery negative terminal (see *Disconnecting the battery*).

2 Remove the driver's side lower trim panel as described in Chapter 11, Section 26.

3 The pedal cluster must be removed complete, in order to allow sufficient room for the brake pedal to be removed

4 Remove the stop-light switch (Section 20).

5 Unhook the clutch cable from the pedal.

6 It is now necessary to release the brake pedal from the ball on the vacuum servo pushrod. To do this, reach up behind the pedal and carefully expand the pedal retaining clip lugs until the pedal can be gently pulled off the servo unit pushrod ball.

7 Drill out the two shear-bolts used to secure the base of the steering column to the pedal bracket.

8 Unscrew and remove the pedal bracket mounting bolts, and remove the assembly from the car.

9 Unscrew the nut on the right-hand end of the pedal pivot shaft, and pull the shaft out. Remove the brake pedal.

10 Carefully clean all components, and renew any that are worn or damaged.

Refitting

11 Refitting is a reversal of removal, noting the following points:
   a) *Prior to refitting, apply a smear of multi-purpose grease to the pivot shaft and pedal bearing surfaces.*
   b) *Fit new shear-bolts and tighten them until their heads break off.*
   c) *Press the brake pedal onto the servo pushrod ball, ensuring that it locates correctly.*
   d) *Refit the stop-light switch as described in Section 20.*

15 Vacuum servo unit – testing, removal and refitting

Testing

1 To test the operation of the servo unit, depress the footbrake several times to exhaust the vacuum, then start the engine whilst keeping the pedal firmly depressed. As the engine starts, there should be a noticeable 'give' in the brake pedal as the vacuum builds-up. Allow the engine to run for at least two minutes, then switch it off. If the brake pedal is now depressed, it should feel normal, but further applications should result in the pedal feeling firmer, with the pedal stroke decreasing with each application.

2 If the servo does not operate as described, first inspect the servo unit check valve as described in Section 16.

3 If the servo unit still fails to operate satisfactorily, the fault lies within the unit itself. Repairs to the unit are not possible – if faulty, the servo unit must be renewed.

Removal

Note: *On left-hand drive models, it is not possible to remove the vacuum servo unit without first removing the hydraulic unit (see Section 22). Therefore, servo unit removal and refitting should be entrusted to a VW dealer.*

4 Remove the master cylinder (Section 13).

5 Carefully ease the vacuum hose out from the servo unit sealing grommet.

6 From inside the car, remove the stop-light switch as described in Section 20.

7 Undo the four retaining nuts securing the servo unit to the pedal mounting bracket, then return to the engine compartment and manoeuvre the servo unit out of position, noting the gasket which is fitted to the rear of the unit. As the servo is withdrawn, it will be necessary to release its pushrod ball from the brake pedal spring clip (see paragraph 6 of Section 14).

Refitting

8 Check the servo unit vacuum hose sealing grommet for signs of damage or deterioration, and renew if necessary.

9 Fit a new gasket to the rear of the servo unit, and reposition the unit in the engine compartment.

10 From inside the car, ensure that the servo unit pushrod is correctly engaged with the brake pedal, and clip the pedal onto the pushrod ball. Check the pedal is securely retained, then refit the servo unit mounting nuts and tighten them to the specified torque.

11 Carefully ease the vacuum hose back into position in the servo, taking great care not to displace the sealing grommet.

12 Refit the master cylinder as described in Section 13 of this Chapter.

13 Refit the stop-light switch (Section 20).

14 On completion, start the engine and check for air leaks at the vacuum hose-to-servo unit connection; check the operation of the braking system.

16 Vacuum servo unit check valve – removal, testing and refitting

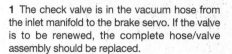

1 The check valve is in the vacuum hose from the inlet manifold to the brake servo. If the valve is to be renewed, the complete hose/valve assembly should be replaced.

Removal

2 Ease the vacuum hose out of the servo unit, taking care not to displace the grommet.

3 Note the routing of the hose, then slacken the retaining clip and disconnect the opposite end of the hose assembly from the manifold/pump and remove it from the car.

Testing

4 Examine the check valve and vacuum hose for signs of damage, and renew if necessary.

5 The valve may be tested by blowing through it in both directions. Air should flow through the valve in one direction only – when blown through from the servo unit end of the

17.5 Unscrew and remove the plastic nuts behind the gear/selector lever . . .

17.6a . . . then lift the rear of the console for access to the handbrake adjuster nuts

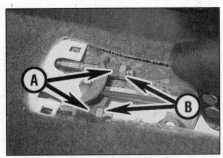

17.6b Cable adjuster nuts (A) and locknuts (B) – seen with centre console removed

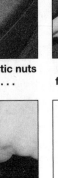

17.7 Adjusting the handbrake cables

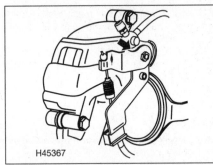

H45367

17.9 Adjust the clearance between the handbrake lever and caliper as described in the text

valve. Renew the valve if this is not the case.

6 Examine the servo unit rubber sealing grommet for signs of damage or deterioration, and renew as necessary.

Refitting

7 Ensure that the sealing grommet is correctly fitted to the servo unit.

8 Ease the hose union into position in the servo, taking great care not to displace or damage the grommet.

9 Ensure that the hose is correctly routed, and connect it to the inlet manifold/pump, tightening its retaining clip securely.

10 On completion, start the engine and check the check valve-to-servo unit connection for signs of air leaks.

17 Handbrake –
adjustment

1 To check the handbrake adjustment, first apply the footbrake firmly several times to establish correct shoe-to-drum/pad-to-disc clearance, then apply and release the handbrake several times.

2 Applying normal moderate pressure, pull the handbrake lever to the fully-applied position, counting the number of clicks emitted from the handbrake ratchet mechanism. If adjustment is correct, there should be approximately 4 to 7 clicks before the handbrake is fully applied. If this is not the case, adjust as follows.

3 Chock the front wheels, then jack up the rear of the car and support it on axle stands.

On rear disc brake models, remove the rear wheels.

4 To gain the best access to the handbrake adjuster nuts (which are behind the lever itself), the centre console should be removed completely, as described in Chapter 11. However, this is a complicated procedure, and sufficient access can be gained as follows.

5 Prise up the gaiter (or selector lever panel) for access to the two plastic nuts securing the front of the console. Remove the nuts **(see illustration)**.

6 Pull upwards on the rear of the console, to release the spring clip which holds it to the floor. Take care that the metal clip does not get pulled out of its floor recess, as it may then fall down and get trapped among the handbrake cables. Though the console can only be lifted a few inches, it should be enough to access the adjuster nuts **(see illustrations)**.

18.2a To improve access to the handbrake lever, prise out the curved panel . . .

Rear drum brake models

7 With the handbrake set on the 4th notch of the ratchet mechanism, slacken the locknuts and rotate the adjusting nuts equally until it is difficult to turn both rear wheels **(see illustration)**. Once this is so, release the handbrake lever, and check that the wheels rotate freely. Check the adjustment by applying the handbrake fully, counting the clicks from the handbrake ratchet and, if necessary, re-adjust.

Rear disc brake models

8 With the handbrake fully released, equally slacken the handbrake locknuts and adjusting sleeves until both the rear caliper handbrake levers are back against their stops.

9 From this point, equally tighten both adjusting sleeves until both handbrake levers just move off the caliper stops. The help of an assistant will be necessary to determine the exact point when the levers lift. Ensure that the gap between each caliper handbrake lever and its stop is less than 1.5 mm, and ensure both the right- and left-hand gaps are equal **(see illustration)**. Check that both wheels/discs rotate freely, then check the adjustment by applying the handbrake fully, counting the clicks emitted from the handbrake ratchet. If necessary, re-adjust.

All models

10 Once adjustment is correct, hold the adjusting nuts and securely tighten the locknuts. Refit the centre console.

18 Handbrake lever and warning light switch –
removal and refitting

Handbrake lever
Removal

1 To gain the best access to the handbrake lever, the centre console should be removed completely, as described in Chapter 11. However, this is a complicated procedure, and sufficient access may be gained by following the procedure in Section 17, paragraphs 5 and 6.

2 In addition, the curved panel in the centre console under the lever can be prised out, and the handbrake lever cover removed using a small screwdriver **(see illustrations)**.

3 Referring to Section 17 if necessary, remove both the handbrake cable locknuts and adjusting nuts, and detach the cables from the compensator plate.
4 Disconnect the wiring connector from the warning light switch, then undo the retaining nuts and remove the lever from the car.

Refitting

5 Refitting is a reversal of the removal. Adjust the handbrake as described in Section 17.

Warning light switch

Removal

6 Proceed as described in paragraphs 1 and 2.
7 Pull the handbrake lever up as far as possible.
8 The switch has a plastic peg moulded into it, which locates through a small hole in the base of the handbrake lever. Press out the peg, and disconnect the wiring plug from the switch **(see illustrations)**.

Refitting

9 Refitting is a reversal of removal.

---

19 Handbrake cables – removal and refitting

Removal

1 The handbrake cable consists of two sections, a right- and a left-hand section, which are linked to the lever by a

18.2b . . . or prise down the securing lug at the base of the handle . . .

18.2c . . . and pull off the handle cover

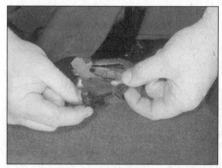

18.8a Release the handbrake warning light switch from the base of the lever . . .

18.8b . . . and disconnect the wiring plug

19.5 Handbrake cable securing clip on rear suspension arm

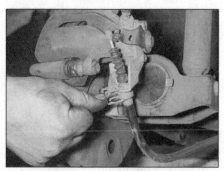

19.7b . . . then remove the retaining clip . . .

19.7a On disc brake models, detach the inner cable from the caliper lever . . .

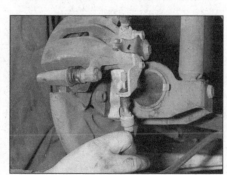

19.7c . . . and free the cable from the caliper bracket

compensator plate. Each section can be removed individually.
2 Gain access to the cables as described in

Section 17. Also referring to Section 17, slacken the relevant handbrake locknut and adjusting nut to obtain maximum free play in the cable, and disengage the inner cable from the handbrake compensator plate.
3 Chock the front wheels, then loosen the relevant rear wheel bolts. Jack up the rear of the car and support it on axle stands.
4 From the underbody, free the front end of the outer cable from the body, and withdraw the cable from its support guide.
5 Working back along the length of the cable, noting its correct routing, and free it from all the relevant retaining clips **(see illustration)**.

Rear drum brake models

6 Remove the rear brake shoes from the relevant side as described in Section 5. Using a hammer and pin punch, carefully tap the outer cable out from the brake backplate, release it from the backplate cable guide, and remove it from underneath the car.

Rear disc brake models

7 Disengage the inner cable from the caliper handbrake lever, then remove the outer cable retaining clip and detach the cable from the caliper **(see illustrations)**.

Refitting

8 Refitting is a reversal of the removal procedure. Where the cable is clipped to the rear trailing arm, note that genuine VW cables have an indentation in the cable outer, which must lie in the centre of the retaining clip when fitted. On completion, adjust the handbrake as described in Section 17.

20.3 Disconnect the stop-light switch wiring plug ...

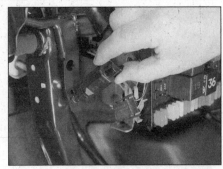

20.4 ... then twist the switch body 90° clockwise and remove it from the brake pedal

20 Stop-light switch – removal and refitting

Removal

1 The stop-light switch is located on the pedal bracket below the facia.
2 Remove the driver's side lower trim panel as described in Chapter 11, Section 26.
3 Reach up behind the facia and disconnect the wiring connector from the switch **(see illustration)**.
4 Twist the switch through 90° clockwise and release it from the mounting bracket **(see illustration)**.

Refitting

5 Prior to installation, fully extend the stop-light switch plunger.
6 Fully depress and hold the brake pedal, then manoeuvre the switch into position. Secure the switch in position it by twisting it through 90° anti-clockwise, and release the brake pedal.
7 Reconnect the wiring connector, and check the operation of the stop-lights. The stop-lights should illuminate after the brake pedal has travelled about 5 mm. If the switch is not functioning correctly, it is faulty and must be renewed; no adjustment is possible.
8 On completion, refit the driver's side lower trim panel as described in Chapter 11, Section 26.

21 Anti-lock braking system (ABS) – general information

ABS is fitted to all models covered in this manual. The system comprises a hydraulic block (which contains the hydraulic solenoid valves and accumulators), the electrically-driven return pump, and four roadwheel sensors (one fitted to each wheel), and the electronic control unit (ECU). The purpose of the system is to prevent the wheel(s) locking during heavy braking. This is achieved by automatic release of the brake on the relevant

wheel, followed by re-application of the brake.
The solenoids are controlled by the ECU, which itself receives signals from the four wheel sensors (one fitted on each hub), which monitor the speed of rotation of each wheel. By comparing these signals, the ECU can determine the speed at which the car is travelling. It can then use this speed to determine when a wheel is decelerating at an abnormal rate, compared to the speed of the car, and therefore predicts when a wheel is about to lock. During normal operation, the system functions in the same way as a non-ABS braking system.
If the ECU senses that a wheel is about to lock, it operates the relevant solenoid valve in the modulator block, which then isolates the brake caliper on the wheel which is about to lock from the master cylinder, effectively sealing-in the hydraulic pressure.
If the speed of rotation of the wheel continues to decrease at an abnormal rate, the ECU switches on the electrically-driven return pump, which pumps the hydraulic fluid back into the master cylinder, releasing pressure on that brake so that the brake is released. Once the speed of rotation of the wheel returns to an acceptable rate, the pump stops; the solenoid valve opens, allowing the hydraulic master cylinder pressure to return to the brake, which then re-applies the brake. This cycle can be carried out at up to 10 times a second.
The action of the solenoid valves and return pump creates pulses in the hydraulic circuit. When the ABS system is functioning, these pulses can be felt through the brake pedal.

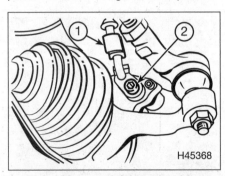

22.5 ABS front wheel sensor wiring plug (1) and retaining bolt (2)

The operation of the ABS system is entirely dependent on electrical signals. To prevent the system responding to any inaccurate signals, a built-in safety circuit monitors all signals received by the ECU. If an inaccurate signal or low battery voltage is detected, the ABS system is automatically shut down, and the warning light on the instrument panel is illuminated, to inform the driver that the ABS system is not operational. Normal braking should still be available, however.
If a fault does develop in the ABS system, the car must be taken to a VW dealer for fault diagnosis and repair.

22 Anti-lock braking system (ABS) components – removal and refitting

Hydraulic unit

1 Removal and refitting of the hydraulic unit should be entrusted to a VW dealer. Great care has to be taken not to allow any fluid to escape from the unit as the pipes are disconnected. If the fluid is allowed to escape, air can enter the unit, causing air locks which cause the hydraulic unit to malfunction.

Electronic control unit (ECU)

2 The anti-lock braking system ECU is secured to the hydraulic unit, and can only be separated from it once the pair have been removed as an assembly. This task should be entrusted to a VW dealer.

Front wheel sensor

Removal

3 Chock the rear wheels, then firmly apply the handbrake and loosen the relevant front wheel bolts. Jack up the front of the car and support on axle stands. Remove the appropriate front roadwheel.
4 Trace the wiring back from the sensor to the connector, freeing it from any retaining clips, and disconnect it from the main loom.
5 Slacken and remove the bolt securing the sensor to the swivel hub **(see illustration)**, and remove the sensor and lead assembly from the car.

Refitting

6 Prior to refitting, apply a thin coat of multi-purpose grease to the sensor body, and to the sensor's location in the swivel hub (VW recommend the use of lubricating paste G 000 650 – available from your dealer).
7 Fit the sensor to the swivel hub, then refit the retaining bolt and tighten it to the specified torque.
8 Ensure that the sensor wiring is correctly routed and retained by necessary clips, and reconnect its wiring connector.
9 Refit the roadwheel, then lower the car to the ground and tighten the roadwheel bolts to the specified torque.

Rear wheel sensor

Removal

10 Chock the front wheels, then loosen the relevant rear wheel bolts. Jack up the rear of the car and support it on axle stands. Remove the appropriate roadwheel.

11 Fold the rear seat forwards, and lift up any floor covering beneath. Locate the wheel sensor wiring connector, and disconnect it.

12 Working under the car, unscrew and remove the sensor retaining bolt from the stub axle **(see illustration)**, and withdraw the sensor from the brake.

13 Trace the sensor wiring back from the sensor, detaching it from the retaining clips. Where the sensor wiring passes into the car's interior, prise out the rubber grommet from the floor, and pull the sensor wiring through. The sensor and its wiring can now be removed from the car.

Refitting

14 Coat the sensor body and its aperture in the stub axle/brake backplate with a thin coat of multi-purpose grease (VW recommend the use of lubricating paste G 000 650 – available from your dealer).

15 Fit the sensor to the stub axle/brake backplate, then refit the retaining bolt and tighten it to the specified torque.

16 Ensure the sensor wiring is routed correctly, and secured by the retaining clips. Feed the wiring through the hole in the floor, and seal the hole with the grommet.

17 Inside the car, reconnect the sensor wiring, then refit the floor covering and fold the rear seat upright.

18 Refit the roadwheel, then lower the car to the ground and tighten the roadwheel bolts to the specified torque.

Front wheel sensor reluctor rings

19 The front reluctor rings are fixed onto the rear of wheel hubs. Examine the rings for damage such as chipped or missing teeth. If renewal is necessary, the complete hub assembly must be dismantled as described in Chapter 10.

Rear wheel sensor reluctor rings

Early models

20 The rear reluctor rings are pressed onto the inside of the rear brake drum, or onto the rear stub axle (rear disc brake models). Examine the rings for signs of damage such as chipped or missing teeth, and renew as necessary. If renewal is necessary, remove the drum as described in Section 8, or the rear disc as described in Section 9 . The reluctor

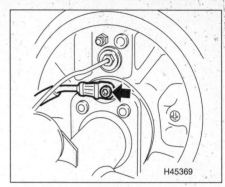

22.12 ABS rear wheel sensor retaining bolt (arrowed)

ring can be prised off using two screwdrivers on opposite sides of the ring. Press the new ring on squarely, using a tube or socket of appropriate diameter.

Later models

21 The rear reluctor rings are pressed onto the rear hub/bearing – remove the drum as described in Section 8, or the rear disc as described in Section 9 . Examine the rings for signs of damage such as chipped or missing teeth, and renew as necessary. At the time of writing, it appears that the rear hub/bearing is only available as a complete assembly.

Chapter 10
Suspension and steering

Contents

Degrees of difficulty

| Easy, suitable for novice with little experience | | Fairly easy, suitable for beginner with some experience | | Fairly difficult, suitable for competent DIY mechanic | | Difficult, suitable for experienced DIY mechanic | | Very difficult, suitable for expert DIY or professional | |

Specifications

General

Front suspension type	Independent, with coil spring struts incorporating telescopic shock absorbers; lower wishbones. Anti-roll bar
Rear suspension type	Transverse torsion beam with trailing arms. Coil spring struts incorporating telescopic shock absorbers
Steering type	Rack-and-pinion. Power assistance on all models

Suspension angles/wheel alignment

Front wheels:
Toe-in	0° ± 10'
Camber:	
Except DOHC engine models	-25' ± 20'
DOHC engine models	-30' ± 20'
Castor	+1°20' ± 30'
Maximum side-to-side difference:	
Camber	20'
Castor	30'
Track angle difference at lock of 20° left and right	-1°05' ± 30'

Rear wheels:
Camber	-1°40' ± 20'
Maximum side-to-side difference	20'
Total track (at specified camber)	+20' ± 10'
Maximum allowable deviation	20'

Tyre pressures . . . . See end of *Weekly checks* on page 0•17

Torque wrench settings

	Nm	lbf ft
Front suspension		
Anti-roll bar connecting link nuts	25	18
Anti-roll bar mounting plate bolts	25	18
Brake disc splash shield bolts	10	7
Piston rod nut	60	44
Strut upper mounting bolts*:		
Stage 1	15	11
Stage 2	Angle-tighten a further 180°	
Strut-to-swivel hub mounting nut*/bolt	95	70
Subframe mounting bolt (M12):		
Stage 1	50	37
Stage 2	Angle-tighten a further 90°	
Wishbone/lower arm balljoint nut	35	26
Wishbone/lower arm balljoint retaining bolts	35	26
Wishbone/lower arm pivot bolt	70	52
Wishbone/lower arm rear mounting through-bolt (M12):		
Stage 1	50	37
Stage 2	Angle-tighten a further 90°	
Rear suspension		
Rear axle pivot bolt nut	65	48
Shock absorber top nuts	15	11
Strut lower mounting nut	55	41
Strut upper mounting nut	25	18
Steering		
Column height adjuster lever nut (**left-hand thread**)	8	6
Column height adjuster lever through-bolt (**left-hand thread**)	23	17
Column lower universal joint (UJ) bolt	30	22
Fluid hose banjo bolt	30	22
Fluid reservoir mounting bolts	5	4
Fluid union nuts	20	15
Steering gear mounting bolts	30	22
Steering gear pinion clamp bolt	30	22
Steering pump mounting bolts	25	18
Steering pump mounting bracket bolts	45	33
Steering pump pulley bolts	25	18
Steering wheel nut	50	37
Track rod adjustment locknut	50	37
Track rod balljoint nut	35	26
Track rod-to-steering gear	80	59
Roadwheels		
Roadwheel bolts	110	81

Use new nuts/bolts

1 General description

The front suspension is of independent, MacPherson strut and wishbone type. The strut on each side incorporates a telescopic shock absorber and coil spring. The wishbone arms are pivoted from large rubber bushes in the subframe, and are attached to the swivel hubs by a large balljoint. An anti-roll bar is fitted to all models, and is located on the wishbone arms at each end, and also at underbody mountings.

The rear suspension consists of a transverse torsion beam axle with trailing arms. The combined axle and arms pivot from large underbody mountings each side. A coil spring and shock absorber strut are located each side, between the top of the wheel arch and the axle arm at the bottom end, to control axle movement.

Rack-and-pinion steering is fitted, with power assistance on all models. The steering column incorporates a telescopic collapsible section as a safety feature in the event of a collision. A height-adjustable steering column is fitted on some models. All models have a steering column equipped with a 'torque overload clutch'. This is an additional security device, which ensures that the steering column lock cannot be broken by excessive force. If a torque of more than 100 Nm is applied through the steering wheel, the clutch disengages the column from the front wheels, preventing damage to the lock. The clutch mechanism is overridden when the ignition key is next inserted.

All models are equipped with an airbag mounted in the steering wheel. For details, refer to Chapter 12.

2 Front suspension strut – removal and refitting

Removal

1 Chock the rear wheels, apply the handbrake, then loosen the relevant front wheel bolts. Jack up and support the front of the car on axle stands (see *Jacking and vehicle support*). Remove the roadwheel on the side concerned.

2 Position a jack under the outer end of the wishbone arm for support.

3 In the engine compartment, unscrew and remove the three strut upper mounting bolts **(see illustration)**. Discard the bolts, as new ones should be used when refitting.

4 Scribe an alignment mark around the periphery of the suspension strut-to-swivel hub location lugs, to ensure accurate

2.3 Front strut upper mounting bolts

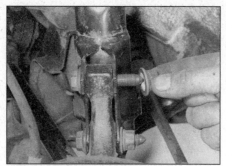

2.4a Loosen and remove the strut-to-swivel hub nuts . . .

2.4b . . . and remove the bolts, noting their direction of fitting

positioning when refitting. Also mark the upper and lower retaining bolts to identify one from the other. This is essential, as the fitted position of the strut to swivel hub (and of the bolts) sets the camber angle. It is therefore critical that they be refitted in exactly the same position during reassembly. Undo the retaining nuts (18 mm on project car), and withdraw the two bolts securing the strut at its bottom end to the swivel hub, noting that the bolts are fitted from the front **(see illustrations)**. Renew the self-locking nuts.

5 Disengage the strut from its top mounting, then prise it free from the swivel hub **(see illustration)**.

6 Note that the lower balljoint must not be detached from the wishbone without first referring to Section 6.

Refitting

7 Refitting is a reversal of the removal procedure, noting the following points:

a) *Tighten all fasteners to the specified torque (see illustration).*

b) *Use new self-locking nuts to secure the strut-to-swivel hub bolts. Insert the bolts from the front of the swivel hubs. Ensure the correct realignment of the two units (as marked during removal), to ensure that the camber angle is maintained.*

c) *Use new strut upper mounting bolts, tightened in the two Stages specified.*

d) *If a new strut and/or swivel hub have been fitted, have the camber angle checked and if necessary adjusted by a VW dealer.*

3 Front suspension strut and coil spring – separation and reassembly

1 Remove the front suspension strut as described in the previous Section.

⚠ **Warning: Before attempting to dismantle the suspension strut, a suitable tool to hold the coil spring in compression must be obtained. Adjustable coil spring compressors are readily available, and are recommended for this operation. Any attempt to dismantle the strut without such a tool is likely to result in damage or personal injury.**

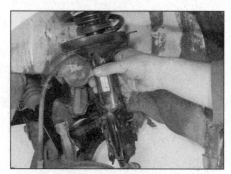

2.5 Removing the suspension strut from under the front wheel arch

2 Support the lower end of the strut in a vice, then fit the coil spring compressor into position, and check that it is securely located.

3 Compress the spring until the upper spring seat is free of tension, then remove the nut from the top of the piston rod. Hold the piston rod with an Allen key while the nut is unscrewed. The need to hold the piston rod means that an ordinary deep socket cannot readily be used; in

2.7 Tighten the strut-to-swivel hub nuts/bolts to the specified torque

the workshop, we used a deep socket with hex flats on it (a box spanner would also work), which could be held using a spanner. The nut is especially tight – don't expect to use makeshift means to loosen it safely.

4 Remove the strut mounting, followed by the bearing **(see illustration)**. Note the fitted order and orientation of all components, for use when refitting.

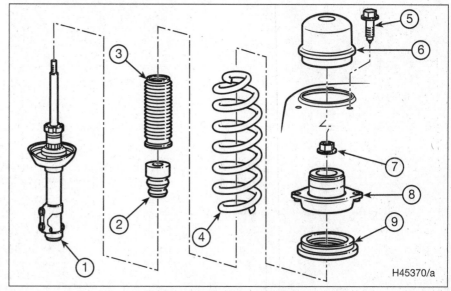

3.4 Front suspension strut details

1 Shock absorber	4 Spring	7 Piston rod nut
2 Bump stop	5 Upper mounting bolts	8 Strut mounting
3 Gaiter	6 Plastic cap	9 Bearing

H45370/a

5 Lift the coil spring from the strut with the compressor still in position. Mark the top of the spring for reference.

6 Withdraw the protective sleeve and bump-stop from the piston rod, noting their order of removal.

7 Move the shock absorber piston rod up-

3.9a Slide on the bump stop . . .

3.9b . . . followed by the protective sleeve

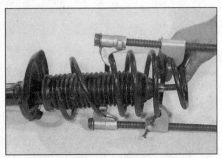

3.9c Taking care that the spring compressor is not accidentally released, fit the spring over the strut . . .

3.9d . . . ensuring that the spring end (arrowed) engages with the recess in the lower spring seat

and-down through its complete stroke, and check that the resistance is even and smooth. If there are any signs or seizing or lack of resistance, or if fluid has been leaking excessively, the shock absorber should be renewed.

8 The coil springs are normally colour-coded, and if the springs are to be renewed (it is advisable to renew both at the same time), be sure to get the correct type with an identical colour code.

9 To reassemble the spring to the strut, follow the accompanying photos **(see illustrations)**. Be sure to stay in order, and carefully read the caption underneath each. On completion, add

the bearing and mounting plate, and secure it all with the shock absorber piston rod nut, tightened to the specified torque (if possible).

---

4 Front swivel hub – removal and refitting

Note: *The swivel hub can be removed and refitted on its own, or together with the front strut. If disconnecting the strut unit from the swivel hub (before or after removal from the car) the instructions given in paragraph 4 of Section 2 must be noted and adhered to.*

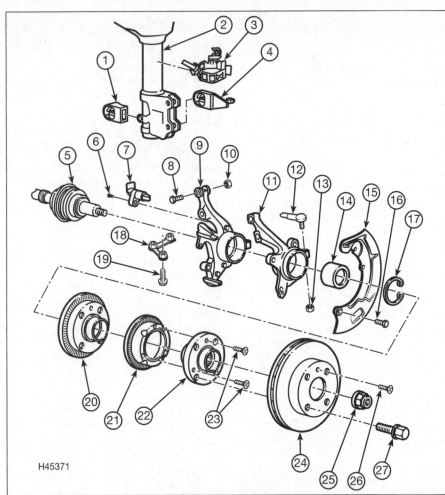

H45371

4.5 Front swivel hub and related components

1 Protective cap
2 Suspension strut
3 Bracket
4 Bracket
5 Driveshaft
6 ABS wheel sensor retaining bolt
7 ABS wheel sensor
8 Strut-to-swivel hub bolt
9 Swivel hub (except 16-valve models)
10 Strut-to-swivel hub nut

11 Swivel hub (16-valve models only)
12 Track rod
13 Track rod nut
14 Wheel bearing
15 Brake splash shield
16 Brake splash shield retaining bolt
17 Wheel bearing retaining circlip
18 Lower balljoint retaining plate

19 Lower balljoint retaining bolts
20 Wheel hub with integral ABS rotor
21 ABS rotor
22 Wheel hub
23 Wheel hub-to-ABS rotor screws
24 Brake disc
25 Driveshaft nut
26 Brake disc securing screw
27 Roadwheel bolt

4.14 Free the swivel hub from the driveshaft splines, and remove it from the car

5.5 Removing the front wheel bearing retaining circlip

Removal

1 Firmly apply the handbrake and chock the rear wheels. Where applicable, remove the relevant front wheel trim to gain access to the driveshaft nut or bolt through the centre of the roadwheel.

2 Loosen, but do not remove, the driveshaft retaining nut or bolt. The weight of the car must be on the ground, as the nut/bolt is tightened to a very high torque, and it would be dangerous to try loosening it with the car raised.

3 Loosen the relevant front wheel bolts.

4 Raise the front of the car and support it on axle stands (see *Jacking and vehicle support*). Remove the relevant front roadwheel.

5 Unscrew and remove the driveshaft nut/bolt, and recover the washer, where applicable **(see illustration opposite)**.

6 Remove the brake caliper and disc as described in Chapter 9. The brake caliper can be tied up out of the way, leaving the hydraulic hose attached but clear of the strut.

7 Where applicable, refer to Chapter 9 and remove the ABS front wheel sensor from the side concerned.

8 Remove the expanding rivets and detach the air deflector from the wishbone/lower arm.

9 Loosen the nut on top of the lower arm balljoint, leaving the nut attached to the balljoint by a couple of threads. If necessary, the balljoint shank can be retained using a cut-down 5 mm Allen key. Using a suitable balljoint splitter tool, separate the balljoint from the swivel hub, then unscrew and remove the balljoint nut.

10 Refer to Section 18 and disconnect the track rod from the swivel hub.

11 Where applicable, refer to Section 7 and disconnect the anti-roll bar connecting link from the wishbone.

12 If the swivel hub is to be separated from the suspension strut, refer to paragraph 4 in Section 2, and mark the relative positions of the items described before removing the retaining bolts. Prise free the strut from the swivel hub.

13 If removing the swivel hub together with the strut, disconnect the strut at the top from the body mounting, as described in Section 2. If the suspension coil spring is still under tension, position a jack under the swivel hub to support the weight of the hub and strut; when the strut is detached at the top end from the body, lower the jack slowly to decompress the coil spring and allow the strut to be disengaged from the body.

14 Remove the swivel hub (and where applicable, the strut), withdrawing it from the driveshaft **(see illustration)**. Withdraw the hub assembly from the shaft, using a suitable puller if necessary, or carefully tap it free.

Refitting

15 Refitting is a reversal of the removal procedure. Refer to Chapter 8 for details on reconnecting the driveshaft, and Chapter 9 when refitting the wheel sensor, brake disc and caliper.

16 When reconnecting the suspension strut to the swivel hub, ensure that the two are correctly realigned before tightening the retaining bolts.

17 When refitting the bottom balljoint nut, hold the balljoint shank stationary using a cut-down 5 mm Allen key.

18 Do not fully tighten the driveshaft retaining nut/bolt or the anti-roll bar connecting link nut until after the car is lowered, and with its full weight on the wheels.

19 All fastenings must be tightened to their specified torque settings.

---

5 Front wheel bearing – renewal

1 Remove the swivel hub, as described in the previous Section.

2 Undo the retaining bolts, and remove the brake disc splash shield.

3 Support the swivel hub with the hub facing down, and press or drive out the hub from the housing. Unscrew and remove the three cross-head screws, and remove the ABS speed sensor reluctor ring.

4 The bearing inner race can be removed from the swivel hub using a suitable puller, but note that the bearing must be renewed once it is removed.

5 Extract the circlip, then supporting the swivel hub, press or drive out the bearing **(see illustration)**.

6 Clean the recess in the housing, then support the swivel hub and press the new bearing into position, so that it is positioned behind the circlip groove. If a tube drift is used, ensure that it butts against the bearing outer race only.

7 Press the inner bearing race onto the swivel hub, using a suitable tube drift.

8 Fit the circlip, and ensure that it is fully engaged in its groove.

9 Refit the ABS wheel sensor reluctor ring to the swivel hub (where applicable), then with the swivel hub positioned and supported with its bearing shoulder facing up, press or drive the bearing housing into position.

10 Refit the brake disc splash shield.

11 Refit the swivel hub as described in the previous Section.

12 When the driveshaft nut/bolt and roadwheel bolts have been tightened to the specified torque, raise the car again so that the front wheels are clear of the ground. Referring to Chapter 1 *Steering and suspension check*, rotate the wheels by hand to ensure that they turn freely, without binding. There should be no excessive lateral play.

---

6 Wishbone/lower arm – removal, overhaul and refitting

Removal

1 Apply the handbrake and chock the rear wheels, then loosen the relevant front

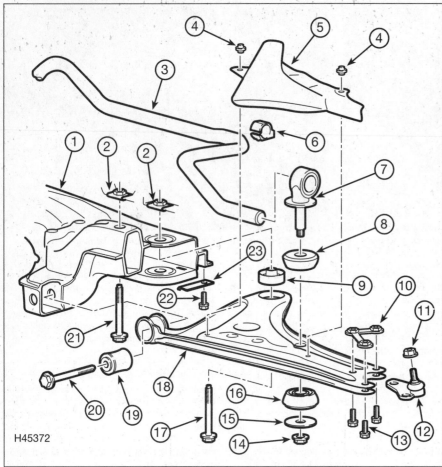

6.2 Wishbone/lower arm and related components

1 Subframe	9 Wishbone rear mounting	18 Wishbone/lower arm
2 Captive nut	10 Retaining plate	19 Wishbone front mounting
3 Anti-roll bar	11 Lower balljoint nut	bush
4 Spreader	12 Lower balljoint	20 Wishbone front mounting
5 Air deflector plate	13 Lower balljoint bolts	bolt
6 Anti-roll bar bush	14 Connecting link nut	21 Subframe mounting bolt
7 Anti-roll bar connecting	15 Washer	22 Anti-roll bar mounting
link	16 Connecting link bush	plate bolt
8 Connecting link	17 Wishbone rear mounting	23 Anti-roll bar mounting
bush	bolt	plate

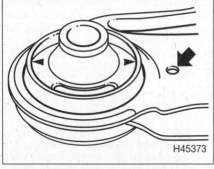

6.14 Fitted position of wishbone rear mounting

One of the embossed arrows must align with the projection (arrowed) on top of the wishbone

roadwheel bolts. Raise and support the front of the car on axle stands (see *Jacking and vehicle support*). Remove the relevant front roadwheel.

2 Remove the expanding rivets and detach the air deflector plate from the wishbone **(see illustration)**.

3 Position a jack under the centre of the subframe and raise it to support (not lift) the subframe.

4 Unbolt and remove the wishbone rear mounting through-bolt.

5 Where applicable, unscrew the connecting link nut, and detach the anti-roll bar from the wishbone. As it is removed, note that the connecting link-to-wishbone mounting bush is fitted with its conical side towards the wishbone.

6 Refer to Section 4, paragraph 9, and

disconnect the bottom balljoint from the swivel hub.

7 Unscrew and remove the pivot bolt from the front inboard end of the wishbone arm (to subframe).

8 Remove the wishbone, manoeuvring it down to clear the front pivot and the balljoint, and twisting it to clear the rear mounting. A suitable lever will assist in freeing the wishbone from its mountings, but take care not to damage adjacent components.

Overhaul

9 With the wishbone removed, clean it for inspection.

10 Check the balljoint for excessive wear, and check the pivot bushes for deterioration. Also examine the wishbone arm for damage and distortion. If necessary, the balljoint and bushes should be renewed.

11 To renew the balljoint, first outline its exact position on the wishbone. This is important as the relative positions of the wishbone and the balljoint are set during production, and the new balljoint must be accurately positioned when fitting it. Unscrew the bolts and remove the balljoint and clamp plate. Fit a new balljoint in the exact outline, and tighten the bolts. If fitting a new wishbone, locate the balljoint centrally in the elongated hole.

12 To renew the front pivot bush, use a long bolt, together with a metal tube and washers, to pull the bush from the wishbone. Fit the new bush using the same method but, to ease insertion, dip the bush into soapy water first.

13 The rear mounting rubber bush can be removed in the same manner as the front pivot bush.

14 Press or drive the new mounting bush into position from the top of the wishbone, but ensure that it is positioned correctly **(see illustration)**.

Refitting

15 Refitting the wishbone is a reverse of removal, noting the following points:

a) *Delay fully tightening the pivot bolts until the weight of the car is on the wheels.*

b) *Tighten all fasteners to the specified torque (where given).*

c) *Refer to Section 4 when reconnecting the balljoint.*

d) *Refer to Section 7 when reconnecting the anti-roll bar.*

e) *Have the front wheel alignment checked and, if necessary, adjusted on completion.*

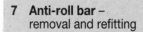

7 Anti-roll bar –
removal and refitting

Removal

1 Apply the handbrake and chock the rear wheels, then loosen the front roadwheel bolts.

Raise and support the front of the car on axle stands (see *Jacking and vehicle support*). For better access, remove the front roadwheels.

2 Unscrew and remove the anti-roll bar mounting plate retaining bolts, then unhook the plates from the subframe locations **(see illustration)**.

3 Unscrew the connecting link nut, and detach the anti-roll bar from the wishbone each side. As they are removed, note that the connecting link-to-wishbone mounting bushes are fitted with their conical side facing the wishbone **(see illustration)**.

4 Lower the anti-roll bar, and remove it from under the car.

5 Renew the anti-roll bar if it is damaged or distorted. Renew the mounting bushes if they are perished or worn.

Refitting

6 Refitting is a reversal of the removal procedure. Ensure that the connecting link mounting bushes are fitted with their conical faces towards the wishbone.

7 Do not fully tighten the retaining bolts to their specified torque settings until after the car is fully lowered onto its wheels.

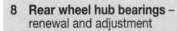

8 Rear wheel hub bearings –
renewal and adjustment

Rear drum brake models

1 Remove the rear brake drum as described in Chapter 9.

Early models

2 Wipe clean the inner bearing and seal. Note the direction of fitting, then lever out the seal. Take care not to damage the ABS sensor rotor. Extract the inner bearing from the hub.

3 The races can be driven out using a soft metal drift – take care not to damage the hub or ABS sensor rotor **(see illustration)**.

4 Clean the bearing race locations in the hub. Use a tube drift of suitable diameter to drive or press the new races into position in the hub each side **(see illustration)**. Ensure that they are squarely and fully inserted. If using the old bearings, be sure to keep the original bearings and races together. Never interchange new bearings with old races, or vice-versa.

5 Lubricate the inner bearing with grease, and insert it into position **(see illustration)**.

6 Support the hub with its outboard face down, and carefully drive the new oil seal into position, taking care not to damage the ABS sensor rotor, where applicable **(see illustration)**. Lubricate the oil seal for refitting to the stub axle.

7 Pack the hub with grease, then refit it to the stub axle. Fit the outer bearing and the thrustwasher, then screw the hub retaining nut into position by hand. Adjust the bearing as described later in this Section.

Later models

8 With the drum removed, the hub/bearing assembly slides off the stub axle.

**7.2 Anti-roll bar mounting plate bolt (A) –
plate is hooked into subframe at point (B)**

9 At the time of writing, the bearing is not available separately from the hub, so the hub and bearing must be renewed complete.

10 Before installing the new assembly, ensure that the reluctor ring for the ABS sensor is clean, then slide the hub onto the stub axle.

11 Refit the brake drum as described in Chapter 9.

Rear disc brake models

12 Chock the front wheels, then jack up the rear of the car and support on axle stands (see *Jacking and vehicle support*). Release the handbrake and remove the relevant rear wheel.

13 Remove the rear brake disc as described in Chapter 9.

Early models

14 Prise the seal from the disc/hub, and remove the inner bearing **(see illustration overleaf)**.

**8.3 Drive out the old outer races using a
hammer and punch**

**8.5 Work grease into the taper-roller inner
bearing prior to fitting to the hub**

**7.3 Anti-roll bar mounting bushes
(arrowed)**

15 Drive out the old bearing inner and outer races, using a soft metal drift.

16 Clean the bearing race locations. Use a tube drift of suitable diameter to drive or press the new races into position each side.

17 Grease and reassemble the new inner bearing and inner seal, tapping the seal home.

18 Wipe clean the stub axle, then refit the disc/hub. Grease and fit the new outer bearing, then refit the thrustwasher and hub nut (by hand only) to secure it

Later models

19 With the disc removed, the hub/bearing assembly slides off the stub axle.

20 At the time of writing, the bearing is not available separately from the hub, so the hub and bearing must be renewed complete.

21 Before installing the new assembly, ensure that the reluctor ring for the ABS

**8.4 Drive the new races in squarely, using
a socket on the outer edge**

**8.6 Grease the lips of the oil seal, and
press it into the rear of the hub**

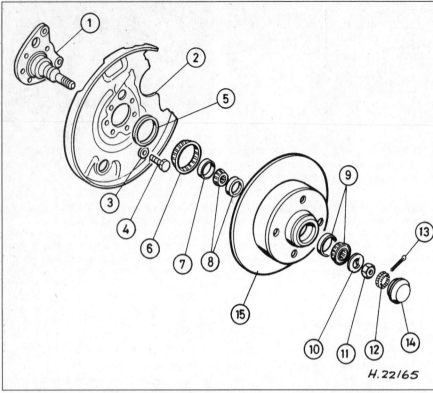

8.14 Rear brake disc/hub and associated components – early models

1 Stub axle	6 Speed sensor rotor (ABS)	11 Nut
2 Splash plate	7 Seal ring	12 Lock ring
3 Dished washer	8 Wheel bearing (inner)	13 Cotter pin
4 Bolt	9 Wheel bearing (outer)	14 Grease cap
5 Cover ring	10 Thrustwasher	15 Disc/hub

sensor is clean, then slide the hub onto the stub axle.

22 Refit the brake disc as described in Chapter 9.

Adjustment

Note: *Adjustment is only possible on early models, with the components described below.*

23 If not already done, extract the split pin, remove the locking ring and loosen the hub nut.

24 Tighten the hub nut slowly, until it only just touches the thrustwasher. Turn the hub as the nut is tightened, to ensure the bearings are correctly seated. Back the nut off a fraction so the washer just moves using a screwdriver tip. Fit the locking ring and insert a new split pin to secure.

25 Beware of overtightening the hub nut, as this will cause premature bearing wear. If adjusting a bearing which has been in service for some time, when play has been noted, do not overtighten to compensate for wear – this is potentially dangerous and unlikely to be more than a temporary solution.

26 Smear a liberal amount of grease into the cap, then carefully drive the grease cap into position. If the grease cap is badly dented or

distorted, such that it is no longer a tight fit, a new one should be fitted.

27 If a new bearing has been fitted, check for play after a few hundred miles. Re-adjust the bearing if necessary.

---

9 Rear stub axle – removal and refitting

Removal

1 Chock the front wheels, engage 1st gear (or P), then loosen the relevant rear wheel bolts. Raise the car at the rear and support on axle stands (see *Jacking and vehicle support*).

2 Refer to the appropriate Sections in Chapter 9, and proceed with the following:

a) *Remove the brake shoes, or the rear brake caliper, rear disc (and hub).*
b) *On rear drum brake models, disconnect the brake pipe from the wheel cylinder.*
c) *Disconnect the handbrake cable.*
d) *Remove the rear wheel sensor.*

3 Undo the four bolts and remove the brake backplate and stub axle. Two of the bolts are used to retain the handbrake cable guide –

recover the guide as the bolts are removed, noting how it is fitted.

Refitting

4 Refit in the reverse order of removal.

5 Refer to Chapter 9 to refit the brake system components. On early models, adjust the wheel hub bearings as described in Section 8 of this Chapter.

6 Bleed the brake hydraulic circuit and adjust the handbrake, as described in Chapter 9.

---

10 Rear suspension strut and coil spring – removal and refitting

Removal

1 Chock the front roadwheels, engage 1st gear (or P), then loosen the relevant rear roadwheel bolts. Raise and support the car at the rear on axle stands (see *Jacking and vehicle support*). Allow the suspension to extend fully.

2 From inside the car, tilt forwards the rear seat backrest. Unhook the support straps and pull out the rear parcel shelf.

3 Remove the two Torx screws from the parcel shelf side support, then unhook the panel from the two retaining lugs on the C-pillar and remove it from the car (**see illustration**).

4 If the right-hand rear strut is being removed on models provided with a first aid kit storage compartment, turn the two fasteners through 90° and lower the side trim panel. Otherwise, prise out the plastic retainer(s) holding the upper part of the carpeted side trim panel in place, and fold the carpet down for access to the strut upper mounting. It may be helpful to remove, or at least loosen, several peripheral trim panels to achieve improved access – see Chapter 11.

5 Pull the domed cover off the strut upper mounting for access to the nut beneath (**see illustration**).

6 Using a small open-ended spanner on the piston rod flats if necessary, unscrew and remove the upper mounting nut (**see illustration**). Recover the large dished washer if it is loose.

10.3 Removing the parcel shelf side support

7 Working underneath the car, engage a spanner on the nut securing the strut bottom mounting bolt, then unscrew the bolt and remove it. Take care that the ABS wheel sensor wiring is not damaged as the strut is being worked on – if preferred, remove the wheel sensor as described in Chapter 9.

8 Disengage the strut at the bottom end, and withdraw the strut downwards (complete with coil spring) from the car.

Refitting

9 Refit in the reverse order of removal. Ensure that the strut is correctly located at the top end, and then engage the lower end with the trailing arm.

10 Tighten the retaining bolts to their specified torque settings, but delay full tightening of the upper mounting nut and lower mounting bolt until after the car is lowered fully, and standing on its wheels.

11 Rear suspension strut and coil spring – separation and reassembly

1 The component parts of the strut and coil spring are as shown **(see illustration)**.

⚠️ *Warning: Before attempting to dismantle the suspension strut, a suitable tool to hold the coil spring in compression must be obtained. Adjustable coil spring compressors are readily available, and are recommended for this operation. Any attempt to dismantle the strut without such a tool is likely to result in damage or personal injury.*

2 Fit the spring compressor, and ensure that it is fully located. Compress the spring so that the tension on the top mounting retainer is relieved.

3 Prise free the cover cap and remove the sealing O-ring.

4 Unscrew and remove the shock absorber top nut, then remove the large cover, rubber bush, small cover and the nut beneath.

5 Withdraw the spacer tube and washer, the lower bush, spring plate and spring seat.

6 Lift the coil spring from the strut with the compressor still in position. Mark the top of the spring for reference.

7 Remove the bump-stop, tube, and plastic cap. Release the circlip and remove the lower spring seat and packing piece(s).

8 Note that the coil springs are colour-coded, and if renewal is necessary, check that the correct one is supplied for your car. It is advisable to renew both rear springs at the same time, to ensure even handling characteristics.

9 Check the operation of the shock absorber in the same manner described for the front units in Section 3, paragraph 7. Renew if necessary, as the shock absorbers cannot be overhauled.

10.5 Pull off the domed cover from the top of the suspension strut

10.6 Hold the piston rod stationary using a suitable spanner, and unscrew the upper mounting nut

10 Reassembly of the shock absorber and coil spring is a reversal of the removal procedure. The spring seat installation position must be as shown **(see illustration)**.

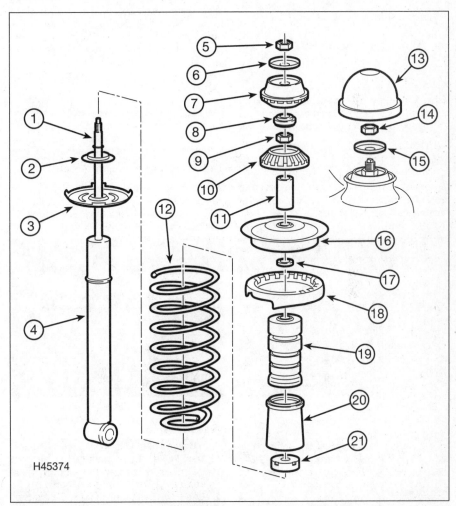

H45374

11.1 Rear suspension strut components

1 Piston rod and circlip	8 Cover	15 Dished washer
2 Packing piece	9 Nut	16 Upper spring plate
3 Lower spring seat	10 Washer	17 Lower mounting rubber
4 Shock absorber	11 Spacer tube	bush
5 Nut	12 Coil spring	18 Upper spring seat
6 Cover	13 Domed cover	19 Bump-stop
7 Upper mounting rubber	14 Upper mounting	20 Protective tube
bush	nut	21 Protective cap

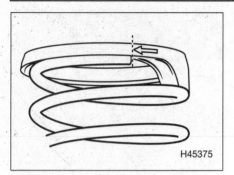

11.10 The spring seat must be installed so that the arrow aligns with the end of the spring

11 Tighten the shock absorber nuts to the specified torque setting. Remove the spring compressor tool before refitting the unit to the car as described in Section 10.

12 Rear torsion beam axle – removal and refitting

Note: *If the rear axle is suspected of being distorted, it must be checked in position by a VW garage, using optical alignment equipment.*

Removal

1 Chock the front wheels, engage 1st gear (or P), then loosen the rear roadwheel bolts. Raise and support the car at the rear on axle stands (see *Jacking and vehicle support*). Remove the rear roadwheels.

2 Refer to Chapter 9 and disconnect the handbrake cable from each rear brake, then detach the cable from the clips securing it to the axle.

3 Disconnect the brake hydraulic line from each rear brake, and from the attachment points on the axle, referring to Chapter 9 for details. Either remove the ABS wheel sensors completely, or disconnect the wiring under the rear seat, pull the wiring through the grommet in the floor, and detach it from the retaining clips on the rear axle – see Chapter 9.

4 Position jacks or stands under the axle each side to support its weight.

5 Unbolt and remove the strut lower mounting bolt each side, and detach the struts from the axle.

6 Check that all associated fittings are clear of the axle. Cover the stub axles and brake assemblies to ensure that they do not get damaged or dirty as the axle assembly is removed. Ensure that the axle is securely supported. If possible, engage the services of an assistant to help in steadying the axle assembly as it is detached and lowered from the car.

7 Unscrew and remove the pivot bolt nut each side, then withdraw the bolts and lower the axle from the pivot/mountings. Lower and remove the axle assembly from under the car.

8 If the mounting/pivot bushes are worn, they must be renewed. Remove the outer bush, then the inner bush, using a suitable puller. It is important that the mounting is not driven out, or else the seating would be enlarged.

9 Dip the new bushes in soapy water, to

lubricate them for ease of fitting. Press each bush in from the outside with a puller, ensuring that the rubber/metal protrusions on the inner face point to the front, and the outer section points to the rear. Insert each half to the point where the conical part is in contact with the axle. Fit each half one at a time.

Refitting

10 Refitting is a reversal of the removal procedure. When the axle is raised into position, loosely assemble the retaining bolts and nuts until the axle is fully located before tightening them fully to the specified torque settings.

11 When reconnecting the brake hydraulic lines, handbrake cables and ABS wiring, ensure that everything is correctly routed and secured. Bleed the hydraulic system and adjust the handbrake as described in Chapter 9.

13 Steering wheel – removal and refitting

Removal

1 Set the front wheels in the straight-ahead position, and release the steering lock by inserting the ignition key. Ensure that the direction indicator lever is in the central 'off' position.

2 Remove the airbag unit from the centre of the steering wheel, as described in Chapter 12.

3 Slacken and remove the three retaining screws underneath, then unclip and remove the lower shroud **(see illustrations)**.

4 Peel back the grey foam cover fitted over the airbag clockspring's yellow wiring connector, and separate the plug halves **(see illustrations)**. This is essential – if the wiring is not disconnected, the clockspring will be damaged when the wheel is removed (the clockspring is attached to the back of the wheel hub, and is removed with the wheel).

5 Prevent the steering wheel turning by grasping the rim firmly, then unscrew and remove the steering wheel securing nut **(see illustration)**. Do not rely on the steering column lock to prevent the wheel turning, as this may damage the lock.

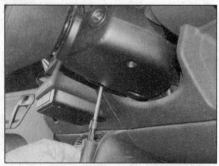

13.3a Remove the three screws . . .

13.3b . . . then unclip and remove the steering column lower shroud

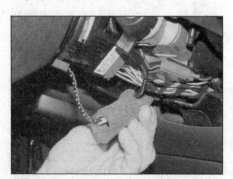

13.4a Peel back the grey foam cover . . .

13.4b . . . and separate the clockspring wiring connector

13.5 Hold the wheel rim while unscrewing the nut

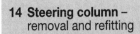

HAYNES HiNT *Don't unscrew the nut all the way – leave it in by a thread or two. This way, if excess effort is needed to pull the wheel off its splines, the wheel won't suddenly fly off and cause injury.*

6 Grip the steering wheel on each side (or top and bottom), then pull and withdraw it from the splines on the end of the column. If not already done, remove the nut completely. As the wheel is removed, withdraw the airbag clockspring wiring through with it.

Refitting

7 Make sure that the front wheels are pointing in the straight-ahead position, then fit the steering wheel to the column, feeding through the clockspring wiring.
8 Refit the steering wheel securing nut, and tighten to the specified torque – again, do not rely on the steering column lock to hold the wheel as the nut is tightened **(see illustration)**.
9 The remainder of the refitting procedure is a reversal of removal. Refit the airbag unit as described in Chapter 12.

14 Steering column – removal and refitting

Removal

1 Disconnect the battery negative lead (see *Disconnecting the battery*).

13.8 Tighten the steering wheel nut to the specified torque

2 Remove the steering wheel, as described in the previous Section.
3 Unclip and withdraw the steering column upper shroud **(see illustration)**.
4 Remove the combination switches as described in Chapter 12, Section 6.
5 Remove the driver's side lower trim panel as described in Chapter 11, Section 26.
6 Unclip the ignition immobiliser key reader coil from the ignition switch **(see illustration)**.
7 Pull the plastic cover from the rear of the ignition switch, then disconnect the main ignition switch wiring connector **(see illustrations)**.
8 If not already done, unscrew the fasteners and detach and remove the lower column/bulkhead cover from above the foot pedals **(see illustration)**. Also remove the floor cover panel at the base of the column, where it passes through the bulkhead.
9 Remove the column mounting bolts. Shear-

14.3 Remove the steering column upper shroud

type bolts are used – to remove them, it will be necessary to drill out the threaded portion and use a stud extractor, tap them round with a centre-punch, or chisel the heads off **(see illustration)**. Access to one of the bolts may be improved by removing the instrument panel – see Chapter 12.
10 Now loosen and remove the column lower universal joint clamp bolt **(see illustration)**.
11 Pull the steering column to the rear, to unhook it from the mounting halfway up the column tube, and pull it from the universal joint. Withdraw the column tube assembly from the car **(see illustration)**.

Inspection

12 Check the various components for excessive wear. If the column has been damaged in any way, it must be renewed as a unit.
13 The column can only be withdrawn from

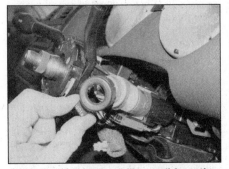

14.6 Unclip the immobiliser coil from the ignition switch

14.7a Unclip the plastic rear cover . . .

14.7b . . . then squeeze the retaining tabs and disconnect the wiring plug

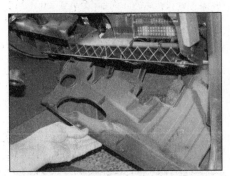

14.8 Remove the lower cover above the foot pedals

14.9 Using a hammer and chisel to remove the column mounting shear-bolts (arrowed)

14.10 Removing the universal joint clamp bolt

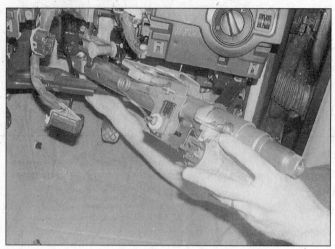

14.11 Withdraw the steering column from inside the car

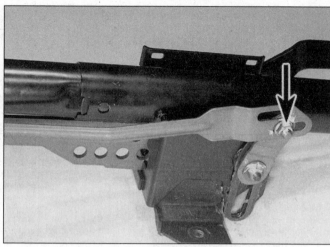

15.1 General view of the steering column height adjuster mechanism (steering column removed) – nut arrowed has a *left-hand thread*

the tube by cutting off the upper universal joint – if the column is to be overhauled, seek the advice of your VW dealer.

Refitting

14 Reassembly and refitting is in general a reversal of the dismantling and removal procedure, but note the following special points:

a) *Tighten the retaining nuts and bolts to the specified torque wrench settings. Fit new shear-bolts and tighten them until their heads break off.*

b) *On completion, ensure that the steering action, and the operation of the column switches, is satisfactory.*

15 Steering column height adjuster – removal and refitting

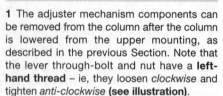

1 The adjuster mechanism components can be removed from the column after the column is lowered from the upper mounting, as described in the previous Section. Note that the lever through-bolt and nut have a **left-hand thread** – ie, they loosen *clockwise* and tighten *anti-clockwise* **(see illustration)**.

2 Any components in the height adjuster mechanism which are broken or excessively worn must be renewed.

3 When refitting the components of the adjuster, note the following points:

a) *Lubricate the sliding surfaces of the adjuster.*

b) *The mounting plate tabs must be guided under the spring pin.*

c) *When refitting the lever, tighten the through-bolt to the specified torque setting with the lever on the upper stop. Refit the locking plate after the bolt is tightened.*

d) *Ensure that the return springs are attached to the mounting bracket.*

16 Steering gear gaiters – renewal

1 The steering gear gaiters can be removed and refitted with the steering gear unit *in situ* or removed from the car.

2 Measure the exposed amount of adjustment thread showing on the inboard side of the track rod end balljoint locknut. This will act as a guide to the adjustment position when refitting the balljoint to the rod. Loosen off the locknut, and detach the balljoint from the track rod as described in Section 18.

3 Unscrew and remove the locking nut from the track rod.

4 Release the retaining clips and withdraw the gaiter from the steering gear and track rod.

5 Refit in the reverse order of removal. Smear the inner bore of the gaiter with lubricant prior to fitting, to ease its assembly. Renew the balljoint locknuts.

6 On completion, have the front wheel alignment checked (see Section 21).

17 Steering gear – removal and refitting

Removal

1 Apply the handbrake and chock the rear wheels, then loosen the front roadwheel bolts.

2 Raise and support the front of the car on axle stands (see *Jacking and vehicle support*). For better access, remove the front roadwheels.

3 Refer to Section 18, and detach the track rod end balljoints from the swivel hub.

4 Either clamp the power steering fluid supply and return hoses with suitable hose clamps, or drain the hydraulic system as described in

Section 19. Clean the area around the fluid hose connections on the steering gear.

5 Unscrew and remove the steering column lower universal joint shaft clamp bolt, as described in Section 14, paragraph 10. Release the large grommet from the bulkhead on the engine side, and push it forward over the lower joint **(see illustration)**. Note the TOP marking on the grommet, which should face into the passenger compartment when fitted.

6 Referring to Chapter 4B, unbolt and lower the exhaust system front downpipe.

7 On manual transmission models, refer to Chapter 7A, Section 3, and disconnect the cable support from the transmission housing.

8 Unscrew the nut and remove the through-bolt from the engine/transmission rear mounting – see Chapter 2A or 2B.

9 Support the subframe from below, using two jacks if available. Loosen, but do not remove, the wishbone/lower arm rear mounting through-bolts and the subframe mounting bolts, then lower the subframe sufficiently to disengage the steering gear pinion from the universal joint splines. Do not lower the subframe any more than is necessary.

10 Disconnect the fluid supply and return lines from the steering gear **(see illustration)**. Recover the seals and O-rings as they are detached. Drain any fluid remaining in the system into a container for disposal. Position the lines out of the way, and seal off their ends to prevent further leakage and the possible ingress of dirt.

11 Check that all connections are free and clear of the steering gear, then withdraw it rearwards and manoeuvre it from the car.

12 If the steering gear is known to be damaged or worn beyond an acceptable level, it may have to be renewed. However, it is possible to have the steering gear overhauled – consult a VW dealer or specialist repairer for further advice.

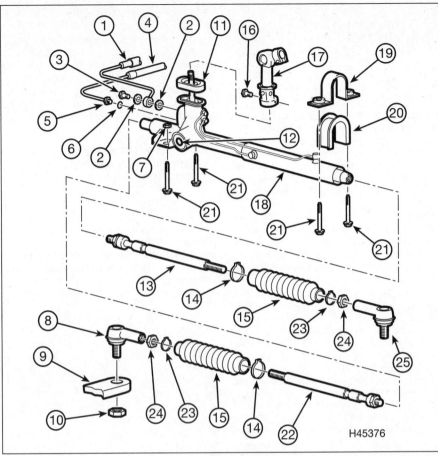

17.5 Power steering gear

1 Supply (pressure) hose
2 Seal
3 Banjo bolt
4 Return hose
5 Union nut
6 O-ring
7 Mounting nut
8 Left-hand track-rod end
   and balljoint
9 Steering arm on swivel hub

10 Track-rod balljoint
    nut
11 Grommet
12 Adjustment bolt
13 Right-hand track-rod
14 Gaiter securing clip
15 Gaiter
16 Clamp bolt
17 Steering column universal
    joint

18 Steering gear
19 Mounting clamp
20 Mounting rubber
21 Steering gear mounting
    bolts
22 Left-hand track-rod
23 Gaiter securing clip
24 Track-rod end locknut
25 Right-hand track-rod end
    and balljoint

Refitting

13 Refitting is a reversal of the removal procedure, noting the following points:

a) Centralise the steering rack and the column shaft before connecting them. An assistant will be required to align and engage the two shafts as the subframe and engine are raised. When the two are reconnected and the clamp bolt is tight, make sure the floor sealing grommet is correctly located, to prevent noise and water ingress.

b) The fluid lines will also need to be connected as the unit is raised. Take care to keep the connections clean. Use new O-rings and seals when reconnecting the fluid lines.

c) Tighten all fasteners to the specified torque wrench settings.

d) Refer to Section 18 to reconnect the track rod ends.

e) Top-up the fluid level as described in 'Weekly checks' and bleed the system as described in Section 19.

f) Finally, have the wheel alignment checked and if necessary adjusted (see Section 21).

18 Track rod end balljoints –
removal and refitting

Removal

1 If the steering track rod end balljoints are worn, play will be evident as the roadwheel is rocked from side-to-side, and the balljoint must then be renewed. Make sure, however,

17.10 Power steering gear fluid supply and return unions

that any lateral play noted is not due to a worn wheel bearing – hold your hand over the balljoint while an assistant rocks the roadwheel; play in the balljoint will be readily apparent **(see illustration)**.

2 Apply the handbrake and chock the rear wheels, then loosen the relevant front roadwheel bolts. Raise and support the front of the car on axle stands (see *Jacking and vehicle support*). Remove the front roadwheel on the side concerned.

3 Measure the distance of the exposed thread inboard of the locknut. Make a note of the distance, so that the new balljoint can be screwed on to the same position, then loosen the locknut. It is advisable to fit a new locknut if the balljoint is being renewed.

4 Loosen the balljoint nut on the side concerned, and unscrew it by a few turns – do not remove it at this stage. Use a balljoint separator tool to release the joint from the swivel hub, then remove the nut completely. With the track rod outer joint separated from the swivel hub, the outer balljoint can be unscrewed from the track rod.

Refitting

5 Screw the new balljoint onto the track rod so that, when the locknut is tightened, the same amount of thread is exposed as noted on removal.

6 Reconnect the outer balljoints to the swivel hub, and tighten the nut to the specified torque wrench setting. Tighten the track rod locknut to the specified torque.

7 On completion, have the front wheel alignment checked (see Section 21).

18.1 Track rod end balljoint (arrowed)

19 Power steering fluid – general information, draining and refilling

General information

1 The power steering fluid level is checked as described in *Weekly checks*. Fluid renewal is not called for by the manufacturer's maintenance schedule, and so should only be necessary if the power steering components are being removed.

2 All models covered by this manual use a special VW hydraulic oil in the power steering system, and normal automatic transmission fluid (ATF) is not recommended, even for topping-up. If the system is being drained and refilled, use **only** the recommended oil.

3 If the system is in need of constant topping-up, check for signs of leakage at the pump, reservoir and steering gear hose unions and make repairs as necessary.

Draining

4 To drain the fluid from the system, detach the fluid suction hose at the pump, and drain the fluid into a container for disposal. When draining, turn the steering wheel from lock-to-lock to expel as much fluid as possible. Do **not** run the engine while this is being done, or the pump will be damaged.

Refilling and bleeding

5 After draining off the fluid, reconnect the suction hose to the pump, then fill the reservoir to the top with new fluid. Restart the engine and switch off as soon as it fires, repeating the starting and stopping sequence several times; this will cause fluid to be drawn into the system quickly. As with draining the fluid, do not leave the engine running while the pump is short of fluid, or the pump will be damaged.

6 Watch the level of fluid, and keep adding fluid so that the reservoir is never sucked dry. When the fluid ceases to drop as a result of the start/stop sequence, start the engine and allow it to run at idle speed.

7 Turn the steering from lock-to-lock several times, being careful not to leave the wheels on full lock because this will cause the pressure in the system to build-up.

8 Watch the level of the fluid in the reservoir, and add fluid if necessary to keep the level at the MAX mark.

9 When the level stops falling and no more air bubbles appear in the reservoir, switch the engine off and fit the reservoir cap. The level of fluid will rise slightly when the engine is switched off.

10 After the car is next used, recheck the fluid level as described in *Weekly checks*, and top-up if necessary.

20 Power steering pump – removal and refitting

Removal

1 If the power steering is suspected of malfunction, have the supply and system pressure checked by your VW dealer. The pump cannot be overhauled or repaired, and if defective, it must be renewed as a unit. Note that the type of pump fitted depends on engine type and equipment level, but removal procedures for each pump are basically the same.

2 Using brake hose clamps, clamp both the supply and return hoses near the power steering fluid reservoir. This will minimise fluid loss during subsequent operations. Alternatively, drain the fluid from the system as described in Section 19.

3 Slacken the steering pump pulley retaining bolts – it may be necessary to counterhold the pulley using a large Allen key in the centre of the pulley mounting flange. Working as described in Chapter 2A or 2B, release the drivebelt tension and unhook the drivebelt from the pump pulley.

4 Unscrew the retaining bolts and remove the pulley from the power steering pump, noting which way around it is fitted.

5 Slacken the retaining clip, and disconnect the fluid supply hose from the pump. Where a spring-type clip is still fitted, cut the clip and discard it; replace it with a standard worm-drive hose clip on refitting. Slacken the union bolt, and disconnect the feed pipe from the pump, along with its sealing washers; discard the washers – new ones should be used on refitting. Be prepared for some fluid spillage as the pipe and hose are disconnected, and plug the hose/pipe end and pump unions, to minimise fluid loss and prevent the entry of dirt into the system.

6 Slacken and remove the bolts securing the power steering pump to its mounting bracket, and remove the pump from the engine compartment.

Refitting

7 Prior to fitting, ensure that the pump is primed by injecting hydraulic oil in through the supply hose union and rotating the pump shaft. This is especially important if a new or reconditioned pump is being fitted, as it will be supplied 'dry'.

8 Manoeuvre the pump into position and refit the mounting bolts, tightening them to the specified torque setting.

9 Position a new sealing washer on each side of the feed pipe union, then fit the union bolt and tighten it to the specified torque setting. Refit the supply pipe to the pump, and securely tighten its retaining clip. Remove the brake hose clamps, if used.

10 Refit the drive pulley, making sure it is the correct way around, and fit its retaining bolts.

11 Check the condition of the drivebelt as described in Chapter 1. If a new pump is being fitted, a new drivebelt should be used.

12 Refit the drivebelt to the pump pulley as described in Chapter 2A or 2B. Once the belt is tensioned, tighten the pulley retaining bolts to the specified torque setting.

13 On completion, fill and/or bleed the hydraulic system as described in Section 19.

21 Wheel alignment and steering angles – general information

Definitions

1 A car's steering and suspension geometry is defined in three basic settings – all angles are expressed in degrees; the steering axis is defined as an imaginary line drawn through the axis of the suspension strut, extended where necessary to contact the ground.

2 **Camber** is the angle between each roadwheel and a vertical line drawn through its centre and tyre contact patch, when viewed from the front or rear of the car. 'Positive' camber is when the roadwheels are tilted outwards from the vertical at the top; 'negative' camber is when they are tilted inwards.

3 Camber angle is adjustable, and can be checked using a camber checking gauge.

4 **Castor** is the angle between the steering axis and a vertical line drawn through each roadwheel's centre and tyre contact patch, when viewed from the side of the car. 'Positive' castor is when the steering axis is tilted so that it contacts the ground ahead of the vertical; 'negative' castor is when it contacts the ground behind the vertical.

5 Castor is not adjustable, and is given for reference only; while it can be checked using a castor checking gauge, if the figure obtained is significantly different from that specified, the car must be taken for careful checking by a professional, as the fault can only be caused by wear or damage to the body or suspension components.

6 **Toe** is the difference, viewed from above, between lines drawn through the roadwheel centres and the car's centre-line. 'Toe-in' is when the roadwheels point inwards, towards each other at the front, while 'toe-out' is when they splay outwards from each other at the front.

7 The front wheel toe setting is adjusted by screwing the right-hand track rod in or out of its balljoint, to alter the effective length of the track rod assembly.

8 Rear wheel toe setting is not adjustable.

Checking and adjustment

Front wheel toe setting

9 Due to the special measuring equipment necessary to check the wheel alignment, and the skill required to use it properly, the

checking and adjustment of these settings is best left to a VW dealer or similar expert. Note that most tyre-fitting centres now possess sophisticated checking equipment.

10 To check the toe setting, a tracking gauge must first be obtained. Two types of gauge are available, and can be obtained from motor accessory shops. The first type measures the distance between the front and rear inside edges of the roadwheels, as previously described, with the car stationary. The second type, known as a 'scuff plate', measures the actual position of the contact surface of the tyre, in relation to the road surface, with the car in motion. This is achieved by pushing or driving the front tyre over a plate, which then moves slightly according to the scuff of the tyre, and shows this movement on a scale. Both types have their advantages and disadvantages, but either can give satisfactory results if used correctly and carefully.

11 Make sure that the steering is in the straight-ahead position when making measurements.

12 If adjustment is necessary, apply the handbrake, then jack up the front of the car and support it securely on axle stands. Adjustment is made on the right-hand track rod (right- and left-hand are as seen from the driver's seat).

13 First clean the track rod threads; if they are corroded, apply penetrating fluid before starting adjustment. Release the rubber gaiter outer clips, peel back the gaiters and apply a smear of grease. This will ensure that both gaiters are free, and will not be twisted or strained as their respective track rods are rotated.

14 Retain the track rod with a suitable spanner, and slacken the balljoint locknut fully. Alter the length of the track rod, by screwing them into or out of the balljoints. Rotate the track rod using an open-ended spanner fitted to the track rod flats provided; shortening the track rods (screwing them onto their balljoints) will reduce toe-in/increase toe-out.

15 When the setting is correct, hold the track rod and tighten the balljoint locknut to the specified torque setting. If after adjustment, the steering wheel spokes are no longer horizontal when the wheels are in the straight-ahead position, remove the steering wheel and reposition it (see Section 13).

16 Check that the toe setting has been correctly adjusted by lowering the car to the ground and rechecking the toe setting; re-adjust if necessary. Ensure that the rubber gaiters are seated correctly and are not twisted or strained, and secure them in position with the retaining clips; where necessary, fit a new retaining clip (refer to Section 16).

Front wheel camber angle

17 Checking and adjusting the front wheel camber angle should be entrusted to a VW dealer or other suitably-equipped specialist. Note that most tyre-fitting centres now possess sophisticated checking equipment. For reference, adjustments are made by slackening the suspension strut-to-swivel hub mounting bolts, and repositioning the swivel hub assembly.

Chapter 11
Bodywork and fittings

Contents

Degrees of difficulty

Easy, suitable for novice with little experience	**Fairly easy,** suitable for beginner with some experience	**Fairly difficult,** suitable for competent DIY mechanic	**Difficult,** suitable for experienced DIY mechanic	**Very difficult,** suitable for expert DIY or professional

Specifications

Torque wrench settings	Nm	lbf ft
Bonnet hinge bolts	23	17
Bonnet lock retaining bolts (use locking fluid)	12	9
Door check link pivot bolt nut	7	5
Door handle retaining bolt	8	6
Door hinge pin grub screw	23	17
Door hinge retaining bolts (Torx)	36	27
Door lock retaining bolts	8	6
Door window glass clamp nuts	10	7
Door window glass regulator retaining bolts:		
Electric windows	23	17
Manual windows	10	7
Lock carrier-to-chassis bolts	23	17
Lock carrier-to-front wing bolts	5	4
Rear bumper inner section retaining nuts	15	11
Seat belt height adjuster bolt	23	17
Seat belt mounting bolts	40	30
Tailgate lock screws	20	15
Tailgate strut lower mounting bolts	10	7
Tailgate strut upper mounting ball-stud	22	16

1 General information

The bodyshell is made of pressed-steel sections, and is available in both three- and five-door Hatchback versions. Most components are welded together, but some use is made of structural adhesives; the front wings are bolted on.

The bonnet, door, and some other vulnerable panels are made of zinc-coated metal, and are further protected by being coated with an anti-chip primer before being sprayed.

Extensive use is made of plastic materials, mainly in the interior, but also in exterior components. The front and rear bumpers are injection-moulded from a synthetic material that is very strong and yet light. Plastic components such as wheel arch liners are fitted to the underside of the car, to improve the body's resistance to corrosion.

2 Maintenance – bodywork and underframe

The general condition of a car's bodywork is the one thing that significantly affects its value. Maintenance is easy, but needs to be regular. Neglect, particularly after minor damage, can lead quickly to further deterioration and costly repair bills. It is important also to keep watch on those parts of the car not immediately visible, for instance the underside, inside all the wheel arches, and the lower part of the engine compartment.

The basic maintenance routine for the bodywork is washing – preferably with a lot of water, from a hose. This will remove all the loose solids which may have stuck to the car. It is important to flush these off in such a way as to prevent grit from scratching the finish. The wheel arches and underframe need washing in the same way, to remove any accumulated mud which will retain moisture and tend to encourage rust. Paradoxically enough, the best time to clean the underframe and wheel arches is in wet weather, when the mud is thoroughly wet and soft. In very wet weather, the underframe is usually cleaned of large accumulations automatically, and this is a good time for inspection.

Periodically, except on cars with a wax-based underbody protective coating, it is a good idea to have the whole of the underframe of the car steam-cleaned, engine compartment included, so that a thorough inspection can be carried out to see what minor repairs and renovations are necessary. Steam cleaning is available at many garages, and is necessary for the removal of the accumulation of oily grime, which sometimes is allowed to become thick in certain areas. If steam-cleaning facilities are not available, there are some excellent grease solvents available which can be brush-applied; the dirt can then be simply hosed off. Note that these methods should not be used on cars with wax-based underbody protective coating, or the coating will be removed. Such cars should be inspected annually, preferably just before Winter, when the underbody should be washed down, and any damage to the wax coating repaired. Ideally, a completely fresh coat should be applied. It would also be worth considering the use of wax-based protection for injection into door panels, sills, box sections, etc, as an additional safeguard against rust damage, where such protection is not provided by the vehicle manufacturer.

After washing paintwork, wipe off with a chamois leather to give an unspotted clear finish. A coat of clear protective wax polish will give added protection against chemical pollutants in the air. If the paintwork sheen has dulled or oxidised, use a cleaner/polisher combination to restore the brilliance of the shine. This requires a little effort, but such dulling is usually caused because regular washing has been neglected. Care needs to be taken with metallic paintwork, as special non-abrasive cleaner/polisher is required to avoid damage to the finish. Always check that the door and ventilator opening drain holes and pipes are completely clear, so that water can be drained out. Brightwork should be treated in the same way as paintwork. Windscreens and windows can be kept clear of the smeary film which often appears, by proprietary glass cleaner. Never use any form of wax or other body or chromium polish on glass.

3 Maintenance – upholstery and carpets

Mats and carpets should be brushed or vacuum-cleaned regularly, to keep them free of grit. If they are badly stained, remove them from the car for scrubbing or sponging, and make quite sure they are dry before refitting. Seats and interior trim panels can be kept clean by wiping with a damp cloth. If they do become stained (which can be more apparent on light-coloured upholstery), use a little liquid detergent and a soft nail brush to scour the grime out of the grain of the material. Do not forget to keep the headlining clean in the same way as the upholstery. When using liquid cleaners inside the car, do not over-wet the surfaces being cleaned. Excessive damp could get into the seams and padded interior, causing stains, offensive odours or even rot. If the inside of the car gets wet accidentally, it is worthwhile taking some trouble to dry it out properly, particularly where carpets are involved. *Do not leave oil or electric heaters inside the car for this purpose.*

4 Minor body damage – repair

Minor scratches

If the scratch is very superficial, and does not penetrate to the metal of the bodywork, repair is very simple. Lightly rub the area of the scratch with a paintwork renovator or a very fine cutting paste to remove loose paint from the scratch, and to clear the surrounding bodywork of wax polish. Rinse the area with clean water.

In the case of metallic paint, the most commonly-found scratches are not in the paint, but in the lacquer top coat, and appear white. If care is taken , these can sometimes be rendered less obvious by very careful use of paintwork renovator (which would otherwise not be used on metallic paintwork); otherwise, repair of these scratches can be achieved by applying lacquer with a fine brush.

Apply touch-up paint to the scratch using a fine paint brush; continue to apply fine layers of paint until the surface of the paint in the scratch is level with the surrounding paintwork. Allow the new paint at least two weeks to harden, then blend it into the surrounding paintwork by rubbing the scratch area with a paintwork renovator or a very fine cutting paste. Finally, apply wax polish.

Where the scratch has penetrated right through to the metal of the bodywork, causing the metal to rust, a different repair technique is required. Remove any loose rust from the bottom of the scratch with a penknife, then apply rust-inhibiting paint to prevent the formation of rust in the future. Using a rubber

or nylon applicator, fill the scratch with bodystopper paste. If required, this paste can be mixed with cellulose thinners to provide a very thin paste which is ideal for filling narrow scratches. Before the stopper-paste in the scratch hardens, wrap a piece of smooth cotton rag around the top of a finger. Dip the finger in cellulose thinners, and quickly sweep it across the surface of the stopper-paste in the scratch; this will ensure that the surface of the stopper-paste is slightly hollowed. The scratch can now be painted over as described earlier in this Section.

Dents

When deep denting of the car's bodywork has taken place, the first task is to pull the dent out, until the affected bodywork almost attains its original shape. There is little point in trying to restore the original shape completely, as the metal in the damaged area will have stretched on impact, and cannot be reshaped fully to its original contour. It is better to bring the level of the dent up to a point which is about 3 mm below the level of the surrounding bodywork. In cases where the dent is very shallow anyway, it is not worth trying to pull it out at all. If the underside of the dent is accessible, it can be hammered out gently from behind, using a mallet with a wooden or plastic head. Whilst doing this, hold a suitable block of wood firmly against the outside of the panel, to absorb the impact from the hammer blows and thus prevent a large area of the bodywork from being 'belled-out'.

Should the dent be in a section of the bodywork which has a double skin, or some other factor making it inaccessible from behind, a different technique is called for. Drill several small holes through the metal inside the area – particularly in the deeper section. Then screw long self-tapping screws into the holes, just sufficiently for them to gain a good purchase in the metal. Now the dent can be pulled out by pulling on the protruding heads of the screws with a pair of pliers.

The next stage of the repair is the removal of the paint from the damaged area, and from an inch or so of the surrounding 'sound' bodywork. This is accomplished most easily by using a wire brush or abrasive pad on a power drill, although it can be done just as effectively by hand, using sheets of abrasive paper. To complete the preparation for filling, score the surface of the bare metal with a screwdriver or the tang of a file, or alternatively, drill small holes in the affected area. This will provide a good 'key' for the filler paste.

To complete the repair, see the Section on filling and respraying.

Rust holes or gashes

Remove all paint from the affected area, and from an inch or so of the surrounding 'sound' bodywork, using an abrasive pad or a wire brush on a power drill. If these are not available, a few sheets of abrasive paper will do the job most effectively. With the paint removed, you will be able to judge the severity of the corrosion, and therefore decide whether to renew the whole panel (if this is possible) or to repair the affected area. New body panels are not as expensive as most people think, and it is often quicker and more satisfactory to fit a new panel than to attempt to repair large areas of corrosion.

Remove all fittings from the affected area, except those which will act as a guide to the original shape of the damaged bodywork (eg sill or wheel arch mouldings, etc). Then, using tin snips or a hacksaw blade, remove all loose metal and any other metal badly affected by corrosion. Hammer the edges of the hole inwards, to create a slight depression for the filler paste.

Wire-brush the affected area to remove the powdery rust from the surface of the remaining metal. Paint the affected area with rust-inhibiting paint; if the back of the rusted area is accessible, treat this also.

Before filling can take place, it will be necessary to block the hole in some way. This can be achieved with aluminium or plastic mesh, or aluminium tape.

Aluminium or plastic mesh, or glass-fibre matting, is probably the best material to use for a large hole. Cut a piece to the approximate size and shape of the hole to be filled, then position it in the hole so that its edges are below the level of the surrounding bodywork. It can be retained in position by several blobs of filler paste around its periphery.

Aluminium tape should be used for small or very narrow holes. Pull a piece off the roll, trim it to the approximate size and shape required, then pull off the backing paper (if used) and stick the tape over the hole; it can be overlapped if the thickness of one piece is insufficient. Burnish down the edges of the tape with the handle of a screwdriver or similar, to ensure that the tape is securely attached to the metal underneath.

Filling and respraying

Before using this Section, see the Sections on dent, deep scratch, rust holes and gash repairs.

Many types of bodyfiller are available, but generally speaking, those proprietary kits which contain a tin of filler paste and a tube of resin hardener are best for this type of repair which can be used directly from the tube. A wide, flexible plastic or nylon applicator will be found invaluable for imparting a smooth and well-contoured finish to the surface of the filler.

Mix up a little filler on a clean piece of card or board – measure the hardener carefully (follow the maker's instructions on the pack), otherwise the filler will set too rapidly or too slowly. Using the applicator, apply the filler paste to the prepared area; draw the applicator across the surface of the filler to achieve the correct contour and to level the surface. When a contour that approximates to

the correct one is achieved, stop working the paste – if you carry on too long, the paste will become sticky and begin to 'pick-up' on the applicator. Continue to add thin layers of filler paste at 20-minute intervals, until the level of the filler is just proud of the surrounding bodywork.

Once the filler has hardened, the excess can be removed using a metal plane or file. From then on, progressively-finer grades of abrasive paper should be used, starting with a 40-grade production paper, and finishing with a 400-grade wet-and-dry paper. Always wrap the abrasive paper around a flat rubber, cork, or wooden block – otherwise the surface of the filler will not be completely flat. During the smoothing of the filler surface, the wet-and-dry paper should be periodically rinsed in water. This will ensure that a very smooth finish is imparted to the filler at the final stage.

At this stage, the 'dent' should be surrounded by a ring of bare metal, which in turn should be encircled by the finely 'feathered' edge of the good paintwork. Rinse the repair area with clean water, until all the dust produced by the rubbing-down operation has gone.

Spray the whole area with a light coat of primer – this will show up any imperfections in the surface of the filler. Repair these imperfections with fresh filler paste or bodystopper, and again smooth the surface with abrasive paper. If bodystopper is used, it can be mixed with cellulose thinners, to form a thin paste which is ideal for filling small holes. Repeat this spray-and-repair procedure until you are satisfied that the surface of the filler, and the feathered edge of the paintwork, are perfect. Clean the repair area with clean water, and allow to dry fully.

The repair area is now ready for final spraying. Paint spraying must be carried out in a warm, dry, windless and dust-free atmosphere. This condition can be created artificially if you have access to a large indoor working area, but if you are forced to work in the open, you will have to pick your day very carefully. If you are working indoors, dousing the floor in the work area with water will help to settle the dust which would otherwise be in the atmosphere. If the repair area is confined to one body panel, mask off the surrounding panels; this will help to minimise the effects of a slight mis-match in paint colours. Bodywork fittings (eg chrome strips, door handles etc) will also need to be masked off. Use genuine masking tape, and several thickness of newspaper, for the masking operations.

Before starting to spray, agitate the aerosol can thoroughly, then spray a test area (an old tin, or similar) until the technique is mastered. Cover the repair area with a thick coat of primer; the thickness should be built up using several thin layers of paint, rather than one thick one. Using 400-grade wet-and-dry paper, rub down the surface of the primer until it is smooth. While doing this, the work area should be thoroughly doused with water,

and the wet-and-dry paper periodically rinsed in water. Allow to dry before spraying on more paint.

Spray on the top coat, again building up the thickness by using several thin layers of paint. Start spraying at the top of the repair area, and then, using a side-to-side motion, work downwards until the whole repair area and about 2 inches of the surrounding original paintwork is covered. Remove all masking material 10 to 15 minutes after spraying on the final coat of paint.

Allow the new paint at least two weeks to harden, then, using a paintwork renovator or a very fine cutting paste, blend the edges of the paint into the existing paintwork. Finally, apply wax polish.

Plastic components

With the use of more and more plastic body components by the car manufacturers (eg bumpers, spoilers, and in some cases major body panels), rectification of more serious damage to such items has become a matter of either entrusting repair work to a specialist in this field, or renewing complete components. Repair of such damage by the DIY owner is not feasible, owing to the cost of the equipment and materials required for effecting such repairs. The basic technique involves making a groove along the line of the crack in the plastic, using a rotary burr in a power drill. The damaged part is then welded back together, using a hot air gun to heat up and fuse a plastic filler rod into the groove. Any excess plastic is then removed, and the area rubbed down to a smooth finish. It is important that a filler rod of the correct plastic is used, as body components can be made of a variety of different types (eg polycarbonate, ABS, polypropylene).

Damage of a less serious nature (abrasions, minor cracks etc) can be repaired by the DIY owner using a two-part epoxy filler repair material which can be used directly from the tube. Once mixed in equal proportions, this is used in similar fashion to the bodywork filler used on metal panels. The filler is usually cured in twenty to thirty minutes, ready for sanding and painting.

If the owner is renewing a complete component himself, or if he has repaired it with epoxy filler, he will be left with the problem of finding a suitable paint for finishing which is compatible with the type of plastic used. At one time, the use of a universal paint was not possible, owing to the complex range of plastics met with in body component applications. Standard paints, generally speaking, will not bond to plastic or rubber satisfactorily, but professional matched paints, to match any plastic or rubber finish, can be obtained from some dealers. However, it is now possible to obtain a plastic body parts finishing kit which consists of a pre-primer treatment, a primer and coloured top coat. Full instructions are normally supplied with a kit, but basically the method of use is to

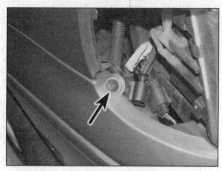

6.3 Remove the front bumper mounting screw inside the indicator aperture

6.4 Remove the four screws at the rear edge of the bumper

6.5 Pull back the wheel arch liner and remove the vertical screw

first apply the pre-primer to the component concerned, and allow it to dry for up to 30 minutes. Then the primer is applied, and left to dry for about an hour before finally applying the special-coloured top coat. The result is a correctly coloured component, where the paint will flex with the plastic or rubber, a property that standard paint does not normally possess.

5 Major body damage – repair

Where serious damage has occurred, or large areas need renewal due to neglect, it means that complete new panels will need welding-in, and this is best left to professionals. If the damage is due to impact, it will also be necessary to check completely

the alignment of the bodyshell, and this can only be carried out accurately by a VW dealer using special jigs. If the body is left misaligned, it is primarily dangerous, as the car will not handle properly, and secondly, uneven stresses will be imposed on the steering, suspension and possibly transmission, causing abnormal wear, or complete failure, particularly to such items as the tyres.

6 Front bumper – removal and refitting

Removal

1 Apply the handbrake, then jack up the front of the car and support it on axle stands (see *Jacking and vehicle support*).

2 On models with headlight washers, prise up the cover for the washer jet (below each headlight) and unclip the jets from the bumper.
3 Remove both front direction indicators as described in Chapter 12, Section 7. Remove the single screw now visible in the indicator aperture, each side **(see illustration)**.
4 Working in each front wheel arch, remove the four screws securing the bumper edge to the wheel arch plastic liner **(see illustration)**.
5 Again on each side, pull the wheel arch liner out slightly, to access a further bumper retaining screw, mounted vertically at the top of the bumper **(see illustration)**.
6 Remove the single screw which secures the bumper lower trim/front foglight trim panel on each side. Unhook the panel at its inner edge, and remove it **(see illustrations)**.
7 Remove the single screw each side, behind the bumper trim panel just removed **(see illustration)**.
8 On models with front foglights, disconnect the wiring plug from each light.
9 Working underneath the front of the car (raise and support it on axle stands if preferred), prise out the four (very stiff) plastic clips which secure the lower edge of the bumper **(see illustration)**.
10 Remove the two screws fitted to the panels either side of the bonnet lock, then (preferably with the help of an assistant) unhook the bumper ends and pull the bumper forwards to remove **(see illustrations)**.

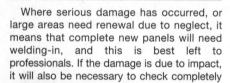
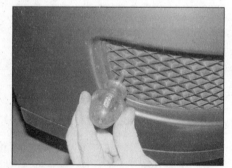

6.6a Remove the screw at the outer edge . . .

6.6b . . . and unhook the bumper lower trim panel

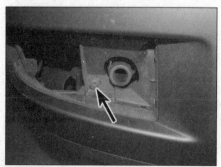

6.7 Remove the screw behind the bumper trim panel

6.9 Prise out the row of four clips under the front edge of the bumper

6.10a Remove the two screws each side of the bonnet lock . . .

6.10b . . . then unhook and remove the bumper

Refitting

11 Refitting is a reverse of removal. Ensure that any wiring is properly reconnected and secured. Tighten all bumper fixings securely.

7 Rear bumper – removal and refitting

Removal

1 To improve access, chock the front wheels, then jack up the rear of the car and support it on axle stands (see *Jacking and vehicle support*).
2 Remove the two screws which secure the ends of the bumper to the rear of the rear wheel arch **(see illustration)**.
3 Open the tailgate and remove the four Torx screws at the top edge of the bumper **(see illustration)**.

4 Pull the bumper rearwards off the four locating pins, disconnect the number plate light wiring, and lower to the ground **(see illustration)**.
5 If the bumper inner section shows signs of damage, it can be removed by unscrewing the four retaining nuts.

Refitting

6 Refitting is a reverse of the removal procedure, ensuring that the bumper engages correctly with the locating pins as it is refitted.

8 Bonnet – removal, refitting and adjustment

Removal

1 Open the bonnet and have an assistant support it. Using a pencil or felt tip pen, mark the outline of each bonnet hinge relative to the bonnet, to use as a guide on refitting.
2 Disconnect the washer hose from the windscreen washer jets, and from the securing clips on the underside of the bonnet **(see illustration)**.
3 Have an assistant support the bonnet. At the top end of the bonnet support strut, prise out the spring clip and then pull the strut off its ball fitting **(see illustration)**.
4 Undo the bonnet retaining bolts and, with the help of an assistant, carefully lift the bonnet clear **(see illustration)**. Store the bonnet out of the way in a safe place.
5 Inspect the bonnet hinges for signs of wear

and free play at the pivots, and if necessary renew. Each hinge is secured to the body by two bolts. Mark the position of the hinge on the body, then undo the retaining bolts and remove it from the car. On refitting, align the new hinge with the marks and securely tighten the retaining bolts.

Refitting and adjustment

6 With the aid of an assistant, offer up the bonnet and loosely fit the retaining bolts. Align the hinges with the marks made on removal, then tighten the retaining bolts securely. Reconnect the earth strap and securely tighten its retaining nut.
7 Refit the bonnet support strut, and secure with the spring clip, making sure the clip is properly engaged before trusting it to support the weight of the bonnet.
8 Close the bonnet, and check for alignment with the adjacent panels. If necessary, slacken the hinge bolts and re-align the bonnet to suit. Once the bonnet is correctly aligned, securely tighten the hinge bolts. Once the bonnet is correctly aligned, check that the bonnet fastens and releases satisfactorily.

9 Bonnet release cable – removal and refitting

Removal

1 Detach the inner cable from the lock body, and release the outer cable from the lock lever **(see illustrations)**.

7.2 Rear bumper-to-wheel arch screws (arrowed)

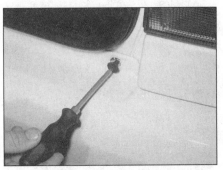

7.3 Removing one of the upper retaining screws

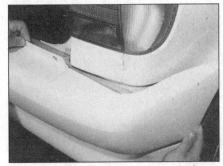

7.4 Pull the bumper rearwards off its retaining pins

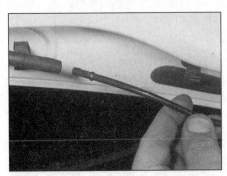

8.2 Unclip the washer hose, and separate it at the rubber connections

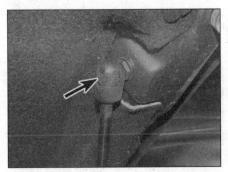

8.3 Prise out the bonnet support strut clip

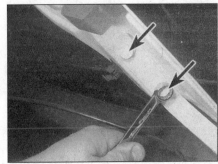

8.4 Bonnet retaining bolts (arrowed)

9.1a Unhook the bonnet release inner cable . . .

9.1b . . . and the outer cable from the lock

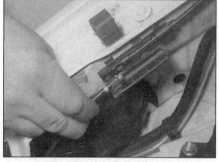

9.3a Unclip the bonnet lock cable connector plastic cover . . .

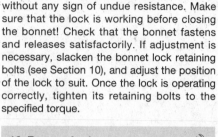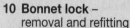

9.3b . . . then unhook the cable end fitting

2 The cable is in two sections, joined in a plastic housing attached to the right-hand inner wing.

3 Prise open the housing cover, and disconnect the cable ball-stud from the housing **(see illustrations)**. The front section of cable can be renewed independently, but it may be advisable to renew both sections if one has failed – the other section may be weak.

4 If required, work back along the cable towards the engine compartment bulkhead, noting its correct routing, and free it from the retaining clips and ties. Tie a length of string to the end of the cable.

5 From inside the car, slacken and remove the screws securing the bonnet release handle to the car.

6 Release the cable grommet from the bulkhead, and withdraw the lever and cable assembly. Once the cable is free, untie the

string and leave it in position in the car; the string can then be used to draw the new cable back into position.

Refitting

7 Tie the inner end of the string to the end of the cable, then use the string to draw the bonnet release cable through into the engine compartment. Once the cable is through, untie the string.

8 Manoeuvre the bonnet release lever back into position, and securely tighten its retaining screws. Seat the rubber grommet in the bulkhead.

9 Ensure that the cable is correctly routed, and secured to all the relevant retaining clips.

10 Clip the cable ball-stud into the plastic connector housing on the inner wing, and close the housing cover.

11 Connect the inner and outer cable to the bonnet lock.

12 Check that the lock operates smoothly, without any sign of undue resistance. Make sure that the lock is working before closing the bonnet! Check that the bonnet fastens and releases satisfactorily. If adjustment is necessary, slacken the bonnet lock retaining bolts (see Section 10), and adjust the position of the lock to suit. Once the lock is operating correctly, tighten its retaining bolts to the specified torque.

10 Bonnet lock – removal and refitting

Removal

1 Unbolt the lock support arm, then unhook and remove it from the lock carrier **(see illustrations)**.

2 Referring to Section 9, free the release cable outer from the lock lever, then detach the inner cable from the lock bracket.

3 Using a suitable marker pen, mark the outline of the bonnet lock on the cross-member, then slacken and remove the two lock retaining bolts **(see illustration)**. Remove the lock from the front of the car.

Refitting

4 Before refitting, remove all traces of old locking compound from the bonnet retaining bolts and their threads in the body.

5 Locate the bonnet release inner cable in the lock bracket and reconnect the outer cable to the lever. Seat the lock on the crossmember.

6 Apply a locking compound (VW recommend the use of locking fluid D 185 400 A2 – available from your VW dealer) to the threads of the lock retaining bolts.

7 Align the lock with the marks made prior to removal, then refit the bolts and tighten them to the specified torque setting.

8 Hook the lock support arm into through the top of the lock carrier, then insert and tighten the securing bolt at the bottom end.

9 Check that the lock operates smoothly, without any sign of undue resistance. Make sure that the lock is working before closing the bonnet! Check that the bonnet fastens and releases satisfactorily. If adjustment is

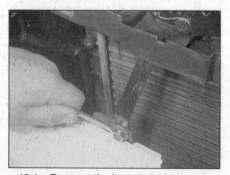

10.1a Remove the bonnet lock support arm securing bolt . . .

10.1b . . . then unhook the arm from the lock carrier, and remove it

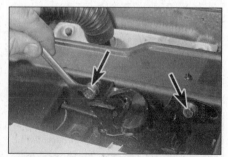

10.3 Unscrew the retaining bolts (arrowed) and remove the bonnet lock from the front of the car

11.2a Unscrew the front door wiring connector using a suitable C-spanner . . .

11.2b . . . and withdraw it from the door pillar

11.2c On 5-door models with central locking, disconnect the vacuum connection to the rear door

necessary, slacken the bonnet lock retaining bolts, and adjust the position of the lock to suit. Once the lock is operating correctly, tighten its retaining bolts to the specified torque.

11 Door –
removal, refitting and adjustment

Removal

1 Disconnect the battery negative terminal (see *Disconnecting the battery*).
2 Open the door. On front doors, rotate the wiring connector anti-clockwise and disconnect it from the pillar – a suitable C-spanner may be required for this. When working on rear doors on models equipped with central locking, disengage the gaiter from the door pillar and disconnect the vacuum pipe **(see illustrations)**.
3 Slacken and remove the nut and pivot bolt securing the check link to the pillar **(see illustration)**.
4 Prise off the cap over the grub screw on each hinge with a small flat-bladed screwdriver. Have an assistant support the door, then slacken and remove the grub screws and lift the door upwards to remove **(see illustration)**.
5 Examine the hinges for signs of wear or damage. If renewal is necessary, mark the position of the hinge(s) then undo the retaining bolts and remove them from the car. Fit the new hinge(s), align with the marks made before removal and tighten the retaining bolts to the specified torque.

Refitting

6 Apply a smear of multi-purpose grease to the hinge pins, then, with the aid of an assistant, refit the door to the car. Once the door is correctly positioned, tighten the grub screws to the specified torque.
7 On all models, align the check link with its bracket and refit the pivot bolt and nut, tightening it to the specified torque setting.
8 Reconnect the front door wiring connector, making sure it is correctly reconnected, and secure it in position. Where necessary, reconnect the central locking vacuum pipe, making sure the connection is pushed firmly

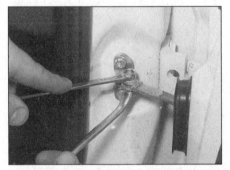

11.3 Removing the check link pivot bolt and nut

together. Fold the rubber gaiter back into position, ensuring it is correctly located on the pillar.
9 Check the door alignment and, if necessary, adjust then reconnect the battery negative terminal. If the paintwork around the hinges has been damaged, paint the area with a suitable touch-in brush to prevent corrosion.

Adjustment

10 Close the door and check the door alignment with surrounding body panels. If necessary, slight adjustment of the door position can be made by slackening the hinge bolts and grub screws, and repositioning the hinge/door as necessary. Once the door is correctly positioned, tighten the hinge bolts and grub screws to the specified torque. If the paintwork around the hinges has been damaged, paint the affected area with a suitable touch-in brush to prevent corrosion.

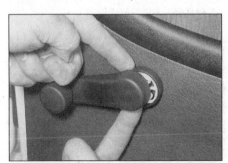

12.2a Slide out the spacer behind the regulator handle (the direction will not necessarily be as shown) . . .

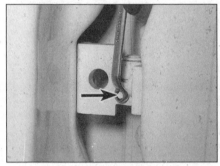

11.4 Loosen the hinge grub screw (arrowed)

12 Door inner trim panel –
removal and refitting

Removal

Front door

1 Disconnect the battery negative terminal (see *Disconnecting the battery*).
2 On models with manual front windows (or when working on the rear door trim panel), ensure that the window is closed, then slide the spacer behind the regulator handle, to release the retaining clip. The direction in which the spacer must be pushed will vary, as the spacer turns with the handle, but it can easily be done by hand. Pull the handle off the spindle **(see illustrations)**.

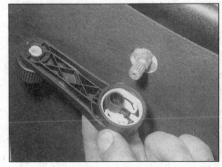

12.2b . . . and remove the handle from the splines

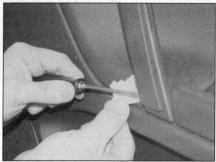

12.3 Remove the door lock operating knob

12.4a Taking care not to damage the finish . . .

12.4b . . . prise out the door handle centre panel

12.5 Remove the two screws behind the handle panel

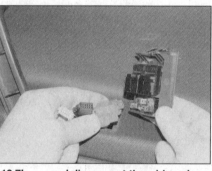

12.6 Remove the screw at the front of the trim panel

6 Remove the small screw at the top of the trim panel, at the front (see illustration).

7 On models with electric windows, carefully prise out the window switch from the trim panel, and disconnect the wiring plugs – note which plug fits where, as they can be mixed up (on our car, the nearest plug was beige in colour) (see illustrations).

8 Release the door trim panel studs, carefully levering between the panel and door with a flat-bladed screwdriver or similar tool. Work around the outside of the panel, and when all the studs are released, ease the panel away from the door (see illustration).

9 Lift the panel over the door lock knob, and release it from the interior lock handle. Lift the panel away (see illustrations).

10 Reach round the back of the panel, and disconnect the mirror switch wiring plug (see illustration). The trim panel is now free to be removed from the car.

3 Unscrew the door lock inner operating knob from its rod (see illustration). This is not essential, but it means the trim panel has to be lifted less high to remove it.

4 Taking care not to damage the finish,

carefully prise out the centre trim panel from the door pull handle (see illustrations).

5 Remove the two screws behind the door pull handle trim panel just removed (see illustration).

12.7a Prise up the window switch panel . . .

12.7b . . . and disconnect the wiring plugs

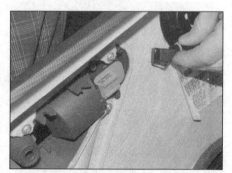

12.8 Prise the panel carefully to release the clips around the outside

12.9a Lift the panel at the rear, to clear the lock knob . . .

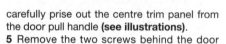

12.9b . . . and lift it away

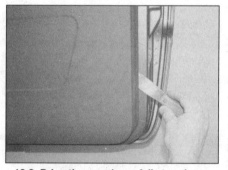

12.10 Disconnect the mirror switch wiring plug at the back of the panel

Bodywork and fittings 11•9

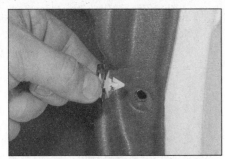

12.12 If any of the trim panel retaining studs are broken, they should be prised out and renewed

Rear door

11 The procedure for removing the rear door trim panel is very similar to that for the front door panel described previously, ignoring all references to the door mirror.

Refitting

12 Refitting the trim panel(s) is the reverse of removal. Before refitting, check whether any of the trim panel retaining studs were broken on removal, and renew them as necessary **(see illustration)**.

---

13 Door handle and lock components – removal and refitting

1 The 'freewheeling' door lock is designed so that the entire lock barrel rotates if excessive force is applied, thereby preventing unauthorised access **(see illustration)**. It is not recommended that the lock cylinder be removed from the later-type door lock assembly, as a special VW tool is required to reassemble the freewheeling mechanism.

Removal

Interior door handle

2 Remove the door inner trim panel as described in Section 12.
3 Release the handle retaining clip at the front with a suitable screwdriver, then slide the handle out of the door in a forwards direction, and free it from the end of the link rod **(see illustrations)**.

Exterior door handle

Note: *This task can be performed with the door inner trim panel in position.*
4 If work is being carried out on the front door, insert the key into the lock.
5 Slacken and remove the Torx screw from the rear edge of the door. Move the handle assembly forwards and pivot it out of position. On the front door, as the handle is being removed, rotate the key through 45° to disengage the handle from the lock operating lever **(see illustrations)**.
6 Recover the handle seals and the lock retaining clips, and inspect them for signs of damage or deterioration; renewing them if necessary. **Note:** *Do not drop the components into the door; if the clip is dropped, it will be necessary to remove the inner trim panel to recover it.*

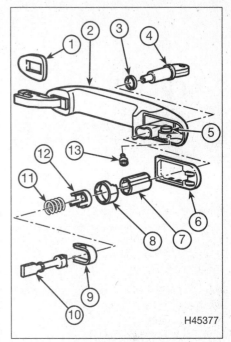

13.1 Front door handle and lock components

1	Back plate	8	Support
2	Door handle	9	Locking plate
3	Seal	10	Paddle
4	Lock cylinder	11	Spring
5	Spring	12	Coupling plate
6	Back plate	13	Torx screw
7	Freewheel sleeve		

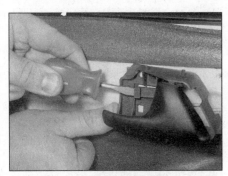

13.3a Release the interior handle retaining clip using a screwdriver . . .

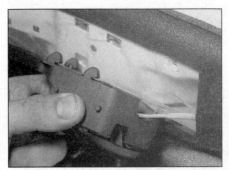

13.3b . . . then slide the handle out of the door . . .

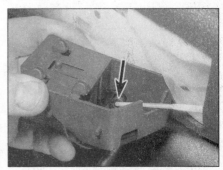

13.3c . . . and release the link rod (arrowed)

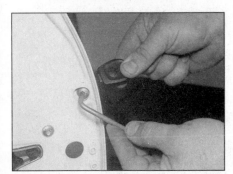

13.5a Remove the handle securing screw using a Torx key or socket . . .

13.5b . . . then turn the key and disengage the rear end . . .

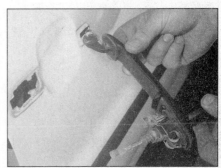

13.5c . . . and unhook the front end of the handle

13.9 Prise out the door inner trim panel retaining studs

13.12a Pull the vacuum pipe off the central locking unit . . .

13.12b . . . together with the main wiring connector

Front door lock cylinder

7 It is not recommended that the lock cylinder be removed from the later-type lock assembly, as a special VW assembly tool is required to ensure that the freewheeling mechanism is refitted correctly. Front door lock cylinder renewal on these models should be entrusted to your VW dealer.

Front door lock

8 Ensure that the window is in the fully-closed position, then remove the interior door handle as described in paragraphs 2 and 3.

9 Carefully lever out the door trim panel retaining studs from the rear edge of the door (see illustration).

10 Carefully peel the foam insulating panel away from the rear edge of the door (see Section 14). We found that a small trimming knife was useful to slice through the bead of

adhesive used to attach the foam panel, but this is a long job, as care must be taken not to cut the panel. If the panel is ripped or damaged, a new one must be used on refitting; any damaged trim clips must also renewed. Continue as described under the relevant sub-heading.

11 Remove the exterior door handle as described in paragraphs 4 to 6.

12 On models with central locking, disconnect the vacuum pipe from the lock assembly, and disconnect the main wiring plug from the central locking positioner **(see illustrations)**.

13 Slacken and remove the lock retaining bolts at the rear edge of the door. Prise out the retaining clips and disconnect the lock link rods from the door frame as necessary. Manoeuvre the lock out through the door inner frame, and disconnect the upper wiring

plug from the central locking positioner, where applicable. Disengage the lock from the link rods and remove it from the door **(see illustrations)**.

Rear door lock

14 Carry out the operations described above in paragraphs 8 to 12, noting that there is no wiring plug on the rear door lock.

15 Using a suitable pin punch, press the spreader pin through the centre of the interior lock button pivot link rod. Free the pivot from the door. Recover the pin from inside the door and detach the pivot from the link rod **(see illustrations)**.

16 Unclip the link rod guide clips from the door.

17 Slacken and remove the lock retaining bolts and manoeuvre the lock and link rod assembly out from the door **(see illustration)**.

13.13a Unscrew the lock retaining bolts . . .

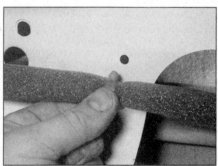

13.13b . . . detach the lock link rod from the door frame . . .

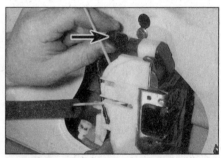

13.13c . . . then pull out the lock and disconnect the upper wiring plug from the central locking unit . . .

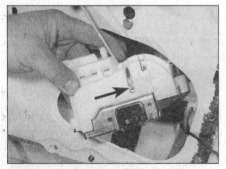

13.13d . . . and disconnect the link rods (arrowed) from the lock

13.15a Using a pin punch, press through the spreader pin . . .

13.15b . . . which fits in the centre of the link rod pivot

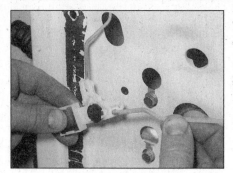

13.15c Unclip the link rods

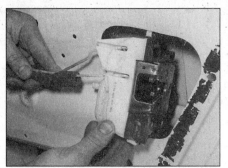

13.17 Removing a rear door lock

13.22 Door lock adjustment screw (arrowed)

If necessary, detach the link rods from the lock noting their correct fitted locations; the link rods are different, and must not be interchanged.

Refitting

Interior door handle

18 Engage the handle with the link rod, and clip it back into position. Make sure the handle operates correctly, then refit the trim panel as described in Section 12.

Exterior door handle

19 Fit the lock retaining clip to the door, and fit the seals to the rear of the handle. **Note:** *Do not drop the clip into the door; if the clip is dropped it will be necessary to remove the inner trim panel to recover it.*

20 Hook the lock front pivot into place, then clip the rear of the handle into position. On the front door, rotate the key through 45° to engage the handle with the lock operating lever.

21 Check the operation of the handle, then refit the Torx screw to the rear edge of the door.

Front door lock

22 Before refitting, slacken the lock adjusting (Torx) screw – this screw is normally hidden behind a plastic plug in the rear edge of the door **(see illustration)**. On the right-hand door, this screw has a **left-hand thread** – ie, it unscrews *clockwise*.

23 Manoeuvre the lock assembly into position, and engage it with the link rod.

24 Refit the lock bolts and tighten them to the specified torque. Where necessary, reconnect the vacuum pipe and wiring connector(s) (as applicable) to the lock assembly.

25 Refit the exterior handle as described in paragraphs 19 to 21.

26 Remove the plastic plug from the door to gain access to the lock adjustment screw. Noting that the screw may have a left-hand thread (see paragraph 22), tighten the screw to 3 Nm (2 lbf ft) then refit the plastic plug.

27 Where necessary, refit the regulator guide rail retaining bolts, and adjust as described in Section 14.

28 Check the operation of the lock and handle, then press the polythene insulating panel back onto the door and refit the door trim panel retaining clips.

29 Refit the interior door handle as described in paragraph 18.

Rear door lock

30 Refit the link rods to the lock, making sure they are correctly refitted.

31 Before refitting, slacken the lock adjusting (Torx) screw – this screw is normally hidden behind a plastic plug in the rear edge of the door. On the right-hand door, this screw has a **left-hand thread** – ie, it unscrews *clockwise*.

32 Manoeuvre the lock assembly into position and tighten the retaining bolts to the specified torque. Where necessary, reconnect the vacuum pipe and wiring connector(s) (as applicable) to the lock assembly.

33 Attach the link rod to the pivot, and clip the pivot into the door. Secure the pivot in position with the spreader pin.

34 Carry out the operations described in paragraphs 25 to 29, ignoring the remark about the regulator bolts.

14 Door window glass and regulator – removal and refitting

Removal

Front door window glass

1 Remove the interior door handle as described in Section 13.

2 Carefully lever out the door trim panel retaining clips from the door.

3 On models with front door speakers, remove four screws and lift away the speaker. Disconnect the speaker wiring as it becomes accessible **(see illustration)**.

4 Carefully peel the foam insulating panel away from the door, and remove the panel, feeding the wiring through the holes provided. We found that a small trimming knife was useful to slice through the bead of adhesive used to attach the foam panel, but this is a long job, as care must be taken not to cut the panel **(see illustrations)**. If the panel is ripped or damaged, a new one must be used on refitting; any damaged trim clips must also renewed.

5 Position the window glass so the glass clamps on the regulator mechanism are accessible through the door panel cutaways.

6 Slacken the window clamp bolts, and release the clamps from the glass. Pull the

14.3 Disconnect the wiring from the rear of the speaker

14.4a Using a small knife to slice through the adhesive securing the foam panel to the door

14.4b Removing the foam panel

14.6a Loosen the window clamp bolts . . .

14.6b . . . then lift the window glass upwards and out of the door frame

14.10a Pull off the rubber guides in front . . .

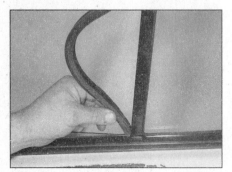

14.10b . . . and to the rear of the rear door window

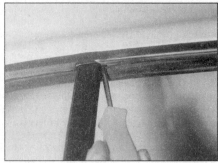

14.11a Remove the rear guide channel upper screw . . .

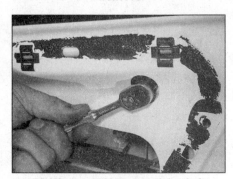

14.11b . . . and lower retaining bolt

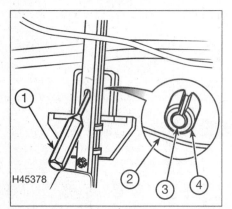

14.12 Rear window glass-to-regulator attachment details

1 Pin punch   *3 Spreader pin*
2 Window glass   *4 Plastic plug*

glass upwards, then tilt it towards the front and manoeuvre the window glass out through the top of the door **(see illustrations)**.

Rear door window glass

7 Remove the interior door handle as described in Section 13.

8 Carefully lever out the door trim panel retaining clips from the door.

9 Carefully peel the foam insulating panel away from the door and remove the panel. We found that a small trimming knife was useful to slice through the bead of adhesive used to attach the foam panel, but this is a long job, as care must be taken not to cut the panel. If the panel is ripped or damaged, a new one must be used on refitting; any damaged trim clips must also be renewed.

10 Pull out the rubber guides in front and to the rear of the window **(see illustrations)**.

11 Remove the rear guide channel upper screw and lower retaining bolt **(see illustrations)**.

12 The window glass is secured to the regulator by a plastic spreader pin and plug – the pin fits inside the plug. Using a 3 mm pin punch, tap out the spreader pin, then use a larger punch to drive out the plug, and recover them both from the door **(see illustration)**.

13 Lift up the window glass to release it from the regulator, and move it down as far as possible.

14 Pull the rear guide channel forwards off the door fixed glass, taking care not to pull off the rubber seal beneath it. Once it is free, pull the channel down a little to release the top from the rubber seal, then remove it upwards from the door **(see illustrations)**.

15 Pull the window glass upwards out of the door **(see illustration)**.

14.14a Pull the guide channel downwards . . .

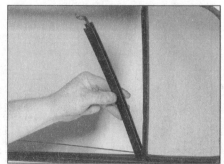

14.14b . . . then remove it from the door

14.15 Lifting out the rear door window glass

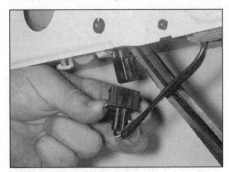

14.18 Disconnecting the electric window motor wiring plug

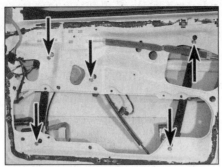

14.19a Front window regulator bolt locations (arrowed)

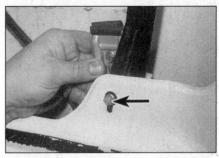

14.19b Lift the regulator so that the bolt heads (arrowed) can pass through the holes in the door frame

16 If necessary, the fixed glass can now be disengaged from the sealing strip and removed from the door.

Front window regulator

17 Remove the window glass as described earlier.

18 Release the retaining clip, and free the regulator cables from the door. On models with electric windows, disconnect the wiring connector from the regulator motor **(see illustration)**.

19 Loosen the regulator retaining bolts, then lift the regulator slightly so that the bolt heads can be passed through the holes in the inner door **(see illustrations)**.

20 Manoeuvre the regulator mechanism downwards and out through the door aperture **(see illustration)**.

Rear window regulator

21 Remove the window glass as described earlier.

22 Loosen the regulator retaining bolts, then lift the regulator slightly so that the bolt heads can be passed through the holes in the inner door **(see illustration)**. Recover the foam spacer from the regulator spindle, where fitted.

23 Manoeuvre the regulator downwards out through the door aperture **(see illustration)**.

Refitting

Front door window glass

24 Manoeuvre the window glass into position and engage it with the regulator clamps. Make sure the glass is correctly seated, then lightly tighten the regulator clamp nuts.

25 Check that the window glass moves smoothly and easily, and closes fully. If necessary, slacken the regulator clamp nuts then reposition the glass as necessary. Once the window operation is correct, tighten the clamp nuts to the specified torque.

26 Once the window is operating correctly, press the foam insulating panel back into position, making sure it is correctly seated, and refit the trim panel clips. Refit the inner trim panel as described in Section 12.

Rear door window glass

27 Where removed, ease the fixed glass into position, making sure it is correctly seated in the sealing strip.

28 Refit the rear guide channel to the fixed glass.

29 Insert the plastic plug and spreader pin into the window glass, so that the assembly protrudes an equal amount either side of the glass **(see illustration)**.

30 Guide the window glass into the top of the door, taking care as it is quite difficult to align. Insert the glass into the top of the lifting rail slot, again ensuring that the edge of the glass is central in the slot.

31 Tap the top of the glass down gently, so that the spreader pin/plug assembly locates in the lifting rail.

32 Refit the rear guide channel upper and lower retaining screws, then fit the front and rear rubber guides.

33 Check that the window glass moves smoothly and easily, and closes fully.

34 Once the window is operating correctly, press the foam insulating panel back into

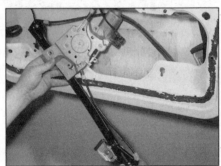

14.20 Removing the window regulator from a front door

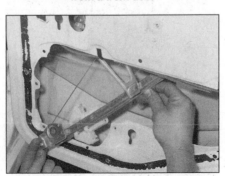

14.23 Removing the rear door window regulator

position, making sure it is correctly seated, and refit the trim panel clips. Refit the inner trim panel as described in Section 12.

Front window regulator

35 Manoeuvre the regulator into position through the door aperture, hooking the bolt heads into engagement with the inner door. Tighten all its fixings to the specified torque. Where necessary, reconnect the wiring connector to the regulator motor.

36 Clip the regulator cables into position then refit the glass as described above.

Rear window regulator

37 Manoeuvre the regulator into position through the door aperture then refit the retaining bolts and tighten them to the specified torque. Where necessary, reconnect the wiring connector to the regulator motor.

38 Refit the glass as described above.

14.22 Rear door window regulator bolts (two of four arrowed)

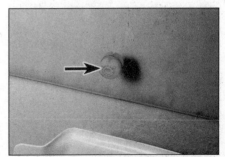

14.29 Fit the plastic plug and spreader pin (arrowed) so that they protrude an equal amount either side of the glass

15.2a Inside the tailgate, remove the handle retaining screw . . .

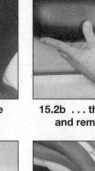

15.2b . . . then release the securing clips and remove the tailgate trim panel

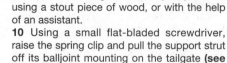

15.6 Tailgate hinge securing bolts (arrowed)

15.10 Prise out the tailgate support strut spring clip (arrowed)

15 Tailgate and support struts – removal and refitting

Removal

Tailgate

1 Open up the tailgate, then disconnect the battery negative terminal (see *Disconnecting the battery*).

2 Slacken and remove the tailgate handle retaining screw, then release the tailgate trim panel clips, carefully levering between the panel and tailgate with a flat-bladed screwdriver. Work around the outside of the panel, and when all the clips are released, remove the panel **(see illustrations)**.

3 Disconnect the wiring connectors situated behind the trim panel, and free the washer hose from the tailgate wiper motor. Also disconnect the wiring connectors from the heated rear screen terminals, and free the wiring grommets from the tailgate.

4 Tie a piece of string to each end of the wiring then, noting the correct routing of the wiring harness, release the harness rubber grommets from the tailgate and withdraw the wiring. When the end of the wiring appears, untie the string and leave it in position in the tailgate; it can then be used on refitting to draw the wiring into position.

5 Using a suitable marker pen, draw around the outline of each hinge, marking its correct position on the tailgate.

6 Have an assistant support the tailgate, then release the support struts from their balljoint mountings on the tailgate as described in paragraph 10. Slacken and remove the bolts securing the hinges to the tailgate, and remove the tailgate from the car **(see**

illustration). Where necessary, recover the gaskets fitted between the hinge and tailgate.

7 Inspect the hinges for signs of wear or damage and renew if necessary.

8 The hinges are secured to the car by nuts or bolts (depending on model) which can be accessed once the headlining has been freed from the trim strip and peeled back. On refitting ensure that the hinge gasket is in good condition, and secure the hinge in position.

Support struts

9 Support the tailgate in the open position, using a stout piece of wood, or with the help of an assistant.

10 Using a small flat-bladed screwdriver, raise the spring clip and pull the support strut off its balljoint mounting on the tailgate **(see illustration)**. Raise the second retaining clip then detach the strut from the balljoint on the body and remove it from the car. If the struts are to be re-used, do not pull the spring clips out completely, or they will be damaged.

Refitting

Tailgate

11 Refitting is the reverse of removal, aligning the hinges with the marks made before removal.

12 On completion, close the tailgate and check its alignment with the surrounding panels. If necessary, slight adjustment can be made by slackening the retaining bolts and repositioning the tailgate slightly on its hinges.

Support struts

13 Refitting is a reverse of the removal procedure, ensuring that the strut is securely held by its retaining clips.

16 Tailgate lock components – removal and refitting

Removal

Tailgate lock

1 Open up the tailgate, then remove the tailgate trim panel as described in paragraph 2 of Section 15.

2 Disconnect the wiring plug for the boot light, then detach the lock and handle operating rod using a suitable flat-bladed screwdriver **(see illustration)**.

3 Loosen and remove the lock retaining screws, then manoeuvre the lock out of position **(see illustrations)**.

Tailgate lock handle

4 Open up the tailgate, then remove the tailgate trim panel as described in paragraph 2 of Section 15.

5 Disconnect the pullrod from the handle assembly, and where applicable, unclip the central locking operating rod **(see illustrations)**.

6 Lever out the securing wire clip and detach

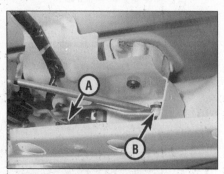

16.2 Boot light wiring plug (A) and lock operating rod (B)

16.3a Tailgate lock retaining screws (arrowed)

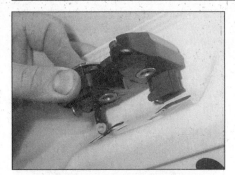

16.3b Removing the tailgate lock

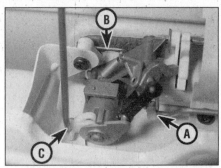

16.5a Tailgate lock cylinder, showing handle pullrod (A), wire clip (B) and central locking rod (C)

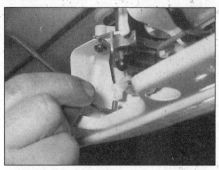

16.5b Disconnecting central locking operating rod

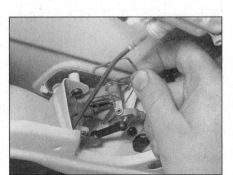

16.6a Prise out the wire clip . . .

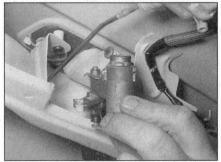

16.6b . . . and withdraw the lock cylinder

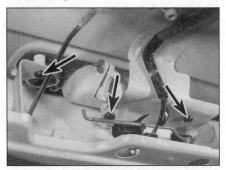

16.7a Unscrew the Torx bolts (arrowed) . . .

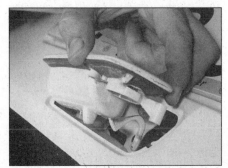

16.7b . . . and withdraw the handle from the tailgate

the lock cylinder from the handle **(see illustrations)**. Recover the O-ring seal.

7 Remove three Torx retaining bolts and remove the handle from the tailgate **(see illustrations)**.

Tailgate lock cylinder

8 The lock cylinder is removed as described in paragraphs 5 and 6 above.

Refitting

9 Refitting is a reversal of the relevant removal procedure. Before refitting the trim panel, check the operation of the lock components and (where necessary) the central locking system.

17 Central locking components – removal and refitting

1 Higher-specification models are equipped with a central door locking system, which automatically locks all doors and the tailgate in unison with the manual locking of either front door. The system is operated by a bi-pressure pump, which supplies vacuum to lock the doors, and pressure to unlock them **(see illustration)**. Apart from the central locking positioners and the bi-pressure pump, the door locks are identical to those on models without central locking.

2 Should the system develop a fault, the condition and security of the hoses should first be checked. A leak will cause the bi-pressure pump to run longer than five seconds, and if it runs for thirty-five seconds, an internal control unit will automatically switch it off.

Removal

Central locking pressure pump

3 The central locking operating pump is located on the right-hand side of the luggage compartment, behind the right-hand side trim panel. Before removal, disconnect the battery negative lead (see *Disconnecting the battery*).

4 Open the tailgate, then lower the right-hand side trim panel by turning the two fasteners through 90°.

5 Lift out the first-aid box tray, where fitted. Lift the pump carefully out of the insulation

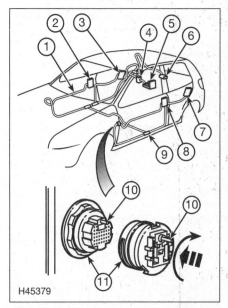

H45379

17.1 Central locking system components

1 Vacuum pipe
2 Front door lock positioner
3 Rear door lock positioner
4 Fuel filler flap positioner
5 Bi-pressure pump
6 Tailgate lock positioner
7 Rear door lock positioner
8 Front door lock positioner
9 T-piece
10 Pipe connector
11 Door pillar connector

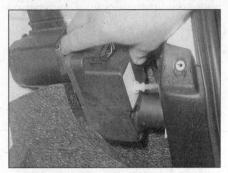

17.5a Pull out the bi-pressure pump . . .

17.5b . . . then disconnect the wiring plug . . .

17.5c . . . and the vacuum connection

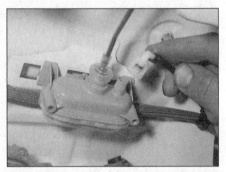

17.9 Pulling off the vacuum pipe from the tailgate lock positioner

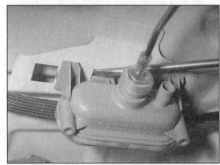

17.11a Lift up the retaining clip . . .

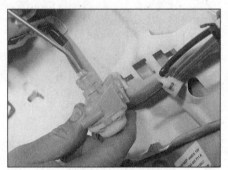

17.11b . . . then slide the positioner to the left and remove

packing, then disconnect the wiring connector and pressure pipe from the pump, and remove the pump from the car (see illustrations).

Door lock positioner

6 The positioner is removed with the door lock, as described in Section 13.

7 To remove the positioner from the lock, first turn the lock latch to the 'locked' position then pull off the door window stop buffer. Unscrew and remove the positioner retaining Torx screw. Release the retaining clips and remove the positioner from the lock, noting how the positioner plunger is engaged with the lock lever.

Tailgate lock positioner

8 Remove the tailgate trim panel as described in paragraph 2 of Section 15.

9 Disconnect the vacuum pipe from the positioner (see illustration).

10 Referring to Section 16, disconnect the operating rod from the lock cylinder.

11 Lift up the retaining clip, and press the positioner to the left to remove it from its location in the tailgate (see illustrations).

Fuel filler flap positioner

12 To gain access to the filler flap positioner, remove the pressure pump as described above. With the pump removed, take out its insulation packing.

13 Slacken and remove the positioner retaining screws. Pull the positioner and its operating rod out of its location, disconnecting its vacuum hose as it becomes accessible.

Note that the rear light cluster will have to be removed (see Chapter 12, Section 7) when refitting the positioner, in order to guide the locking rod into the filler cap.

Refitting

14 Refitting is a reverse of the relevant removal procedure, making sure all vacuum pipe connections are securely remade. On completion, check the operation of all central locking system components.

18 Electric window components – removal and refitting

Window switches

1 Refer to Chapter 12, Section 6.

Window motors

Removal

2 Remove the regulator assembly as described in Section 14.

3 Remove the three cross-head motor retaining screws from one side of the motor, and recover the plastic spacer sleeves.

4 Turn the regulator assembly around, and remove the five cable drum securing screws. Open the hinged cover and remove the wiring connector from its location.

5 Pull the cable drum off the gear housing by hand – it may be necessary to rock it loose.

Refitting

6 If a new motor is being fitted, remove the fitting cover. Pull the drive gear off the old motor shaft, and recover the spacer washer. Fit the drive gear and washer to the cable drum.

7 Make sure that the motor drivegear components are sufficiently lubricated (VW recommend grease G 000 450 02 – available from your VW dealer) and free from dust and dirt.

8 Check that the cable is correctly located on the drum, then engage the cable drum with the motor. It may be necessary to turn the drum and motor slightly to achieve satisfactory engagement.

9 Refit the cable drum securing screws, and tighten in a diagonal sequence. Refit the wiring connector, and secure by closing the hinged cover.

10 Turn the assembly over, and refit the motor retaining screws.

11 Refit the regulator assembly as described in Section 14.

19 Exterior mirrors and associated components – removal and refitting

Removal

1 Remove the door inner trim panel as described in Section 12.

2 Remove the screw at the base of the mirror

trim panel, and unclip the panel from the door **(see illustrations)**.

3 Disconnect the speaker wiring plug **(see illustration)**.

4 Disconnect the mirror wiring plug **(see illustration)**.

5 Support the mirror, then remove the three mirror mounting screws and withdraw it from the car **(see illustrations)**.

Mirror glass

Note: *The mirror glass is clipped into place. Removal of the glass without the VW special tool (number 80-200) is likely to result in breakage of the glass.*

 Warning: Wear thick gloves and eye protection when removing the mirror glass – even if the glass is not broken, it may break during removal.

6 Insert a wide plastic or wooden wedge between the mirror glass and mirror housing, and carefully prise the glass out. Take great care when removing the glass; do not use excessive force, as the glass is easily broken.

7 Remove the glass from the mirror. Where applicable, disconnect the wiring connectors from the mirror heating element.

Mirror switch

8 Refer to Chapter 12, Section 6.

Mirror motor

9 Remove the mirror glass as described above.
10 Undo the retaining screws and remove the motor, disconnecting its wiring connector as it becomes accessible.

Refitting

11 Refitting is the reverse of the relevant removal procedure.

20 Windscreen, tailgate and fixed window glass (3-door models) – general information

These areas of glass are secured by the tight fit of the weatherstrip in the body aperture, and are bonded in position with a special adhesive. Renewal of such fixed glass is a difficult, messy and time-consuming task, which is beyond the scope of the home mechanic. It is difficult, unless one has plenty of practice, to obtain a secure, waterproof fit.

19.2a Remove the mirror trim panel screw . . .

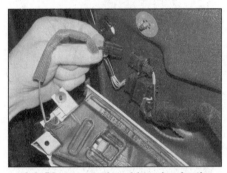

19.3 Disconnect the wiring plug for the tweeter speaker . . .

Furthermore, the task carries a high risk of breakage; this applies especially to the laminated glass windscreen. In view of this, owners are strongly advised to have this sort of work carried out by one of the many specialist windscreen fitters.

21 Sunroof – general information

Due to the complexity of the sunroof mechanism, considerable expertise is needed to repair, renew or adjust the sunroof components successfully. Removal of the roof first requires the headlining to be removed, which is a complex and tedious operation, and not a task to be undertaken lightly. Therefore, any problems with the sunroof should be referred to a VW dealer.

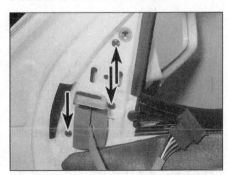

19.5b Remove the three mounting screws (arrowed) . . .

19.2b . . . and unclip the panel from the door

19.4 . . . and the one below it, for the mirror electrics

22 Body exterior fittings – removal and refitting

Wheel arch liners and body under-panels

1 The various plastic covers fitted to the underside of the car are secured in position by a mixture of screws, nuts and retaining clips, and removal will be fairly obvious on inspection. Work methodically around the panel, removing its retaining screws and releasing its retaining clips until the panel is free and can be removed from the underside of the car. Most clips are simply prised out of position.

2 On refitting, renew any retaining clips that may have been broken on removal, and ensure that the panel is securely retained by all the relevant clips and screws.

19.5c . . . and remove the mirror from the door

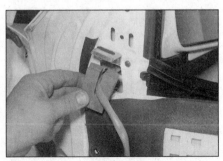

19.5a Mirror wiring is protected from the metal edge of the door frame by a foam insulation block

23.1a Unclip the trim cover from the front seat inner rail . . .

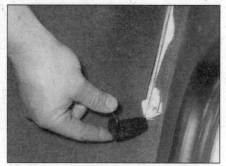

23.1b . . . and the cover or end plug from the outer rail

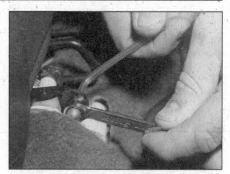

23.2 Removing the rearward travel limiter nut and bolt

Body trim strips and badges

3 The various body trim strips and badges are held in position with a special adhesive tape. Removal requires the trim/badge to be heated, to soften the adhesive, and then cut away from the surface. Due to the high risk of damage to the paintwork during this operation, it is recommended that this task should be entrusted to a VW dealer.

23 Seats – removal and refitting

Removal

Front seat

1 Slide the seat forwards and unclip the trim cover from the seat inner guide rail. Remove the cover rearwards. Repeat the operation on the outer seat rail **(see illustrations)**.
2 Slide the seat backwards and remove the rearward travel limiter Allen bolt and nut from the front of the seat centre guide rail **(see illustration)**.
3 Slide the seat fully backwards, disengaging it from the outer guide rails and remove it from the car. Recover the plastic guide pieces from each of the seat guides, and renew them if they show signs of damage or deterioration.

Rear seat assembly

4 Lift up the rear seat cushion(s), then press together the spring legs and release from the hinges. Remove the seat cushion(s) from the car.
5 Fold down the rear seat backrest(s).
6 On models with a split folding rear seat, carefully prise out the double-ended retaining clip out from the top of the centre hinge pivot.
7 Using a small flat-bladed screwdriver, depress the locking hook at the side of the backrest, then move the backrest upwards to release its pivot pin. Disengage the backrest from the centre hinge, or from the other locking hook (as applicable), and remove it from the car. On models with a split folding rear seat, remove the opposite seat back in the same way.

Refitting

Front seats

8 Before refitting, examine the seat guide pieces for signs of wear or damage, and renew if necessary. Refitting is a reverse of the removal procedure, ensuring that the seat adjustment lever engages correctly with the centre guide locking plunger as the seat is refitted.

Rear seat assembly

9 Refitting is the reverse of removal, making sure the seat backs and cushions are clipped securely in position.

24 Front seat belt tensioning mechanism – general information

Most models covered in this manual are fitted with a front seat belt tensioner system. The system is designed to instantaneously take up any slack in the seat belt in the case of a sudden frontal impact, therefore reducing the possibility of injury to the front seat occupants. Each front seat is fitted with its system, the tensioner being situated behind the sill trim panel.

The seat belt tensioner is triggered by a frontal impact above a predetermined force. Lesser impacts, including impacts from behind, will not trigger the system.

When the system is triggered, the explosive gas in the tensioner mechanism retracts and locks the seat belt through a cable which acts

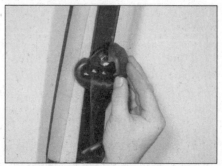

25.1 Unclip the cover from the seat belt upper mounting . . .

on the inertia reel. This prevents the seat belt moving and keeps the occupant firmly in position in the seat. Once the tensioner has been triggered, the seat belt will be permanently locked and the assembly must be renewed. If any abnormal rattling noises are heard when pulling out or retracting the belt this also indicates that the tensioner has been triggered.

There is a risk of injury if the system is triggered inadvertently when working on the car, and it is therefore strongly recommended that any work involving the seat belt tensioner system is entrusted to a VW dealer. Note the following warnings before contemplating any work on the front seat belts.

⚠ **Warning: Do not expose the tensioner mechanism to temperatures in excess of 100°C (212°F).**
• **If the tensioner mechanism is dropped, it must be renewed, even it has suffered no apparent damage.**
• **Do not allow any solvents to come into contact with the tensioner mechanism.**
• **Do not attempt to open the tensioner mechanism as it contains explosive gas.**
• **Tensioners must be discharged before they are disposed of, but this task should be entrusted to a VW dealer.**

25 Seat belt components – removal and refitting

⚠ **Warning: On models equipped with seat belt tensioners refer to Section 24 before proceeding; under no circumstances should you attempt to separate the tensioner assembly from the inertia reel.**

Removal

Front seat belt – three-door models

1 Pull the cover off the seat belt upper mounting, for access to the mounting bolt beneath **(see illustration)**.
2 Unscrew and remove the upper mounting bolt, recovering any washers or spacers, and noting the correct fitted order of all components **(see illustrations)**.
3 Pull off the rubber door weatherstrip in the area around the B-pillar trim panels. Carefully

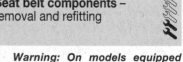

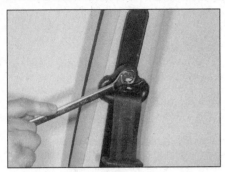
25.2a . . . loosen the mounting bolt . . .

25.2b . . . and remove it from the car, noting the fitted order of all components

25.12a Pulling off the weatherstrip from the door aperture

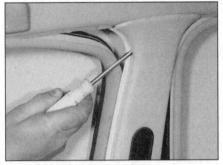
25.12b Prise off the B-pillar upper trim panel . . .

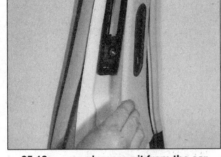
25.12c . . . and remove it from the car

25.12d If required, the seat belt height adjuster can be unbolted and removed

prise off the B-pillar upper trim panel, releasing it from its clips on the door side first.
4 Remove the screw at the bottom of the door aperture securing the side trim panel to the door sill trim panel. Loosen the sill trim panel in the area where it joins the side trim panel.
5 Fold the rear seat backrest forwards.
6 Unscrew the seat backrest locating pin from the side trim panel.
7 Unscrew the two oval-shaped buttons from the rear of the side trim panel.
8 Working around the edges of the side trim panel, release the panel from its retaining clips and remove it from the car.
9 Remove two cross-head screws and detach the seat belt guide clip from the B-pillar.
10 Loosen and remove the seat belt reel mounting bolt, and remove the belt reel from its location. **Note:** *Removing the reel mounting bolt disables the seat belt tensioner mechanism – do not refit the bolt while the seat belt is removed from the car, as this enables the system once more.*
11 The seat belt side/sliding anchor and the seat belt stalk can be simply unbolted and removed with the seat belt – fold back the carpet for access to the bolts, as required. Note the correct fitted order and position of all bolts and washers, for refitting.

Front seat belt – five-door models

12 Remove the seat belt upper mounting bolt and B-pillar upper trim panel as described in paragraphs 1 to 3. With the trim panel removed, the seat belt height adjuster can be unbolted and removed, if required **(see illustrations)**.

13 Loosen the door sill trim panels in the area around the base of the B-pillar. Prise off the lower trim panel, releasing it from its retaining clips, and pulling it forward off the mounting pin at the base of the panel **(see illustrations)**.

14 The seat belt guide clip, inertia reel, side anchor and seat belt stalk can be removed as described in paragraphs 9 to 11 **(see illustrations)**.

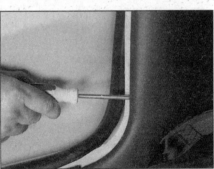
25.13a Carefully prise away the B-pillar lower trim panel . . .

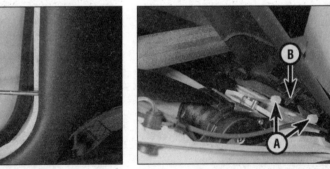
25.13b . . . to release the retaining clips (A) and the mounting pin (B)

25.14a Loosening the seat belt side anchor bolt . . .

25.14b . . . and the inertia reel mounting bolt

25.20 Cover removed from rear seat belt upper mounting

Rear seat belt – three-door models

15 Remove the rear parcel shelf, and fold the rear seat cushions and backrest forwards.
16 Remove the side trim panel as described in paragraphs 6 to 8.
17 Remove the two Torx screws from the parcel shelf side support, then unhook the panel from the two retaining lugs on the C-pillar and remove it from the car.
18 Unscrew the two nuts from the base of the C-pillar trim panel, then prise off the C-pillar trim panel and remove it from the car.
19 Depending on model and the amount of access required, it may be necessary to partially remove and fold back the carpeted trim panel from the rear wheel housing.
20 Pull the cover off the seat belt upper mounting, for access to the mounting bolt beneath **(see illustration)**.
21 Unscrew and remove the upper mounting

25.22 Rear seat belt inertia reel mounting bolt (arrowed)

bolt, recovering any washers or spacers, and noting the correct fitted order of all components.
22 Loosen and remove the inertia reel mounting bolt **(see illustration)**, and lower the reel out of position.
23 The seat belt side anchorages and seat belt stalks can be simply unbolted and removed with the seat belt. Note the correct fitted order and position of all bolts and washers, for refitting.

Rear seat belt – five-door models

24 Remove the rear parcel shelf, and fold the rear seat cushions and backrest forwards.
25 Unscrew the seat backrest locating pin from the rear door aperture trim panel, and unscrew the two oval-shaped buttons.
26 Working along the panel, release the door aperture trim panel from its retaining clips and remove it from the car.
27 The remainder of the removal procedure

is as described for three-door models, in paragraphs 17 to 23.

Refitting

28 Refitting is a reversal of the removal procedure, ensuring that all the seat belt mounting bolts are securely tightened. Also ensure that all disturbed trim panels are correctly located and securely retained by all the relevant retaining clips. When refitting the upper trim panels, the height adjustment lever must engage correctly with the seat belt upper mounting bolt.

26 Interior trim – removal and refitting

Interior trim panels

1 The interior trim panels are secured using either screws or various types of trim fasteners, usually studs or clips.
2 Check that there are no other panels overlapping the one to be removed; usually there is a sequence that has to be followed, and this will only become obvious on close inspection.
3 Remove all obvious fasteners, such as screws. If the panel will not come free, it is held by hidden clips or fasteners. These are usually situated around the edge of the panel, and can be prised up to release them; note, however, that they can break quite easily so new ones should be available. The best way of releasing such clips without the correct type of tool, is to use a large flat-bladed screwdriver. Note in many cases that the adjacent sealing strip must be prised back to release a panel.
4 When removing a panel, **never** use excessive force or the panel may be damaged; always check carefully that all fasteners or other relevant components have been removed or released before attempting to withdraw a panel.
5 Refitting is the reverse of the removal procedure; secure the fasteners by pressing them firmly into place and ensure that all disturbed components are correctly secured to prevent rattles.

Driver's side lower trim panel

6 Release the steering column height adjuster (to the left of the steering column), and raise the column to its maximum height.
7 Remove the three screws securing the steering column lower shroud, then unclip the shroud from the upper half and remove it **(see illustration)**.
8 Remove the single screw from the curved trim panel below the main light switch, and unclip the small panel **(see illustration)**.
9 Now remove a total of six further screws from the lower trim panel/storage compartment, and remove it from the facia panel **(see illustrations)**.
10 If required, a further panel above the foot

26.7 Remove the three screws and lower the bottom shroud

26.8 Unscrew and remove the curved panel below the lighting switch

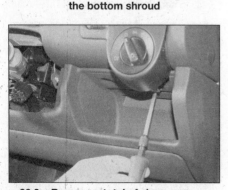

26.9a Remove a total of six screws ...

26.9b ... and take down the lower trim panel

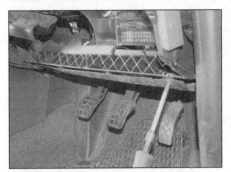

26.10a Remove the various fasteners . . .

26.10b . . . and remove the panel above the foot pedals if required

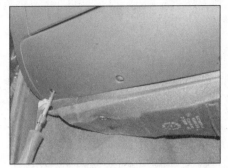

26.13 Remove the three screws from the panel below the glovebox

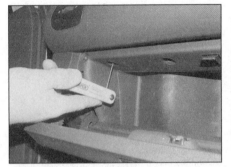

26.14 Remove the three screws inside the glovebox

26.15a Remove two screws under the cup holder/storage tray . . .

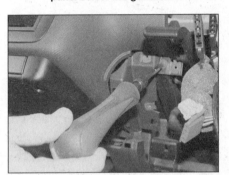

26.15b . . . and a further screw to the left of the steering wheel . . .

pedals can be removed, after removing the various plastic fasteners **(see illustrations)**.
11 Refitting is a reversal of removal.

Glovebox

12 Remove the driver's side lower trim panel as described previously in this Section, and the centre console as described in Section 27.
13 Remove the three screws along the base of the trim panel below the glovebox **(see illustration)**.
14 Open the glovebox, and remove the three screws at the top, inside **(see illustration)**.
15 The glovebox is unusual in having an 'arm' built onto its left-hand side, which extends back across the facia. This arm must be unscrewed before the glovebox assembly can be removed (three screws) **(see illustrations)**.
16 Release the glovebox support arm from the centre of the facia, and withdraw the glovebox **(see illustration)**.

17 Refitting is a reversal of removal.

Cup holder/storage tray

18 Remove the driver's side lower trim panel as described previously in this Section.

26.16 . . . then remove the glovebox and arm from the facia

19 Remove two screws on the driver's side, and a single screw on the passenger's side (open the glovebox), and remove the facia trim panel fitted around the base of the cup holder unit **(see illustrations)**.

26.19a Remove one lower . . .

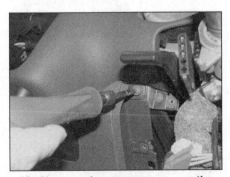

26.19b . . . and one upper screw on the driver's side . . .

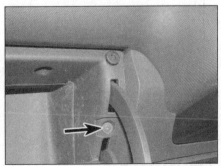

26.19c . . . then the lower screw of the two visible with the glovebox open . . .

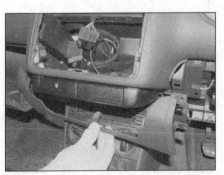

26.19d . . . and remove the trim panel from the base of the cup holder

26.20a Remove the four screws . . .

26.20b . . . and withdraw the cup holder from the facia

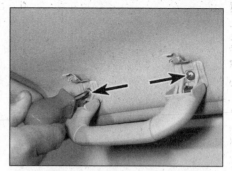

26.26 Removing the grab handle securing screws (arrowed)

20 Remove the four screws underneath securing the cup holder unit, and withdraw it from the facia **(see illustrations)**.

Carpets

21 The passenger compartment floor carpet is in one piece and is secured at its edges by screws or clips, usually the same fasteners used to secure the various adjoining trim panels.

22 Carpet removal and refitting is reasonably straightforward but very time-consuming because all adjoining trim panels must be removed first, as must components such as the seats, the centre console and seat belt lower anchorages.

Headlining

23 The headlining is clipped to the roof and can be withdrawn only once all fittings such as the grab handles, sun visors, sunroof (if fitted), windscreen and rear quarter windows and related trim panels have been removed, and the door, tailgate and sunroof aperture sealing strips have been prised clear.

24 Note that headlining removal requires considerable skill and experience if it is to be carried out without damage, and is therefore best entrusted to an expert.

Grab handles

25 Pull the grab handle down and hold it in this position.

26 The grab handle securing screws are located under two flaps, which can be unclipped and swung upwards for access **(see illustration)**.

27 Remove the two screws and take off the grab handle.

28 Refitting is a reversal of removal.

27 Centre console – removal and refitting

Removal

1 Remove the driver's side lower trim panel as described in Section 26.

2 Remove two screws on the driver's side, and a single screw on the passenger's side (open the glovebox), and remove the facia trim panel fitted around the base of the cup holder unit **(see illustrations 26.19a and 26.19b)**.

3 Remove the coin tray above the heater control panel by pressing downwards on its base, and pull it out **(see illustration)**.

4 With the coin tray removed, carefully unclip the trim panel from around the heater controls, and remove it **(see illustration)**.

5 Prise out and remove the rectangular trim pieces fitted at either end of the switch panel below the heater controls **(see illustration)**.

6 Remove the top two screws each side above the heater control panel, and the lower one either side of the switch panel **(see illustrations)**.

7 Remove the screw either side at the top of the console where it meets the facia panel **(see illustration)**.

8 On manual transmission models, unclip the gear lever gaiter from the console, and lift it up the gear lever **(see illustration)**.

9 On automatic transmission models, undo the screw under the detent button on the lever handle, and lift the handle from the lever.

27.3 Pull out the coin tray above the heater panel

27.4 Unclip and remove the heater panel surround

27.5 Prise out and remove the trim pieces at either end of the switch panel

27.6a Remove the two top screws each side . . .

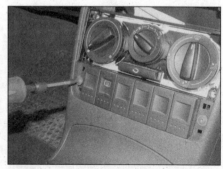

27.6b . . . and the lower screws either side of the switch panel

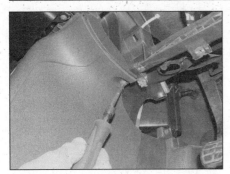

27.7 Remove the centre console-to-facia screws

27.8 Unclip the gear lever gaiter and lift it up the gear lever

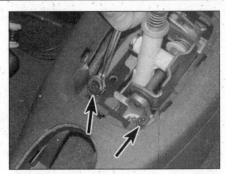

27.10 Unscrew the two plastic nuts behind the gear lever

Detach and lift the selector cover up from the centre console.

10 Unscrew and remove the two plastic nuts fitted inside the console, behind the gear/ selector lever **(see illustration)**.

11 Pull upwards on the rear of the console, to release the spring clip which holds it to the floor **(see illustration)**. Take care that the metal clip does not get pulled out of its floor recess, as it may then fall down and get trapped among the handbrake cables. Feed the gear lever gaiter/selector cover down through the console as it is lifted up and removed.

12 Underneath the console, remove the two screws securing the ashtray, and separate the ashtray from the console **(see illustration)**. The console can now be completely removed.

Refitting

13 Refitting is the reverse of removal, making sure all fasteners are securely tightened.

27.11 Pull up at the back of the console to release the spring clip

27.12 Lift the console and remove the ashtray securing screws underneath

facia mounting nuts found behind the instrument panel location.

6 Remove the two screws either side of the fuse panel, and carefully cut through any cable-ties at the side of the fusebox **(see illustrations)**.

7 Unclip the footwell side trim panel each side, and remove the single facia mounting screw fitted behind each one **(see illustration)**.

8 Open both front doors (if not already done). Prise off the plug at each end of the facia

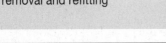

28 Facia panel –
removal and refitting

Label each wiring connector as it is disconnected from its component. The labels will prove useful on refitting, when routing the wiring and feeding the wiring through the facia apertures.

Removal

1 Disconnect the battery negative terminal (see *Disconnecting the battery*).

2 Remove the glovebox (Section 26) – this procedure also involves removing the driver's side lower trim panel and the centre console. When removing the driver's lower trim panel, also remove the cover panel fitted above the foot pedals.

3 Remove the steering wheel (Chapter 10).

4 Remove the steering column switches and headlight adjuster switch as described in Chapter 12, Section 6.

5 Remove the instrument panel as described in Chapter 12. Unscrew and remove the two

28.6a Remove the fuse panel screws

28.7 Facia side mounting screw

28.6b Cut through the cable-ties next to the fuse panel

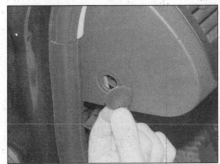

28.8a Prise off the cover plug . . .

28.8b ... and remove the end screw underneath

28.9a Remove the two screws ...

28.9b ... and the nut from the central mounting bracket

panel, and remove the facia mounting screw beneath **(see illustrations)**.

9 Remove the two screws and the single nut securing the facia central mounting bracket to the facia and the floor **(see illustrations)**.

10 Remove the centre air vent as described in Chapter 3.

11 Below and to either side of the centre vent location, remove two screws which are deeply recessed inside cut-outs in the facia **(see illustrations)**.

12 Remove the pollen filter as described in Chapter 1. Unscrew and remove the two nuts fitted below the filter, and lift out the pollen filter housing. Below the housing location, remove a further four bolts (two are clearly visible, two are fitted vertically, tucked under the base of the windscreen).

13 With the help of an assistant, carefully ease the facia assembly away from the bulkhead. As it is withdrawn, release the wiring harness from its retaining clips on the rear of the facia, whilst noting its correct routing (see **Haynes Hint** at the start of this Section). Remove the facia assembly from the car. Recover the sealing grommets which are

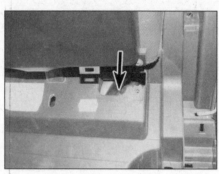

28.11a Remove the recessed screw on the driver's side ...

28.11b ... and the one on the passenger's side

fitted to the facia mounting studs; renew them if they are worn or damaged.

Refitting

14 Refitting is a reversal of the removal procedure, noting the following points:

a) Fit the sealing grommets to the facia studs and manoeuvre the facia into position. Using the labels stuck on during removal, ensure that the wiring is

correctly routed and securely retained by its facia clips.

b) Clip the facia back into position, making sure all the wiring connectors are fed through their respective apertures, then refit all the facia fasteners, and tighten them securely.

c) On completion, reconnect the battery and check that all the electrical components and switches function correctly.

Chapter 12
Body electrical system

Contents

Degrees of difficulty

| Easy, suitable for novice with little experience | Fairly easy, suitable for beginner with some experience | Fairly difficult, suitable for competent DIY mechanic | Difficult, suitable for experienced DIY mechanic | Very difficult, suitable for expert DIY or professional |

Specifications

System type ....   12-volt, negative-earth

Fuses

Refer to label on back of fusebox cover

Torque wrench settings	Nm	lbf ft
Rear wiper arm outer nut	15	11
Rear wiper arm spindle nut	7	5
Rear wiper motor mounting bolts	5	4
Windscreen wiper arm nuts	20	15
Windscreen wiper motor mounting nuts/bolts	20	15

1 General information and precautions

⚠ Warning: Before carrying out any work on the electrical system, read through the precautions given in 'Safety first!' at the beginning of this manual, and in Chapter 5A.

The electrical system is of 12 volt negative-earth type. Power for the lights and all electrical accessories is supplied by a lead-acid type battery which is charged by the alternator.

This Chapter covers repair and service procedures for the various electrical components not associated with the engine. Information on the battery, alternator and starter motor can be found in Chapter 5A.

It should be noted that prior to working on any component in the electrical system, the battery negative terminal should first be disconnected to prevent the possibility of electrical short-circuits and/or fires (see *Disconnecting the battery*).

2 Electrical fault finding – general information

Note: *Refer to the precautions given in 'Safety first!' and in Chapter 5A before starting work. The following tests relate to testing of the main electrical circuits, and should not be used to test delicate electronic circuits (such as anti-lock braking systems), particularly where an electronic control unit is used.*

General

1 A typical electrical circuit consists of an electrical component, any switches, relays, motors, fuses, fusible links or circuit breakers related to that component, and the wiring and connectors which link the component to both the battery and the chassis. To help to pinpoint a problem in an electrical circuit, wiring diagrams are included at the end of this Chapter.

2 Before attempting to diagnose an electrical fault, first study the appropriate wiring diagram to obtain a complete understanding of the components included in the particular circuit concerned. The possible sources of a fault can be narrowed down by noting if other components related to the circuit are operating properly. If several components or circuits fail at one time, the problem is likely to be related to a shared fuse or earth connection.

3 Electrical problems usually stem from simple causes, such as loose or corroded connections, a faulty earth connection, a blown fuse, a melted fusible link, or a faulty relay (refer to Section 3 for details of testing relays). Visually inspect the condition of all fuses, wires and connections in a problem circuit before testing the components. Use the wiring diagrams to determine which terminal connections will need to be checked in order to pinpoint the trouble-spot.

4 The basic tools required for electrical fault-finding include a circuit tester or voltmeter (a 12 volt bulb with a set of test leads can also be used for certain tests); a self-powered test light (sometimes known as a continuity tester); an ohmmeter (to measure resistance); a battery and set of test leads; and a jumper wire, preferably with a circuit breaker or fuse incorporated, which can be used to bypass suspect wires or electrical components. Before attempting to locate a problem with test instruments, use the wiring diagram to determine where to make the connections.

5 To find the source of an intermittent wiring fault (usually due to a poor or dirty connection, or damaged wiring insulation), a 'wiggle' test can be performed on the wiring. This involves wiggling the wiring by hand to see if the fault occurs as the wiring is moved. It should be possible to narrow down the source of the fault to a particular section of wiring. This method of testing can be used in conjunction with any of the tests described in the following sub-Sections.

6 Apart from problems due to poor connections, two basic types of fault can occur in an electrical circuit – open-circuit, or short-circuit.

7 Open-circuit faults are caused by a break somewhere in the circuit, which prevents current from flowing. An open-circuit fault will prevent a component from working, but will not cause the relevant circuit fuse to blow.

8 Short-circuit faults are caused by a 'short' somewhere in the circuit, which allows the current flowing in the circuit to 'escape' along an alternative route, usually to earth. Short-circuit faults are normally caused by a breakdown in wiring insulation, which allows a feed wire to touch either another wire, or an earthed component such as the bodyshell. A short circuit fault will normally cause the relevant circuit fuse to blow.

Finding an open-circuit

9 To check for an open-circuit, connect one lead of a circuit tester or voltmeter to either the negative battery terminal or a known good earth.

10 Connect the other lead to a connector in the circuit being tested, preferably nearest to the battery or fuse.

11 Switch on the circuit, bearing in mind that some circuits are live only when the ignition switch is moved to a particular position.

12 If voltage is present (indicated either by the tester bulb lighting or a voltmeter reading, as applicable), this means that the section of the circuit between the relevant connector and the battery is problem-free.

13 Continue to check the remainder of the circuit in the same fashion.

14 When a point is reached at which no voltage is present, the problem must lie between that point and the previous test point with voltage. Most problems can be traced to a broken, corroded or loose connection.

Finding a short-circuit

15 To check for a short-circuit, first disconnect the load(s) from the circuit (loads are the components which draw current from a circuit, such as bulbs, motors, heating elements, etc).

16 Remove the relevant fuse from the circuit, and connect a circuit tester or voltmeter to the fuse connections.

17 Switch on the circuit, bearing in mind that some circuits are live only when the ignition switch is moved to a particular position.

18 If voltage is present (indicated either by the tester bulb lighting or a voltmeter reading, as applicable), this means that there is a short-circuit.

19 If no voltage is present, but the fuse still blows with the load(s) connected, this indicates an internal fault in the load(s).

Finding an earth fault

20 The battery negative terminal is connected to 'earth' – the metal of the engine/transmission and the car body – and most systems are wired so that they only receive a positive feed, the current returning through the metal of the car body. This means that the component mounting and the body form part of that circuit. Loose or corroded mountings can therefore cause a range of electrical faults, ranging from total failure of a circuit, to a puzzling partial fault. In particular, lights may shine dimly (especially when another circuit sharing the same earth point is in operation), motors (eg, wiper motors or the radiator cooling fan motor) may run slowly, and the operation of one circuit may have an apparently unrelated effect on another. Note that on many vehicles, earth straps are used between certain components, such as the engine/transmission and the body, usually where there is no metal-to-metal contact between components due to flexible rubber mountings, etc.

21 To check whether a component is properly earthed, disconnect the battery and connect one lead of an ohmmeter to a known good earth point. Connect the other lead to the wire or earth connection being tested. The resistance reading should be zero; if not, check the connection as follows.

22 If an earth connection is thought to be faulty, dismantle the connection and clean back to bare metal both the bodyshell and the wire terminal or the component earth connection mating surface. Be careful to remove all traces of dirt and corrosion, then use a knife to trim away any paint, so that a clean metal-to-metal joint is made. On reassembly, tighten the joint fasteners securely; if a wire terminal is being refitted, use serrated washers between the terminal and the bodyshell to ensure a clean and secure connection. When the connection is remade, prevent the onset of corrosion in the future by applying a coat of petroleum jelly or silicone-based grease, or by spraying on (at regular intervals) a proprietary ignition sealer or a water-dispersant lubricant.

3 Fuses and relays – general information

Main fuses

1 Some of the fuses are located on a panel fixed to the top of the battery in the engine compartment. The rest of the fuses are located in the lower facia on the driver's side.

2 Access to the passenger compartment fuses is gained by removing the driver's side lower facia trim panel, as described in Chapter 11, Section 26.

3 The fuses attached to the top of the battery can be accessed by pressing together the fuse cover locking lugs, and taking off the cover.

4 All the fuses are numbered, and the circuits which they protect are listed on the back of the fusebox cover.

5 To remove a fuse, first switch off the circuit concerned (or the ignition), then pull the fuse out of its terminals. A fuse removal tool is attached to the rear of the fuse cover **(see illustrations)**. The wire within the fuse should be visible; if the fuse is blown, it will be broken or melted.

6 Always renew a fuse with one of an identical rating; never use a fuse with a different rating from the original or substitute anything else. Never renew a fuse more than once without tracing the source of the trouble. The fuse rating is stamped on top of the fuse;

3.5a Remove the fuse cover, noting the removal tool clipped to it

3.5b Removing one of the fuses from the main panel inside the car

3.5c Removing a fuse from the engine compartment fusebox, on top of the battery

note that the fuses are also colour-coded for easy recognition. A list of fuses, and the circuits they protect, appears on the back of the glovebox and in the Wiring diagrams at the end of this Chapter.

7 If a new fuse blows immediately, find the cause before renewing it again; a short to earth as a result of faulty insulation is most likely. Where a fuse protects more than one circuit, try to isolate the defect by switching on each circuit in turn (if possible) until the fuse blows again. Always carry a supply of spare fuses of each relevant rating on the car, a spare of each rating should be clipped into the base of the fusebox.

Fusible links

8 If any of the fusible links blows, this indicates a serious wiring fault. Repairing or renewing a fusible link should not be attempted without consulting a VW dealer or automotive electrical specialist – all circuits protected by a fusible link carry a high current, and a fire could result from improper repair.

Relays

9 The relays are of sealed construction, and cannot be repaired if faulty. The relays are of the plug-in type, and may be removed by pulling directly from their terminals. On some of the relays located behind the facia, it is necessary to prise the two plastic clips outwards before removing the relay.

10 If a circuit or system controlled by a relay develops a fault and the relay is suspect, operate the system; if the relay is functioning, it should be possible to hear it click as it is energised. If this is the case, the fault lies with the components or wiring of the system. If the relay is not being energised, then either the relay is not receiving a main supply or a switching voltage, or the relay itself is faulty. Testing is by the substitution of a known good unit, but be careful; while some relays are identical in appearance and in operation, others look similar but perform different functions.

11 To renew a relay, first ensure that the ignition switch is off. The relay can then simply be pulled out from the socket and the new relay pressed in.

Fuse/relay panel

12 The passenger compartment fuse panel

and relay panel are separate, each panel being secured by two screws. Once the screws are removed, disconnect the wiring plugs from the rear of the panel, labelling the plugs as necessary for refitting.

13 Removal of the engine compartment fusebox on top of the battery is described in Chapter 5A, as part of the battery removal procedure.

14 When refitting, ensure that all wiring connections are securely made.

**4 Ignition switch/
steering column lock –
removal and refitting**

Removal

1 Disconnect the battery negative lead (refer to *Disconnecting the battery*).

4.5a Unclip the ignition switch plastic cover . . .

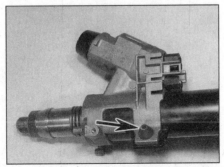

4.6 Ignition switch/steering column lock shear-bolt (arrowed)

2 Remove the steering wheel as described in Chapter 10.

3 Remove the steering column combination switch as described in Section 5.

4 Detach the immobiliser reader coil from the ignition switch, and remove it from the steering lock housing (see Chapter 10, Section 14).

5 Unclip the plastic cover, then disconnect the wiring plug from the ignition switch **(see illustrations)**. On models with automatic transmission, press the Park Lock cable clip out of its mounting bracket next to the ignition switch, and prise the cable end fitting off its ball-stud.

6 Drill out the shear-bolt securing the ignition switch/steering column lock, or chisel its head off **(see illustration)**.

7 Pull off the splined adapter sleeve from the top of the steering column, using a suitable two-legged puller **(see illustration)**.

4.5b . . . then squeeze the retaining tabs and disconnect the wiring plug

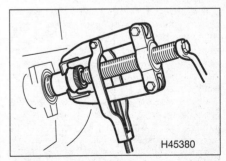

H45380

4.7 Pulling off the splined adapter sleeve from the steering column, using a suitable puller

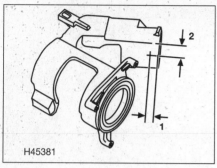

4.9 Drilling point for removing ignition lock cylinder

1 = 9.5 mm   2 = 10 mm

8 The ignition switch/steering column lock and spring can now be pulled off the column, and removed.
9 To remove the lock cylinder from the housing, a 3 mm hole must be drilled in the housing (**see illustration**). When the hole has been drilled, the lock cylinder retaining spring should be visible. Use the drill bit inserted in the drilled hole to release the lock spring, then pull out the lock cylinder using the ignition key. **Note:** *Once the lock housing has been drilled, it obviously reduces the security of the car, since the lock cylinder could be removed with the housing installed. Consideration should be given to renewing the housing along with the lock cylinder in this instance.*

Refitting

10 Insert the new lock cylinder into position in the housing. As it is fitted, turn the key gently in the cylinder to engage the cylinder onto its stop.
11 Slide the ignition lock housing and spring onto the steering column.

12 Drive the splined adapter sleeve onto the column using a suitable piece of tubing.
13 The remainder of refitting is the reverse of removal. Where the column does not project fully from the tube, pull it further up by fitting a nut and spacer washer onto the column, and tighten the washer against the housing to pull the column up so that it projects. Fit a new ignition switch shear-bolt and tighten until the head breaks off.
14 Refer to Section 5 to refit the steering column combination switch.
15 Refer to Chapter 10 to refit the steering wheel.

5 Steering column combination switch – removal and refitting

Removal

1 Disconnect the battery negative lead (refer to *Disconnecting the battery*).
2 Refer to Chapter 10 and remove the steering wheel.
3 Undo the three retaining screws on the front of the combination switch assembly (**see illustration**).
4 To remove the left-hand column switch, disconnect the large black multi-plug on the left-hand side of the steering column, and remove the switch (**see illustration**).
5 If the right-hand switch has to be removed as well, this means disconnecting all the red plugs underneath the steering column as well as the two large black plugs behind each switch. If both switches are removed together, they can be separated and removed individually if required (**see illustrations**).

Refitting

6 Refitting is a reversal of the removal procedure. Ensure that the wiring connections are securely made. Check for satisfactory operation on completion.

5.3 Remove the three screws on the front

5.4 If required, the left-hand stalk can be removed separately

5.5a Unclip and disconnect the wiring plugs below the steering column . . .

5.5b . . . and remove the complete switch assembly

5.5c The right-hand stalk can be separated after removal

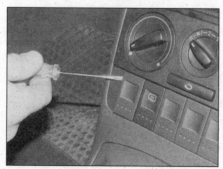

6.2a Prise out one of the blank switches . . .

6 Switches – removal and refitting

1 Disconnect the battery negative lead (see *Disconnecting the battery*) then proceed as described under the relevant heading below.

Facia pushbutton switches

2 Using a small screwdriver or similar tool, carefully prise the switch out of the facia. To make this easier, and to avoid damage to the switch itself, first prise out either one of the blank switches or the blanking plate next to the switch (**see illustrations**).
3 Disconnect the multi-plug from the rear of the switch (**see illustration**).
4 Refitting is a reversal of removal.

Lighting switch

5 Remove the driver's side lower trim panel, as described in Chapter 11, Section 26.

6 Press in and twist the switch knob clockwise to release the switch body from the surround **(see illustration)**. Some trial-and-error will be required until the switch releases.

7 Pull the lighting switch from the facia panel, and disconnect its wiring connector **(see illustration)**.

8 Refitting is a reversal of removal.

Headlight adjuster switch

9 Remove the lighting switch as described previously in this Section.

10 Remove the screw fitted behind the lighting switch location **(see illustration)**.

11 The switch surround and vent assembly now has to be carefully prised from the facia – there are two clips on the right, and one on the left **(see illustration)**.

12 Disconnect the wiring plug from the back of the adjuster switch, then squeeze the two retaining lugs together and remove from the back of the surround/vent panel **(see illustrations)**.

13 Refitting is a reversal of removal.

Hazard warning light switch

14 Remove the centre air vent as described in Chapter 3.

15 Release the spring clip on the base of the switch, then press and remove the switch rearwards out of the vent panel **(see illustrations)**.

16 Refitting is a reversal of removal.

6.2b . . . to improve access to the switch being removed

6.3 Disconnect the switch wiring plug

6.6 Press in and twist the switch knob clockwise to release the switch . . .

6.7 . . . then pull it out and disconnect the wiring plug

Air conditioning/ recirculation switches

17 These switches are fitted to the rear of the heater control panel (see Chapter 3).

Courtesy light switches

18 Pull off the rubber cover **(see illustration)**.

19 Using two small flat-bladed screwdrivers at the prise points indicated by the

6.10 Remove the screw behind the lighting switch

6.11 Prise out and remove the switch surround and driver's side vent

6.12a Disconnect the headlight adjuster wiring plug . . .

6.12b . . . then squeeze and release the switch from the vent panel

6.15a Release the spring clip and push the switch out of the vent panel . . .

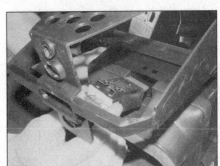

6.15b . . . to remove it completely

6.18 Pull the rubber cover off the courtesy light switch . . .

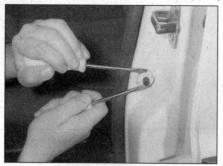

6.19 . . . then use two screwdrivers to release the switch from the door pillar

6.20 Disconnect the switch wiring, but make sure it does not fall back into the pillar

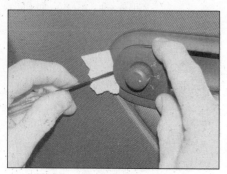

6.22 Prise the switch from the door panel . . .

6.23 . . . and disconnect the wiring plug

6.25 Prise the window switch from the armrest . . .

arrowheads on the switch body, prise the switch out of the door pillar (see illustration).
20 Disconnect the wiring plug and remove the switch (see illustration). Make sure that the wiring does not drop back into the aperture by using tape or string to secure it.
21 Refitting is a reversal of removal. Fit the rubber cover to the switch before reconnecting the wiring and pressing it back into position.

Door mirror switch

22 Carefully prise out the switch panel and remove it from the door trim panel (see illustration).
23 Detach the wiring connector (see illustration).
24 Refit in the reverse order of removal.

Electric window switches

25 Carefully prise out the switch panel and remove it from the armrest (see illustration).

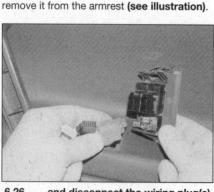

6.26 . . . and disconnect the wiring plug(s)

26 Detach the wiring connectors (see illustration). Note that, on the driver's door panel, it is possible to mix up the connectors for the left and right switches, though they are different colours – on our car, the beige plug was for the left-hand switch.
27 Refit in the reverse order of removal.

Handbrake-on warning switch

28 Refer to Chapter 9, Section 18.

Stop-light switch

29 Refer to Chapter 9.

Indicator/wiper switches

30 Refer to Section 5.

Sunroof switch

31 Remove the interior light as described in Section 8.
32 Unclip the sunroof switch trim panel from the roof.
33 Remove the two Torx screws securing the sunroof switch, then lower the switch out of its location, and disconnect the wiring plug.
34 Refitting is a reversal of removal.

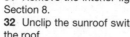

7   Exterior light bulbs – renewal

1 Whenever a bulb is renewed, note the following points:
 a) *Disconnect the battery negative lead before starting work (see 'Disconnecting the battery').*

 b) *Remember that if the light has just been in use, the bulb may be extremely hot.*
 c) *Always check the bulb contacts and holder, ensuring that there is clean metal-to-metal contact between the bulb and its live(s) and earth. Clean off any corrosion or dirt before fitting a new bulb.*
 d) *Wherever bayonet-type bulbs are fitted, ensure that the live contact(s) bear firmly against the bulb contact.*
 e) *Always ensure that the new bulb is of the correct rating and that it is completely clean before fitting it; this applies particularly to headlight/foglight bulbs (see below).*

Headlight bulbs

2 Open the bonnet, and release the headlight rear cover by swinging the wire clip to the side (see illustration).

7.2 Release the wire clip and remove the headlight rear cover

7.3 Disconnect the wiring connector from the bulb

7.4 Unhook the bulb retaining clip

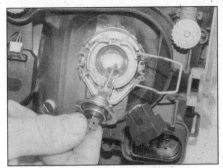

7.5 Remove the headlight bulb

7.7 Disconnect the main beam bulb wiring plug

7.8 Swing down the bulb retaining clip

7.9 Remove the main beam bulb

Dipped beam (outer) bulb

3 Pull the wiring connector from the rear of the headlight bulb **(see illustration)**.
4 Unhook the ends of the bulb retaining wire clip at the side, and swing the clip to the side **(see illustration)**.
5 Withdraw the bulb from the rear of the headlight **(see illustration)**.
6 Refitting is a reversal of removal. Do not touch the glass of the new headlight bulb with bare fingers. If the glass is accidentally touched, clean it with methylated spirit. Check the light for satisfactory operation, on completion.

Main beam (inner) bulb

7 Pull the wiring connector from the rear of the bulb **(see illustration)**.
8 Unhook the ends of the bulb retaining wire clip at the top, and swing the clip diagonally down **(see illustration)**.

9 Withdraw the bulb from the rear of the headlight **(see illustration)**.
10 Refitting is a reversal of removal. Do not touch the glass of the new headlight bulb with bare fingers. If the glass is accidentally touched, clean it with methylated spirit. Check the light for satisfactory operation, on completion.

Sidelight bulb

11 Pull the bulbholder and wiring connector out from the reflector **(see illustration)**.
12 Pull the wedge-type bulb out and remove it **(see illustration)**.
13 Refit in the reverse order of removal, and check the light for satisfactory operation.

Front foglight

14 Reach in behind the foglight, and twist off the light rear cover anti-clockwise.
15 Disconnect the wiring plug inside the cap,

then release the bulb securing clip and remove the H3 bulb from the light unit.
16 To remove the foglight, refer to Chapter 11 and remove the front bumper components as necessary for access to the foglight securing screws.
17 Refitting is a reversal of removal. Do not touch the glass of the new bulb with bare fingers. If the glass is accidentally touched, clean it with methylated spirit. Check the light for satisfactory operation, on completion.

Front direction indicator

18 Turn the securing catch on top of the light unit anti-clockwise, and pull the catch upwards to release the spring on the light unit mounting **(see illustration)**.
19 Pull the direction indicator forwards to remove it, then twist the bulbholder anti-clockwise, and pull it from the rear of the light unit **(see illustration)**.

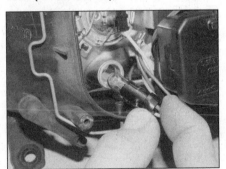

7.11 Remove the sidelight bulbholder

7.12 Pull out the sidelight bulb

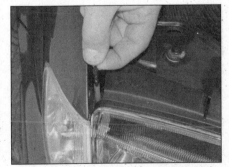

7.18 Twist the securing catch next to the headlight, and pull upwards

7.19 Twist and pull out the bulbholder . . .

7.20 . . . then remove the bayonet-fit bulb

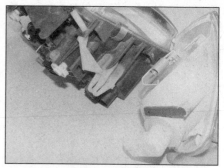

7.21 Showing the headlight/indicator catch mechanism

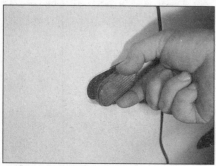

7.22 Push the side repeater light to the rear, and pull out at the front

7.23 Remove the bulbholder from the rear of the light unit

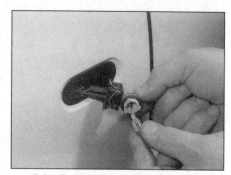

7.24 Pull out the wedge-type bulb

20 Depress and twist the bulb to remove it from its holder **(see illustration)**.
21 Refit in the reverse order of removal. Make sure the catch is raised as the light is

offered into position, then press the catch down to tension the mounting spring, and turn it clockwise to lock it **(see illustration)**. Check the light for satisfactory operation.

Direction indicator side repeater

22 Push the lens to the rear, then prise it out at the front to release the lens **(see illustration)**.
23 Turn the bulbholder fully to the right, and extract the bulbholder from the lens **(see illustration)**.
24 Pull the bulb from the holder **(see illustration)**.
25 To remove the light unit, disconnect the wiring multi-plug **(see illustration)**. Tape the plug or its wire to the wing, to stop it disappearing inside.
26 Refit in the reverse order of removal, and check the light for satisfactory operation.

Rear combination lights

27 On the left-hand rear light, pull open the access flap in the rear luggage area carpet on the side concerned.
28 On the right-hand rear light unit, turn the two trim panel fasteners through 90°, and lower the trim panel for access to the light unit **(see illustration)**.
29 Depress the retaining lug towards the outside of the car, and withdraw the bulbholder **(see illustration)**.
30 Press and untwist the relevant bulb to remove it **(see illustration)**.
31 To remove the light unit, disconnect the wiring plug from the bulbholder, then undo three retaining nuts and withdraw the unit from the body **(see illustrations)**.
32 Refit in the reverse order of removal, and check the lights for satisfactory operation.

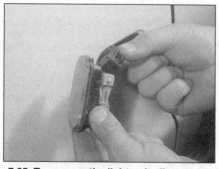

7.25 To remove the light unit, disconnect the wiring plug

7.28 Turn the trim panel fasteners and pull the panel down

7.29 Press the bulbholder lug and pull the holder out from the back of the light

7.30 Push and twist the bulb to remove it

7.31a Remove the three light unit nuts . . .

7.31b . . . and remove the light unit from outside

7.34 Prise out the cover plugs at the top of the tailgate

7.35 Prise and pull the catches with a screwdriver

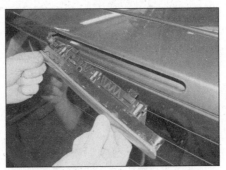

7.36a Withdraw the light from the tailgate . . .

7.36b . . . and disconnect the wiring plug

High-level brake light

33 The high-level brake light consists of a number of LEDs, not conventional bulbs. If the light stops working, therefore, bulb renewal is not an option. To remove the light unit for investigation, proceed as follows.

34 Open the tailgate, then prise out the two cover plugs at the top **(see illustration)**.

35 The brake light unit can be tricky to release. There are two plastic retaining catches inside the access holes now uncovered – these must be prised down and pulled towards you to release **(see illustration)**.

36 Withdraw the light from the outside of the tailgate, and disconnect the wiring plug **(see illustrations)**.

37 Refitting is a reversal of removal. Make sure the light is pushed home so that both clips engage.

Number plate light

38 Open the tailgate, and remove the two screws securing the light unit.

39 Withdraw the light unit, then pull the bulb from the spring contacts.

40 Refitting is a reversal of removal, noting the following points:

a) *Ensure that the new bulb is a firm fit in the contacts – carefully bend them inwards if necessary.*

b) *When refitting the light, note that the silver strip on the lens must face the bumper.*

8 Interior light bulbs – renewal

1 Whenever a bulb is renewed, note the following points:

a) *Disconnect the battery negative lead before starting work (see 'Disconnecting the battery').*

b) *Remember that if the light has just been in use, the bulb may be extremely hot.*

c) *Always check the bulb contacts and holder, ensuring that there is clean metal-to-metal contact between the bulb and its live(s) and earth. Clean off any corrosion or dirt before fitting a new bulb.*

d) *Wherever bayonet-type bulbs are fitted, ensure that the live contact(s) bear firmly against the bulb contact.*

e) *Always ensure that the new bulb is of the correct rating and that it is completely clean before fitting it.*

Interior light

2 Using a suitable screwdriver, prise the interior light from the headlining. If wished, the light unit can be removed by disconnecting its wiring plug **(see illustrations)**.

3 Slide the light rear cover upwards in the direction of the arrow moulded into the cover, for access to the bulb **(see illustration)**.

4 Unclip the festoon type bulb from its contacts and remove it **(see illustration)**.

5 Refit in the reverse order of removal.

Luggage area light

6 Prise free the light lens/unit and extract the festoon bulb from its holder.

7 Refit in the reverse order of removal, and check for satisfactory operation.

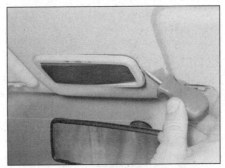

8.2a Prise the interior light out of the headlining . . .

8.2b . . . and disconnect the wiring plug, if required

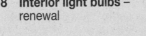

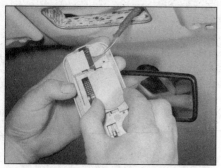

8.3 To renew the bulb, slide up the cover . . .

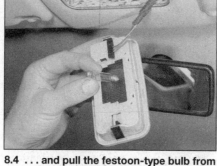

8.4 . . . and pull the festoon-type bulb from the contacts

8.12 Pull off the central control knob

8.13 The push-fit bulb can most safely be removed using a piece of tubing

Sunvisor/vanity mirror light

8 Prise free the lens from the sunvisor. The festoon bulbs can be extracted from their holders in the visor.

9 Refit in the reverse order of removal.

9.3a Remove the headlight retaining screws . . .

Instrument panel bulbs

10 The warning light and illumination bulbs are an integral part of the instrument panel, and cannot be removed or renewed separately. If more than one light has failed,

9.3b . . . then move the light unit to the centre of the car, to release the lower tab

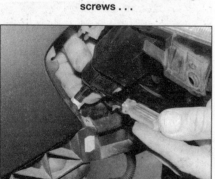

9.4a Disconnect the headlight wiring plug using a screwdriver if necessary . . .

9.4b . . . then withdraw the light from the car

remove the instrument panel as described in Section 10, and check that the multi-pin wiring connectors are securely attached to the rear of the panel, and that all pins are making good contact in the wiring plugs.

Switch illumination bulbs

11 Switch illumination bulbs are usually built into the switch itself, and cannot be renewed separately. Refer to Section 6 and remove the switch – bulb renewal should then be self-evident, if it is possible; otherwise, renew the switch.

Heater control illumination bulb

12 Carefully pull off the central control knob for access to the bulb **(see illustration)**.

13 The bulb can be withdrawn using thin-nosed pliers, but this carries a risk of damaging the bulb (this won't matter when removing a blown bulb, but would be inconvenient when fitting the new one). Instead, use a section of washer jet tubing (or similar plastic/rubber pipe to withdraw/refit the wedge-base bulb **(see illustration)**.

14 Refit the control knob to complete.

| 9 | Headlight – removal, refitting and beam adjustment | |

Removal

1 Remove the front bumper as described in Chapter 11.

2 Remove both the front direction indicators as described in Section 7.

3 Remove the three retaining screws (two under the light, one on top). Move the headlight towards the centre of the car first, to disengage the retaining tab from the plastic bumper support, then slide the headlight forwards for access to the wiring plug **(see illustrations)**.

4 Disconnect the wiring plug from the rear of the headlight, and remove the headlight from the car **(see illustrations)**.

Refitting

5 Reassembly and refitting is a reversal of the removal procedure. On completion check for satisfactory operation, and have the headlight beam adjustment checked as soon as possible (see below).

Beam adjustment

6 Accurate adjustment of the headlight beam is only possible using optical beam-setting equipment, and this work should therefore be carried out by a VW dealer or suitably-equipped workshop.

7 For reference, the headlights can be adjusted using the adjuster assemblies fitted to the top of each light unit, accessed through the cut-outs in the light housing **(see illustration)**.

8 Some models are equipped with an

9.7 The headlight adjusters are accessed through cut-outs in the top of the housing

10.2 Remove the screw inside the instrument cowl

10.3a Press in the edges of the outer cover . . .

electrically-operated headlight beam adjustment system, which is controlled through a switch in the facia. On these models, ensure that the switch is set to the basic (-) position before adjusting the headlight aim.

10 Instrument panel – removal and refitting

Removal

1 Disconnect the battery negative lead (refer to *Disconnecting the battery*).
2 Remove the single screw inside the cowl **(see illustration)**.
3 The outer part of the cowl panel must now be unclipped – this is especially tricky, as the

four mounting clips (equally-spaced around the front edge of the panel) are extremely stiff. We found the best method is to press inwards on the outer cover, either side – prising the panel with any tools is not advisable. When the clips are released, pull the panel towards you to remove it **(see illustrations)**.
4 To remove the inner part of the cowl panel, remove three further screws and lift the panel away **(see illustrations)**.
5 The instrument panel itself is secured by two screws at the top. Remove the screws, and slide the panel upwards to remove it **(see illustrations)**.
6 Disconnect the wiring connectors on the back of the panel by pivoting the hinged locking clips to one side of the connector **(see illustrations)**.
7 It is recommended that no attempt is made

to dismantle the instrument panel. Any faults with the panel can be diagnosed by a VW dealer, using dedicated fault diagnosis equipment.

Refitting

8 Refitting the panel is a reversal of removal. Ensure that the wiring connector locking clips engage correctly.

11 Instruments – removal and refitting

The instrument panel should not be dismantled. In the event of a problem occurring, remove the panel as described in Section 10, and take it to a VW dealer for diagnosis.

10.3b . . . to release the four clips, then pull the cover backwards to remove it

10.4a Remove the three inner cowl securing screws . . .

10.4b . . . and lift the cowl away

10.5a Remove the two instrument panel screws . . .

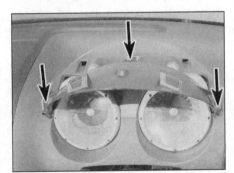

10.5b . . . then lift the panel out

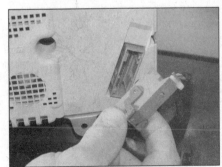

10.6 Pivot the wiring plug hinged locking clips over to release the plugs

12.3a Disconnect the lighter wiring plug . . .

12.3b . . . and the one from the bulbholder

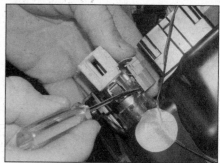

12.4 Slide off the bulbholder using a screwdriver

12 Cigar lighter –
removal and refitting

Removal

1 Disconnect the battery negative lead (refer to *Disconnecting the battery*).
2 Remove the centre console as described in Chapter 11.
3 Disconnect the wiring plugs from the rear of the lighter, and from its illumination bulb **(see illustrations)**.
4 Using a small screwdriver, slide off the bulbholder from the side of the lighter body **(see illustration)**.
5 Release the side clips, and slide the lighter unit out of the ashtray **(see illustration)**.
6 If required, the orange outer section can similarly be released and removed.

Refitting

7 Refit in the reverse order of removal.

13 Windscreen wiper components –
removal and refitting

Wiper blades

1 Refer to *Weekly checks*.

Wiper arms

2 If the wipers are not in their parked position, switch on the ignition, and allow the motor to automatically 'park'. Depending which wiper arm is to be removed, it may be necessary to open the bonnet for access.
3 Before removing an arm, mark its 'parked' position on the glass with a strip of adhesive tape. Prise off the cover and unscrew the

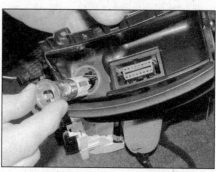

12.5 Removing the cigar lighter body

outer nut **(see illustrations)**. Remove the washer or circlip, and ease the arm from the spindle by rocking it slowly from side-to-side.
4 Refitting is a reversal of removal, but before tightening the spindle nuts, position the wiper blades on the motor shaft splines so that the blades sit on the glass as marked before removal.

Wiper motor

5 Disconnect the battery negative lead (refer to *Disconnecting the battery*).
6 Remove the wiper arms as described in paragraphs 2 and 3.
7 Open the bonnet, then pull off the rubber weatherstrip from the top of the engine compartment bulkhead. Peel back the rubber sealing strip from the base of the windscreen, then prise out the retaining clips and remove the plastic cowling panels from below the windscreen **(see illustrations)**.

13.3a Prise off the cover . . .

13.3b . . . then unscrew the nut and remove the wiper arm

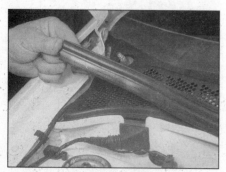

13.7a Pull off the weatherstrip . . .

13.7b . . . then peel back the sealing strip and prise out the cowl panel retaining clips

13.7c Removing one of the cowl panels

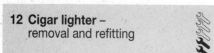

8 Disconnect the wiring plug from the wiper motor **(see illustration)**.

9 Undo the three wiper frame-to-body bolts (next to the wiper arm spindles, and one beside the motor), noting the fitted order of all washers. Withdraw the wiper motor and mounting frame assembly **(see illustrations)**.

10 If required, unbolt and remove the motor from the frame **(see illustration)**. If the assembly is to be completely dismantled, note the fitted order of all washers and spacers, etc.

11 Refit in the reverse order of removal. Lubricate the connecting link pivots with a little molybdenum disulphide grease. If a new wiper motor is being fitted, the crank arm must be set in the 'parked' position.

12 On completion, check for satisfactory operation.

14 Washer system – general

1 All models are fitted with a windscreen washer system and a tailgate washer.

2 The fluid reservoir for the windscreen washer and tailgate washer is located in the engine compartment on the left-hand side. The fluid pump is attached to the side of the reservoir body, and can be pulled out once the wiring plug has been disconnected **(see illustration)**.

3 The reservoir fluid level must be regularly topped-up with proper washer fluid containing an antifreeze agent, but not cooling system antifreeze – see *Weekly checks*.

4 The supply hoses are attached by rubber couplings to their various connections, and if required, can be detached by simply pulling them free from the appropriate connector **(see illustration)**.

5 The windscreen washer jets can be prised from their locations in the bonnet, after disconnecting the fluid hoses and electric heating wiring, where applicable.

6 The rear washer jet is integral with the rear wiper motor – to remove the wiper motor, see Section 15.

7 The washer jets can be cleaned and

13.8 Wiper motor wiring plug (arrowed)

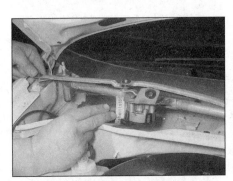

13.9b Removing the wiper frame and motor assembly

adjusted using a needle. Later models may be fitted with additional preset washer jets which only have a limited amount of adjustment. Height adjustment on these later jets is effected by turning an eccentric on the spray jet. When adjusted correctly, the jets should be aimed at a point just above the centre of the wiper swept area.

15 Tailgate wiper motor – removal and refitting

Removal

1 Disconnect the battery negative lead, with reference to Section 1.

2 Open the tailgate and detach the trim panel from it. Slacken and remove the tailgate handle retaining screw, then release the

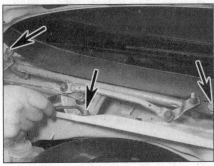

13.9a Wiper frame-to-body bolts (arrowed)

13.10 Wiper motor-to-frame bolts (arrowed)

tailgate trim panel clips, carefully levering between the panel and tailgate with a flat-bladed screwdriver. Work around the outside of the panel, and when all the clips are released, remove the panel (see Chapter 11, Section 15).

3 Make sure that the wiper arm is in the 'parked' position by switching the rear wiper on and then off, so that the arm moves through a complete sweep. Mark the position of the wiper blade on the glass by sticking a strip of masking tape along the line of the blade. Lift up the hinged cover from the wiper arm nut, then remove the nut and pull the wiper arm off the splines **(see illustrations)**.

4 Detach the wiring connector from the wiper motor, and pull off the washer fluid pipe.

5 Undo the three mounting nuts, and remove the wiper motor, complete with the mounting rubbers and spacers, from the tailgate. Recover the seal from the rear window glass,

14.2 Washer pump is attached to the side of the washer fluid reservoir

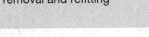
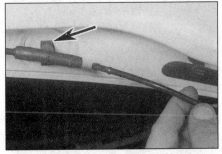

14.4 Disconnecting a washer supply hose from a T-piece connection – washer jet arrowed

15.3a Lift up the hinged cover . . .

15.3b . . . then remove the wiper arm nut . . .

15.3c . . . and pull the wiper arm off the splines

16.1 Horn location under left-hand wing – mounting bolt arrowed

and check its condition – obtain a new one for refitting if necessary.

Refitting

6 Refit in the reverse order of removal. Make sure the rubber seal is fitted to the tailgate glass before offering the motor in. Refit the wiper arm and blade so that the arm is parked correctly.

16 Horn – removal and refitting

Removal

1 The horn is located at the front end of the car, on the left-hand side between the front bumper and the inner wing. Access to the horn is best gained from below (see illustration).

17.1 In an emergency, it may be possible to use feeler blades as substitute removal tools

18.4a Release the trim panel from the C-pillar trim . . .

2 Disconnect the battery negative lead (see Section 1).
3 Apply the handbrake, then jack up the front left-hand corner of the car, and support securely on an axle stand (see Jacking and vehicle support).
4 Disconnect the horn wiring, then unscrew the horn-to-body mounting bolt, and remove the horn unit from under the car.

Refitting

5 Refit in the reverse order of removal. Check for satisfactory operation on completion.

17 Radio/cassette unit – removal and refitting

Note: This Section applies only to standard-fit audio equipment.

17.4 Disconnect the aerial lead and wiring plugs from the back of the set

18.4b . . . and remove it from the car

Removal

1 The radio is fitted with special mounting clips, requiring the use of special removal tools, which should be supplied with the car, or may be obtained from an in-car entertainment specialist. Alternatively, it may be possible to make up some removal tools (see illustration).
2 Disconnect the battery negative lead – refer to Disconnecting the battery.
3 Slide the removal tools into the slots in the radio front panel until they locate, or until the retaining tags are released.
4 Withdraw the radio from the mounting cage, then disconnect the loudspeaker, supply and aerial plugs (and the CD changer lead, where applicable) (see illustration).
5 Where applicable, release the radio removal tools once the unit has been withdrawn from the facia panel, by depressing the spring-loaded locating lugs on each side of the radio/cassette unit.

Refitting

6 Refitting is a reversal of removal, but push the radio fully into its case until the spring clips are engaged. If the radio is of the security code type, it will be necessary to enter the code number before switching on the radio.

18 Radio aerial (roof-mounted) – removal and refitting

1 Gaining access to the aerial mounting involves lowering the headlining at the rear. Removing the headlining is not normally a task to be undertaken lightly, and this job may have to be entrusted to a VW dealer. If you are satisfied that this can be accomplished easily, the procedure is given below. The aerial lead is in two sections, joined behind the facia panel at the left-hand windscreen pillar.
2 If just the aerial mast has been damaged, this can be unscrewed from the aerial base and renewed separately, with no further dismantling.
3 To remove the aerial base, open the tailgate and pull down the rubber seal from the top of the tailgate opening.
4 Prise down the trim panel which fits between the top of the tailgate and the rear of

the moulded headlining, releasing its retaining clips. Unhook the panel from the C-pillar trim, and remove it from the car **(see illustrations)**.

5 Carefully prise down the rear of the headlining for access to the aerial lead and aerial securing nut – don't pull the headlining down more than is necessary **(see illustration)**.

6 Disconnect the aerial cable at the connector.

7 If the aerial lead to the front of the car is to be removed, remove its foam insulation, then tie a piece of string to it at the roof aerial end – the string must be long enough to easily reach the front of the car. Remove the radio/cassette unit as described in Section 17. Pull the aerial lead through from the front, until the end of the lead with the string attached appears. Untie the string, and leave it in position in the car – when fitting the new lead, use the string to pull it through into place.

8 Unscrew the aerial mounting nut from inside the roof. Lift off the aerial base from the top of the roof, pulling the aerial lead through and recovering the roof seal.

9 Refitting the aerial is a reversal of removal. Check that the aerial works before refitting the headlining, where applicable.

19 Speakers – removal and refitting

Note: *This Section applies only to standard-fit audio equipment.*

1 Depending on equipment level, four or six speakers will be fitted as standard. Tweeter speakers are fitted in the door mirror trim panels, with bass units in the front door trim panels – higher-specification models also have tweeters in the rear doors.

Front tweeter speakers

2 Remove the door inner trim panel as described in Chapter 11.

3 Remove the screw at the base of the mirror trim panel, and unclip the panel from the door **(see illustrations)**.

4 Disconnect the speaker wiring plug **(see illustration)**. The speaker is an integral part of the trim panel, and no further dismantling is possible.

5 Refitting is a reversal of removal.

18.5 Pull down the headlining for access to the roof aerial mounting nut

Front bass speakers

6 Remove the door inner trim panel as described in Chapter 11.

7 Remove the four securing screws, then withdraw the speaker from the panel and disconnect the wiring plug.

8 Refitting is a reversal of removal.

Rear tweeter speakers

9 Remove the door inner trim panel as described in Chapter 11.

10 The tweeter speaker is integral with the door inner handle assembly, which is secured to the rear of the panel by four bolts. Remove the bolts, disconnect the speaker wiring, and remove the assembly.

11 Refitting is a reversal of removal.

20 Airbag system – general information and precautions

⚠️ *Warning: Before carrying out any operations on the airbag system, disconnect the battery negative terminal, and wait for two minutes before proceeding. When operations are complete, make sure no one is inside the car when the battery is reconnected, and ensure that the ignition is switched off.*

• *Note that the airbags must not be subjected to temperatures in excess of 90°C (194°F). When an airbag is removed, ensure that it is stored with the padded surface upwards to prevent possible inflation.*

• *Do not allow any solvents or cleaning agents to contact the airbag assemblies. They must be cleaned using only a damp cloth.*

• *The airbags and control unit are both sensitive to impact. If either is dropped or damaged they should be renewed.*

• *Disconnect the airbag control unit wiring plug prior to using arc-welding equipment on the car.*

1 Driver's and passenger's airbags are fitted as standard to all models in the Polo range. Later models may also be fitted with side airbags, built into the outside bolsters of the front seats. The airbag system comprises the airbag units (complete with gas generator), an impact sensor, the control unit and a warning light in the instrument panel.

2 The airbag system is triggered in the event of a heavy frontal (or side) impact above a predetermined force; depending on the point of impact. The airbag is inflated within milliseconds, and forms a safety cushion between the driver and the steering wheel, or the front seat passenger and the facia. This prevents contact between the upper body and the wheel/facia, and therefore greatly reduces the risk of injury. The airbag then deflates almost immediately.

3 Every time the ignition is switched on, the airbag control unit performs a self-test. The self-test takes approximately 3 seconds, and during this time the airbag warning light on the facia is illuminated. After the self-test has been completed, the warning light should go out. If the warning light fails to come on, remains illuminated after the initial 3-second period, flashes, or comes on at any time when the car is being driven, there is a fault in the airbag system. The car should then be taken to a VW dealer for examination at the earliest possible opportunity.

21 Airbag system components – removal and refitting

Note: *Refer to the warnings in Section 20 before carrying out the following operations.*

1 Disconnect the battery negative terminal (see *Disconnecting the battery*).

19.3a Remove the screw from the mirror trim panel . . .

19.3b . . . then unclip and remove the panel from the door

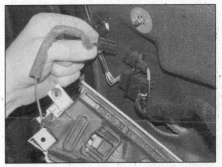

19.4 Disconnecting the speaker wiring plug

21.3 Using a piece of bent wire to unhook the airbag spring clip

21.4 When both ends of the spring have been released, lift the airbag out

9 Making sure that no-one is inside the car, reconnect the battery negative lead.

Passenger's airbag

Removal

10 Remove the facia panel as described in Chapter 11.
11 Disconnect the wiring plug from the back of the airbag unit.
12 Remove the airbag mounting nuts, and swing the airbag unit down from its mounting bracket.

Refitting

13 Manoeuvre the airbag into position, secure with the mounting nuts and reconnect the wiring connector.
14 Making sure that no-one is inside the car, reconnect the battery negative lead.

Side airbags

15 The side airbags are located internally within the front seat backrest, and no attempt should be made to remove them. Any suspected problems with the side airbag system should be referred to a VW dealer.

Airbag control unit

Removal

16 The airbag control unit is fitted in the centre of the car, under the facia.
17 Remove the centre console as described in Chapter 11, then remove three screws and take out the footwell vent.
18 It may be necessary to make a small cut in the carpet for access to the control unit.
19 Release the securing catch and disconnect the wiring plug from the side of the unit.
20 Undo the securing nuts and remove the control unit from the car **(see illustration)**.

Refitting

21 Refitting is a reversal of removal.

Airbag clockspring (rotary connector)

Removal

22 Remove the airbag unit as described above, and the steering wheel as described in Chapter 10.
23 Taking care not to rotate the contact unit,

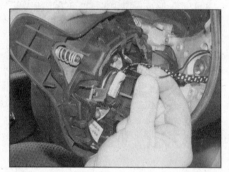

21.5a Disconnect the horn wiring plug . . .

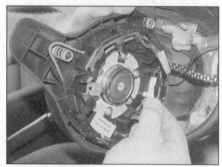

21.5b . . . and the airbag plug in the centre

Driver's airbag

Removal

2 The airbag is mounted in the centre of the steering wheel, and is secured by a circular spring ring on the back, the ends of which can be accessed and released through two holes in the back of the wheel hub.
3 Turn the steering wheel through 90° from the straight-ahead position (to the side) to access the first of the airbag retaining clips. Use a small screwdriver (or a piece of wire) in the hole provided at the back of the wheel, to prise the end of the spring clip used to retain the airbag – as this is done, pull gently on the steering wheel centre pad to release it **(see illustration)**.
4 Turn the wheel through 180° (to the other side), and repeat the process to free the airbag unit completely. Either have an assistant hold the released side of the airbag clear of the steering wheel, or wedge it clear,

otherwise trying to release the second clip will re-engage the first one. Patience is required for this job **(see illustration)**.
5 Disconnect the horn wiring plug (grey) at the top of the airbag, and the airbag wiring plug (yellow) in the centre **(see illustrations)**.
6 Carefully lift the airbag assembly away from the steering wheel. Note that the airbag must not be knocked or dropped, and should be stored the correct way up, with its padded surface uppermost.

Refitting

7 Make sure that the steering wheel is in the straight-ahead position, and that the battery is still disconnected.
8 Reconnect the airbag and horn wiring connectors and seat the airbag unit in the steering wheel, ensuring that the wiring does not become trapped. Align the airbag with the wheel spokes, and press firmly into position to engage the ends of the spring clip.

21.20 Airbag control unit

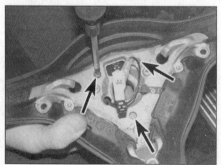

21.23a Undo the three screws . . .

21.23b . . . and remove the clockspring from the back of the wheel

22.1 Removing the immobiliser control unit

22.3 Disconnect the wiring plug and lift off the reader coil

the immobiliser and allow the engine to be started.

3 The immobiliser reader coil can be unplugged and removed from the ignition switch, after removing the steering column shrouds as described in Chapter 10, Section 13 **(see illustration)**.

4 Any problems or work involving the immobiliser system should be entrusted to a VW dealer, as dedicated electronic equipment is required to diagnose faults, or to 'match' the various components.

undo the three retaining screws and remove it from the steering wheel **(see illustrations)**.

24 On refitting, fit the unit to the steering wheel and securely tighten its retaining screws. If a new contact unit is being fitted, cut the cable-tie which is fitted to prevent the unit accidentally rotating.

25 Refit the steering wheel as described in Chapter 10, and the airbag unit as described above.

22 Anti-theft immobiliser system – general information

Note: *This information is applicable only to the anti-theft immobiliser system fitted by VW as standard equipment.*

1 All models are equipped with an electronic immobiliser as standard, which is automatically activated when the ignition key is removed from the ignition switch. A control unit, fitted under the driver's side lower facia above the fuse/relay panel **(see illustration)**, cuts the ignition circuit.

2 The system is disarmed when the ignition key is inserted into the ignition switch, as follows. The head of the ignition key contains a transponder microchip, and the ignition lock contains a reader coil. When the key enters the lock, the reader coil recognises the signal from the microchip, and de-activates the immobiliser. It is essential that the key tag showing the key number is not lost (this will be supplied with the car when new). Any duplicate keys will have to be obtained from a VW dealer, who will need the key number to supply a duplicate – any keys cut elsewhere will work the door locks, but will not contain the transponder chip necessary to de-activate

23 Heated front seat components – removal and refitting

Heater mats

1 On models equipped with heated front seats, a heater pad is fitted to both the seat back and the seat cushion. Renewal of either heater mat involves peeling back the upholstery, removing the old mat, sticking the new mat in position and then refitting the upholstery. Note that upholstery removal and refitting requires considerable skill and experience if it is to be carried out successfully and is therefore best entrusted to your VW dealer. In practice, it will be very difficult for the home mechanic to carry out the job without ruining the upholstery.

Heated seat switches

2 Refer to Section 6.

VW POLO wiring diagrams

Diagram 1

Key to symbols

Bulb	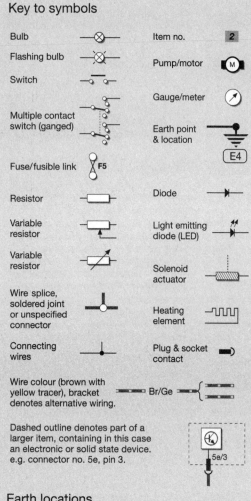	Item no.	**2**
Flashing bulb		Pump/motor	M
Switch		Gauge/meter	
Multiple contact switch (ganged)		Earth point & location	E4
Fuse/fusible link	F5		
Resistor		Diode	
Variable resistor		Light emitting diode (LED)	
Variable resistor		Solenoid actuator	
Wire splice, soldered joint or unspecified connector		Heating element	
Connecting wires		Plug & socket contact	

Wire colour (brown with yellow tracer), bracket denotes alternative wiring. — Br/Ge

Dashed outline denotes part of a larger item, containing in this case an electronic or solid state device. e.g. connector no. 5e, pin 3. 5e/3

Earth locations

E1 Earth strap - battery to body
E2 Earth strap - engine to body
E3 On left of engine compartment
E4 Near LH tail light
E5 Near gear selector mechanism
E6 In engine compartment wiring harness
E7 Earth point on cylinder head
E8 Earth connection 1 in headlight harness
E9 Earth connection 2 in headlight harness
E10 Earth point 1 in dashboard harness
E11 Lower RH 'A' pillar
E12 Near RH tail light
E13 Earth connection in front passenger's door wiring harness
E14 Earth connection in front driver's door wiring harness

Passenger compartment fuses 6

Fuse	Rating	Circuit protected
F1	10A	Oxygen sensor heater
F2	5A	Number plate light
F3	10A	Fuel injectors
F4	5A	LH sidelight
F5	5A	RH sidelight
F6	15A	Rear window wiper
F7	7.5A	Direction indicators
F8	5A	ABS with EDL/ESP
F9	5A	Headlight levelling
F10	7.5A	Interior lighting, glovebox light, vanity mirror light, luggage compartment light
F11	5A	Diagnostic connector, instrument cluster, air conditioning
F12	10A	RH headlight main beam and warning light
F13	10A	LH headlight main beam
F14	10A	Hazard warning lights
F15	10A	Stop lights
F16	5A	Ignition switch 'S' contact
F17	-	Not used
F18	5A	Heated mirrors
F19	15A	Horn
F20	-	Not used
F21	-	Not used
F22	15A	Alarm system
F23	5A	EGR, air mass meter, additional heater relay, glow plug relay
F24	5A	Clutch pedal switch (Diesel)
F25	5A	Selector lever switch (automatic transmission)
F26	7.5A	Air conditioning, central locking, electric windows, electric mirrors, navigation system
F27	5A	Instrument cluster
F28	5A	Speedometer sensor unit, immobilizer
F29	7.5A	Reversing lights, heated washer jets, headlight levelling
F30	5A	EGR valve, charcoal filter solenoid
F31	10A	Engine management
F32	5A	Fuel shut-off control unit (Diesel)
F33	-	Not used
F34	10A	Ignition transformer
F35	25A	Sunroof
F36	15A	Engine management
F37	15A	Engine management
F38	25A	Driver's electric window
F39	25A	Passenger's electric window
F40	15A	Fuel pump
F41	15A	Central locking, alarm system
F42	15A	Radio, navigation
F43	15A	Front and rear foglights
F44	15A	LH dip beam headlight
F45	15A	RH dip beam headlight
F46	15A	Cigar lighter
F47	20A	Headlight washer
F48	20A	Heated rear window
F49	25A	Heater blower motor
F50	15A	Front wash/wipe
F51	15A	Heated seats

Passenger fusebox 6

Wire colours

Ws White   **Bl** Blue
Ge Yellow   **Ro** Red
Br Brown   **Gr** Grey
Gn Green   **Li** Lilac
Sw Black

Key to items

1 Battery
2 Starter motor
3 Alternator
4 Ignition switch
5 Battery fusebox
6 Passenger fusebox
7 Engine cooling fan
8 Engine cooling fan switch
9 Starter inhibitor relay (auto.)
10 Light switch
   a = side/headlight switch
11 Combination switch
   a = direction indicators/
        parking light switch
12 LH headlight unit
   a = sidelight
13 RH headlight unit
   a = sidelight
14 Number plate light
15 LH rear light unit
   a = tail light
   b = stop light
16 RH rear light unit
   a = tail light
   b = stop light
   c = reversing light
17 High level stop light
18 Stop light switch
19 Reversing light switch

Diagram 2

H33013

Starting, charging & engine cooling fan

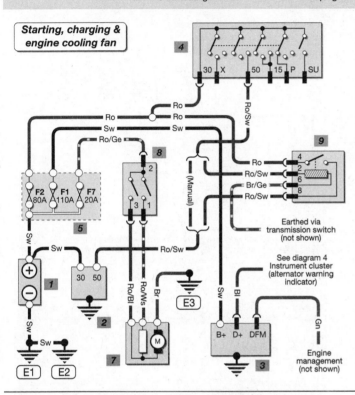

Stop & reversing lights

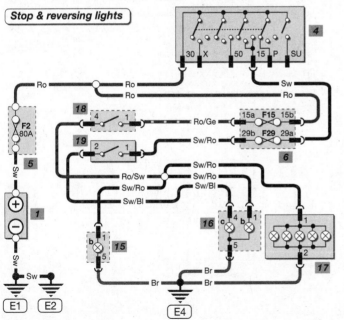

Side, tail & number plate lights

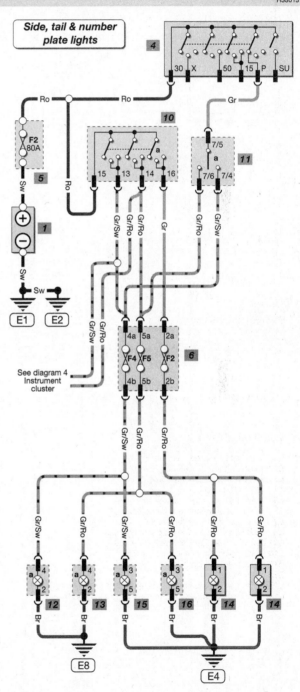

Wire colours

Ws	White	**Bl**	Blue
Ge	Yellow	**Ro**	Red
Br	Brown	**Gr**	Grey
Gn	Green	**Li**	Lilac
Sw	Black		

Key to items

1 Battery
4 Ignition switch
5 Battery fusebox
6 Passenger fusebox
10 Light switch
  a = side/headlight switch
  b = front/rear foglight switch
  c = foglight indicator
  d = control unit
11 Combination switch
  a = direction indicator/parking light
  b = dip/main/flash

12 LH headlight unit
  b = dip/main beam
13 RH headlight unit
  b = dip/main beam
15 LH rear light unit
  c = foglight
  d = direction indicator
16 RH rear light unit
  d = direction indicator
22 LH front foglight
23 RH front foglight
24 'X contact' relay

25 LH front direction indicator
26 RH front direction indicator
27 LH direction indicator side repeater
28 RH direction indicator side repeater
29 Hazard warning light switch

Diagram 3

H33014

Headlights & foglights

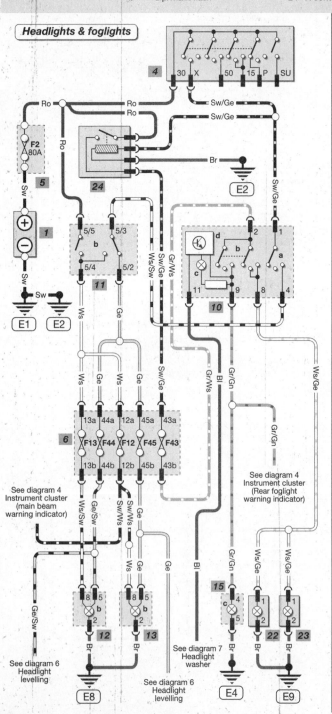

Direction indicator & hazard warning lights

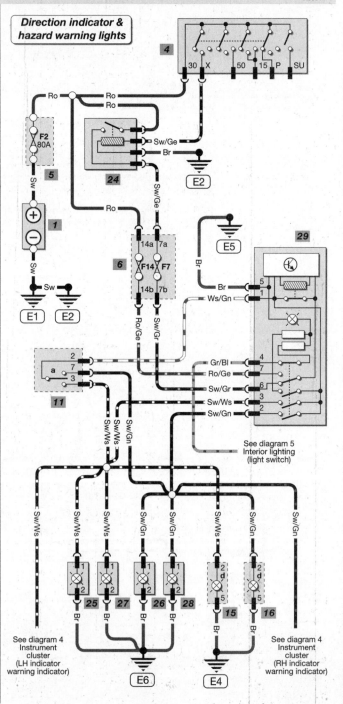

Wire colours

Ws	White	Bl	Blue
Ge	Yellow	Ro	Red
Br	Brown	Gr	Grey
Gn	Green	Li	Lilac
Sw	Black		

* Models without ABS

Key to items

1 = Battery
4 = Ignition switch
5 = Battery fusebox
6 = Passenger fusebox
33 = Speedometer sensor
34 = Driver's seatbelt switch
35 = Handbrake switch
36 = Low brake fluid switch
37 = Oil pressure switch
38 = Low coolant level switch
39 = Fuel gauge sender
40 = Coolant temperature sender

41 Instrument cluster
a = seatbelt warning indicator
b = digital display illumination
c = brake system warning indicator
d = coolant temp./level warning indicator
e = oil pressure warning indicator
f = main beam warning indicator
g = rear foglight warning indicator
h = alternator warning indicator
i = RH direction indicator
j = LH direction indicator
k = display control unit

41 Instrument cluster continued
l = handbrake/low brake fluid indicator
m = tachometer
n = voltage stabiliser
o = odometer
p = digital clock
q = oil pressure warning buzzer
r = instrument illumination
s = sidelight warning indicator
t = coolant temp. gauge
u = fuel gauge
v = control unit for Can-bus

Diagram 4

H33015

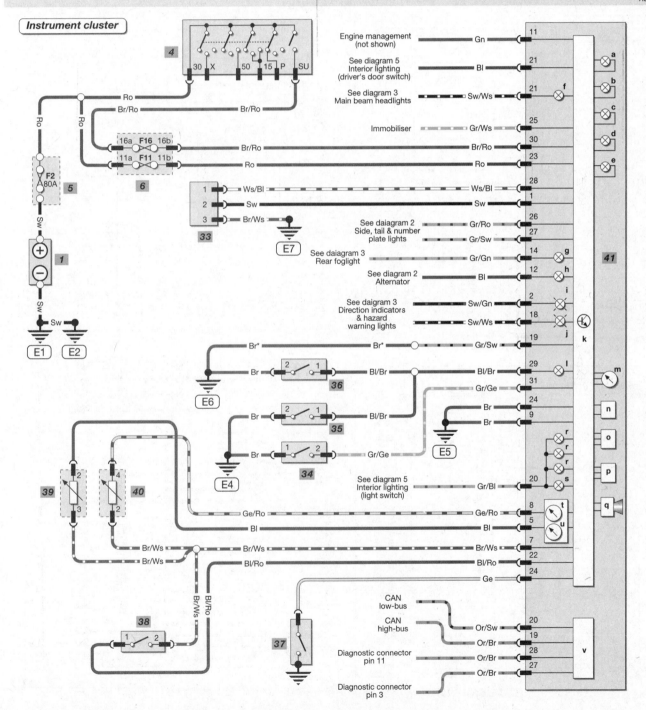

Wire colours

Ws	White	**Bl**	Blue
Ge	Yellow	**Ro**	Red
Br	Brown	**Gr**	Grey
Gn	Green	**Li**	Lilac
Sw	Black		

Key to items

1 Battery
4 Ignition switch
5 Battery fusebox
6 Passenger fusebox
10 Light switch
   a = side/headlight switch
   d = control unit
   e = switch illumination
   f = interior lighting rheostat
24 'X contact' relay

45 Interior light
46 Driver's door switch
47 Passenger's door switch
48 Luggage compartment light
49 Luggage compartment light switch
50 Horn
51 Horn switch
52 Cigar lighter
53 Wash/wipe switch
54 Heated rear window switch

55 Heated rear window
56 Heater blower switch
57 Heater blower resitors
58 Heater blower motor

Diagram 5

H33016

Interior lighting

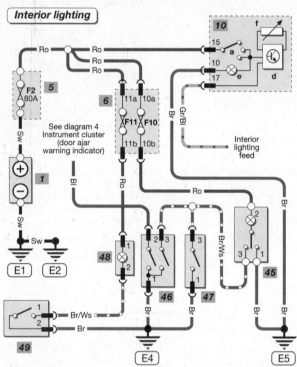

Heated rear window

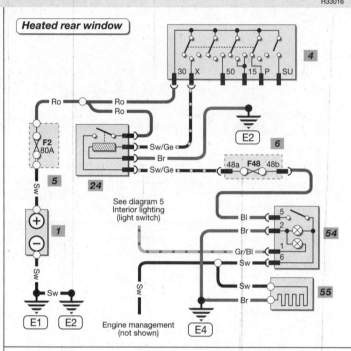

Horn & cigar lighter

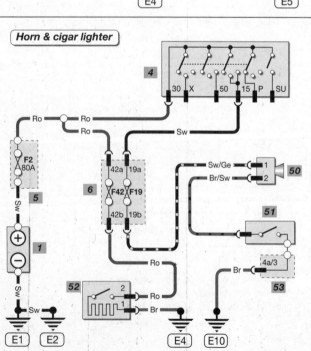

Heater blower

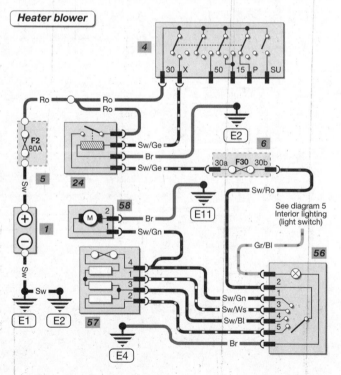

Wire colours

Ws White   **Bl** Blue
Ge Yellow   **Ro** Red
Br Brown   **Gr** Grey
Gn Green   **Li** Lilac
Sw Black

Key to items

1   Battery
4   Ignition switch
5   Battery fusebox
6   Passenger fusebox
10   Light switch
   a = side/headlight switch
11   Combination switch
   a = dip/main/flash
24   'X' contact relay

60   Wash/wipe switch
   a = rear wiper switch
   b = washer switch
   c = front wiper switch
61   Front/rear washer pump
62   Front wiper motor
63   Rear wiper motor
64   Front wiper relay
65   Audio unit

66   Aerial amplifier
67   LH front base speaker
68   LH front tweeter
69   RH front base speaker
70   RH front tweeter
71   Headlight levelling switch
72   LH headlight levelling adjuster
73   RH headlight levelling adjuster

Diagram 6

H33017

Wash/wipe

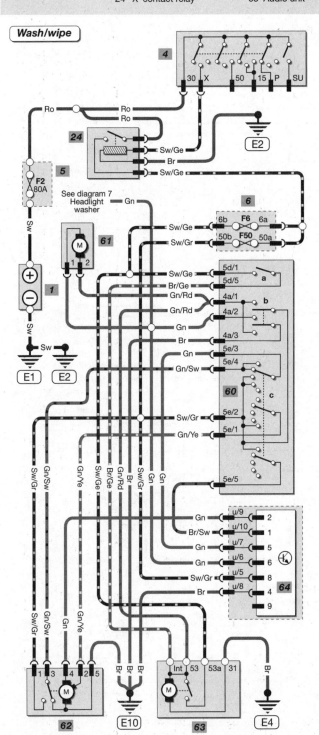

Typical audio system

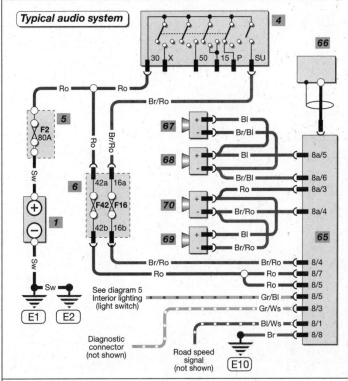

Headlight levelling

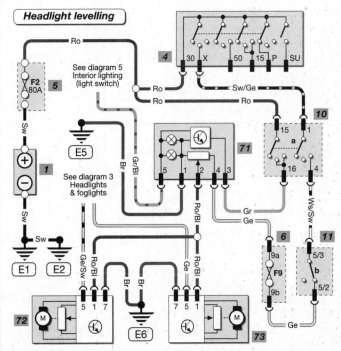

Wire colours

Ws White   **Bl** Blue
Ge Yellow   **Ro** Red
Br Brown   **Gr** Grey
Gn Green   **Li** Lilac
Sw Black

Key to items

1   Battery
4   Ignition switch
5   Battery fusebox
6   Passenger fusebox
75   Heated washer jet
76   Mirror control switch
77   Driver's mirror assembly
78   Passenger's mirror assembly
79   Sunroof control unit & motor
80   Sunroof adjustment regulator
81   Headlight washer relay
82   Headlight washer motor
83   Heated mirror relay

Diagram 7

H33018

Heated washer jets

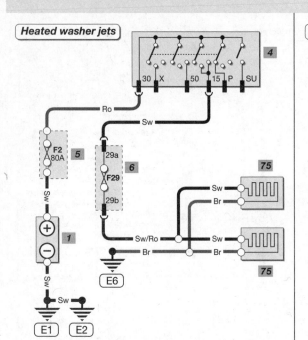

Heated mirrors

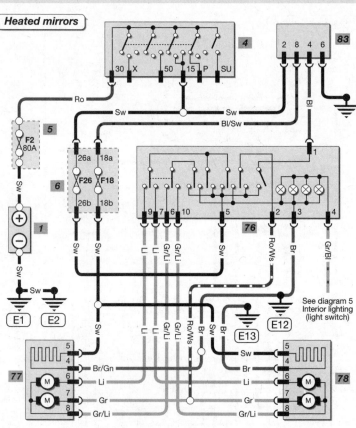

Sunroof

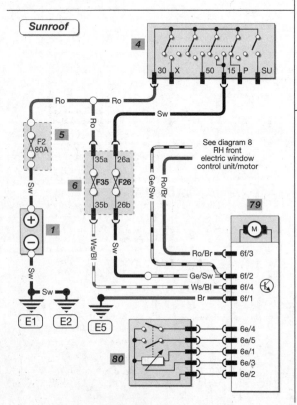

Headlight washer

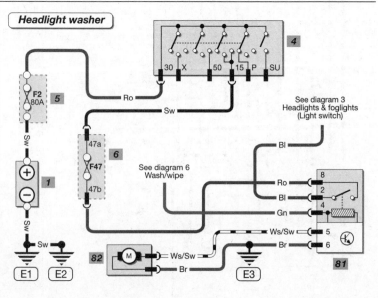

Wire colours

Ws	White	**Bl**	Blue
Ge	Yellow	**Ro**	Red
Br	Brown	**Gr**	Grey
Gn	Green	**Li**	Lilac
Sw	Black		

Key to items

1 Battery
4 Ignition switch
5 Battery fusebox
6 Passenger fusebox
85 Front LH central locking actuator
86 Central locking pump with control unit
87 Driver's central locking switch
88 Passenger's central locking switch
89 Electric window control switch
90 Front electric window switch
91 Front LH window control unit/motor
92 Front RH window control unit/motor

Diagram 8

H33019

Central locking

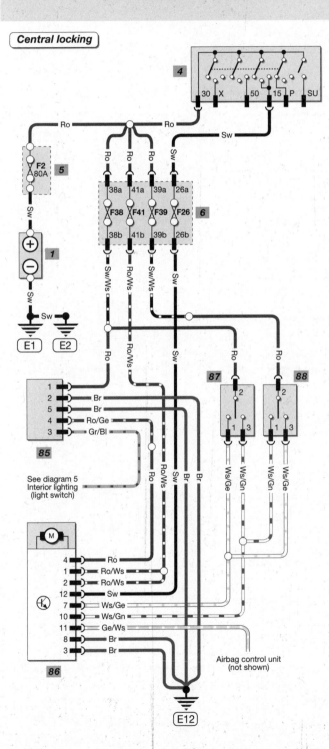

Electric windows

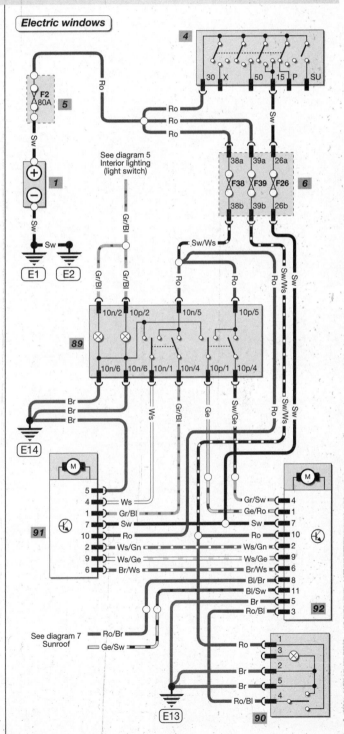

Notes

Dimensions and weights

Note: *All figures are approximate, and may vary according to model. Refer to manufacturer's data for exact figures.*

Dimensions

Overall length	3743 mm
Overall width	1632 mm
Overall height (unladen)	1418 mm
Wheelbase	2407 mm

Weights

Kerb weight	923 to 987 kg*
Maximum gross vehicle weight**	1410 to 1500 kg*
Maximum roof rack load	50 kg
Maximum towing weight**:	
Braked trailer	650 to 800 kg*
Unbraked trailer	450 kg
Maximum trailer nose weight	50 kg

* Depending on model and specification.
** Refer to VW dealer for exact recommendations.

Length (distance)
Inches (in)	x 25.4	= Millimetres (mm)	x 0.0394	= Inches (in)
Feet (ft)	x 0.305	= Metres (m)	x 3.281	= Feet (ft)
Miles	x 1.609	= Kilometres (km)	x 0.621	= Miles

Volume (capacity)
Cubic inches (cu in; in³)	x 16.387	= Cubic centimetres (cc; cm³)	x 0.061	= Cubic inches (cu in; in³)
Imperial pints (Imp pt)	x 0.568	= Litres (l)	x 1.76	= Imperial pints (Imp pt)
Imperial quarts (Imp qt)	x 1.137	= Litres (l)	x 0.88	= Imperial quarts (Imp qt)
Imperial quarts (Imp qt)	x 1.201	= US quarts (US qt)	x 0.833	= Imperial quarts (Imp qt)
US quarts (US qt)	x 0.946	= Litres (l)	x 1.057	= US quarts (US qt)
Imperial gallons (Imp gal)	x 4.546	= Litres (l)	x 0.22	= Imperial gallons (Imp gal)
Imperial gallons (Imp gal)	x 1.201	= US gallons (US gal)	x 0.833	= Imperial gallons (Imp gal)
US gallons (US gal)	x 3.785	= Litres (l)	x 0.264	= US gallons (US gal)

Mass (weight)
Ounces (oz)	x 28.35	= Grams (g)	x 0.035	= Ounces (oz)
Pounds (lb)	x 0.454	= Kilograms (kg)	x 2.205	= Pounds (lb)

Force
Ounces-force (ozf; oz)	x 0.278	= Newtons (N)	x 3.6	= Ounces-force (ozf; oz)
Pounds-force (lbf; lb)	x 4.448	= Newtons (N)	x 0.225	= Pounds-force (lbf; lb)
Newtons (N)	x 0.1	= Kilograms-force (kgf; kg)	x 9.81	= Newtons (N)

Pressure
Pounds-force per square inch (psi; lbf/in²; lb/in²)	x 0.070	= Kilograms-force per square centimetre (kgf/cm²; kg/cm²)	x 14.223	= Pounds-force per square inch (psi; lbf/in²; lb/in²)
Pounds-force per square inch (psi; lbf/in²; lb/in²)	x 0.068	= Atmospheres (atm)	x 14.696	= Pounds-force per square inch (psi; lbf/in²; lb/in²)
Pounds-force per square inch (psi; lbf/in²; lb/in²)	x 0.069	= Bars	x 14.5	= Pounds-force per square inch (psi; lbf/in²; lb/in²)
Pounds-force per square inch (psi; lbf/in²; lb/in²)	x 6.895	= Kilopascals (kPa)	x 0.145	= Pounds-force per square inch (psi; lbf/in²; lb/in²)
Kilopascals (kPa)	x 0.01	= Kilograms-force per square centimetre (kgf/cm²; kg/cm²)	x 98.1	= Kilopascals (kPa)
Millibar (mbar)	x 100	= Pascals (Pa)	x 0.01	= Millibar (mbar)
Millibar (mbar)	x 0.0145	= Pounds-force per square inch (psi; lbf/in²; lb/in²)	x 68.947	= Millibar (mbar)
Millibar (mbar)	x 0.75	= Millimetres of mercury (mmHg)	x 1.333	= Millibar (mbar)
Millibar (mbar)	x 0.401	= Inches of water (inH$_2$O)	x 2.491	= Millibar (mbar)
Millimetres of mercury (mmHg)	x 0.535	= Inches of water (inH$_2$O)	x 1.868	= Millimetres of mercury (mmHg)
Inches of water (inH$_2$O)	x 0.036	= Pounds-force per square inch (psi; lbf/in²; lb/in²)	x 27.68	= Inches of water (inH$_2$O)

Torque (moment of force)
Pounds-force inches (lbf in; lb in)	x 1.152	= Kilograms-force centimetre (kgf cm; kg cm)	x 0.868	= Pounds-force inches (lbf in; lb in)
Pounds-force inches (lbf in; lb in)	x 0.113	= Newton metres (Nm)	x 8.85	= Pounds-force inches (lbf in; lb in)
Pounds-force inches (lbf in; lb in)	x 0.083	= Pounds-force feet (lbf ft; lb ft)	x 12	= Pounds-force inches (lbf in; lb in)
Pounds-force feet (lbf ft; lb ft)	x 0.138	= Kilograms-force metres (kgf m; kg m)	x 7.233	= Pounds-force feet (lbf ft; lb ft)
Pounds-force feet (lbf ft; lb ft)	x 1.356	= Newton metres (Nm)	x 0.738	= Pounds-force feet (lbf ft; lb ft)
Newton metres (Nm)	x 0.102	= Kilograms-force metres (kgf m; kg m)	x 9.804	= Newton metres (Nm)

Power
Horsepower (hp)	x 745.7	= Watts (W)	x 0.0013	= Horsepower (hp)

Velocity (speed)
Miles per hour (miles/hr; mph)	x 1.609	= Kilometres per hour (km/hr; kph)	x 0.621	= Miles per hour (miles/hr; mph)

Fuel consumption*
Miles per gallon, Imperial (mpg)	x 0.354	= Kilometres per litre (km/l)	x 2.825	= Miles per gallon, Imperial (mpg)
Miles per gallon, US (mpg)	x 0.425	= Kilometres per litre (km/l)	x 2.352	= Miles per gallon, US (mpg)

Temperature
Degrees Fahrenheit = (°C x 1.8) + 32   Degrees Celsius (Degrees Centigrade; °C) = (°F - 32) x 0.56

It is common practice to convert from miles per gallon (mpg) to litres/100 kilometres (l/100km), where mpg x l/100 km = 282

Spare parts are available from many sources, including maker's appointed garages, accessory shops, and motor factors. To be sure of obtaining the correct parts, it will sometimes be necessary to quote the vehicle identification number (see *Vehicle identification*). If possible, it can also be useful to take the old parts along for positive identification. Items such as starter motors and alternators may be available under a service exchange scheme – any parts returned should always be clean.

Our advice regarding spare part sources is as follows.

Officially-appointed garages

This is the best source of parts which are peculiar to your car, and which are not otherwise generally available (eg, badges, interior trim, certain body panels, etc). It is also the only place at which you should buy parts if the car is still under warranty.

Accessory shops

These are very good places to buy materials and components needed for the maintenance of your car (oil, air and fuel filters, spark plugs, light bulbs, drivebelts, oils and greases, brake pads, touch-up paint, etc). Components of this nature sold by a reputable shop are of the same standard as those used by the car manufacturer.

Besides components, these shops also sell tools and general accessories, usually have convenient opening hours, charge lower prices, and can often be found not far from home. Some accessory shops have parts counters where the components needed for almost any repair job can be purchased or ordered.

Motor factors

Good factors will stock all the more important components which wear out comparatively quickly, and can sometimes supply individual components needed for the overhaul of a larger assembly (eg brake seals and hydraulic parts, bearing shells, pistons, valves, alternator brushes). They may also handle work such as cylinder block reboring, crankshaft regrinding and balancing, etc.

Tyre and exhaust specialists

These outlets may be independent, or members of a local or national chain. They frequently offer competitive prices when compared with a main dealer or local garage, but it will pay to obtain several quotes before making a decision. When researching prices, also ask what 'extras' may be added – for instance, fitting a new valve and balancing the wheel are both commonly charged on top of the price of a new tyre.

Other sources

Beware of parts or materials obtained from market stalls, car boot sales or similar outlets. Such items are not invariably sub-standard, but there is little chance of compensation if they do prove unsatisfactory. In the case of safety-critical components such as brake pads, there is the risk not only of financial loss but also of an accident causing injury or death.

Second-hand components or assemblies obtained from a car breaker can be a good buy in some circumstances, but this sort of purchase is best made by the experienced DIY mechanic.

Vehicle identification

Modifications are a continuing and unpublicised process in car manufacture, quite apart from major model changes. Spare parts manuals and lists are compiled upon a numerical basis, the individual vehicle identification numbers being essential to correct identification of the component concerned.

When ordering spare parts, always give as much information as possible. Quote the car model, year of manufacture, body and engine numbers as appropriate.

The vehicle identification number (VIN) plate or chassis number may be found in the engine compartment, on top of the bulkhead **(see illustration)**. On some models, this information may appear on the passenger door pillar. Some models may have the chassis number on a small plate on the top of the facia panel (visible VIN).

The engine number is stamped on the transmission end of cylinder block (on some models, it can also be found on a sticker attached to the timing belt cover) **(see illustrations)**.

Note: *The first part of the engine number gives the engine code – eg, AUA.*

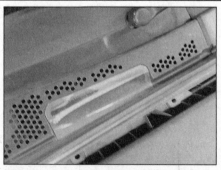

VIN number is visible through a clear panel on top of the bulkhead

VIN plate on engine compartment bulkhead

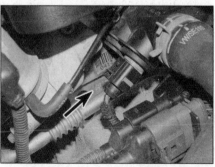

The engine number is stamped on the transmission end of the block . . .

. . . and may appear on the timing belt cover

Whenever servicing, repair or overhaul work is carried out on the car or its components, observe the following procedures and instructions. This will assist in carrying out the operation efficiently and to a professional standard of workmanship.

Joint mating faces and gaskets

When separating components at their mating faces, never insert screwdrivers or similar implements into the joint between the faces in order to prise them apart. This can cause severe damage which results in oil leaks, coolant leaks, etc upon reassembly. Separation is usually achieved by tapping along the joint with a soft-faced hammer in order to break the seal. However, note that this method may not be suitable where dowels are used for component location.

Where a gasket is used between the mating faces of two components, a new one must be fitted on reassembly; fit it dry unless otherwise stated in the repair procedure. Make sure that the mating faces are clean and dry, with all traces of old gasket removed. When cleaning a joint face, use a tool which is unlikely to score or damage the face, and remove any burrs or nicks with an oilstone or fine file.

Make sure that tapped holes are cleaned with a pipe cleaner, and keep them free of jointing compound, if this is being used, unless specifically instructed otherwise.

Ensure that all orifices, channels or pipes are clear, and blow through them, preferably using compressed air.

Oil seals

Oil seals can be removed by levering them out with a wide flat-bladed screwdriver or similar implement. Alternatively, a number of self-tapping screws may be screwed into the seal, and these used as a purchase for pliers or some similar device in order to pull the seal free.

Whenever an oil seal is removed from its working location, either individually or as part of an assembly, it should be renewed.

The very fine sealing lip of the seal is easily damaged, and will not seal if the surface it contacts is not completely clean and free from scratches, nicks or grooves. If the original sealing surface of the component cannot be restored, and the manufacturer has not made provision for slight relocation of the seal relative to the sealing surface, the component should be renewed.

Protect the lips of the seal from any surface which may damage them in the course of fitting. Use tape or a conical sleeve where possible. Lubricate the seal lips with oil before fitting and, on dual-lipped seals, fill the space between the lips with grease.

Unless otherwise stated, oil seals must be fitted with their sealing lips toward the lubricant to be sealed.

Use a tubular drift or block of wood of the appropriate size to install the seal and, if the seal housing is shouldered, drive the seal down to the shoulder. If the seal housing is unshouldered, the seal should be fitted with its face flush with the housing top face (unless otherwise instructed).

Screw threads and fastenings

Seized nuts, bolts and screws are quite a common occurrence where corrosion has set in, and the use of penetrating oil or releasing fluid will often overcome this problem if the offending item is soaked for a while before attempting to release it. The use of an impact driver may also provide a means of releasing such stubborn fastening devices, when used in conjunction with the appropriate screwdriver bit or socket. If none of these methods works, it may be necessary to resort to the careful application of heat, or the use of a hacksaw or nut splitter device.

Studs are usually removed by locking two nuts together on the threaded part, and then using a spanner on the lower nut to unscrew the stud. Studs or bolts which have broken off below the surface of the component in which they are mounted can sometimes be removed using a stud extractor. Always ensure that a blind tapped hole is completely free from oil, grease, water or other fluid before installing the bolt or stud. Failure to do this could cause the housing to crack due to the hydraulic action of the bolt or stud as it is screwed in.

When tightening a castellated nut to accept a split pin, tighten the nut to the specified torque, where applicable, and then tighten further to the next split pin hole. Never slacken the nut to align the split pin hole, unless stated in the repair procedure.

When checking or retightening a nut or bolt to a specified torque setting, slacken the nut or bolt by a quarter of a turn, and then retighten to the specified setting. However, this should not be attempted where angular tightening has been used.

For some screw fastenings, notably cylinder head bolts or nuts, torque wrench settings are no longer specified for the latter stages of tightening, "angle-tightening" being called up instead. Typically, a fairly low torque wrench setting will be applied to the bolts/nuts in the correct sequence, followed by one or more stages of tightening through specified angles.

Locknuts, locktabs and washers

Any fastening which will rotate against a component or housing during tightening should always have a washer between it and the relevant component or housing.

Spring or split washers should always be renewed when they are used to lock a critical component such as a big-end bearing retaining bolt or nut. Locktabs which are folded over to retain a nut or bolt should always be renewed.

Self-locking nuts can be re-used in non-critical areas, providing resistance can be felt when the locking portion passes over the bolt or stud thread. However, it should be noted that self-locking stiffnuts tend to lose their effectiveness after long periods of use, and should then be renewed as a matter of course.

Split pins must always be replaced with new ones of the correct size for the hole.

When thread-locking compound is found on the threads of a fastener which is to be re-used, it should be cleaned off with a wire brush and solvent, and fresh compound applied on reassembly.

Special tools

Some repair procedures in this manual entail the use of special tools such as a press, two or three-legged pullers, spring compressors, etc. Wherever possible, suitable readily-available alternatives to the manufacturer's special tools are described, and are shown in use. In some instances, where no alternative is possible, it has been necessary to resort to the use of a manufacturer's tool, and this has been done for reasons of safety as well as the efficient completion of the repair operation. Unless you are highly-skilled and have a thorough understanding of the procedures described, never attempt to bypass the use of any special tool when the procedure described specifies its use. Not only is there a very great risk of personal injury, but expensive damage could be caused to the components involved.

Environmental considerations

When disposing of used engine oil, brake fluid, antifreeze, etc, give due consideration to any detrimental environmental effects. Do not, for instance, pour any of the above liquids down drains into the general sewage system, or onto the ground to soak away. Many local council refuse tips provide a facility for waste oil disposal, as do some garages. If none of these facilities are available, consult your local Environmental Health Department, or the National Rivers Authority, for further advice.

With the universal tightening-up of legislation regarding the emission of environmentally-harmful substances from motor vehicles, most vehicles have tamperproof devices fitted to the main adjustment points of the fuel system. These devices are primarily designed to prevent unqualified persons from adjusting the fuel/air mixture, with the chance of a consequent increase in toxic emissions. If such devices are found during servicing or overhaul, they should, wherever possible, be renewed or refitted in accordance with the manufacturer's requirements or current legislation.

OIL CARE
FOLLOW THE CODE

OIL BANK LINE
0800 66 33 66
www.oilbankline.org.uk

Note: It is antisocial and illegal to dump oil down the drain. To find the location of your local oil recycling bank, call this number free.

The jack supplied with the car's tool kit should only be used for changing the roadwheels – see *Wheel changing* at the front of this book. When carrying out any other kind of work, raise the car using a hydraulic (or 'trolley') jack, and always supplement the jack with axle stands positioned under the jacking/support points **(see illustration)**. If the roadwheels do not have to be removed, consider using wheel ramps – if wished, these can be placed under the wheels once the car has been raised using a hydraulic jack, and then lowered onto the ramps so that it is resting on its wheels.

Only ever jack the car up on a solid, level surface. If there is even a slight slope, take great care that the car cannot move as the wheels are lifted off the ground. Jacking up on an uneven or gravelled surface is not recommended, as the weight of the car will not be evenly distributed, and the jack may slip as the car is raised.

As far as possible, do not leave the car unattended once it has been raised, particularly if children are playing nearby.

Before jacking up the front of the car, ensure that the handbrake is firmly applied. When jacking up the rear of the car, place wooden chocks in front of the front wheels, and engage first gear.

To raise the front and/or rear of the car, use the jacking/support points at the front and rear ends of the door sills, which are located at the places marked by triangular depressions in the sill panel **(see illustrations)**. Position a block of wood with a groove cut in it on the jack head to prevent the car's weight resting on the sill edge; align the sill edge with the groove in the wood so that the car's weight is spread evenly over the surface of the block. Supplement the jack with axle stands (also with slotted blocks of wood) positioned as close as possible to the jacking points.

When using a hydraulic jack or axle stands, always try to position the jack head or axle stand head under one of the relevant jacking points.

Providing care is taken (and a block of wood is used to spread the load), the centre of the front subframe and centre of the rear axle beam, may be used as support points. It may be safe also to use reinforced areas of the floor pan ('chassis legs'), particularly those in the region of suspension mountings, as support points – consult a VW dealer for advice before using anything other than the approved jacking points, however.

Do not jack the car under any other part of the sill, sump, floor pan, or directly under any of the steering or suspension components.

Never work under, around, or near a raised car, unless it is adequately supported on stands. Do not rely on a jack alone, as even a hydraulic jack could fail under load.

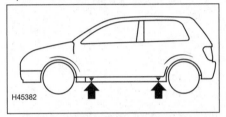

Front and rear jacking points (arrowed)

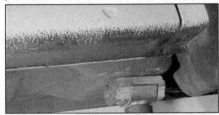

Axle stand and block of wood under front support point

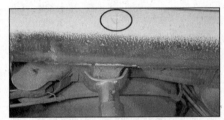

Axle stand under rear jacking/support point

Disconnecting the battery

Several systems fitted to the car require battery power to be available at all times, either to ensure that their continued operation (such as the clock) or to maintain control unit memories (such as that in the engine management system's ECU) which would be wiped if the battery were to be disconnected. Whenever the battery is to be disconnected therefore, first note the following, to ensure that there are no unforeseen consequences of this action:

a) First, on any vehicle with central locking, it is a wise precaution to remove the key from the ignition, and to keep it with you, so that it does not get locked in, if the central locking should engage accidentally when the battery is reconnected.

b) On cars equipped with an engine management system, the system's ECU will lose the information stored in its memory – referred to by VW as the 'KAM' (Keep-Alive Memory) – when the battery is disconnected. This includes idling and operating values, and any fault codes detected – in the case of the fault codes, if it is thought likely that the system has developed a fault for which the corresponding code has been logged, the car must be taken to a VW dealer for the codes to be read, using the special diagnostic equipment necessary for this.

Whenever the battery is disconnected, the information relating to idle speed control and other operating values will have to be re-programmed into the unit's memory. The ECU does this by itself, but until then, there may be surging, hesitation, erratic idle and a generally inferior level of performance. To allow the ECU to relearn these values, start the engine and run it as close to idle speed as possible until it reaches its normal operating temperature, then run it for approximately two minutes at 1200 rpm. Next, drive the car as far as necessary – approximately 5 miles of varied driving conditions is usually sufficient – to complete the relearning process.

c) *If the battery is disconnected while the alarm system is armed or activated, the alarm will remain in the same state when the battery is reconnected. The same applies to the engine immobiliser system.*

d) *If a coded audio unit is fitted, and the unit and/or the battery is disconnected, the unit will not function again on reconnection until the correct security code is entered. Details of this procedure, which varies according to the unit and model year, are given in the handbook supplied with the car when new, with the code itself being given in a 'Radio Passport' and/or a 'Keycode Label' at the*

same time. Ensure you have the correct code before you disconnect the battery. For obvious security reasons, the procedure is not given in this manual. If you do not have the code or details of the correct procedure, but can supply proof of ownership and a legitimate reason for wanting this information, the car's selling dealer may be able to help.

Devices known as 'memory-savers' (or 'code-savers') can be used to avoid some of the above problems. Precise details vary according to the device used. Typically, it is plugged into the cigarette lighter, and is connected by its own wires to a spare battery; the car's own battery is then disconnected from the electrical system, leaving the 'memory-saver' to pass sufficient current to maintain audio unit security codes and ECU memory values, and also to run permanently-live circuits such as the clock, all the while isolating the battery in the event of a short-circuit occurring while work is carried out.

⚠️ *Warning: Some of these devices allow a considerable amount of current to pass, which can mean that many of the car's systems are still operational when the main battery is disconnected. If a 'memory-saver' is used, ensure that the circuit concerned is actually 'dead' before carrying out any work on it!*

Introduction

A selection of good tools is a fundamental requirement for anyone contemplating the maintenance and repair of a motor vehicle. For the owner who does not possess any, their purchase will prove a considerable expense, offsetting some of the savings made by doing-it-yourself. However, provided that the tools purchased meet the relevant national safety standards and are of good quality, they will last for many years and prove an extremely worthwhile investment.

To help the average owner to decide which tools are needed to carry out the various tasks detailed in this manual, we have compiled three lists of tools under the following headings: *Maintenance and minor repair, Repair and overhaul*, and *Special*. Newcomers to practical mechanics should start off with the *Maintenance and minor repair* tool kit, and confine themselves to the simpler jobs around the vehicle. Then, as confidence and experience grow, more difficult tasks can be undertaken, with extra tools being purchased as, and when, they are needed. In this way, a *Maintenance and minor repair* tool kit can be built up into a *Repair and overhaul* tool kit over a considerable period of time, without any major cash outlays. The experienced do-it-yourselfer will have a tool kit good enough for most repair and overhaul procedures, and will add tools from the *Special* category when it is felt that the expense is justified by the amount of use to which these tools will be put.

Maintenance and minor repair tool kit

The tools given in this list should be considered as a minimum requirement if routine maintenance, servicing and minor repair operations are to be undertaken. We recommend the purchase of combination spanners (ring one end, open-ended the other); although more expensive than open-ended ones, they do give the advantages of both types of spanner.

☐ *Combination spanners:*
  Metric - 8 to 19 mm inclusive
☐ *Adjustable spanner - 35 mm jaw (approx.)*
☐ *Spark plug spanner (with rubber insert) - petrol models*
☐ *Spark plug gap adjustment tool - petrol models*
☐ *Set of feeler gauges*
☐ *Brake bleed nipple spanner*
☐ *Screwdrivers:*
  Flat blade - 100 mm long x 6 mm dia
  Cross blade - 100 mm long x 6 mm dia
  Torx - various sizes (not all vehicles)
☐ *Combination pliers*
☐ *Hacksaw (junior)*
☐ *Tyre pump*
☐ *Tyre pressure gauge*
☐ *Oil can*
☐ *Oil filter removal tool*
☐ *Fine emery cloth*
☐ *Wire brush (small)*
☐ *Funnel (medium size)*
☐ *Sump drain plug key (not all vehicles)*

Repair and overhaul tool kit

These tools are virtually essential for anyone undertaking any major repairs to a motor vehicle, and are additional to those given in the *Maintenance and minor repair* list. Included in this list is a comprehensive set of sockets. Although these are expensive, they will be found invaluable as they are so versatile - particularly if various drives are included in the set. We recommend the half-inch square-drive type, as this can be used with most proprietary torque wrenches.

The tools in this list will sometimes need to be supplemented by tools from the *Special* list:

☐ *Sockets (or box spanners) to cover range in previous list (including Torx sockets)*
☐ *Reversible ratchet drive (for use with sockets)*
☐ *Extension piece, 250 mm (for use with sockets)*
☐ *Universal joint (for use with sockets)*
☐ *Flexible handle or sliding T "breaker bar" (for use with sockets)*
☐ *Torque wrench (for use with sockets)*
☐ *Self-locking grips*
☐ *Ball pein hammer*
☐ *Soft-faced mallet (plastic or rubber)*
☐ *Screwdrivers:*
  Flat blade - long & sturdy, short (chubby), and narrow (electrician's) types
  Cross blade - long & sturdy, and short (chubby) types
☐ *Pliers:*
  Long-nosed
  Side cutters (electrician's)
  Circlip (internal and external)
☐ *Cold chisel - 25 mm*
☐ *Scriber*
☐ *Scraper*
☐ *Centre-punch*
☐ *Pin punch*
☐ *Hacksaw*
☐ *Brake hose clamp*
☐ *Brake/clutch bleeding kit*
☐ *Selection of twist drills*
☐ *Steel rule/straight-edge*
☐ *Allen keys (inc. splined/Torx type)*
☐ *Selection of files*
☐ *Wire brush*
☐ *Axle stands*
☐ *Jack (strong trolley or hydraulic type)*
☐ *Light with extension lead*
☐ *Universal electrical multi-meter*

Sockets and reversible ratchet drive

Brake bleeding kit

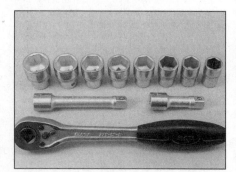
Torx key, socket and bit

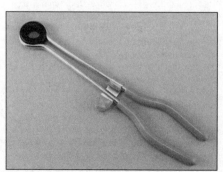
Hose clamp

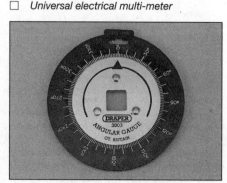
Angular-tightening gauge

Special tools

The tools in this list are those which are not used regularly, are expensive to buy, or which need to be used in accordance with their manufacturers' instructions. Unless relatively difficult mechanical jobs are undertaken frequently, it will not be economic to buy many of these tools. Where this is the case, you could consider clubbing together with friends (or joining a motorists' club) to make a joint purchase, or borrowing the tools against a deposit from a local garage or tool hire specialist. It is worth noting that many of the larger DIY superstores now carry a large range of special tools for hire at modest rates.

The following list contains only those tools and instruments freely available to the public, and not those special tools produced by the vehicle manufacturer specifically for its dealer network. You will find occasional references to these manufacturers' special tools in the text of this manual. Generally, an alternative method of doing the job without the vehicle manufacturers' special tool is given. However, sometimes there is no alternative to using them. Where this is the case and the relevant tool cannot be bought or borrowed, you will have to entrust the work to a dealer.

- [ ] Angular-tightening gauge
- [ ] Valve spring compressor
- [ ] Valve grinding tool
- [ ] Piston ring compressor
- [ ] Piston ring removal/installation tool
- [ ] Cylinder bore hone
- [ ] Balljoint separator
- [ ] Coil spring compressors (where applicable)
- [ ] Two/three-legged hub and bearing puller
- [ ] Impact screwdriver
- [ ] Micrometer and/or vernier calipers
- [ ] Dial gauge
- [ ] Stroboscopic timing light
- [ ] Dwell angle meter/tachometer
- [ ] Fault code reader
- [ ] Cylinder compression gauge
- [ ] Hand-operated vacuum pump and gauge
- [ ] Clutch plate alignment set
- [ ] Brake shoe steady spring cup removal tool
- [ ] Bush and bearing removal/installation set
- [ ] Stud extractors
- [ ] Tap and die set
- [ ] Lifting tackle
- [ ] Trolley jack

Buying tools

Reputable motor accessory shops and superstores often offer excellent quality tools at discount prices, so it pays to shop around.

Remember, you don't have to buy the most expensive items on the shelf, but it is always advisable to steer clear of the very cheap tools. Beware of 'bargains' offered on market stalls or at car boot sales. There are plenty of good tools around at reasonable prices, but always aim to purchase items which meet the relevant national safety standards. If in doubt, ask the proprietor or manager of the shop for advice before making a purchase.

Care and maintenance of tools

Having purchased a reasonable tool kit, it is necessary to keep the tools in a clean and serviceable condition. After use, always wipe off any dirt, grease and metal particles using a clean, dry cloth, before putting the tools away. Never leave them lying around after they have been used. A simple tool rack on the garage or workshop wall for items such as screwdrivers and pliers is a good idea. Store all normal spanners and sockets in a metal box. Any measuring instruments, gauges, meters, etc, must be carefully stored where they cannot be damaged or become rusty.

Take a little care when tools are used. Hammer heads inevitably become marked, and screwdrivers lose the keen edge on their blades from time to time. A little timely attention with emery cloth or a file will soon restore items like this to a good finish.

Working facilities

Not to be forgotten when discussing tools is the workshop itself. If anything more than routine maintenance is to be carried out, a suitable working area becomes essential.

It is appreciated that many an owner-mechanic is forced by circumstances to remove an engine or similar item without the benefit of a garage or workshop. Having done this, any repairs should always be done under the cover of a roof.

Wherever possible, any dismantling should be done on a clean, flat workbench or table at a suitable working height.

Any workbench needs a vice; one with a jaw opening of 100 mm is suitable for most jobs. As mentioned previously, some clean dry storage space is also required for tools, as well as for any lubricants, cleaning fluids, touch-up paints etc, which become necessary.

Another item which may be required, and which has a much more general usage, is an electric drill with a chuck capacity of at least 8 mm. This, together with a good range of twist drills, is virtually essential for fitting accessories.

Last, but not least, always keep a supply of old newspapers and clean, lint-free rags available, and try to keep any working area as clean as possible.

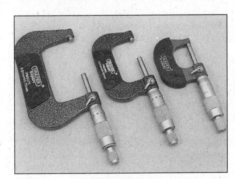
Micrometers

Dial test indicator ("dial gauge")

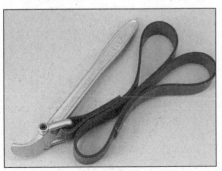
Strap wrench

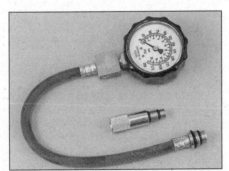
Compression tester

Fault code reader

This is a guide to getting your vehicle through the MOT test. Obviously it will not be possible to examine the vehicle to the same standard as the professional MOT tester. However, working through the following checks will enable you to identify any problem areas before submitting the vehicle for the test.

It has only been possible to summarise the test requirements here, based on the regulations in force at the time of printing. Test standards are becoming increasingly stringent, although there are some exemptions for older vehicles.

An assistant will be needed to help carry out some of these checks.

The checks have been sub-divided into four categories, as follows:

1 Checks carried out **FROM THE DRIVER'S SEAT**

2 Checks carried out **WITH THE VEHICLE ON THE GROUND**

3 Checks carried out **WITH THE VEHICLE RAISED AND THE WHEELS FREE TO TURN**

4 Checks carried out on **YOUR VEHICLE'S EXHAUST EMISSION SYSTEM**

---

1 Checks carried out **FROM THE DRIVER'S SEAT**

Handbrake

☐ Test the operation of the handbrake. Excessive travel (too many clicks) indicates incorrect brake or cable adjustment.
☐ Check that the handbrake cannot be released by tapping the lever sideways. Check the security of the lever mountings.

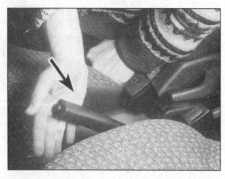

Footbrake

☐ Depress the brake pedal and check that it does not creep down to the floor, indicating a master cylinder fault. Release the pedal, wait a few seconds, then depress it again. If the pedal travels nearly to the floor before firm resistance is felt, brake adjustment or repair is necessary. If the pedal feels spongy, there is air in the hydraulic system which must be removed by bleeding.

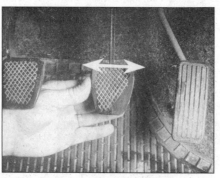

☐ Check that the brake pedal is secure and in good condition. Check also for signs of fluid leaks on the pedal, floor or carpets, which would indicate failed seals in the brake master cylinder.
☐ Check the servo unit (when applicable) by operating the brake pedal several times, then keeping the pedal depressed and starting the engine. As the engine starts, the pedal will move down slightly. If not, the vacuum hose or the servo itself may be faulty.

Steering wheel and column

☐ Examine the steering wheel for fractures or looseness of the hub, spokes or rim.
☐ Move the steering wheel from side to side and then up and down. Check that the steering wheel is not loose on the column, indicating wear or a loose retaining nut. Continue moving the steering wheel as before, but also turn it slightly from left to right.
☐ Check that the steering wheel is not loose on the column, and that there is no abnormal

movement of the steering wheel, indicating wear in the column support bearings or couplings.

Windscreen, mirrors and sunvisor

☐ The windscreen must be free of cracks or other significant damage within the driver's field of view. (Small stone chips are acceptable.) Rear view mirrors must be secure, intact, and capable of being adjusted.

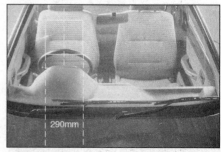

☐ The driver's sunvisor must be capable of being stored in the "up" position.

Seat belts and seats

Note: *The following checks are applicable to all seat belts, front and rear.*

☐ Examine the webbing of all the belts (including rear belts if fitted) for cuts, serious fraying or deterioration. Fasten and unfasten each belt to check the buckles. If applicable, check the retracting mechanism. Check the security of all seat belt mountings accessible from inside the vehicle.

☐ Seat belts with pre-tensioners, once activated, have a "flag" or similar showing on the seat belt stalk. This, in itself, is not a reason for test failure.

☐ The front seats themselves must be securely attached and the backrests must lock in the upright position.

Doors

☐ Both front doors must be able to be opened and closed from outside and inside, and must latch securely when closed.

2 Checks carried out WITH THE VEHICLE ON THE GROUND

Vehicle identification

☐ Number plates must be in good condition, secure and legible, with letters and numbers correctly spaced – spacing at (A) should be at least twice that at (B).

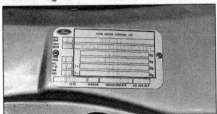

☐ The VIN plate and/or homologation plate must be legible.

Electrical equipment

☐ Switch on the ignition and check the operation of the horn.

☐ Check the windscreen washers and wipers, examining the wiper blades; renew damaged or perished blades. Also check the operation of the stop-lights.

☐ Check the operation of the sidelights and number plate lights. The lenses and reflectors must be secure, clean and undamaged.

☐ Check the operation and alignment of the headlights. The headlight reflectors must not be tarnished and the lenses must be undamaged.

☐ Switch on the ignition and check the operation of the direction indicators (including the instrument panel tell-tale) and the hazard warning lights. Operation of the sidelights and stop-lights must not affect the indicators - if it does, the cause is usually a bad earth at the rear light cluster.

☐ Check the operation of the rear foglight(s), including the warning light on the instrument panel or in the switch.

☐ The ABS warning light must illuminate in accordance with the manufacturers' design. For most vehicles, the ABS warning light should illuminate when the ignition is switched on, and (if the system is operating properly) extinguish after a few seconds. Refer to the owner's handbook.

Footbrake

☐ Examine the master cylinder, brake pipes and servo unit for leaks, loose mountings, corrosion or other damage.

☐ The fluid reservoir must be secure and the fluid level must be between the upper (**A**) and lower (**B**) markings.

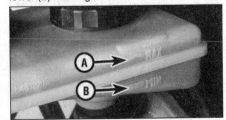

☐ Inspect both front brake flexible hoses for cracks or deterioration of the rubber. Turn the steering from lock to lock, and ensure that the hoses do not contact the wheel, tyre, or any part of the steering or suspension mechanism. With the brake pedal firmly depressed, check the hoses for bulges or leaks under pressure.

Steering and suspension

☐ Have your assistant turn the steering wheel from side to side slightly, up to the point where the steering gear just begins to transmit this movement to the roadwheels. Check for excessive free play between the steering wheel and the steering gear, indicating wear or insecurity of the steering column joints, the column-to-steering gear coupling, or the steering gear itself.

☐ Have your assistant turn the steering wheel more vigorously in each direction, so that the roadwheels just begin to turn. As this is done, examine all the steering joints, linkages, fittings and attachments. Renew any component that shows signs of wear or damage. On vehicles with power steering, check the security and condition of the steering pump, drivebelt and hoses.

☐ Check that the vehicle is standing level, and at approximately the correct ride height.

Shock absorbers

☐ Depress each corner of the vehicle in turn, then release it. The vehicle should rise and then settle in its normal position. If the vehicle continues to rise and fall, the shock absorber is defective. A shock absorber which has seized will also cause the vehicle to fail.

Exhaust system

☐ Start the engine. With your assistant holding a rag over the tailpipe, check the entire system for leaks. Repair or renew leaking sections.

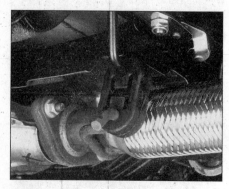

3 Checks carried out **WITH THE VEHICLE RAISED AND THE WHEELS FREE TO TURN**

Jack up the front and rear of the vehicle, and securely support it on axle stands. Position the stands clear of the suspension assemblies. Ensure that the wheels are clear of the ground and that the steering can be turned from lock to lock.

Steering mechanism

☐ Have your assistant turn the steering from lock to lock. Check that the steering turns smoothly, and that no part of the steering mechanism, including a wheel or tyre, fouls any brake hose or pipe or any part of the body structure.
☐ Examine the steering rack rubber gaiters for damage or insecurity of the retaining clips. If power steering is fitted, check for signs of damage or leakage of the fluid hoses, pipes or connections. Also check for excessive stiffness or binding of the steering, a missing split pin or locking device, or severe corrosion of the body structure within 30 cm of any steering component attachment point.

Front and rear suspension and wheel bearings

☐ Starting at the front right-hand side, grasp the roadwheel at the 3 o'clock and 9 o'clock positions and rock gently but firmly. Check for free play or insecurity at the wheel bearings, suspension balljoints, or suspension mountings, pivots and attachments.
☐ Now grasp the wheel at the 12 o'clock and 6 o'clock positions and repeat the previous inspection. Spin the wheel, and check for roughness or tightness of the front wheel bearing.

☐ If excess free play is suspected at a component pivot point, this can be confirmed by using a large screwdriver or similar tool and levering between the mounting and the component attachment. This will confirm whether the wear is in the pivot bush, its retaining bolt, or in the mounting itself (the bolt holes can often become elongated).

☐ Carry out all the above checks at the other front wheel, and then at both rear wheels.

Springs and shock absorbers

☐ Examine the suspension struts (when applicable) for serious fluid leakage, corrosion, or damage to the casing. Also check the security of the mounting points.
☐ If coil springs are fitted, check that the spring ends locate in their seats, and that the spring is not corroded, cracked or broken.
☐ If leaf springs are fitted, check that all leaves are intact, that the axle is securely attached to each spring, and that there is no deterioration of the spring eye mountings, bushes, and shackles.

☐ The same general checks apply to vehicles fitted with other suspension types, such as torsion bars, hydraulic displacer units, etc. Ensure that all mountings and attachments are secure, that there are no signs of excessive wear, corrosion or damage, and (on hydraulic types) that there are no fluid leaks or damaged pipes.
☐ Inspect the shock absorbers for signs of serious fluid leakage. Check for wear of the mounting bushes or attachments, or damage to the body of the unit.

Driveshafts (fwd vehicles only)

☐ Rotate each front wheel in turn and inspect the constant velocity joint gaiters for splits or damage. Also check that each driveshaft is straight and undamaged.

Braking system

☐ If possible without dismantling, check brake pad wear and disc condition. Ensure that the friction lining material has not worn excessively, (A) and that the discs are not fractured, pitted, scored or badly worn (B).

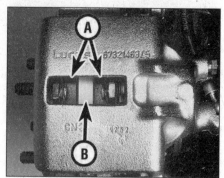

☐ Examine all the rigid brake pipes underneath the vehicle, and the flexible hose(s) at the rear. Look for corrosion, chafing or insecurity of the pipes, and for signs of bulging under pressure, chafing, splits or deterioration of the flexible hoses.
☐ Look for signs of fluid leaks at the brake calipers or on the brake backplates. Repair or renew leaking components.
☐ Slowly spin each wheel, while your assistant depresses and releases the footbrake. Ensure that each brake is operating and does not bind when the pedal is released.

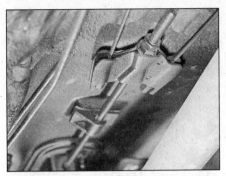

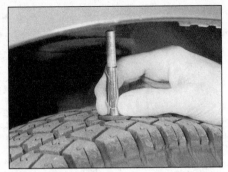

CO emissions (mixture)

☐ The MOT tester has access to the CO limits for all vehicles. The CO level is measured at idle speed, and at 'fast idle' (2500 to 3000 rpm). The following limits are given as a general guide:

At idle speed – Less than 0.5% CO
At 'fast idle' – Less than 0.3% CO
Lambda reading – 0.97 to 1.03

☐ If the CO level is too high, this may point to poor maintenance, a fuel injection system problem, faulty lambda (oxygen) sensor or catalytic converter. Try an injector cleaning treatment, and check the vehicle's ECU for fault codes.

☐ Examine the handbrake mechanism, checking for frayed or broken cables, excessive corrosion, or wear or insecurity of the linkage. Check that the mechanism works on each relevant wheel, and releases fully, without binding.

☐ It is not possible to test brake efficiency without special equipment, but a road test can be carried out later to check that the vehicle pulls up in a straight line.

Fuel and exhaust systems

☐ Inspect the fuel tank (including the filler cap), fuel pipes, hoses and unions. All components must be secure and free from leaks.

☐ Examine the exhaust system over its entire length, checking for any damaged, broken or missing mountings, security of the retaining clamps and rust or corrosion.

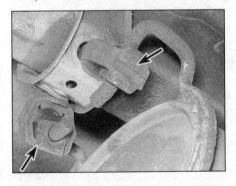

Wheels and tyres

☐ Examine the sidewalls and tread area of each tyre in turn. Check for cuts, tears, lumps, bulges, separation of the tread, and exposure of the ply or cord due to wear or damage. Check that the tyre bead is correctly seated on the wheel rim, that the valve is sound and properly seated, and that the wheel is not distorted or damaged.

☐ Check that the tyres are of the correct size for the vehicle, that they are of the same size

and type on each axle, and that the pressures are correct.

☐ Check the tyre tread depth. The legal minimum at the time of writing is 1.6 mm over at least three-quarters of the tread width. Abnormal tread wear may indicate incorrect front wheel alignment.

Body corrosion

☐ Check the condition of the entire vehicle structure for signs of corrosion in load-bearing areas. (These include chassis box sections, side sills, cross-members, pillars, and all suspension, steering, braking system and seat belt mountings and anchorages.) Any corrosion which has seriously reduced the thickness of a load-bearing area is likely to cause the vehicle to fail. In this case professional repairs are likely to be needed.

☐ Damage or corrosion which causes sharp or otherwise dangerous edges to be exposed will also cause the vehicle to fail.

4 Checks carried out on YOUR VEHICLE'S EXHAUST EMISSION SYSTEM

Petrol models

☐ The engine should be warmed up, and running well (ignition system in good order, air filter element clean, etc).

☐ Before testing, run the engine at around 2500 rpm for 20 seconds. Let the engine drop to idle, and watch for smoke from the exhaust. If the idle speed is too high, or if dense blue or black smoke emerges for more than 5 seconds, the vehicle will fail. Typically, blue smoke signifies oil burning (engine wear); black smoke means unburnt fuel (dirty air cleaner element, or other fuel system fault).

☐ An exhaust gas analyser for measuring carbon monoxide (CO) and hydrocarbons (HC) is now needed. If one cannot be hired or borrowed, have a local garage perform the check.

HC emissions

☐ The MOT tester has access to HC limits for all vehicles. The HC level is measured at 'fast idle' (2500 to 3000 rpm). The following limits are given as a general guide:

At 'fast idle' – Less then 200 ppm

☐ Excessive HC emissions are typically caused by oil being burnt (worn engine), or by a blocked crankcase ventilation system ('breather'). If the engine oil is old and thin, an oil change may help. If the engine is running badly, check the vehicle's ECU for fault codes.

Diesel models

☐ The only emission test for diesel engines is measuring exhaust smoke density, using a calibrated smoke meter. The test involves accelerating the engine at least 3 times to its maximum unloaded speed.

Note: *On engines with a timing belt, it is VITAL that the belt is in good condition before the test is carried out.*

☐ With the engine warmed up, it is first purged by running at around 2500 rpm for 20 seconds. A governor check is then carried out, by slowly accelerating the engine to its maximum speed. After this, the smoke meter is connected, and the engine is accelerated quickly to maximum speed three times. If the smoke density is less than the limits given below, the vehicle will pass:

Non-turbo vehicles: 2.5m-1
Turbocharged vehicles: 3.0m-1

☐ If excess smoke is produced, try fitting a new air cleaner element, or using an injector cleaning treatment. If the engine is running badly, where applicable, check the vehicle's ECU for fault codes. Also check the vehicle's EGR system, where applicable. At high mileages, the injectors may require professional attention.

Engine

- [ ] Engine fails to rotate when attempting to start
- [ ] Engine rotates, but will not start
- [ ] Engine difficult to start when cold
- [ ] Engine difficult to start when hot
- [ ] Starter motor noisy or excessively-rough in engagement
- [ ] Engine starts, but stops immediately
- [ ] Engine idles erratically
- [ ] Engine misfires at idle speed
- [ ] Engine misfires throughout the driving speed range
- [ ] Engine hesitates on acceleration
- [ ] Engine stalls
- [ ] Engine lacks power
- [ ] Engine backfires
- [ ] Oil pressure warning light illuminated with engine running
- [ ] Engine runs-on after switching off
- [ ] Engine noises

Cooling system

- [ ] Overheating
- [ ] Overcooling
- [ ] External coolant leakage
- [ ] Internal coolant leakage
- [ ] Corrosion

Fuel and exhaust systems

- [ ] Excessive fuel consumption
- [ ] Fuel leakage and/or fuel odour
- [ ] Excessive noise or fumes from exhaust system

Clutch

- [ ] Pedal travels to floor – no pressure or very little resistance
- [ ] Clutch fails to disengage (unable to select gears)
- [ ] Clutch slips (engine speed increases, with no increase in vehicle speed)
- [ ] Judder as clutch is engaged
- [ ] Noise when depressing or releasing clutch pedal

Manual transmission

- [ ] Noisy in neutral with engine running
- [ ] Noisy in one particular gear
- [ ] Difficulty engaging gears
- [ ] Jumps out of gear
- [ ] Vibration
- [ ] Lubricant leaks

Automatic transmission

- [ ] Fluid leakage
- [ ] Transmission fluid brown, or has burned smell
- [ ] General gear selection problems
- [ ] Transmission will not downshift (kickdown) with accelerator fully depressed
- [ ] Engine will not start in any gear, or starts in gears other than Park or Neutral
- [ ] Transmission slips, shifts roughly, is noisy, or has no drive in forward or reverse gears

Driveshafts

- [ ] Clicking or knocking noise on turns (at slow speed on full-lock)
- [ ] Vibration when accelerating or decelerating

Braking system

- [ ] Car pulls to one side under braking
- [ ] Noise (grinding or high-pitched squeal) when brakes applied
- [ ] Excessive brake pedal travel
- [ ] Brake pedal feels spongy when depressed
- [ ] Excessive brake pedal effort required to stop car
- [ ] Judder felt through brake pedal or steering wheel when braking
- [ ] Brakes binding
- [ ] Rear wheels locking under normal braking

Suspension and steering systems

- [ ] Car pulls to one side
- [ ] Wheel wobble and vibration
- [ ] Excessive pitching and/or rolling around corners, or during braking
- [ ] Wandering or general instability
- [ ] Excessively-stiff steering
- [ ] Excessive play in steering
- [ ] Lack of power assistance
- [ ] Tyre wear excessive

Electrical system

- [ ] Battery will not hold a charge for more than a few days
- [ ] Ignition/no-charge warning light remains illuminated with engine running
- [ ] Ignition/no-charge warning light fails to come on
- [ ] Lights inoperative
- [ ] Instrument readings inaccurate or erratic
- [ ] Horn inoperative, or unsatisfactory in operation
- [ ] Windscreen/tailgate wipers inoperative, or unsatisfactory in operation
- [ ] Windscreen/tailgate washers inoperative, or unsatisfactory in operation
- [ ] Electric windows inoperative, or unsatisfactory in operation
- [ ] Central locking system inoperative, or unsatisfactory in operation

Introduction

The car owner who does his or her own maintenance according to the recommended service schedules should not have to use this section of the manual very often. Modern component reliability is such that, provided those items subject to wear or deterioration are inspected or renewed at the specified intervals, sudden failure is comparatively rare. Faults do not usually just happen as a result of sudden failure, but develop over a period of time. Major mechanical failures in particular are usually preceded by characteristic symptoms over hundreds or even thousands of miles. Those components which do occasionally fail without warning are often small and easily carried in the car.

With any fault-finding, the first step is to decide where to begin investigations. Sometimes this is obvious, but on other occasions, a little detective work will be necessary. The owner who makes half a dozen haphazard adjustments or replacements may be successful in curing a fault (or its symptoms), but will be none the wiser if the fault recurs, and ultimately may have spent more time and money than was necessary. A calm and logical approach will be found to be more satisfactory in the long run. Always take into account any warning signs or abnormalities that may have been noticed in the period preceding the fault – power loss, high or low gauge readings, unusual smells, etc – and remember that failure of components such as fuses or spark plugs may only be pointers to some underlying fault.

The pages which follow provide an easy-reference guide to the more common problems which may occur during the operation of the vehicle. These problems and their possible causes are grouped under headings denoting various components or systems, such as Engine, Cooling system, etc. The general Chapter which deals with the problem is also shown in brackets; refer to the relevant part of that Chapter for system-specific information. Whatever the fault, certain basic principles apply. These are as follows:

Verify the fault. This is simply a matter of being sure you know exactly what the symptoms are before starting work. This is particularly important if you are investigating a fault for someone else, who may not have described it very accurately.

Don't overlook the obvious. For example, if it won't start, is there fuel in the tank? (Don't take anyone else's word on this particular point, and don't trust the fuel gauge either!) If an electrical fault is indicated, look for loose or broken wires before digging out the test gear.

Cure the disease, not the symptom. Substituting a flat battery with a fully-charged one will get you off the hard shoulder, but if the underlying cause is not attended to, the new battery will go the same way.

Don't take anything for granted. Particularly, don't forget that a 'new' component may itself be defective (especially if it's been rattling around in the boot for months), and don't leave components out of a fault diagnosis sequence just because they are new or recently-fitted. When you do finally diagnose a difficult fault, you'll probably realise that all the evidence was there from the start.

Consider what work, if any, has recently been carried out. Many faults arise through careless or hurried work. For instance, if any work has been performed under the bonnet, could some of the wiring have been dislodged or incorrectly routed, or a hose trapped? Have all the fasteners been properly tightened? Were new, genuine parts and new gaskets used? There is often a certain amount of detective work to be done in this case, as an apparently-unrelated task can have far-reaching consequences.

Engine

Engine fails to rotate when attempting to start

☐ Battery terminal connections loose or corroded (Weekly checks).
☐ Battery discharged or faulty (Chapter 5A).
☐ Broken, loose or disconnected wiring in the starting circuit (Chapter 5A).
☐ Automatic transmission not in P or N (Chapter 7B).
☐ Defective starter solenoid or switch (Chapter 5A).
☐ Defective starter motor (Chapter 5A).
☐ Starter pinion or flywheel ring gear teeth loose or broken (Chapters 2A, 2B, 2C and 5A).
☐ Engine earth strap broken or disconnected (Chapter 5A).

Engine rotates, but will not start

☐ Fuel tank empty.
☐ Battery discharged (engine rotates slowly) (Chapter 5A).
☐ Battery terminal connections loose or corroded (Weekly checks).
☐ Immobiliser fault (Chapter 12).
☐ Ignition components damp or damaged (Chapters 1 and 5B).
☐ Broken, loose or disconnected wiring in the ignition circuit (Chapter 5B).
☐ Worn, faulty or incorrectly-gapped spark plugs (Chapter 1).
☐ Fuel injection system fault (Chapter 4A).
☐ Major mechanical failure (eg camshaft drive) (Chapter 2A, 2B or 2C).

Engine difficult to start when cold

☐ Battery discharged (Chapter 5A).
☐ Battery terminal connections loose or corroded (Weekly checks).
☐ Worn, faulty or incorrectly-gapped spark plugs (Chapter 1).
☐ Fuel injection system fault (Chapter 4A).
☐ Other ignition system fault (Chapter 5B).
☐ Low cylinder compressions (Chapter 2A or 2B).

Engine difficult to start when hot

☐ Air filter element dirty or clogged (Chapter 1).
☐ Fuel injection system fault (Chapter 4A).
☐ Low cylinder compressions (Chapter 2A or 2B).

Starter motor noisy or excessively-rough in engagement

☐ Starter pinion or flywheel ring gear teeth loose or broken (Chapters 2A, 2B and 5A).
☐ Starter motor mounting bolts loose or missing (Chapter 5A).
☐ Starter motor internal components worn or damaged (Chapter 5A).

Engine starts, but stops immediately

☐ Loose or faulty electrical connections in the ignition circuit (Chapter 5B).
☐ Vacuum leak at the throttle body or inlet manifold (Chapter 4A).
☐ Blocked injector/fuel injection system fault (Chapter 4A).

Engine idles erratically

☐ Air filter element clogged (Chapter 1).
☐ Vacuum leak at the throttle body, inlet manifold or associated hoses (Chapter 4A).
☐ Worn, faulty or incorrectly-gapped spark plugs (Chapter 1).
☐ Uneven or low cylinder compressions (Chapter 2A or 2B).
☐ Camshaft lobes worn (Chapter 2A or 2B).
☐ Timing belt incorrectly tensioned (Chapter 2A or 2B).
☐ Blocked injector/fuel injection system fault (Chapter 4A).

Engine misfires at idle speed

☐ Worn, faulty or incorrectly-gapped spark plugs (Chapter 1).
☐ Faulty spark plug HT leads (Chapter 5B).
☐ Vacuum leak at the throttle body, inlet manifold or associated hoses (Chapter 4A).
☐ Blocked injector/fuel injection system fault (Chapter 4A).
☐ Distributor cap cracked or tracking internally (where applicable) (Chapter 5B).
☐ Uneven or low cylinder compressions (Chapter 2A or 2B).
☐ Disconnected, leaking, or perished crankcase ventilation hoses (Chapter 4B).

Engine misfires throughout the driving speed range

☐ Fuel filter choked (Chapter 1).
☐ Fuel pump faulty, or delivery pressure low (Chapter 4A).
☐ Fuel tank vent blocked, or fuel pipes restricted (Chapter 4A).
☐ Vacuum leak at the throttle body, inlet manifold or associated hoses (Chapter 4A).
☐ Worn, faulty or incorrectly-gapped spark plugs (Chapter 1).
☐ Faulty spark plug HT leads (Chapter 5B).
☐ Faulty DIS module (Chapter 5B).
☐ Uneven or low cylinder compressions (Chapter 2A or 2B).
☐ Blocked injector/fuel injection system fault (Chapter 4A).

Engine hesitates on acceleration

☐ Worn, faulty or incorrectly-gapped spark plugs (Chapter 1).
☐ Vacuum leak at the throttle body, inlet manifold or associated hoses (Chapter 4A).
☐ Blocked injector/fuel injection system fault (Chapter 4A).

Engine (continued)

Engine stalls

- ☐ Vacuum leak at the throttle body, inlet manifold or associated hoses (Chapter 4A).
- ☐ Fuel filter choked (Chapter 1).
- ☐ Fuel pump faulty, or delivery pressure low (Chapter 4A).
- ☐ Fuel tank vent blocked, or fuel pipes restricted (Chapter 4A).
- ☐ Blocked injector/fuel injection system fault (Chapter 4A).

Engine lacks power

- ☐ Timing belt incorrectly fitted or tensioned (Chapter 2A or 2B).
- ☐ Fuel filter choked (Chapter 1).
- ☐ Ignition timing incorrect (Chapter 5B)
- ☐ Fuel pump faulty, or delivery pressure low (Chapter 4A).
- ☐ Uneven or low cylinder compressions (Chapter 2A or 2B).
- ☐ Worn, faulty or incorrectly-gapped spark plugs (Chapter 1).
- ☐ Vacuum leak at the throttle body, inlet manifold or associated hoses (Chapter 4A).
- ☐ Blocked injector/fuel injection system fault (Chapter 4A).
- ☐ Brakes binding (Chapters 1 and 9).
- ☐ Clutch slipping (Chapter 6).

Engine backfires

- ☐ Timing belt incorrectly fitted or tensioned (Chapter 2A or 2B).
- ☐ Vacuum leak at the throttle body, inlet manifold or associated hoses (Chapter 4A).
- ☐ Blocked injector/fuel injection system fault (Chapter 4A).
- ☐ Ignition timing incorrect (Chapter 5B)

Oil pressure warning light illuminated with engine running

- ☐ Low oil level, or incorrect oil grade (Weekly checks).
- ☐ Worn engine bearings and/or oil pump (Chapter 2C).
- ☐ High engine operating temperature (Chapter 3).
- ☐ Oil pressure relief valve defective (Chapter 2A or 2B).
- ☐ Oil pick-up strainer clogged (Chapter 2A or 2B).

Engine runs-on after switching off

- ☐ Excessive carbon build-up in engine (Chapter 2C).
- ☐ High engine operating temperature (Chapter 3).
- ☐ Fuel injection system fault (Chapter 4A).

Engine noises

Pre-ignition (pinking) or knocking during acceleration or under load

- ☐ Ignition timing incorrect/ignition system fault (Chapter 5B).
- ☐ Incorrect grade of spark plug (Chapter 1).
- ☐ Incorrect grade of fuel (Chapter 1).
- ☐ Vacuum leak at the throttle body, inlet manifold or associated hoses (Chapter 4A).
- ☐ Excessive carbon build-up in engine (Chapter 2C).
- ☐ Blocked injector/fuel injection system fault (Chapter 4A).

Whistling or wheezing noises

- ☐ Leaking inlet manifold or throttle body gasket (Chapter 4A).
- ☐ Leaking exhaust manifold gasket or pipe-to-manifold joint (Chapter 4A).
- ☐ Leaking vacuum hose (Chapters 4, 5B and 9).
- ☐ Blowing cylinder head gasket (Chapter 2A or 2B).

Tapping or rattling noises

- ☐ Worn hydraulic tappet or camshaft (Chapter 2A or 2B).
- ☐ Ancillary component fault (water pump, alternator, etc) (Chapters 3, 5A, etc).

Knocking or thumping noises

- ☐ Worn big-end bearings (regular heavy knocking, perhaps less under load) (Chapter 2C).
- ☐ Worn main bearings (rumbling and knocking, perhaps worsening under load) (Chapter 2C).
- ☐ Piston slap (most noticeable when cold) (Chapter 2C).
- ☐ Ancillary component fault (water pump, alternator, etc) (Chapters 3, 5A, etc).

Cooling system

Overheating

- ☐ Insufficient coolant in system (Weekly checks).
- ☐ Auxiliary drivebelt broken or drivebelt tensioner faulty (Chapter 1 or 2)
- ☐ Thermostat faulty (Chapter 3).
- ☐ Radiator core blocked, or grille restricted (Chapter 3).
- ☐ Electric cooling fan or thermoswitch faulty (Chapter 3).
- ☐ Pressure cap faulty (Chapter 3).
- ☐ Ignition timing incorrect/ignition system fault (Chapter 5B).
- ☐ Inaccurate temperature gauge sender unit (Chapter 3).
- ☐ Airlock in cooling system (Chapter 1).

Overcooling

- ☐ Thermostat faulty (Chapter 3).
- ☐ Inaccurate temperature gauge sender unit (Chapter 3).

External coolant leakage

- ☐ Deteriorated or damaged hoses or hose clips (Chapter 1).
- ☐ Radiator core or heater matrix leaking (Chapter 3).
- ☐ Pressure cap faulty (Chapter 3).
- ☐ Water pump seal leaking (Chapter 3).
- ☐ Boiling due to overheating (Chapter 3).
- ☐ Core plug leaking (Chapter 2C).

Internal coolant leakage

- ☐ Leaking cylinder head gasket (Chapter 2A or 2B).
- ☐ Cracked cylinder head or cylinder bore (Chapter 2A or 2B).

Corrosion

- ☐ Infrequent draining and flushing (Chapter 1).
- ☐ Incorrect coolant mixture or inappropriate coolant type (Chapter 1).

Fuel and exhaust systems

Excessive fuel consumption

☐ Air filter element dirty or clogged (Chapter 1).
☐ Fuel injection system fault (Chapter 4A).
☐ Ignition timing incorrect/ignition system fault (Chapter 5B).
☐ Tyres under-inflated (Weekly checks).
☐ Brakes binding (Chapter 9).

Fuel leakage and/or fuel odour

☐ Damaged or corroded fuel tank, pipes or connections (Chapter 4).

Excessive noise or fumes from exhaust system

☐ Leaking exhaust system or manifold joints (Chapters 1 and 4).
☐ Leaking, corroded or damaged silencers or pipe (Chapters 1 and 4).
☐ Broken mountings causing body or suspension contact (Chapter 1).

Clutch

Pedal travels to floor – no pressure or very little resistance

☐ Broken clutch cable (Chapter 6).
☐ Cable automatic adjuster faulty, or cable out of adjustment (Chapter 6).
☐ Broken clutch release bearing or fork (Chapter 6).
☐ Broken diaphragm spring in clutch pressure plate (Chapter 6).

Clutch fails to disengage (unable to select gears)

☐ Cable automatic adjuster faulty, or cable out of adjustment (Chapter 6).
☐ Clutch disc sticking on gearbox input shaft splines (Chapter 6).
☐ Clutch disc sticking to flywheel or pressure plate (Chapter 6).
☐ Faulty pressure plate assembly (Chapter 6).
☐ Clutch release mechanism worn or incorrectly assembled (Chapter 6).
☐ Clutch pedal bracket distorted or partly collapsed (Chapter 9, Section 14).

Clutch slips (engine speed increases, with no increase in vehicle speed)

☐ Cable automatic adjuster faulty, or cable out of adjustment (Chapter 6).
☐ Clutch disc linings excessively worn (Chapter 6).
☐ Clutch disc linings contaminated with oil or grease (Chapter 6).
☐ Faulty pressure plate or weak diaphragm spring (Chapter 6).

Judder as clutch is engaged

☐ Clutch disc linings contaminated with oil or grease (Chapter 6).
☐ Clutch disc linings excessively worn (Chapter 6).
☐ Clutch cable sticking or frayed – cable-operated clutch (Chapter 6).
☐ Faulty or distorted pressure plate or diaphragm spring (Chapter 6).
☐ Worn or loose engine or gearbox mountings (Chapter 2A or 2B).
☐ Clutch disc hub or gearbox input shaft splines worn (Chapter 6).

Noise when depressing or releasing clutch pedal

☐ Worn clutch release bearing (Chapter 6).
☐ Worn or dry clutch pedal bushes (Chapter 6).
☐ Faulty pressure plate assembly (Chapter 6).
☐ Pressure plate diaphragm spring broken (Chapter 6).
☐ Broken clutch disc cushioning springs (Chapter 6).

Manual transmission

Noisy in neutral with engine running

☐ Input shaft bearings worn (noise apparent with clutch pedal released, but not when depressed) (Chapter 7A).*
☐ Clutch release bearing worn (noise apparent with clutch pedal depressed, possibly less when released) (Chapter 6).

Noisy in one particular gear

☐ Worn, damaged or chipped gear teeth (Chapter 7A).*

Difficulty engaging gears

☐ Clutch fault (Chapter 6).
☐ Worn or damaged gearchange linkage/cable (Chapter 7A).
☐ Incorrectly-adjusted gearchange linkage/cable (Chapter 7A).
☐ Worn synchroniser units (Chapter 7A).*

Jumps out of gear

☐ Worn or damaged gearchange linkage/cable (Chapter 7A).

☐ Incorrectly-adjusted gearchange linkage/cable (Chapter 7A).
☐ Worn synchroniser units (Chapter 7A).*
☐ Worn selector forks (Chapter 7A).*

Vibration

☐ Lack of oil (Chapter 1).
☐ Worn bearings (Chapter 7A).*

Lubricant leaks

☐ Leaking differential output oil seal (Chapter 7A).
☐ Leaking housing joint (Chapter 7A).*
☐ Leaking input shaft oil seal (Chapter 7A).*

Although the corrective action necessary to remedy the symptoms described is beyond the scope of the home mechanic, the above information should be helpful in isolating the cause of the condition, so that the owner can communicate clearly with a professional mechanic.

Automatic transmission

Note: *Due to the complexity of the automatic transmission, it is difficult for the home mechanic to properly diagnose and service this unit. For problems other than the following, the car should be taken to a dealer service department or automatic transmission specialist. Do not be too hasty in removing the transmission if a fault is suspected, as most of the testing is carried out with the unit still fitted.*

Fluid leakage

☐ Automatic transmission fluid is usually dark in colour. Fluid leaks should not be confused with engine oil, which can easily be blown onto the transmission by airflow.

☐ To determine the source of a leak, first remove all built-up dirt and grime from the transmission housing and surrounding areas using a degreasing agent, or by steam-cleaning. Drive the car at low speed, so airflow will not blow the leak far from its source. Raise and support the car, and determine where the leak is coming from.

General gear selection problems

☐ Chapter 7B deals with checking and adjusting the selector cable on automatic transmissions. The following are common problems which may be caused by a poorly-adjusted cable:

a) *Engine starting in gears other than Park or Neutral.*

b) *Indicator panel indicating a gear other than the one actually being used.*

c) *Car moves when in Park or Neutral.*

d) *Poor gear shift quality or erratic gear changes.*

☐ Refer to Chapter 7B for the selector cable adjustment procedure.

Transmission will not downshift (kickdown) with accelerator pedal fully depressed

☐ Low transmission fluid level (Chapter 1).

☐ Incorrect selector cable adjustment (Chapter 7B).

Engine will not start in any gear, or starts in gears other than Park or Neutral

☐ Incorrect selector cable adjustment (Chapter 7B).

Transmission slips, shifts roughly, is noisy, or has no drive in forward or reverse gears

☐ There are many probable causes for the above problems, but unless there is a very obvious reason (such as a loose or corroded wiring plug connection on or near the transmission), the car should be taken to a VW dealer for the fault to be diagnosed. The transmission control unit incorporates a self-diagnosis facility, and any fault codes can quickly be read and interpreted by a VW dealer with the proper diagnostic equipment.

Driveshafts

Clicking or knocking noise on turns (at slow speed on full-lock)

☐ Lack of constant velocity joint lubricant, possibly due to damaged gaiter (Chapter 8).

☐ Worn outer constant velocity joint (Chapter 8).

Vibration when accelerating or decelerating

☐ Worn inner constant velocity joint (Chapter 8).

☐ Bent or distorted driveshaft (Chapter 8).

Braking system

Note: *Before assuming that a brake problem exists, make sure that the tyres are in good condition and correctly inflated, that the front wheel alignment is correct, the front wheels are balanced, and that the car is not loaded with weight in an unequal manner. Apart from checking the condition of all pipe and hose connections, any faults occurring on the anti-lock braking system should be referred to a VW dealer for diagnosis.*

Car pulls to one side under braking

- ☐ Worn, defective, damaged or contaminated brake pads/shoes on one side (Chapters 1 and 9).
- ☐ Seized or partially-seized front brake caliper/wheel cylinder piston (Chapters 1 and 9).
- ☐ A mixture of brake pad/shoe lining materials fitted between sides (Chapters 1 and 9).
- ☐ Brake caliper or backplate mounting bolts loose (Chapter 9).
- ☐ Worn or damaged steering or suspension components (Chapters 1 and 10).

Noise (grinding or high-pitched squeal) when brakes applied

- ☐ Brake pad or shoe friction lining material worn down to metal backing (Chapters 1 and 9).
- ☐ Excessive corrosion of brake disc or drum. (May be apparent after the car has been standing for some time (Chapters 1 and 9).
- ☐ Foreign object (stone chipping, etc) trapped between brake disc and shield (Chapters 1 and 9).

Excessive brake pedal travel

- ☐ Inoperative rear brake self-adjust mechanism – drum brakes (Chapters 1 and 9).
- ☐ Faulty master cylinder (Chapter 9).
- ☐ Air in hydraulic system (Chapters 1 and 9).
- ☐ Faulty vacuum servo unit (Chapter 9).

Brake pedal feels spongy when depressed

- ☐ Air in hydraulic system (Chapters 1 and 9).
- ☐ Deteriorated flexible rubber brake hoses (Chapters 1 and 9).
- ☐ Master cylinder mounting nuts loose (Chapter 9).
- ☐ Faulty master cylinder (Chapter 9).

Excessive brake pedal effort required to stop car

- ☐ Faulty vacuum servo unit (Chapter 9).
- ☐ Disconnected, damaged or insecure brake servo vacuum hose (Chapter 9).
- ☐ Primary or secondary hydraulic circuit failure (Chapter 9).
- ☐ Seized brake caliper or wheel cylinder piston(s) (Chapter 9).
- ☐ Brake pads or brake shoes incorrectly fitted (Chapters 1 and 9).
- ☐ Incorrect grade of brake pads or brake shoes fitted (Chapters 1 and 9).
- ☐ Brake pads or brake shoe linings contaminated (Chapters 1 and 9).

Judder felt through brake pedal or steering wheel when braking

- ☐ Excessive run-out or distortion of discs/drums (Chapters 1 and 9).
- ☐ Brake pad or brake shoe linings worn (Chapters 1 and 9).
- ☐ Brake caliper or brake backplate mounting bolts loose (Chapter 9).
- ☐ Wear in suspension or steering components or mountings (Chapters 1 and 10).
- ☐ Vibration through pedal – Anti-lock Braking System (ABS) in operation – no fault (models with ABS).

Brakes binding

- ☐ Seized brake caliper or wheel cylinder piston(s) (Chapter 9).
- ☐ Incorrectly-adjusted handbrake mechanism (Chapter 9).
- ☐ Faulty master cylinder (Chapter 9).

Rear wheels locking under normal braking

- ☐ Rear brake shoe linings contaminated (Chapters 1 and 9).
- ☐ Faulty brake pressure regulator (Chapter 9).

Suspension and steering

Note: *Before diagnosing suspension or steering faults, be sure that the trouble is not due to incorrect tyre pressures, mixtures of tyre types, worn tyres, or binding brakes.*

Car pulls to one side

- ☐ Defective or worn tyre (Weekly checks).
- ☐ Tyre pressure low on one side of the car (Weekly checks).
- ☐ Excessive wear in suspension or steering components (Chapters 1 and 10).
- ☐ Incorrect front wheel alignment (Chapter 10).
- ☐ Accident damage to steering or suspension components (Chapter 1).

Wheel wobble and vibration

- ☐ Front roadwheels out of balance (vibration felt mainly through the steering wheel) (Weekly checks).
- ☐ Rear roadwheels out of balance (vibration felt throughout the car) (Weekly checks).
- ☐ Roadwheels damaged or distorted (Weekly checks).
- ☐ Faulty, worn or damaged tyre (Weekly checks).
- ☐ Worn steering or suspension joints, bushes or components (Chapters 1 and 10).
- ☐ Wheel bolts loose (Chapter 1).

Excessive pitching and/or rolling around corners, or during braking

- ☐ Defective shock absorbers (Chapters 1 and 10).
- ☐ Broken or weak spring and/or suspension component (Chapters 1 and 10).
- ☐ Worn or damaged anti-roll bar or mountings (Chapter 10).

Wandering or general instability

- ☐ Incorrect front wheel alignment (Chapter 10).
- ☐ Worn steering or suspension joints, bushes or components (Chapters 1 and 10).
- ☐ Roadwheels out of balance (Weekly checks).
- ☐ Faulty or damaged tyre (Weekly checks).
- ☐ Wheel bolts loose (Chapter 1).
- ☐ Defective shock absorbers (Chapters 1 and 10).

Excessively-stiff steering

- ☐ Incorrect power steering fluid level (Weekly checks).
- ☐ Lack of steering gear lubricant (Chapter 10).
- ☐ Seized track rod end balljoint or suspension balljoint (Chapters 1 and 10).

- ☐ Broken auxiliary drivebelt or drivebelt tensioner fault (Chapter 1).
- ☐ Incorrect front wheel alignment (Chapter 10).
- ☐ Steering rack or column bent or damaged (Chapter 10).

Excessive play in steering

- ☐ Worn steering column intermediate shaft universal joint (Chapter 10).
- ☐ Worn steering track rod end balljoints (Chapters 1 and 10).
- ☐ Worn rack-and-pinion steering gear (Chapter 10).
- ☐ Worn steering or suspension joints, bushes or components (Chapters 1 and 10).

Lack of power assistance

- ☐ Broken, contaminated or incorrectly-adjusted auxiliary drivebelt (Chapter 1 or 2).
- ☐ Incorrect power steering fluid level (Weekly checks).
- ☐ Restriction in power steering fluid hoses (Chapter 1).
- ☐ Faulty power steering pump (Chapter 10).
- ☐ Faulty rack-and-pinion steering gear (Chapter 10).

Tyre wear excessive

Tyres worn on inside or outside edges

- ☐ Tyres under-inflated (wear on both edges) (Weekly checks).
- ☐ Incorrect camber or castor angles (wear on one edge only) (Chapter 10).
- ☐ Worn steering or suspension joints, bushes or components (Chapters 1 and 10).
- ☐ Excessively-hard cornering.
- ☐ Accident damage.

Tyre treads exhibit feathered edges

- ☐ Incorrect toe setting (Chapter 10).

Tyres worn in centre of tread

- ☐ Tyres over-inflated (Weekly checks).

Tyres worn on inside and outside edges

- ☐ Tyres under-inflated (Weekly checks).

Tyres worn unevenly

- ☐ Tyres/wheels out of balance (Weekly checks).
- ☐ Excessive wheel or tyre run-out (Weekly checks).
- ☐ Worn shock absorbers (Chapters 1 and 10).
- ☐ Faulty tyre (Weekly checks).

Electrical system

Note: *For problems associated with the starting system, refer to the faults listed under 'Engine' earlier in this Section.*

Battery will not hold a charge for more than a few days

- ☐ Battery defective internally (Chapter 5A).
- ☐ Battery terminal connections loose or corroded (Weekly checks).
- ☐ Auxiliary drivebelt worn or incorrectly adjusted (Chapter 1 or 2).
- ☐ Alternator not charging at correct output (Chapter 5A).
- ☐ Alternator or voltage regulator faulty (Chapter 5A).
- ☐ Short-circuit causing continual battery drain (Chapters 5A and 12).

Ignition/no-charge warning light remains illuminated with engine running

- ☐ Auxiliary drivebelt broken, worn, or incorrectly adjusted (Chapter 1).
- ☐ Alternator brushes worn, sticking, or dirty (Chapter 5A).
- ☐ Alternator brush springs weak or broken (Chapter 5A).
- ☐ Internal fault in alternator or voltage regulator (Chapter 5A).
- ☐ Broken, disconnected, or loose wiring in charging circuit (Chapter 5A).

Electrical system (continued)

Ignition/no-charge warning light fails to come on

- [ ] Warning light bulb blown (Chapter 12).
- [ ] Broken, disconnected, or loose wiring in warning light circuit (Chapter 12).
- [ ] Alternator faulty (Chapter 5A).

Lights inoperative

- [ ] Bulb blown (Chapter 12).
- [ ] Corrosion of bulb or bulbholder contacts (Chapter 12).
- [ ] Blown fuse (Chapter 12).
- [ ] Faulty relay (Chapter 12).
- [ ] Broken, loose, or disconnected wiring (Chapter 12).
- [ ] Faulty switch (Chapter 12).

Instrument readings inaccurate or erratic

Instrument readings increase with engine speed

- [ ] Faulty voltage stabiliser (Chapter 12).

Fuel or temperature gauges give no reading

- [ ] Faulty gauge sender unit (Chapters 3 and 4A, 4B or 4C).
- [ ] Wiring open-circuit (Chapter 12).
- [ ] Faulty gauge (Chapter 12).

Fuel or temperature gauges give continuous maximum reading

- [ ] Faulty gauge sender unit (Chapters 3 and 4A, 4B or 4C).
- [ ] Wiring short-circuit (Chapter 12).
- [ ] Faulty gauge (Chapter 12).

Horn inoperative, or unsatisfactory in operation

Horn operates all the time

- [ ] Horn push either earthed or stuck down (Chapter 12).
- [ ] Horn cable-to-horn push earthed (Chapter 12).

Horn fails to operate

- [ ] Blown fuse (Chapter 12).
- [ ] Cable or cable connections loose, broken or disconnected (Chapter 12).
- [ ] Faulty horn (Chapter 12).

Horn emits intermittent or unsatisfactory sound

- [ ] Cable connections loose (Chapter 12).
- [ ] Horn mountings loose (Chapter 12).
- [ ] Faulty horn (Chapter 12).

Windscreen/tailgate wipers inoperative, or unsatisfactory in operation

Wipers fail to operate, or operate very slowly

- [ ] Wiper blades stuck to screen, or linkage seized or binding (Weekly checks or Chapter 12).
- [ ] Blown fuse (Weekly checks or Chapter 12).
- [ ] Cable or cable connections loose, broken or disconnected (Chapter 12).
- [ ] Faulty relay (Chapter 12).
- [ ] Faulty wiper motor (Chapter 12).

Wiper blades sweep over too large or too small an area of the glass

- [ ] Wiper arms incorrectly positioned on spindles (Chapter 12).
- [ ] Excessive wear of wiper linkage (Chapter 12).
- [ ] Wiper motor or linkage mountings loose or insecure (Chapter 12).

Wiper blades fail to clean the glass effectively

- [ ] Wiper blade rubbers worn or perished (Weekly checks).
- [ ] Wiper arm tension springs broken, or arm pivots seized (Chapter 12).
- [ ] Insufficient windscreen washer additive to adequately remove road film (Weekly checks).

Windscreen/tailgate washers inoperative, or unsatisfactory in operation

One or more washer jets inoperative

- [ ] Blocked washer jet (Chapter 1).
- [ ] Disconnected, kinked or restricted fluid hose (Chapter 12).
- [ ] Insufficient fluid in washer reservoir (Weekly checks).

Washer pump fails to operate

- [ ] Broken or disconnected wiring or connections (Chapter 12).
- [ ] Blown fuse (Weekly checks or Chapter 12).
- [ ] Faulty washer switch (Chapter 12).
- [ ] Faulty washer pump (Chapter 12).

Washer pump runs for some time before fluid is emitted from jets

- [ ] Faulty one-way valve in fluid supply hose (Chapter 12).

Electric windows inoperative, or unsatisfactory in operation

Window glass will only move in one direction

- [ ] Faulty switch (Chapter 12).

Window glass slow to move

- [ ] Regulator seized or damaged, or in need of lubrication (Chapter 11).
- [ ] Door internal components or trim fouling regulator (Chapter 11).
- [ ] Faulty motor (Chapter 11).

Window glass fails to move

- [ ] Blown fuse (Chapter 12).
- [ ] Faulty relay (Chapter 12).
- [ ] Broken or disconnected wiring or connections (Chapter 12).
- [ ] Faulty motor (Chapter 11).

Central locking system inoperative, or unsatisfactory in operation

Complete system failure

- [ ] Blown fuse (Weekly checks or Chapter 12).
- [ ] Faulty relay (Chapter 12).
- [ ] Broken or disconnected wiring or connections (Chapter 12).
- [ ] Faulty bi-pressure pump (Chapter 11).

Latch locks but will not unlock, or unlocks but will not lock

- [ ] Broken or disconnected latch operating rods or levers (Chapter 11).
- [ ] Faulty relay (Chapter 12).
- [ ] Faulty bi-pressure pump (Chapter 11).

One solenoid/motor fails to operate

- [ ] Broken or disconnected wiring or connections (Chapter 12).
- [ ] Faulty operating assembly (Chapter 11).
- [ ] Broken, binding or disconnected latch operating rods or levers (Chapter 11).
- [ ] Fault in door latch (Chapter 11).

A

ABS (Anti-lock brake system) A system, usually electronically controlled, that senses incipient wheel lockup during braking and relieves hydraulic pressure at wheels that are about to skid.

Air bag An inflatable bag hidden in the steering wheel (driver's side) or the dash or glovebox (passenger side). In a head-on collision, the bags inflate, preventing the driver and front passenger from being thrown forward into the steering wheel or windscreen.

Air cleaner A metal or plastic housing, containing a filter element, which removes dust and dirt from the air being drawn into the engine.

Air filter element The actual filter in an air cleaner system, usually manufactured from pleated paper and requiring renewal at regular intervals.

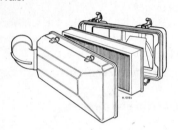

Air filter

Allen key A hexagonal wrench which fits into a recessed hexagonal hole.

Alligator clip A long-nosed spring-loaded metal clip with meshing teeth. Used to make temporary electrical connections.

Alternator A component in the electrical system which converts mechanical energy from a drivebelt into electrical energy to charge the battery and to operate the starting system, ignition system and electrical accessories.

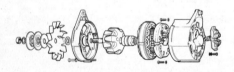

Alternator (exploded view)

Ampere (amp) A unit of measurement for the flow of electric current. One amp is the amount of current produced by one volt acting through a resistance of one ohm.

Anaerobic sealer A substance used to prevent bolts and screws from loosening. Anaerobic means that it does not require oxygen for activation. The Loctite brand is widely used.

Antifreeze A substance (usually ethylene glycol) mixed with water, and added to a vehicle's cooling system, to prevent freezing of the coolant in winter. Antifreeze also contains chemicals to inhibit corrosion and the formation of rust and other deposits that

would tend to clog the radiator and coolant passages and reduce cooling efficiency.

Anti-seize compound A coating that reduces the risk of seizing on fasteners that are subjected to high temperatures, such as exhaust manifold bolts and nuts.

Anti-seize compound

Asbestos A natural fibrous mineral with great heat resistance, commonly used in the composition of brake friction materials. Asbestos is a health hazard and the dust created by brake systems should never be inhaled or ingested.

Axle A shaft on which a wheel revolves, or which revolves with a wheel. Also, a solid beam that connects the two wheels at one end of the vehicle. An axle which also transmits power to the wheels is known as a live axle.

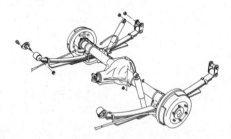

Axle assembly

Axleshaft A single rotating shaft, on either side of the differential, which delivers power from the final drive assembly to the drive wheels. Also called a driveshaft or a halfshaft.

B

Ball bearing An anti-friction bearing consisting of a hardened inner and outer race with hardened steel balls between two races.

Bearing

Bearing The curved surface on a shaft or in a bore, or the part assembled into either, that permits relative motion between them with minimum wear and friction.

Big-end bearing The bearing in the end of the connecting rod that's attached to the crankshaft.

Bleed nipple A valve on a brake wheel cylinder, caliper or other hydraulic component that is opened to purge the hydraulic system of air. Also called a bleed screw.

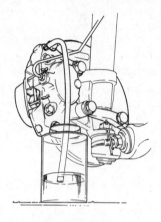

Brake bleeding

Brake bleeding Procedure for removing air from lines of a hydraulic brake system.

Brake disc The component of a disc brake that rotates with the wheels.

Brake drum The component of a drum brake that rotates with the wheels.

Brake linings The friction material which contacts the brake disc or drum to retard the vehicle's speed. The linings are bonded or riveted to the brake pads or shoes.

Brake pads The replaceable friction pads that pinch the brake disc when the brakes are applied. Brake pads consist of a friction material bonded or riveted to a rigid backing plate.

Brake shoe The crescent-shaped carrier to which the brake linings are mounted and which forces the lining against the rotating drum during braking.

Braking systems For more information on braking systems, consult the *Haynes Automotive Brake Manual*.

Breaker bar A long socket wrench handle providing greater leverage.

Bulkhead The insulated partition between the engine and the passenger compartment.

C

Caliper The non-rotating part of a disc-brake assembly that straddles the disc and carries the brake pads. The caliper also contains the hydraulic components that cause the pads to pinch the disc when the brakes are applied. A caliper is also a measuring tool that can be set to measure inside or outside dimensions of an object.

Camshaft A rotating shaft on which a series of cam lobes operate the valve mechanisms. The camshaft may be driven by gears, by sprockets and chain or by sprockets and a belt.

Canister A container in an evaporative emission control system; contains activated charcoal granules to trap vapours from the fuel system.

Canister

Carburettor A device which mixes fuel with air in the proper proportions to provide a desired power output from a spark ignition internal combustion engine.

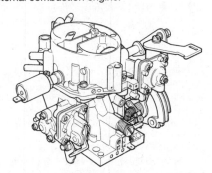

Carburettor

Castellated Resembling the parapets along the top of a castle wall. For example, a castellated balljoint stud nut.

Castellated nut

Castor In wheel alignment, the backward or forward tilt of the steering axis. Castor is positive when the steering axis is inclined rearward at the top.

Catalytic converter A silencer-like device in the exhaust system which converts certain pollutants in the exhaust gases into less harmful substances.

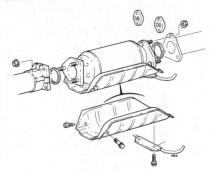

Catalytic converter

Circlip A ring-shaped clip used to prevent endwise movement of cylindrical parts and shafts. An internal circlip is installed in a groove in a housing; an external circlip fits into a groove on the outside of a cylindrical piece such as a shaft.

Clearance The amount of space between two parts. For example, between a piston and a cylinder, between a bearing and a journal, etc.

Coil spring A spiral of elastic steel found in various sizes throughout a vehicle, for example as a springing medium in the suspension and in the valve train.

Compression Reduction in volume, and increase in pressure and temperature, of a gas, caused by squeezing it into a smaller space.

Compression ratio The relationship between cylinder volume when the piston is at top dead centre and cylinder volume when the piston is at bottom dead centre.

Constant velocity (CV) joint A type of universal joint that cancels out vibrations caused by driving power being transmitted through an angle.

Core plug A disc or cup-shaped metal device inserted in a hole in a casting through which core was removed when the casting was formed. Also known as a freeze plug or expansion plug.

Crankcase The lower part of the engine block in which the crankshaft rotates.

Crankshaft The main rotating member, or shaft, running the length of the crankcase, with offset "throws" to which the connecting rods are attached.

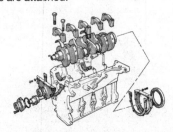

Crankshaft assembly

Crocodile clip See Alligator clip

D

Diagnostic code Code numbers obtained by accessing the diagnostic mode of an engine management computer. This code can be used to determine the area in the system where a malfunction may be located.

Disc brake A brake design incorporating a rotating disc onto which brake pads are squeezed. The resulting friction converts the energy of a moving vehicle into heat.

Double-overhead cam (DOHC) An engine that uses two overhead camshafts, usually one for the intake valves and one for the exhaust valves.

Drivebelt(s) The belt(s) used to drive accessories such as the alternator, water pump, power steering pump, air conditioning compressor, etc. off the crankshaft pulley.

Accessory drivebelts

Driveshaft Any shaft used to transmit motion. Commonly used when referring to the axleshafts on a front wheel drive vehicle.

Driveshaft

Drum brake A type of brake using a drum-shaped metal cylinder attached to the inner surface of the wheel. When the brake pedal is pressed, curved brake shoes with friction linings press against the inside of the drum to slow or stop the vehicle.

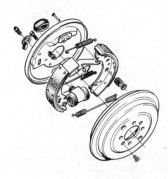

Drum brake assembly

E

EGR valve A valve used to introduce exhaust gases into the intake air stream.

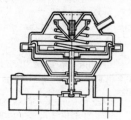

EGR valve

Electronic control unit (ECU) A computer which controls (for instance) ignition and fuel injection systems, or an anti-lock braking system. For more information refer to the *Haynes Automotive Electrical and Electronic Systems Manual.*

Electronic Fuel Injection (EFI) A computer controlled fuel system that distributes fuel through an injector located in each intake port of the engine.

Emergency brake A braking system, independent of the main hydraulic system, that can be used to slow or stop the vehicle if the primary brakes fail, or to hold the vehicle stationary even though the brake pedal isn't depressed. It usually consists of a hand lever that actuates either front or rear brakes mechanically through a series of cables and linkages. Also known as a handbrake or parking brake.

Endfloat The amount of lengthwise movement between two parts. As applied to a crankshaft, the distance that the crankshaft can move forward and back in the cylinder block.

Engine management system (EMS) A computer controlled system which manages the fuel injection and the ignition systems in an integrated fashion.

Exhaust manifold A part with several passages through which exhaust gases leave the engine combustion chambers and enter the exhaust pipe.

Exhaust manifold

F

Fan clutch A viscous (fluid) drive coupling device which permits variable engine fan speeds in relation to engine speeds.

Feeler blade A thin strip or blade of hardened steel, ground to an exact thickness, used to check or measure clearances between parts.

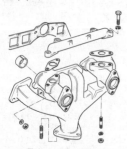

Feeler blade

Firing order The order in which the engine cylinders fire, or deliver their power strokes, beginning with the number one cylinder.

Flywheel A heavy spinning wheel in which energy is absorbed and stored by means of momentum. On cars, the flywheel is attached to the crankshaft to smooth out firing impulses.

Free play The amount of travel before any action takes place. The "looseness" in a linkage, or an assembly of parts, between the initial application of force and actual movement. For example, the distance the brake pedal moves before the pistons in the master cylinder are actuated.

Fuse An electrical device which protects a circuit against accidental overload. The typical fuse contains a soft piece of metal which is calibrated to melt at a predetermined current flow (expressed as amps) and break the circuit.

Fusible link A circuit protection device consisting of a conductor surrounded by heat-resistant insulation. The conductor is smaller than the wire it protects, so it acts as the weakest link in the circuit. Unlike a blown fuse, a failed fusible link must frequently be cut from the wire for replacement.

G

Gap The distance the spark must travel in jumping from the centre electrode to the side

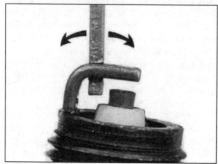

Adjusting spark plug gap

electrode in a spark plug. Also refers to the spacing between the points in a contact breaker assembly in a conventional points-type ignition, or to the distance between the reluctor or rotor and the pickup coil in an electronic ignition.

Gasket Any thin, soft material - usually cork, cardboard, asbestos or soft metal - installed between two metal surfaces to ensure a good seal. For instance, the cylinder head gasket seals the joint between the block and the cylinder head.

Gasket

Gauge An instrument panel display used to monitor engine conditions. A gauge with a movable pointer on a dial or a fixed scale is an analogue gauge. A gauge with a numerical readout is called a digital gauge.

H

Halfshaft A rotating shaft that transmits power from the final drive unit to a drive wheel, usually when referring to a live rear axle.

Harmonic balancer A device designed to reduce torsion or twisting vibration in the crankshaft. May be incorporated in the crankshaft pulley. Also known as a vibration damper.

Hone An abrasive tool for correcting small irregularities or differences in diameter in an engine cylinder, brake cylinder, etc.

Hydraulic tappet A tappet that utilises hydraulic pressure from the engine's lubrication system to maintain zero clearance (constant contact with both camshaft and valve stem). Automatically adjusts to variation in valve stem length. Hydraulic tappets also reduce valve noise.

I

Ignition timing The moment at which the spark plug fires, usually expressed in the number of crankshaft degrees before the piston reaches the top of its stroke.

Inlet manifold A tube or housing with passages through which flows the air-fuel mixture (carburettor vehicles and vehicles with throttle body injection) or air only (port fuel-injected vehicles) to the port openings in the cylinder head.

J

Jump start Starting the engine of a vehicle with a discharged or weak battery by attaching jump leads from the weak battery to a charged or helper battery.

L

Load Sensing Proportioning Valve (LSPV) A brake hydraulic system control valve that works like a proportioning valve, but also takes into consideration the amount of weight carried by the rear axle.

Locknut A nut used to lock an adjustment nut, or other threaded component, in place. For example, a locknut is employed to keep the adjusting nut on the rocker arm in position.

Lockwasher A form of washer designed to prevent an attaching nut from working loose.

M

MacPherson strut A type of front suspension system devised by Earle MacPherson at Ford of England. In its original form, a simple lateral link with the anti-roll bar creates the lower control arm. A long strut - an integral coil spring and shock absorber - is mounted between the body and the steering knuckle. Many modern so-called MacPherson strut systems use a conventional lower A-arm and don't rely on the anti-roll bar for location.

Multimeter An electrical test instrument with the capability to measure voltage, current and resistance.

N

NOx Oxides of Nitrogen. A common toxic pollutant emitted by petrol and diesel engines at higher temperatures.

O

Ohm The unit of electrical resistance. One volt applied to a resistance of one ohm will produce a current of one amp.

Ohmmeter An instrument for measuring electrical resistance.

O-ring A type of sealing ring made of a special rubber-like material; in use, the O-ring is compressed into a groove to provide the sealing action.

O-ring

Overhead cam (ohc) engine An engine with the camshaft(s) located on top of the cylinder head(s).

Overhead valve (ohv) engine An engine with the valves located in the cylinder head, but with the camshaft located in the engine block.

Oxygen sensor A device installed in the engine exhaust manifold, which senses the oxygen content in the exhaust and converts this information into an electric current. Also called a Lambda sensor.

P

Phillips screw A type of screw head having a cross instead of a slot for a corresponding type of screwdriver.

Plastigage A thin strip of plastic thread, available in different sizes, used for measuring clearances. For example, a strip of Plastigage is laid across a bearing journal. The parts are assembled and dismantled; the width of the crushed strip indicates the clearance between journal and bearing.

Plastigage

Propeller shaft The long hollow tube with universal joints at both ends that carries power from the transmission to the differential on front-engined rear wheel drive vehicles.

Proportioning valve A hydraulic control valve which limits the amount of pressure to the rear brakes during panic stops to prevent wheel lock-up.

R

Rack-and-pinion steering A steering system with a pinion gear on the end of the steering shaft that mates with a rack (think of a geared wheel opened up and laid flat). When the steering wheel is turned, the pinion turns, moving the rack to the left or right. This movement is transmitted through the track rods to the steering arms at the wheels.

Radiator A liquid-to-air heat transfer device designed to reduce the temperature of the coolant in an internal combustion engine cooling system.

Refrigerant Any substance used as a heat transfer agent in an air-conditioning system. R-12 has been the principle refrigerant for many years; recently, however, manufacturers have begun using R-134a, a non-CFC substance that is considered less harmful to the ozone in the upper atmosphere.

Rocker arm A lever arm that rocks on a shaft or pivots on a stud. In an overhead valve engine, the rocker arm converts the upward movement of the pushrod into a downward movement to open a valve.

Rotor In a distributor, the rotating device inside the cap that connects the centre electrode and the outer terminals as it turns, distributing the high voltage from the coil secondary winding to the proper spark plug. Also, that part of an alternator which rotates inside the stator. Also, the rotating assembly of a turbocharger, including the compressor wheel, shaft and turbine wheel.

Runout The amount of wobble (in-and-out movement) of a gear or wheel as it's rotated. The amount a shaft rotates "out-of-true." The out-of-round condition of a rotating part.

S

Sealant A liquid or paste used to prevent leakage at a joint. Sometimes used in conjunction with a gasket.

Sealed beam lamp An older headlight design which integrates the reflector, lens and filaments into a hermetically-sealed one-piece unit. When a filament burns out or the lens cracks, the entire unit is simply replaced.

Serpentine drivebelt A single, long, wide accessory drivebelt that's used on some newer vehicles to drive all the accessories, instead of a series of smaller, shorter belts. Serpentine drivebelts are usually tensioned by an automatic tensioner.

Serpentine drivebelt

Shim Thin spacer, commonly used to adjust the clearance or relative positions between two parts. For example, shims inserted into or under bucket tappets control valve clearances. Clearance is adjusted by changing the thickness of the shim.

Slide hammer A special puller that screws into or hooks onto a component such as a shaft or bearing; a heavy sliding handle on the shaft bottoms against the end of the shaft to knock the component free.

Sprocket A tooth or projection on the periphery of a wheel, shaped to engage with a chain or drivebelt. Commonly used to refer to the sprocket wheel itself.

Starter inhibitor switch On vehicles with an automatic transmission, a switch that prevents starting if the vehicle is not in Neutral or Park.
Strut See MacPherson strut.

T

Tappet A cylindrical component which transmits motion from the cam to the valve stem, either directly or via a pushrod and rocker arm. Also called a cam follower.
Thermostat A heat-controlled valve that regulates the flow of coolant between the cylinder block and the radiator, so maintaining optimum engine operating temperature. A thermostat is also used in some air cleaners in which the temperature is regulated.
Thrust bearing The bearing in the clutch assembly that is moved in to the release levers by clutch pedal action to disengage the clutch. Also referred to as a release bearing.
Timing belt A toothed belt which drives the camshaft. Serious engine damage may result if it breaks in service.
Timing chain A chain which drives the camshaft.
Toe-in The amount the front wheels are closer together at the front than at the rear. On rear wheel drive vehicles, a slight amount of toe-in is usually specified to keep the front wheels running parallel on the road by offsetting other forces that tend to spread the wheels apart.

Toe-out The amount the front wheels are closer together at the rear than at the front. On front wheel drive vehicles, a slight amount of toe-out is usually specified.
Tools For full information on choosing and using tools, refer to the *Haynes Automotive Tools Manual.*
Tracer A stripe of a second colour applied to a wire insulator to distinguish that wire from another one with the same colour insulator.
Tune-up A process of accurate and careful adjustments and parts replacement to obtain the best possible engine performance.
Turbocharger A centrifugal device, driven by exhaust gases, that pressurises the intake air. Normally used to increase the power output from a given engine displacement, but can also be used primarily to reduce exhaust emissions (as on VW's "Umwelt" Diesel engine).

U

Universal joint or U-joint A double-pivoted connection for transmitting power from a driving to a driven shaft through an angle. A U-joint consists of two Y-shaped yokes and a cross-shaped member called the spider.

V

Valve A device through which the flow of liquid, gas, vacuum, or loose material in bulk may be started, stopped, or regulated by a movable part that opens, shuts, or partially obstructs one or more ports or passageways. A valve is also the movable part of such a device.
Valve clearance The clearance between the valve tip (the end of the valve stem) and the rocker arm or tappet. The valve clearance is measured when the valve is closed.
Vernier caliper A precision measuring instrument that measures inside and outside dimensions. Not quite as accurate as a micrometer, but more convenient.
Viscosity The thickness of a liquid or its resistance to flow.
Volt A unit for expressing electrical "pressure" in a circuit. One volt that will produce a current of one ampere through a resistance of one ohm.

W

Welding Various processes used to join metal items by heating the areas to be joined to a molten state and fusing them together. For more information refer to the *Haynes Automotive Welding Manual.*
Wiring diagram A drawing portraying the components and wires in a vehicle's electrical system, using standardised symbols. For more information refer to the *Haynes Automotive Electrical and Electronic Systems Manual.*

Note: *References throughout this index are in the form "***Chapter number***" • "***Page number***"*

Haynes Manuals – The Complete UK Car List

Title	Book No.
ALFA ROMEO Alfasud/Sprint (74 - 88) up to F *	0292
Alfa Romeo Alfetta (73 - 87) up to E *	0531
AUDI 80, 90 & Coupe Petrol (79 - Nov 88) up to F	0605
Audi 80, 90 & Coupe Petrol (Oct 86 - 90) D to H	1491
Audi 100 & 200 Petrol (Oct 82 - 90) up to H	0907
Audi 100 & A6 Petrol & Diesel (May 91 - May 97) H to P	3504
Audi A3 Petrol & Diesel (96 - May 03) P to 03	4253
Audi A4 Petrol & Diesel (95 - 00) M to X	3575
Audi A4 Petrol & Diesel (01 - 04) X to 54	4609
AUSTIN A35 & A40 (56 - 67) up to F *	0118
Austin/MG/Rover Maestro 1.3 & 1.6 Petrol (83 - 95) up to M	0922
Austin/MG Metro (80 - May 90) up to G	0718
Austin/Rover Montego 1.3 & 1.6 Petrol (84 - 94) A to L	1066
Austin/MG/Rover Montego 2.0 Petrol (84 - 95) A to M	1067
Mini (59 - 69) up to H *	0527
Mini (69 - 01) up to X	0646
Austin/Rover 2.0 litre Diesel Engine (86 - 93) C to L	1857
Austin Healey 100/6 & 3000 (56 - 68) up to G *	0049
BEDFORD CF Petrol (69 - 87) up to E	0163
Bedford/Vauxhall Rascal & Suzuki Supercarry (86 - Oct 94) C to M	3015
BMW 316, 320 & 320i (4-cyl) (75 - Feb 83) up to Y *	0276
BMW 320, 320i, 323i & 325i (6-cyl) (Oct 77 - Sept 87) up to E	0815
BMW 3- & 5-Series Petrol (81 - 91) up to J	1948
BMW 3-Series Petrol (Apr 91 - 99) H to V	3210
BMW 3-Series Petrol (Sept 98 - 03) S to 53	4067
BMW 520i & 525e (Oct 81 - June 88) up to E	1560
BMW 525, 528 & 528i (73 - Sept 81) up to X *	0632
BMW 5-Series 6-cyl Petrol (April 96 - Aug 03) N to 03	4151
BMW 1500, 1502, 1600, 1602, 2000 & 2002 (59 - 77) up to S *	0240
CHRYSLER PT Cruiser Petrol (00 - 03) W to 53	4058
CITROËN 2CV, Ami & Dyane (67 - 90) up to H	0196
Citroën AX Petrol & Diesel (87 - 97) D to P	3014
Citroën Berlingo & Peugeot Partner Petrol & Diesel (96 - 05) P to 55	4281
Citroën BX Petrol (83 - 94) A to L	0908
Citroën C15 Van Petrol & Diesel (89 - Oct 98) F to S	3509
Citroën C3 Petrol & Diesel (02 - 05) 51 to 05	4197
Citroën CX Petrol (75 - 88) up to F	0528
Citroën Saxo Petrol & Diesel (96 - 04) N to 54	3506
Citroën Visa Petrol (79 - 88) up to F	0620
Citroën Xantia Petrol & Diesel (93 - 01) K to Y	3082
Citroën XM Petrol & Diesel (89 - 00) G to X	3451
Citroën Xsara Petrol & Diesel (97 - Sept 00) R to W	3751
Citroën Xsara Picasso Petrol & Diesel (00 - 02) W to 52	3944
Citroën ZX Diesel (91 - 98) J to S	1922
Citroën ZX Petrol (91 - 98) H to S	1881
Citroën 1.7 & 1.9 litre Diesel Engine (84 - 96) A to N	1379
FIAT 126 (73 - 87) up to E *	0305
Fiat 500 (57 - 73) up to M *	0090
Fiat Bravo & Brava Petrol (95 - 00) N to W	3572
Fiat Cinquecento (93 - 98) K to R	3501
Fiat Panda (81 - 95) up to M	0793
Fiat Punto Petrol & Diesel (94 - Oct 99) L to V	3251
Fiat Punto Petrol (Oct 99 - July 03) V to 03	4066
Fiat Regata Petrol (84 - 88) A to F	1167
Fiat Tipo Petrol (88 - 91) E to J	1625
Fiat Uno Petrol (83 - 95) up to M	0923
Fiat X1/9 (74 - 89) up to G *	0273
FORD Anglia (59 - 68) up to G *	0001
Ford Capri II (& III) 1.6 & 2.0 (74 - 87) up to E *	0283
Ford Capri II (& III) 2.8 & 3.0 V6 (74 - 87) up to E	1309

Title	Book No.
Ford Cortina Mk I & Corsair 1500 ('62 - '66) up to D*	0214
Ford Cortina Mk III 1300 & 1600 (70 - 76) up to P *	0070
Ford Escort Mk I 1100 & 1300 (68 - 74) up to N *	0171
Ford Escort Mk I Mexico, RS 1600 & RS 2000 (70 - 74) up to N *	0139
Ford Escort Mk II Mexico, RS 1800 & RS 2000 (75 - 80) up to W *	0735
Ford Escort (75 - Aug 80) up to V *	0280
Ford Escort Petrol (Sept 80 - Sept 90) up to H	0686
Ford Escort & Orion Petrol (Sept 90 - 00) H to X	1737
Ford Escort & Orion Diesel (Sept 90 - 00) H to X	4081
Ford Fiesta (76 - Aug 83) up to Y	0334
Ford Fiesta Petrol (Aug 83 - Feb 89) A to F	1030
Ford Fiesta Petrol (Feb 89 - Oct 95) F to N	1595
Ford Fiesta Petrol & Diesel (Oct 95 - Mar 02) N to 02	3397
Ford Fiesta Petrol & Diesel (Apr 02 - 05) 02 to 54	4170
Ford Focus Petrol & Diesel (98 - 01) S to Y	3759
Ford Focus Petrol & Diesel (Oct 01 - 05) 51 to 05	4167
Ford Galaxy Petrol & Diesel (95 - Aug 00) M to W	3984
Ford Granada Petrol (Sept 77 - Feb 85) up to B *	0481
Ford Granada & Scorpio Petrol (Mar 85 - 94) B to M	1245
Ford Ka (96 - 02) P to 52	3570
Ford Mondeo Petrol (93 - Sept 00) K to X	1923
Ford Mondeo Petrol & Diesel (Oct 00 - Jul 03) X to 03	3990
Ford Mondeo Petrol & Diesel (July 03 - 07) 03 to 56	4619
Ford Mondeo Diesel (93 - 96) L to N	3465
Ford Orion Petrol (83 - Sept 90) up to H	1009
Ford Sierra 4-cyl Petrol (82 - 93) up to K	0903
Ford Sierra V6 Petrol (82 - 91) up to J	0904
Ford Transit Petrol (Mk 2) (78 - Jan 86) up to C	0719
Ford Transit Petrol (Mk 3) (Feb 86 - 89) C to G	1468
Ford Transit Diesel (Feb 86 - 99) C to T	3019
Ford 1.6 & 1.8 litre Diesel Engine (84 - 96) A to N	1172
Ford 2.1, 2.3 & 2.5 litre Diesel Engine (77 - 90) up to H	1606
FREIGHT ROVER Sherpa Petrol (74 - 87) up to E	0463
HILLMAN Avenger (70 - 82) up to Y	0037
Hillman Imp (63 - 76) up to R *	0022
HONDA Civic (Feb 84 - Oct 87) A to E	1226
Honda Civic (Nov 91 - 96) J to N	3199
Honda Civic Petrol (Mar 95 - 00) M to X	4050
Honda Civic Petrol & Diesel (01 - 05) X to 55	4611
Honda Jazz (01 - Feb 08) 51 - 57	4735
HYUNDAI Pony (85 - 94) C to M	3398
JAGUAR E Type (61 - 72) up to L *	0140
Jaguar MkI & II, 240 & 340 (55 - 69) up to H *	0098
Jaguar XJ6, XJ & Sovereign; Daimler Sovereign (68 - Oct 86) up to D	0242
Jaguar XJ6 & Sovereign (Oct 86 - Sept 94) D to M	3261
Jaguar XJ12, XJS & Sovereign; Daimler Double Six (72 - 88) up to F	0478
JEEP Cherokee Petrol (93 - 96) K to N	1943
LADA 1200, 1300, 1500 & 1600 (74 - 91) up to J	0413
Lada Samara (87 - 91) D to J	1610
LAND ROVER 90, 110 & Defender Diesel (83 - 07) up to 56	3017
Land Rover Discovery Petrol & Diesel (89 - 98) G to S	3016
Land Rover Discovery Diesel (Nov 98 - Jul 04) S to 04	4606
Land Rover Freelander Petrol & Diesel (97 - Sept 03) R to 53	3929
Land Rover Freelander Petrol & Diesel (Oct 03 - Oct 06) 53 to 56	4623
Land Rover Series IIA & III Diesel (58 - 85) up to C	0529
Land Rover Series II, IIA & III 4-cyl Petrol (58 - 85) up to C	0314

Title	Book No.
MAZDA 323 (Mar 81 - Oct 89) up to G	1608
Mazda 323 (Oct 89 - 98) G to R	3455
Mazda 626 (May 83 - Sept 87) up to E	0929
Mazda B1600, B1800 & B2000 Pick-up Petrol (72 - 88) up to F	0267
Mazda RX-7 (79 - 85) up to C *	0460
MERCEDES-BENZ 190, 190E & 190D Petrol & Diesel (83 - 93) A to L	3450
Mercedes-Benz 200D, 240D, 240TD, 300D & 300TD 123 Series Diesel (Oct 76 - 85)	1114
Mercedes-Benz 250 & 280 (68 - 72) up to L *	0346
Mercedes-Benz 250 & 280 123 Series Petrol (Oct 76 - 84) up to B *	0677
Mercedes-Benz 124 Series Petrol & Diesel (85 - Aug 93) C to K	3253
Mercedes-Benz C-Class Petrol & Diesel (93 - Aug 00) L to W	3511
MGA (55 - 62) *	0475
MGB (62 - 80) up to W	0111
MG Midget & Austin-Healey Sprite (58 - 80) up to W *	0265
MINI Petrol (July 01 - 05) Y to 05	4273
MITSUBISHI Shogun & L200 Pick-Ups Petrol (83 - 94) up to M	1944
MORRIS Ital 1.3 (80 - 84) up to B	0705
Morris Minor 1000 (56 - 71) up to K	0024
NISSAN Almera Petrol (95 - Feb 00) N to V	4053
Nissan Almera & Tino Petrol (Feb 00 - 07) V to 56	4612
Nissan Bluebird (May 84 - Mar 86) A to C	1223
Nissan Bluebird Petrol (Mar 86 - 90) C to H	1473
Nissan Cherry (Sept 82 - 86) up to D	1031
Nissan Micra (83 - Jan 93) up to K	0931
Nissan Micra (93 - 02) K to 52	3254
Nissan Primera Petrol (90 - Aug 99) H to T	1851
Nissan Stanza (82 - 86) up to D	0824
Nissan Sunny Petrol (May 82 - Oct 86) up to D	0895
Nissan Sunny Petrol (Oct 86 - Mar 91) D to H	1378
Nissan Sunny Petrol (Apr 91 - 95) H to N	3219
OPEL Ascona & Manta (B Series) (Sept 75 - 88) up to F *	0316
Opel Ascona Petrol (81 - 88)	3215
Opel Astra Petrol (Oct 91 - Feb 98)	3156
Opel Corsa Petrol (83 - Mar 93)	3160
Opel Corsa Petrol (Mar 93 - 97)	3159
Opel Kadett Petrol (Nov 79 - Oct 84) up to B	0634
Opel Kadett Petrol (Oct 84 - Oct 91)	3196
Opel Omega & Senator Petrol (Nov 86 - 94)	3157
Opel Rekord Petrol (Feb 78 - Oct 86) up to D	0543
Opel Vectra Petrol (Oct 88 - Oct 95)	3158
PEUGEOT 106 Petrol & Diesel (91 - 04) J to 53	1882
Peugeot 205 Petrol (83 - 97) A to P	0932
Peugeot 206 Petrol & Diesel (98 - 01) S to X	3757
Peugeot 206 Petrol & Diesel (02 - 06) 51 to 06	4613
Peugeot 306 Petrol & Diesel (93 - 02) K to 02	3073
Peugeot 307 Petrol & Diesel (01 - 04) Y to 54	4147
Peugeot 309 Petrol (86 - 93) C to K	1266
Peugeot 405 Petrol (88 - 97) E to P	1559
Peugeot 405 Diesel (88 - 97) E to P	3198
Peugeot 406 Petrol & Diesel (96 - Mar 99) N to T	3394
Peugeot 406 Petrol & Diesel (Mar 99 - 02) T to 52	3982
Peugeot 505 Petrol (79 - 89) up to G	0762
Peugeot 1.7/1.8 & 1.9 litre Diesel Engine (82 - 96) up to N	0950
Peugeot 2.0, 2.1, 2.3 & 2.5 litre Diesel Engines (74 - 90) up to H	1607
PORSCHE 911 (65 - 85) up to C	0264

* Classic reprint

Title	Book No.
Porsche 924 & 924 Turbo (76 - 85) up to C	0397
PROTON (89 - 97) F to P	3255
RANGE ROVER V8 Petrol (70 - Oct 92) up to K	0606
RELIANT Robin & Kitten (73 - 83) up to A *	0436
RENAULT 4 (61 - 86) up to D *	0072
Renault 5 Petrol (Feb 85 - 96) B to N	1219
Renault 9 & 11 Petrol (82 - 89) up to F	0822
Renault 18 Petrol (79 - 86) up to D	0598
Renault 19 Petrol (89 - 96) F to N	1646
Renault 19 Diesel (89 - 96) F to N	1946
Renault 21 Petrol (86 - 94) C to M	1397
Renault 25 Petrol & Diesel (84 - 92) B to K	1228
Renault Clio Petrol (91 - May 98) H to R	1853
Renault Clio Diesel (91 - June 96) H to N	3031
Renault Clio Petrol & Diesel (May 98 - May 01) R to Y	3906
Renault Clio Petrol & Diesel (June '01 - '05) Y to 55	4168
Renault Espace Petrol & Diesel (85 - 96) C to N	3197
Renault Laguna Petrol & Diesel (94 - 00) L to W	3252
Renault Laguna Petrol & Diesel (Feb 01 - Feb 05) X to 54	4283
Renault Mégane & Scénic Petrol & Diesel (96 - 99) N to T	3395
Renault Mégane & Scénic Petrol & Diesel (Apr 99 - 02) T to 52	3916
Renault Megane Petrol & Diesel (Oct 02 - 05) 52 to 55	4284
Renault Scenic Petrol & Diesel (Sept 03 - 06) 53 to 06	4297
ROVER 213 & 216 (84 - 89) A to G	1116
Rover 214 & 414 Petrol (89 - 96) G to N	1689
Rover 216 & 416 Petrol (89 - 96) G to N	1830
Rover 211, 214, 216, 218 & 220 Petrol & Diesel (Dec 95 - 99) N to V	3399
Rover 25 & MG ZR Petrol & Diesel (Oct 99 - 04) V to 54	4145
Rover 414, 416 & 420 Petrol & Diesel (May 95 - 98) M to R	3453
Rover 45 / MG ZS Petrol & Diesel (99 - 05) V to 55	4384
Rover 618, 620 & 623 Petrol (93 - 97) K to P	3257
Rover 75 / MG ZT Petrol & Diesel (99 - 06) S to 06	4292
Rover 820, 825 & 827 Petrol (86 - 95) D to N	1380
Rover 3500 (76 - 87) up to E *	0365
Rover Metro, 111 & 114 Petrol (May 90 - 98) G to S	1711
SAAB 95 & 96 (66 - 76) up to R *	0198
Saab 90, 99 & 900 (79 - Oct 93) up to L	0765
Saab 900 (Oct 93 - 98) L to R	3512
Saab 9000 (4-cyl) (85 - 98) C to S	1686
Saab 9-3 Petrol & Diesel (98 - Aug 02) R to 02	4614
Saab 9-5 4-cyl Petrol (97 - 04) R to 54	4156
SEAT Ibiza & Cordoba Petrol & Diesel (Oct 93 - Oct 99) L to V	3571
Seat Ibiza & Malaga Petrol (85 - 92) B to K	1609
SKODA Estelle (77 - 89) up to G	0604
Skoda Fabia Petrol & Diesel (00 - 06) W to 06	4376
Skoda Favorit (89 - 96) F to N	1801
Skoda Felicia Petrol & Diesel (95 - 01) M to X	3505
Skoda Octavia Petrol & Diesel (98 - Apr 04) R to 04	4285
SUBARU 1600 & 1800 (Nov 79 - 90) up to H *	0995
SUNBEAM Alpine, Rapier & H120 (67 - 74) up to N *	0051
SUZUKI SJ Series, Samurai & Vitara (4-cyl) Petrol (82 - 97) up to P	1942
Suzuki Supercarry & Bedford/Vauxhall Rascal (86 - Oct 94) C to M	3015
TALBOT Alpine, Solara, Minx & Rapier (75 - 86) up to D	0337

Title	Book No.
Talbot Horizon Petrol (78 - 86) up to D	0473
Talbot Samba (82 - 86) up to D	0823
TOYOTA Avensis Petrol (98 - Jan 03) R to 52	4264
Toyota Carina E Petrol (May 92 - 97) J to P	3256
Toyota Corolla (80 - 85) up to C	0683
Toyota Corolla (Sept 83 - Sept 87) A to E	1024
Toyota Corolla (Sept 87 - Aug 92) E to K	1683
Toyota Corolla Petrol (Aug 92 - 97) K to P	3259
Toyota Corolla Petrol (July 97 - Feb 02) P to 51	4286
Toyota Hi-Ace & Hi-Lux Petrol (69 - Oct 83) up to A	0304
Toyota Yaris Petrol (99 - 05) T to 05	4265
TRIUMPH GT6 & Vitesse (62 - 74) up to N *	0112
Triumph Herald (59 - 71) up to K *	0010
Triumph Spitfire (62 - 81) up to X	0113
Triumph Stag (70 - 78) up to T *	0441
Triumph TR2, TR3, TR3A, TR4 & TR4A (52 - 67) up to F *	0028
Triumph TR5 & 6 (67 - 75) up to P *	0031
Triumph TR7 (75 - 82) up to Y *	0322
VAUXHALL Astra Petrol (80 - Oct 84) up to B	0635
Vauxhall Astra & Belmont Petrol (Oct 84 - Oct 91) B to J	1136
Vauxhall Astra Petrol (Oct 91 - Feb 98) J to R	1832
Vauxhall/Opel Astra & Zafira Petrol (Feb 98 - Apr 04) R to 04	3758
Vauxhall/Opel Astra & Zafira Diesel (Feb 98 - Apr 04) R to 04	3797
Vauxhall/Opel Astra Petrol (04 - 07) 04 - 07	4732
Vauxhall/Opel Astra Diesel (04 - 07) 04 - 07	4733
Vauxhall/Opel Calibra (90 - 98) G to S	3502
Vauxhall Carlton Petrol (Oct 78 - Oct 86) up to D	0480
Vauxhall Carlton & Senator Petrol (Nov 86 - 94) D to L	1469
Vauxhall Cavalier Petrol (81 - Oct 88) up to F	0812
Vauxhall Cavalier Petrol (Oct 88 - 95) F to N	1570
Vauxhall Chevette (75 - 84) up to B	0285
Vauxhall/Opel Corsa Diesel (Mar 93 - Oct 00) K to X	4087
Vauxhall Corsa Petrol (Mar 93 - 97) K to R	1985
Vauxhall/Opel Corsa Petrol (Apr 97 - Oct 00) P to X	3921
Vauxhall/Opel Corsa Petrol & Diesel (Oct 00 - Sept 03) X to 53	4079
Vauxhall/Opel Corsa Petrol & Diesel (Oct 03 - Aug 06) 53 to 06	4617
Vauxhall/Opel Frontera Petrol & Diesel (91 - Sept 98) J to S	3454
Vauxhall Nova Petrol (83 - 93) up to K	0909
Vauxhall/Opel Omega Petrol (94 - 99) L to T	3510
Vauxhall/Opel Vectra Petrol & Diesel (95 - Feb 99) N to S	3396
Vauxhall/Opel Vectra Petrol & Diesel (Mar 99 - May 02) T to 02	3930
Vauxhall/Opel Vectra Petrol & Diesel (June 02 - Sept 05) 02 to 55	4618
Vauxhall/Opel 1.5, 1.6 & 1.7 litre Diesel Engine (82 - 96) up to N	1222
VW 411 & 412 (68 - 75) up to P *	0091
VW Beetle 1200 (54 - 77) up to S	0036
VW Beetle 1300 & 1500 (65 - 75) up to P	0039
VW 1302 & 1302S (70 - 72) up to L *	0110
VW Beetle 1303, 1303S & GT (72 - 75) up to P	0159
VW Beetle Petrol & Diesel (Apr 99 - 01) T to 51	3798
VW Golf & Jetta Mk 1 Petrol 1.1 & 1.3 (74 - 84) up to A	0716
VW Golf, Jetta & Scirocco Mk 1 Petrol 1.5, 1.6 & 1.8 (74 - 84) up to A	0726

Title	Book No.
VW Golf & Jetta Mk 1 Diesel (78 - 84) up to A	0451
VW Golf & Jetta Mk 2 Petrol (Mar 84 - Feb 92) A to J	1081
VW Golf & Vento Petrol & Diesel (Feb 92 - Mar 98) J to R	3097
VW Golf & Bora Petrol & Diesel (April 98 - 00) R to X	3727
VW Golf & Bora 4-cyl Petrol & Diesel (01 - 03) X to 53	4169
VW Golf & Jetta Petrol & Diesel (04 - 07) 53 to 07	4610
VW LT Petrol Vans & Light Trucks (76 - 87) up to E	0637
VW Passat & Santana Petrol (Sept 81 - May 88) up to E	0814
VW Passat 4-cyl Petrol & Diesel (May 88 - 96) E to P	3498
VW Passat 4-cyl Petrol & Diesel (Dec 96 - Nov 00) P to X	3917
VW Passat Petrol & Diesel (Dec 00 - May 05) X to 05	4279
VW Polo & Derby (76 - Jan 82) up to X	0335
VW Polo (82 - Oct 90) up to H	0813
VW Polo Petrol (Nov 90 - Aug 94) H to L	3245
VW Polo Hatchback Petrol & Diesel (94 - 99) M to S	3500
VW Polo Hatchback Petrol (00 - Jan 02) V to 51	4150
VW Polo Petrol & Diesel (02 - May 05) 51 to 05	4608
VW Scirocco (82 - 90) up to H *	1224
VW Transporter 1600 (68 - 79) up to V	0082
VW Transporter 1700, 1800 & 2000 (72 - 79) up to V *	0226
VW Transporter (air-cooled) Petrol (79 - 82) up to Y *	0638
VW Transporter (water-cooled) Petrol (82 - 90) up to H	3452
VW Type 3 (63 - 73) up to M *	0084
VOLVO 120 & 130 Series (& P1800) (61 - 73) up to M *	0203
Volvo 142, 144 & 145 (66 - 74) up to N *	0129
Volvo 240 Series Petrol (74 - 93) up to K	0270
Volvo 262, 264 & 260/265 (75 - 85) up to C *	0400
Volvo 340, 343, 345 & 360 (76 - 91) up to J	0715
Volvo 440, 460 & 480 Petrol (87 - 97) D to P	1691
Volvo 740 & 760 Petrol (82 - 91) up to J	1258
Volvo 850 Petrol (92 - 96) J to P	3260
Volvo 940 petrol (90 - 98) H to R	3249
Volvo S40 & V40 Petrol (96 - Mar 04) N to 04	3569
Volvo S40 & V50 Petrol & Diesel (Mar 04 - Jun 07) 04 to 07	4731
Volvo S70, V70 & C70 Petrol (96 - 99) P to V	3573
Volvo V70 / S80 Petrol & Diesel (98 - 05) S to 55	4263

AUTOMOTIVE TECHBOOKS

Title	Book No.
Automotive Electrical and Electronic Systems Manual	3049
Automotive Gearbox Overhaul Manual	3473
Automotive Service Summaries Manual	3475
Automotive Timing Belts Manual – Austin/Rover	3549
Automotive Timing Belts Manual – Ford	3474
Automotive Timing Belts Manual – Peugeot/Citroën	3568
Automotive Timing Belts Manual – Vauxhall/Opel	3577

DIY MANUAL SERIES

Title	Book No.
The Haynes Air Conditioning Manual	4192
The Haynes Car Electrical Systems Manual	4251
The Haynes Manual on Bodywork	4198
The Haynes Manual on Brakes	4178
The Haynes Manual on Carburettors	4177
The Haynes Manual on Diesel Engines	4174
The Haynes Manual on Engine Management	4199
The Haynes Manual on Fault Codes	4175
The Haynes Manual on Practical Electrical Systems	4267
The Haynes Manual on Small Engines	4250
The Haynes Manual on Welding	4176

* Classic reprint

CL23.12/07

Preserving Our Motoring Heritage

< *The Model J Duesenberg Derham Tourster. Only eight of these magnificent cars were ever built – this is the only example to be found outside the United States of America*

Almost every car you've ever loved, loathed or desired is gathered under one roof at the Haynes Motor Museum. Over 300 immaculately presented cars and motorbikes represent every aspect of our motoring heritage, from elegant reminders of bygone days, such as the superb Model J Duesenberg to curiosities like the bug-eyed BMW Isetta. There are also many old friends and flames. Perhaps you remember the 1959 Ford Popular that you did your courting in? The magnificent 'Red Collection' is a spectacle of classic sports cars including AC, Alfa Romeo, Austin Healey, Ferrari, Lamborghini, Maserati, MG, Riley, Porsche and Triumph.

A Perfect Day Out

Each and every vehicle at the Haynes Motor Museum has played its part in the history and culture of Motoring. Today, they make a wonderful spectacle and a great day out for all the family. Bring the kids, bring Mum and Dad, but above all bring your camera to capture those golden memories for ever. You will also find an impressive array of motoring memorabilia, a comfortable 70 seat video cinema and one of the most extensive transport book shops in Britain. The Pit Stop Cafe serves everything from a cup of tea to wholesome, home-made meals or, if you prefer, you can enjoy the large picnic area nestled in the beautiful rural surroundings of Somerset.

John Haynes O.B.E., Founder and Chairman of the museum at the wheel of a Haynes Light 12. >

< *Graham Hill's Lola Cosworth Formula 1 car next to a 1934 Riley Sports.*

The Museum is situated on the A359 Yeovil to Frome road at Sparkford, just off the A303 in Somerset. It is about 40 miles south of Bristol, and 25 minutes drive from the M5 intersection at Taunton.

Open 9.30am - 5.30pm (10.00am - 4.00pm Winter) 7 days a week, *except Christmas Day, Boxing Day and New Years Day*

Special rates available for schools, coach parties and outings Charitable Trust No. 292048